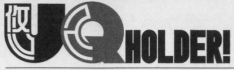

UQ HOLDER!

Ken Akamatsu Presents

Fate Aver-runcus

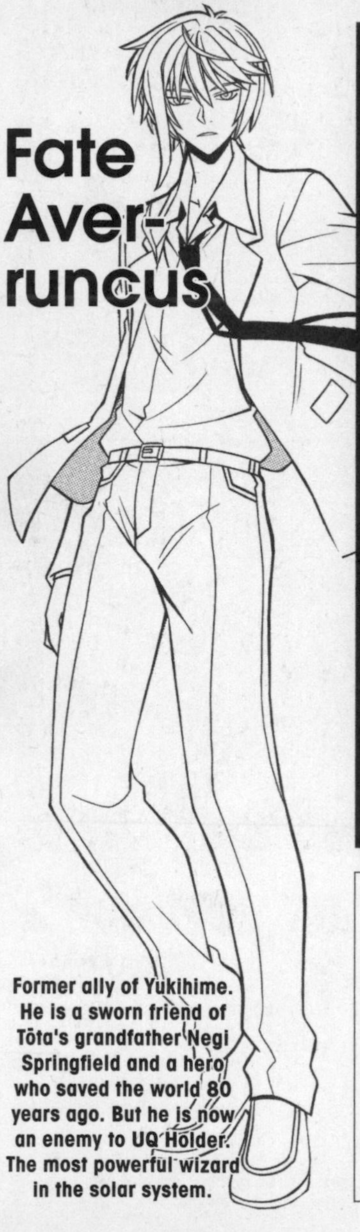

Former ally of Yukihime. He is a sworn friend of Tōta's grandfather Negi Springfield and a hero who saved the world 80 years ago. But he is now an enemy to UQ Holder. The most powerful wizard in the solar system.

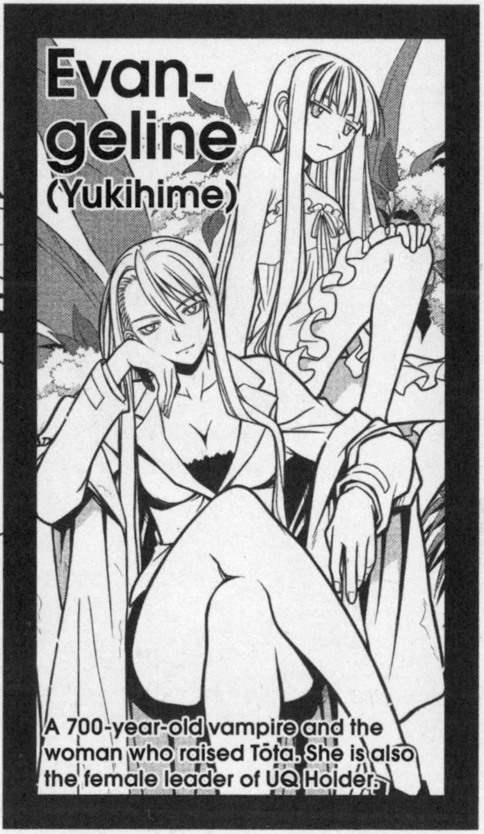
Evan-geline (Yukihime)
A 700-year-old vampire and the woman who raised Tōta. She is also the female leader of UQ Holder.

"UQ Holder Numbers"

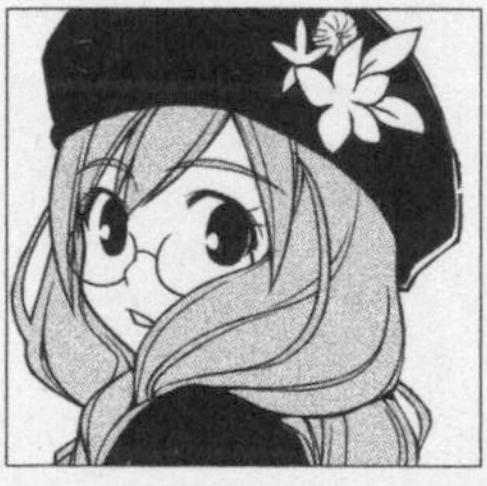

UQ HOLDER NO. 9

Kirië Sakurame

The greatest financial contributor to UQ Holder, who constantly calls Tōta incompetent. Her ability is "Reset and Restart."

THE STORY SO FAR

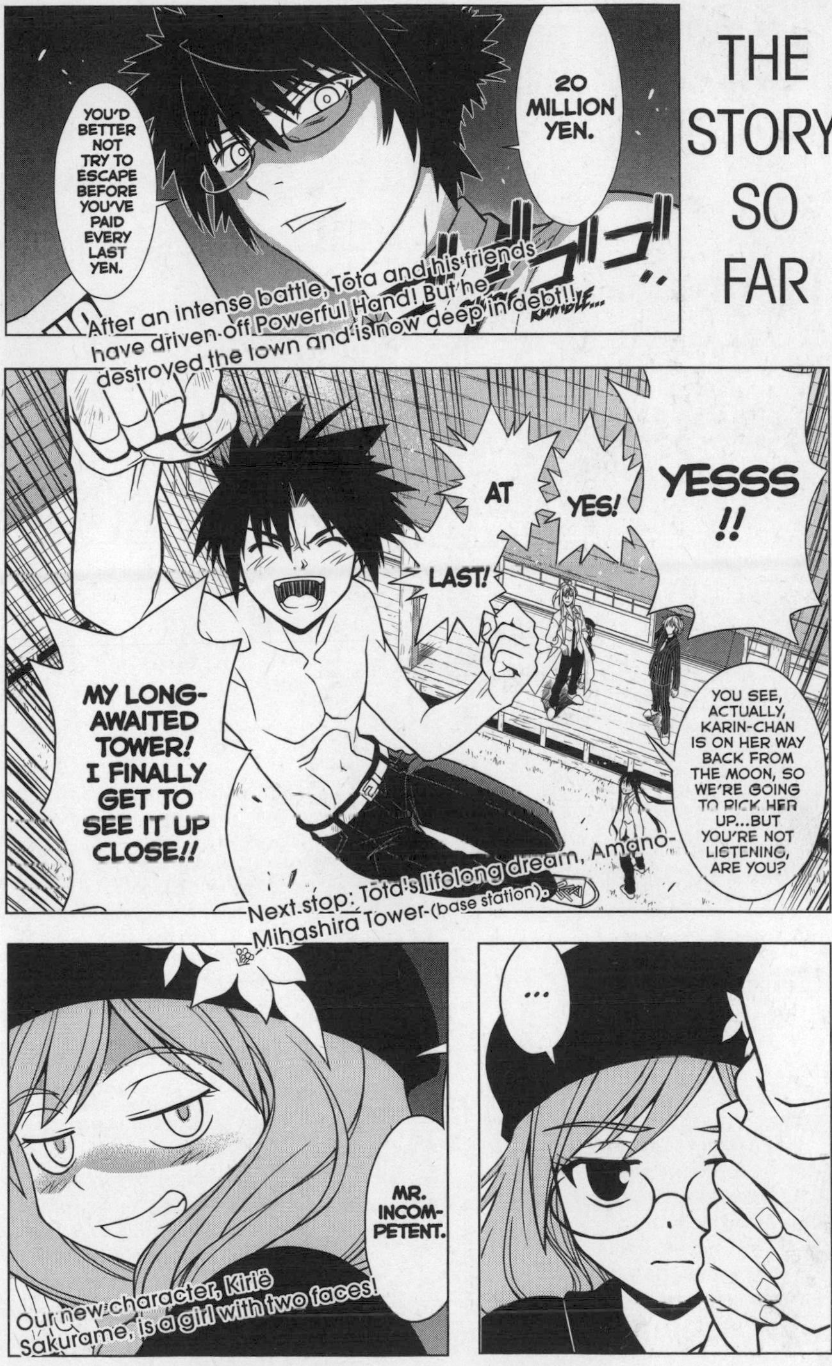

20 MILLION YEN.
YOU'D BETTER NOT TRY TO ESCAPE BEFORE YOU'VE PAID EVERY LAST YEN.
RUMBLE...
After an intense battle, Tōta and his friends have driven off Powerful Hand! But he destroyed the town and is now deep in debt!!
YESSS!!
YES!
AT
LAST!
YOU SEE, ACTUALLY, KARIN-CHAN IS ON HER WAY BACK FROM THE MOON, SO WE'RE GOING TO PICK HER UP...BUT YOU'RE NOT LISTENING, ARE YOU?
MY LONG-AWAITED TOWER! I FINALLY GET TO SEE IT UP CLOSE!!
Next stop: Tōta's lifelong dream, Amano-Mihashira Tower (base station).
...
MR. INCOMPETENT.
Our new character, Kiriё Sakurame, is a girl with two faces!

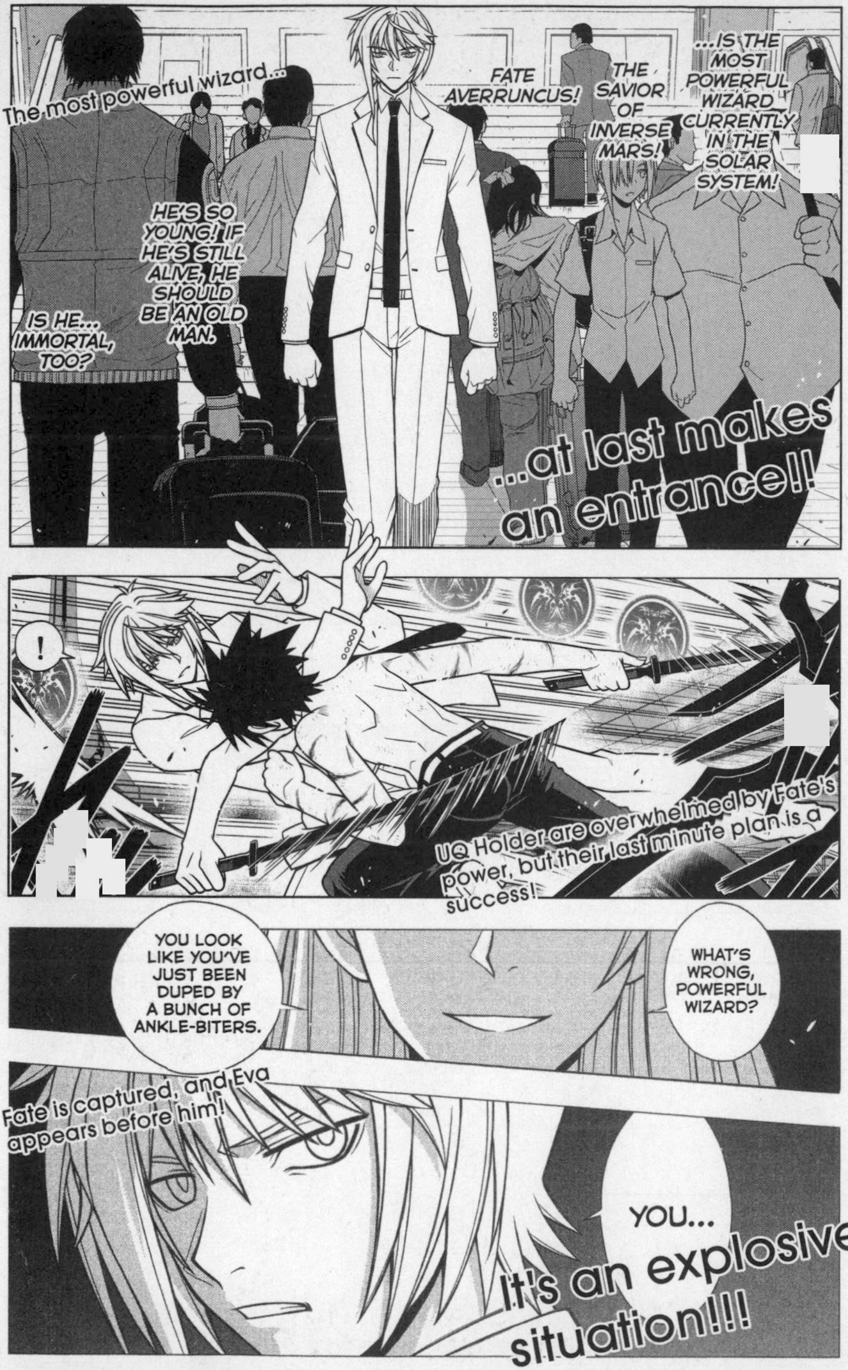
The most powerful wizard...
FATE AVERRUNCUS!
THE SAVIOR OF INVERSE MARS!
...IS THE MOST POWERFUL WIZARD CURRENTLY IN THE SOLAR SYSTEM!
HE'S SO YOUNG! IF HE'S STILL ALIVE, HE SHOULD BE AN OLD MAN.
IS HE... IMMORTAL, TOO?
...at last makes an entrance!!
!
UQ Holder are overwhelmed by Fate's power, but their last minute plan is a success!
WHAT'S WRONG, POWERFUL WIZARD?
YOU LOOK LIKE YOU'VE JUST BEEN DUPED BY A BUNCH OF ANKLE-BITERS.
Fate is captured, and Eva appears before him!
YOU...
It's an explosive situation!!!

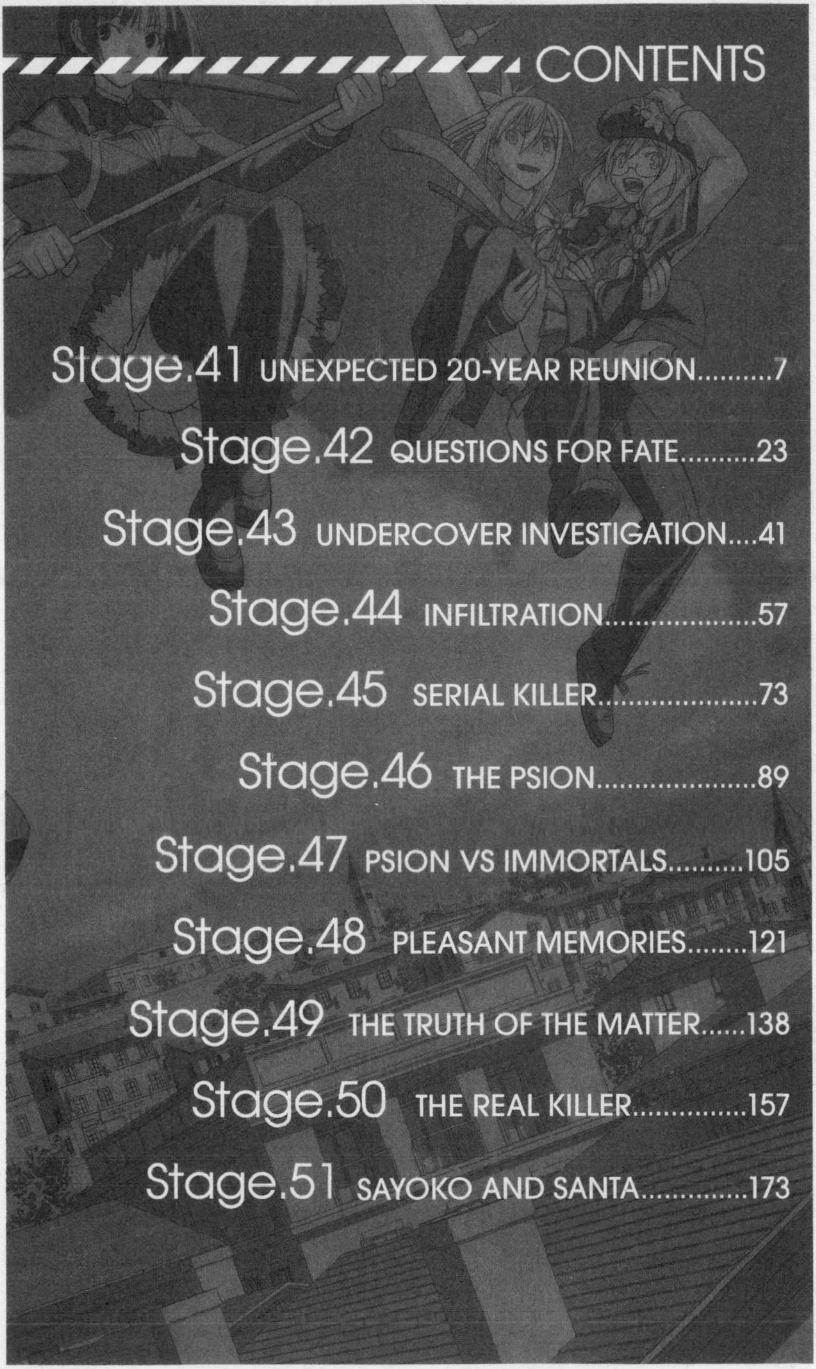

CONTENTS

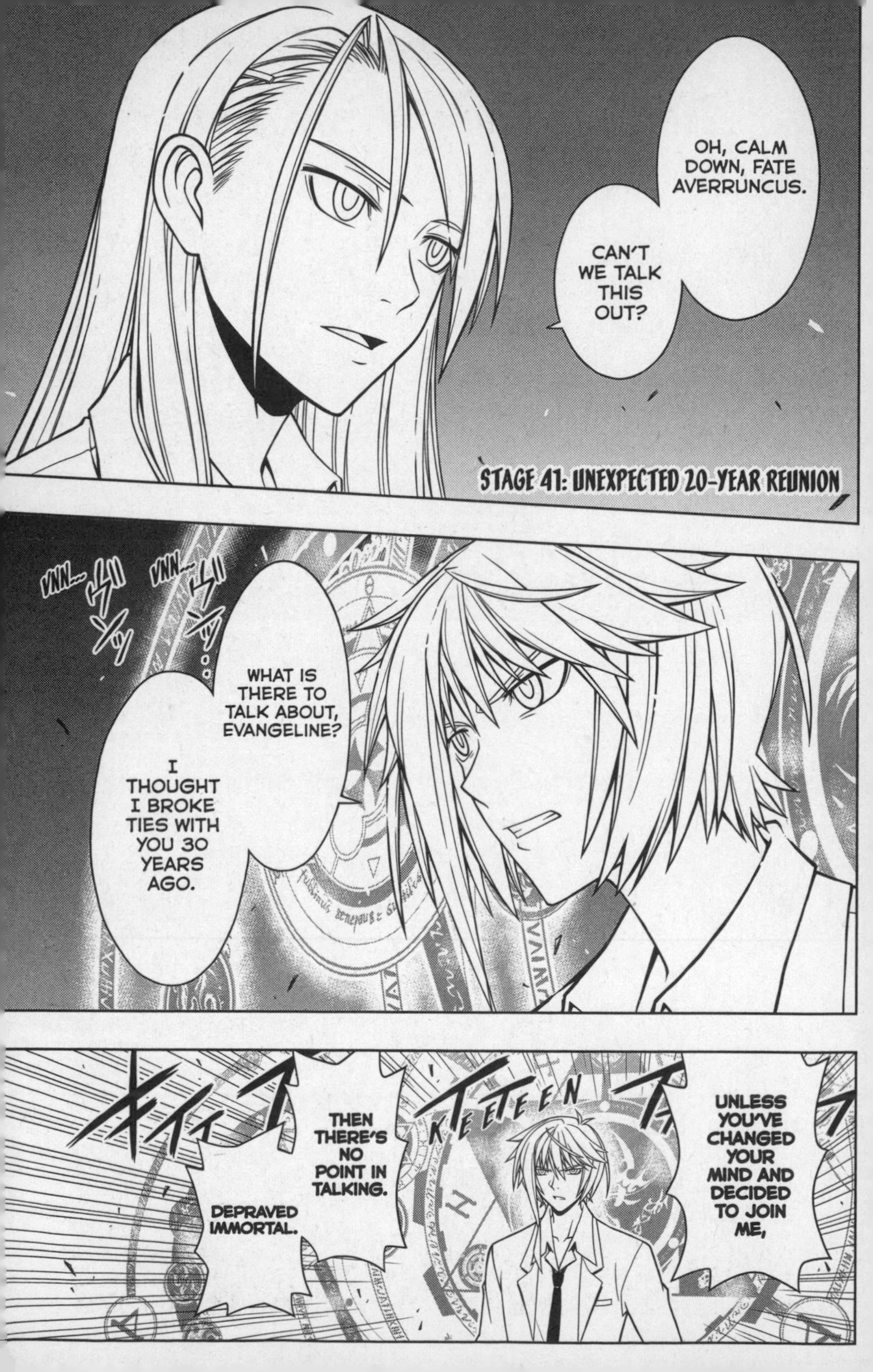
OH, CALM DOWN, FATE AVERRUNCUS.
CAN'T WE TALK THIS OUT?
STAGE 41: UNEXPECTED 20-YEAR REUNION
VNN...
VNN...
WHAT IS THERE TO TALK ABOUT, EVANGELINE?
I THOUGHT I BROKE TIES WITH YOU 30 YEARS AGO.
UNLESS YOU'VE CHANGED YOUR MIND AND DECIDED TO JOIN ME,
KEEEEN
THEN THERE'S NO POINT IN TALKING.
DEPRAVED IMMORTAL.

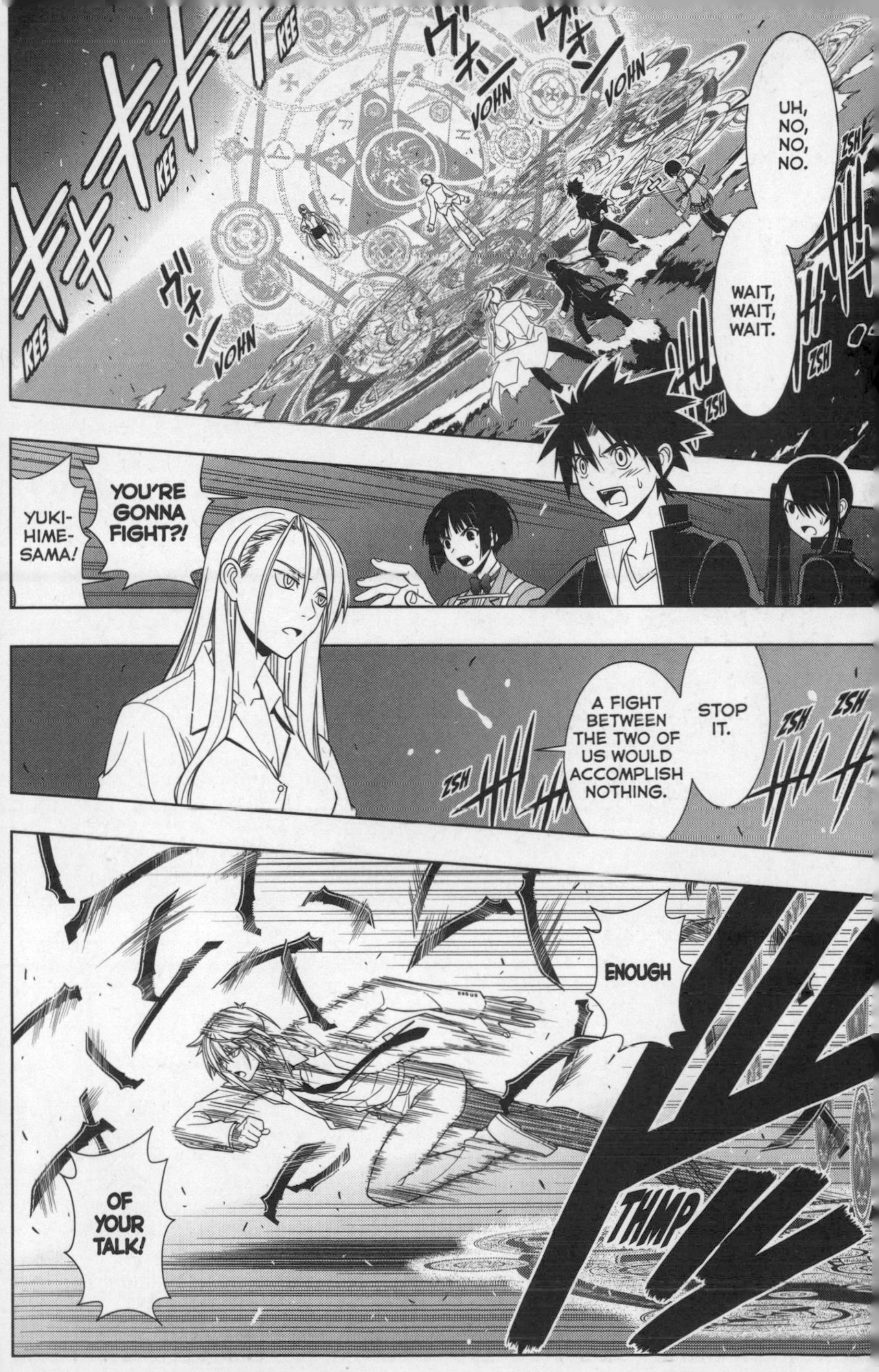
UH, NO, NO, NO.
WAIT, WAIT, WAIT.
ZSH
ZSH
ヴォン
VOHN
ヴォン
VOHN
ヴォン
VOHN
KEE
KEE
KEE
YOU'RE GONNA FIGHT?!
YUKI-HIME-SAMA!
STOP IT.
A FIGHT BETWEEN THE TWO OF US WOULD ACCOMPLISH NOTHING.
ZSH
ZSH
ZSH
ENOUGH
OF YOUR TALK!
THMP

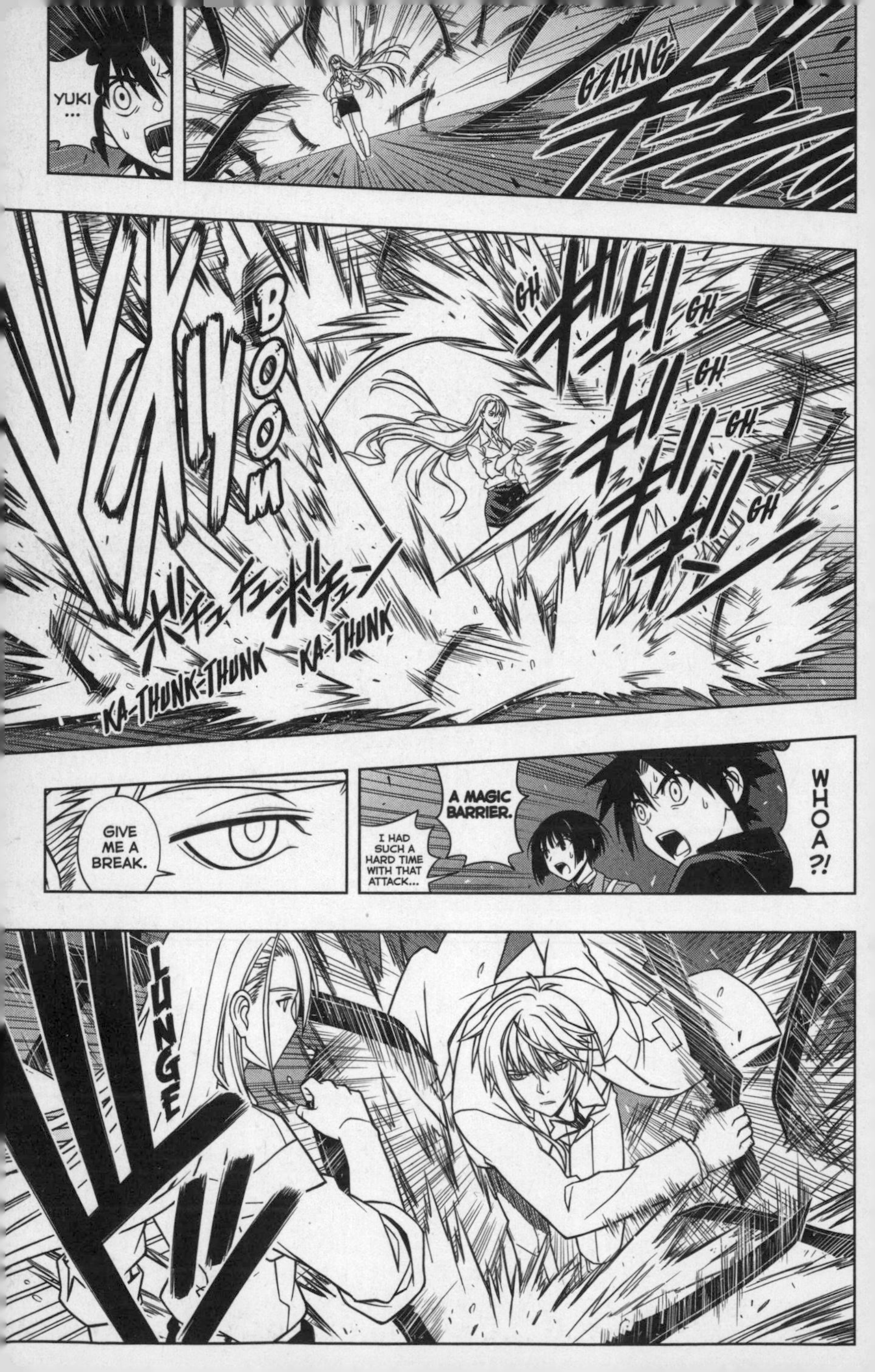
GZHNG
YUKI...
GH GH GH GH GH
BOOM
KA-THUNK
KA-THUNK-THUNK
WHOA?!
A MAGIC BARRIER.
I HAD SUCH A HARD TIME WITH THAT ATTACK...
GIVE ME A BREAK.
LUNGE

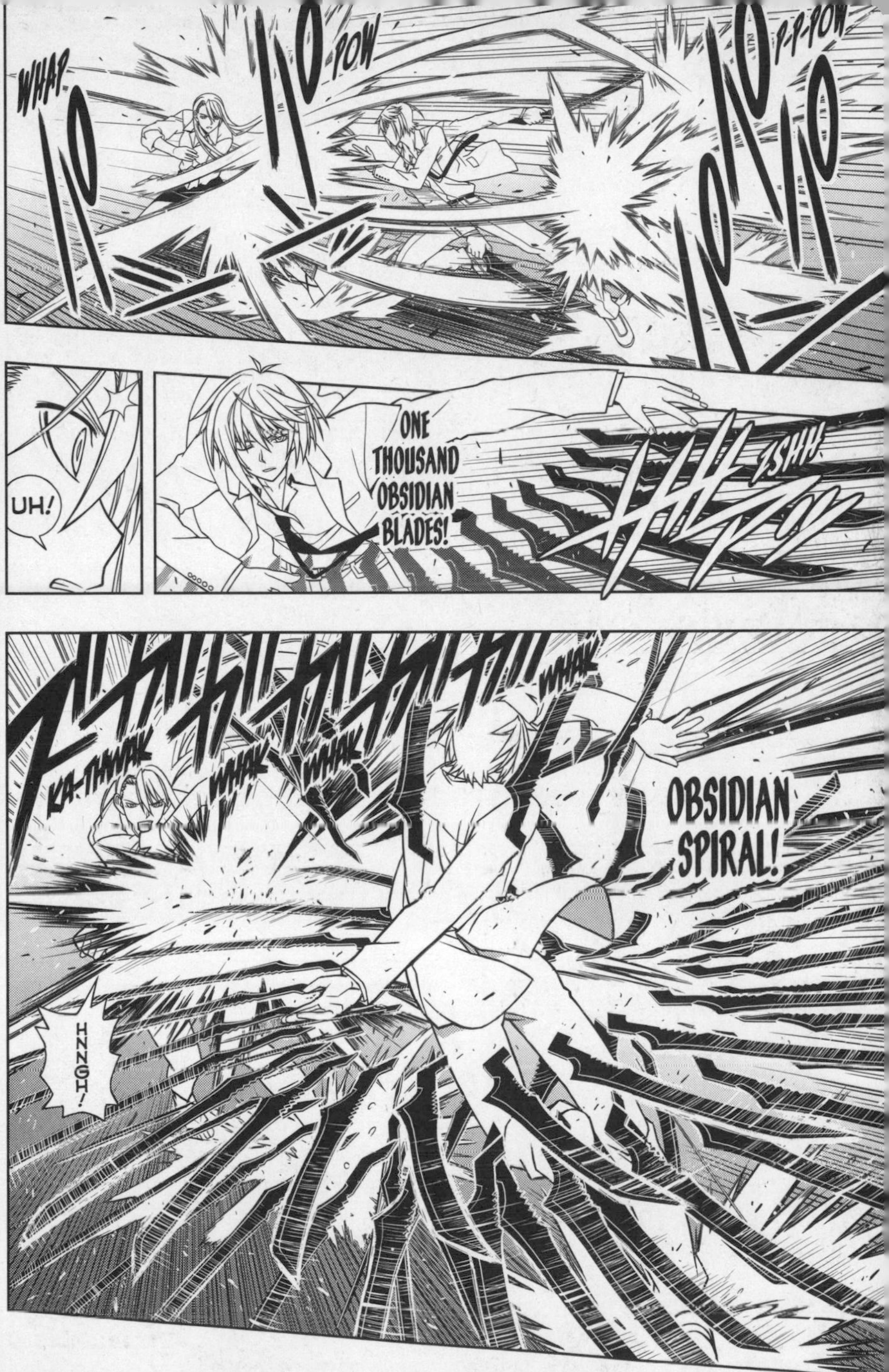
P-P-POW
POW
WHAP
ZSHH
ONE THOUSAND OBSIDIAN BLADES!
UH!
OBSIDIAN SPIRAL!
WHAK
WHAK
WHAK
KA-THWAK
HNNGH!

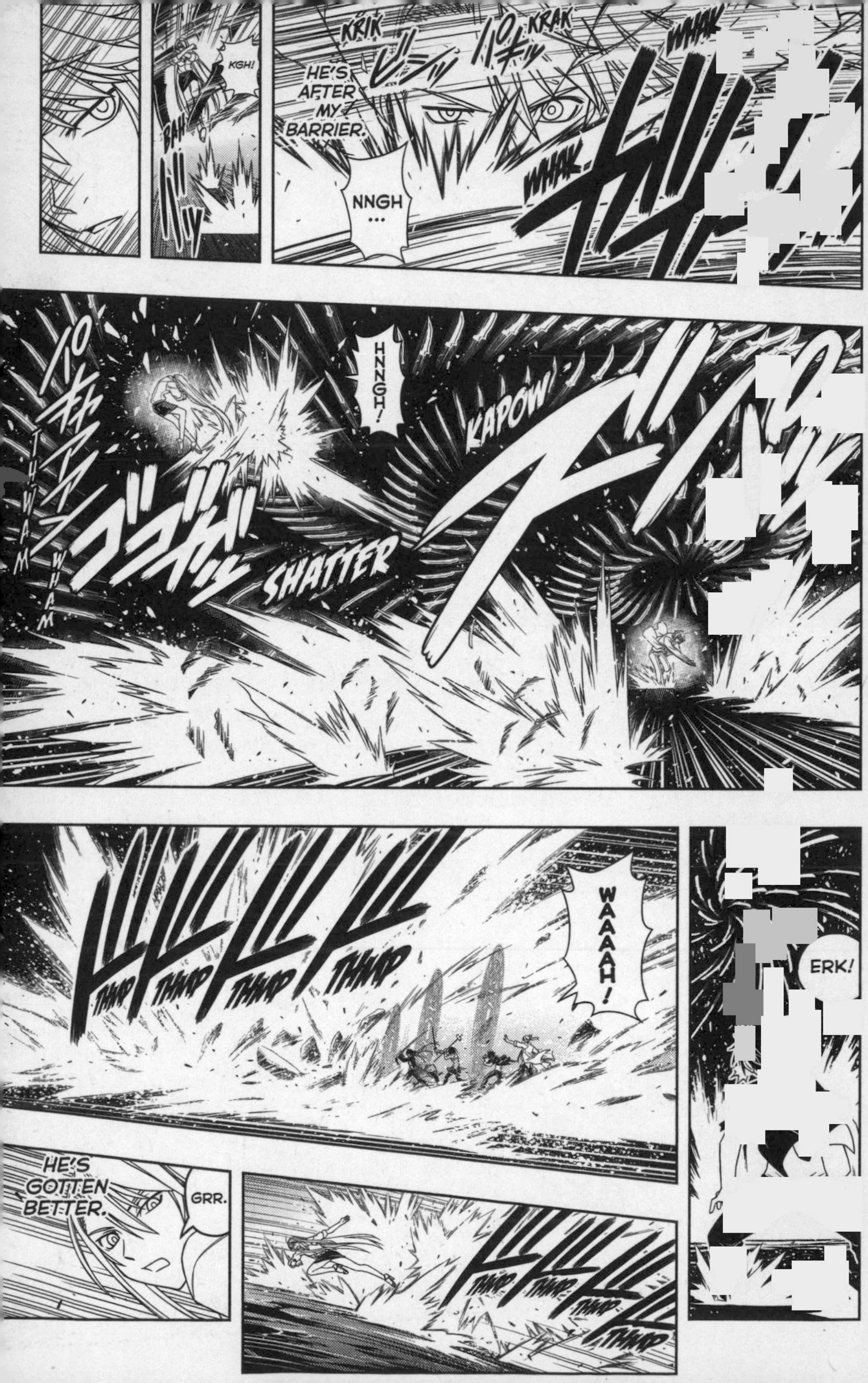
WHAK
KRAK
KRIK
HE'S AFTER MY BARRIER.
WHAK
NNGH...
KGH!
BAM
KAPOW
HNNGH!
SHATTER
THWAM
WHAM
ERK!
WAAAAH!
THWP
THWP
THWP
THWP
THWP
THWP
THWP
THWP
THWP
GRR.
HE'S GOTTEN BETTER.

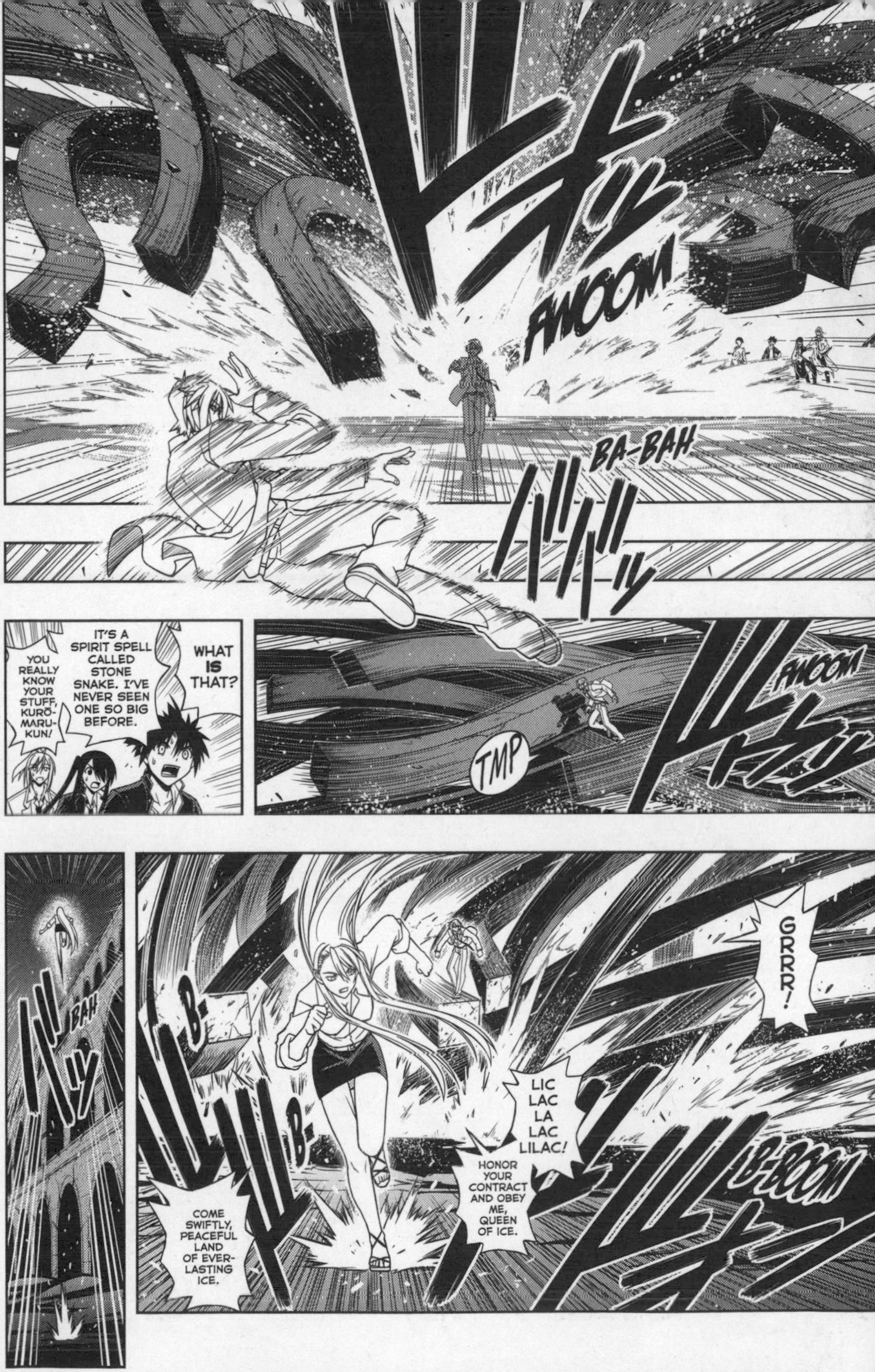
FWOOM
BA-BAH
FWOOM
TMP
WHAT IS THAT?
IT'S A SPIRIT SPELL CALLED STONE SNAKE. I'VE NEVER SEEN ONE SO BIG BEFORE.
YOU REALLY KNOW YOUR STUFF, KURŌMARU-KUN!
GRRR!
B-BOOM
LIC LAC LA LAC LILAC!
HONOR YOUR CONTRACT AND OBEY ME, QUEEN OF ICE.
B-
B-
COME SWIFTLY, PEACEFUL LAND OF EVER-LASTING ICE.
BAH

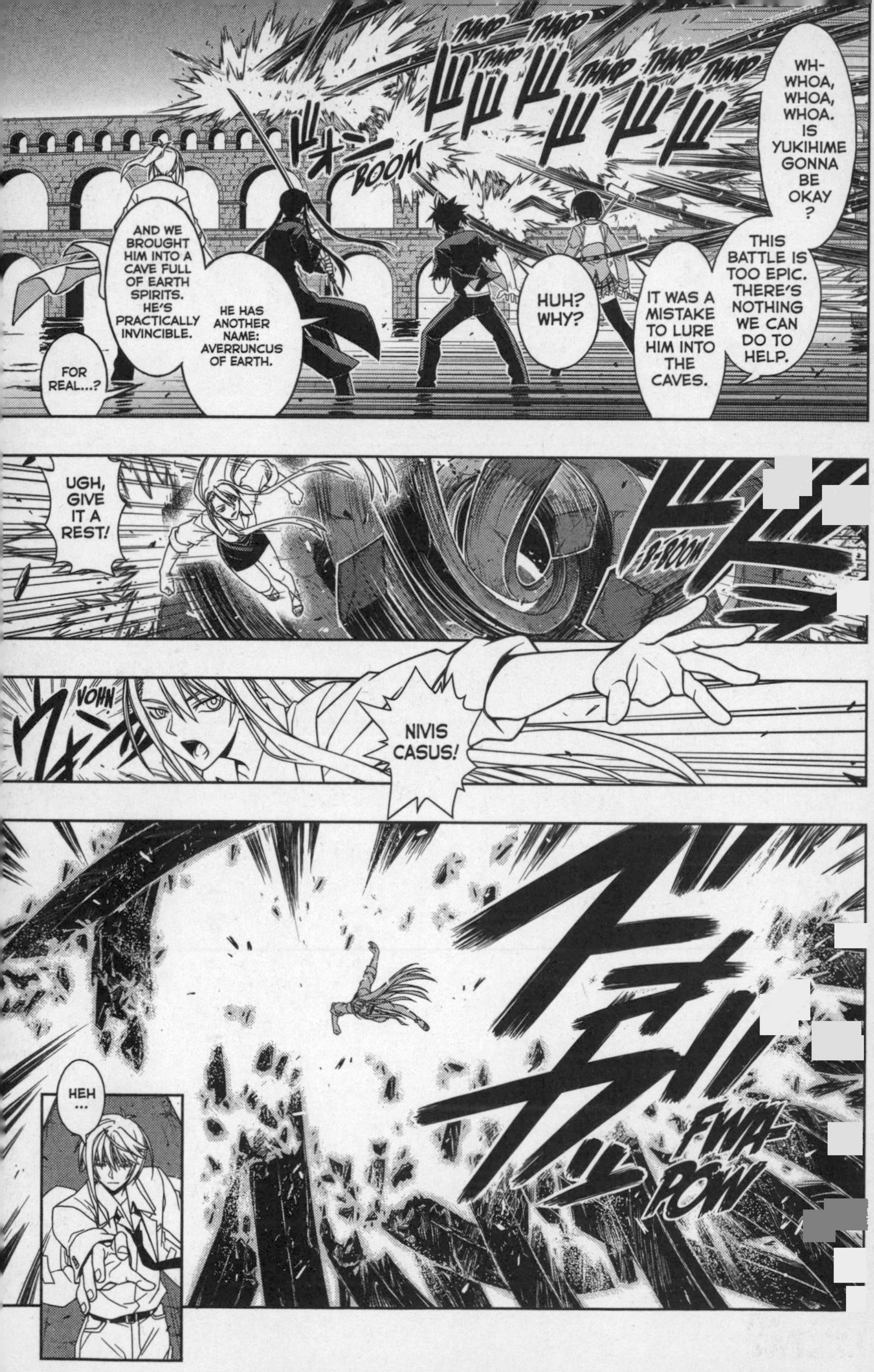
THMP THMP THMP THMP THMP THMP THMP
BOOM
WH-WHOA, WHOA, WHOA. IS YUKIHIME GONNA BE OKAY?
THIS BATTLE IS TOO EPIC. THERE'S NOTHING WE CAN DO TO HELP.
IT WAS A MISTAKE TO LURE HIM INTO THE CAVES.
HUH? WHY?
HE HAS ANOTHER NAME: AVERRUNCUS OF EARTH.
AND WE BROUGHT HIM INTO A CAVE FULL OF EARTH SPIRITS. HE'S PRACTICALLY INVINCIBLE.
FOR REAL...?
B-BOOM
UGH, GIVE IT A REST!
NIVIS CASUS!
VOHN
FWA-POW
HEH...

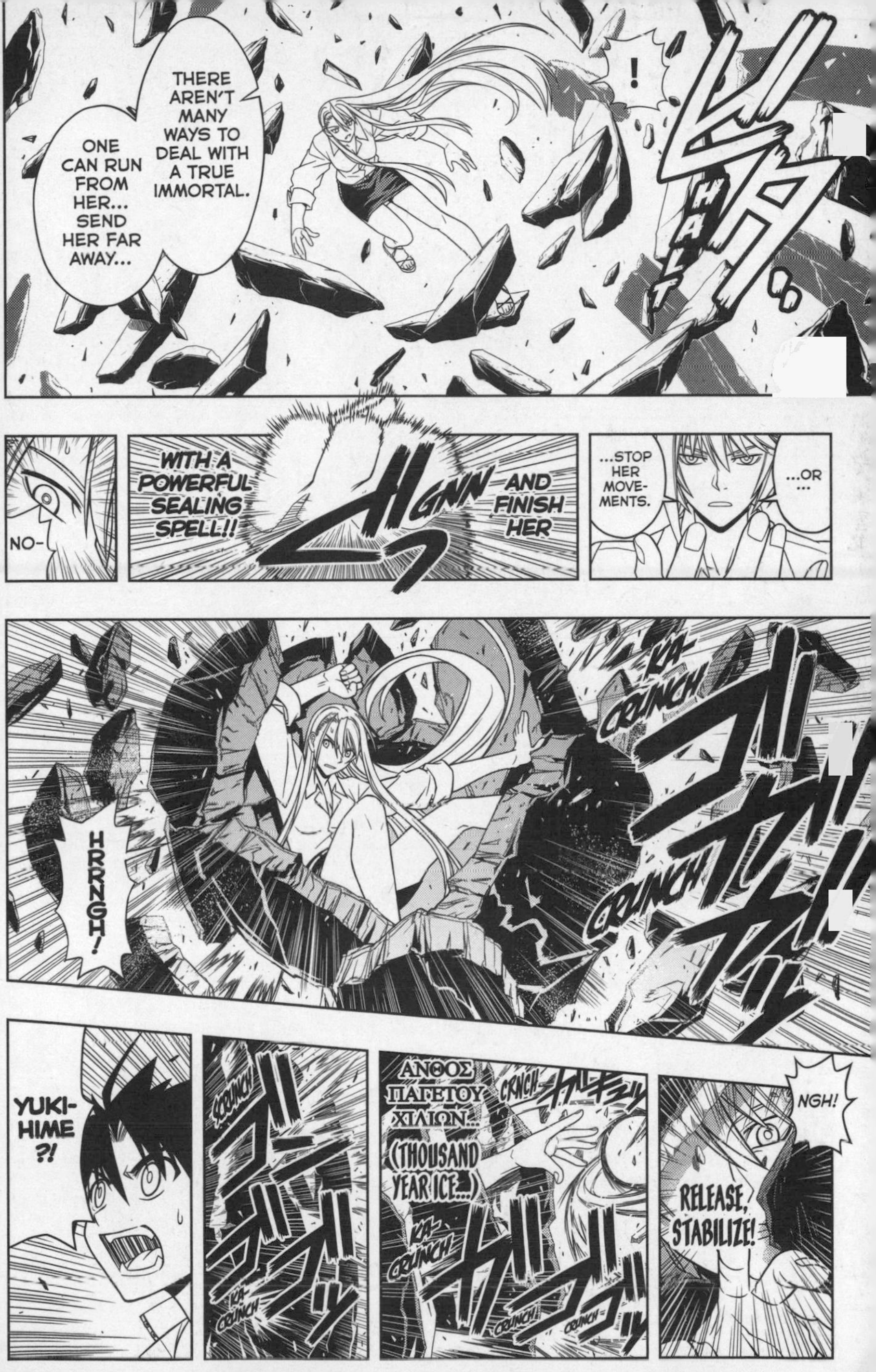
!
HALT
THERE AREN'T MANY WAYS TO DEAL WITH A TRUE IMMORTAL.
ONE CAN RUN FROM HER... SEND HER FAR AWAY...
...OR ...
...STOP HER MOVEMENTS.
WITH A POWERFUL SEALING SPELL!!
HGNN
AND FINISH HER
NO-
KA-CRUNCH
CRUNCH
HRRNGH!
NGH!
RELEASE, STABILIZE!
ΑΝΘΟΣ ΠΑΓΕΤΟΥ ΧΙΛΙΩΝ...
(THOUSAND YEAR ICE...)
CRNCH
KA-CRUNCH
CRUNCH
CRUNCH
SCRUNCH
KA-CRUNCH
YUKI-HIME ?!

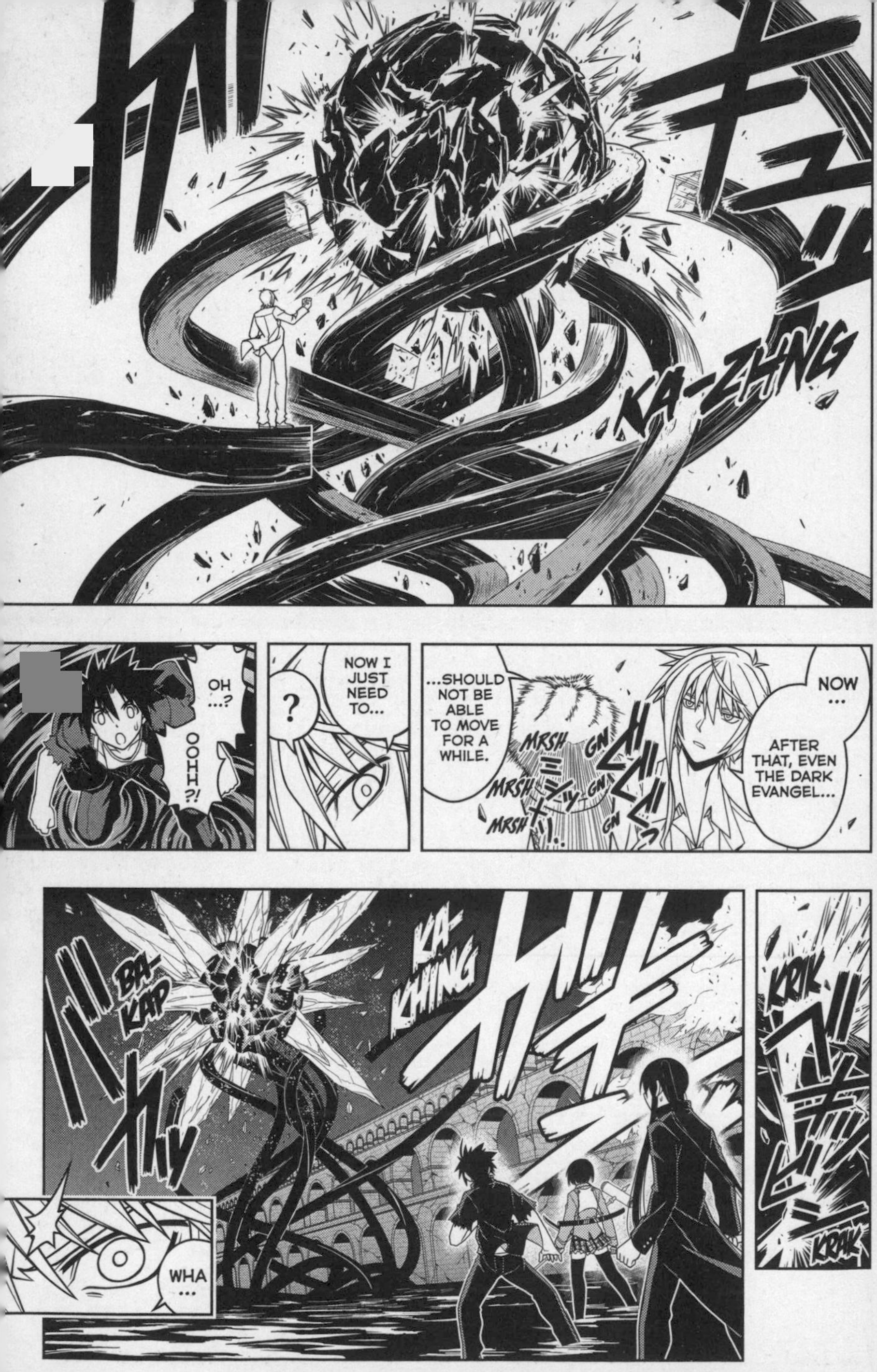
KA-ZHING
NOW...
AFTER THAT, EVEN THE DARK EVANGEL...
...SHOULD NOT BE ABLE TO MOVE FOR A WHILE.
MRSH
MRSH
MRSH
GN
GN
GN
NOW I JUST NEED TO...
?
OH...?
OOHH?!
KRIK
KRAK
KA-KHING
BA-KAP
WHA...

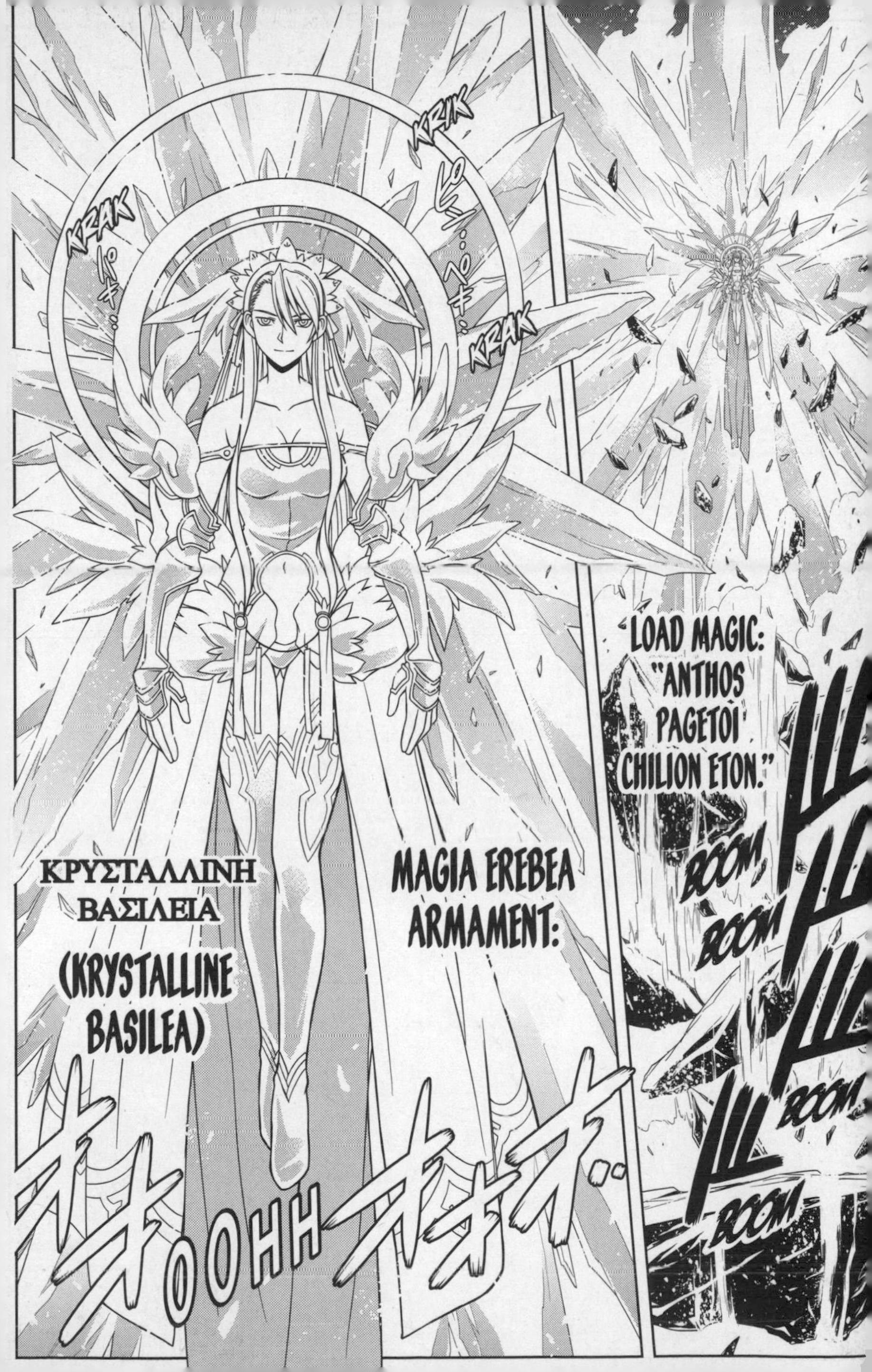
LOAD MAGIC: "ANTHOS PAGETOI CHILION ETON."
BOOM
BOOM
BOOM
BOOM
KRAK
KRAK
KRAK
MAGIA EREBEA ARMAMENT:
ΚΡΥΣΤΑΛΛΙΝΗ ΒΑΣΙΛΕΙΑ
(KRYSTALLINE BASILEA)
OOHH

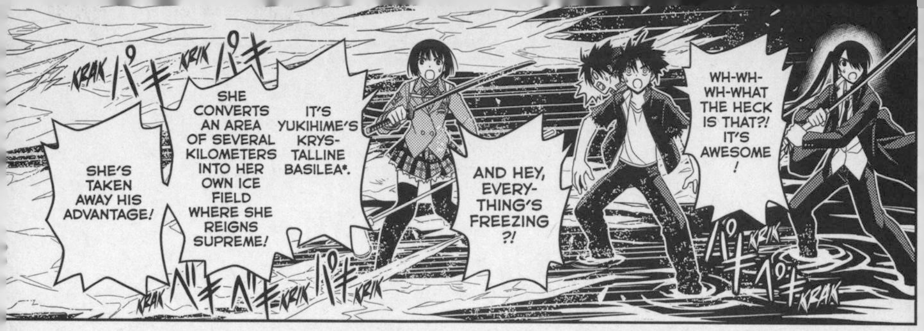
KRAK
KRIK
WH-WH-WH-WHAT THE HECK IS THAT?! IT'S AWESOME!
AND HEY, EVERYTHING'S FREEZING?!
IT'S YUKIHIME'S KRYSTALLINE BASILEA*.
SHE CONVERTS AN AREA OF SEVERAL KILOMETERS INTO HER OWN ICE FIELD WHERE SHE REIGNS SUPREME!
SHE'S TAKEN AWAY HIS ADVANTAGE!
KRAK
KRIK
KRIK
KRAK

*Queen of Ice

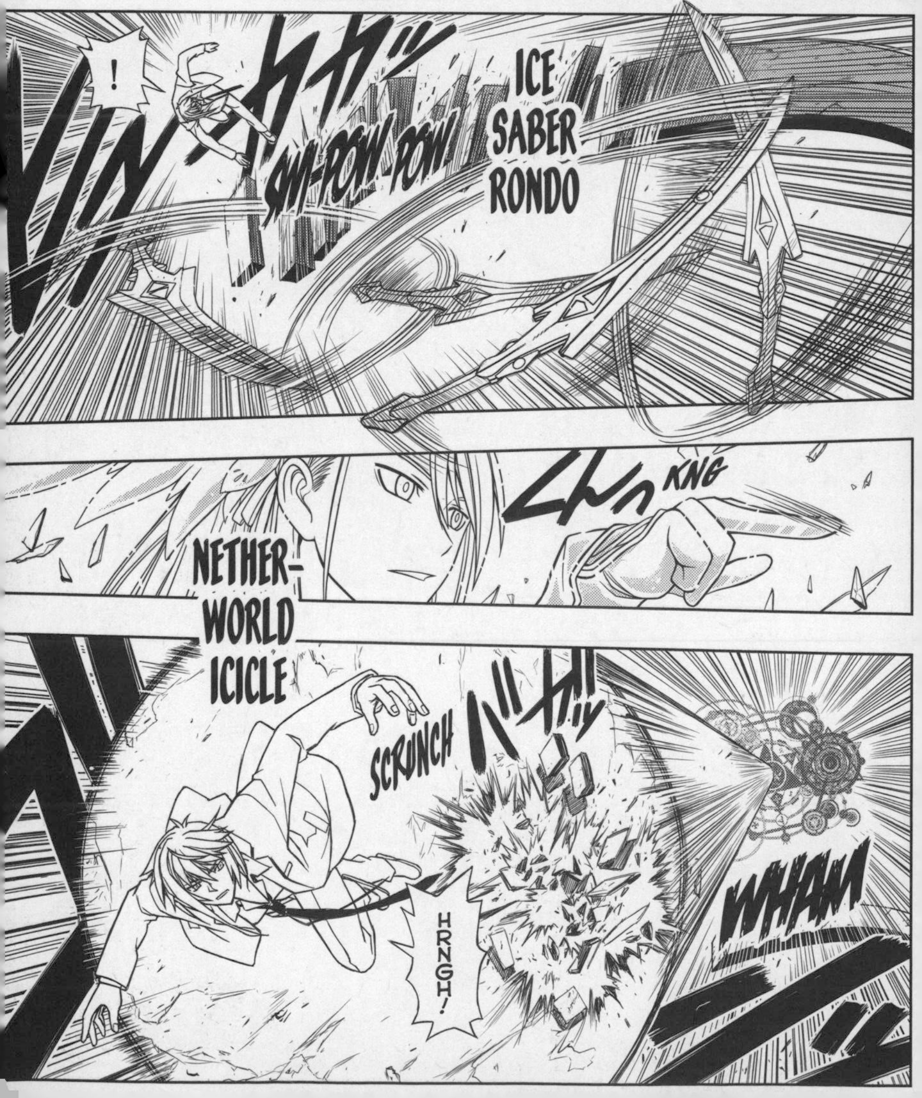
ICE SABER RONDO
SWI-POW POW POW
!
KNG
NETHER-WORLD ICICLE
SCRUNCH
WHAM
HRNGH!

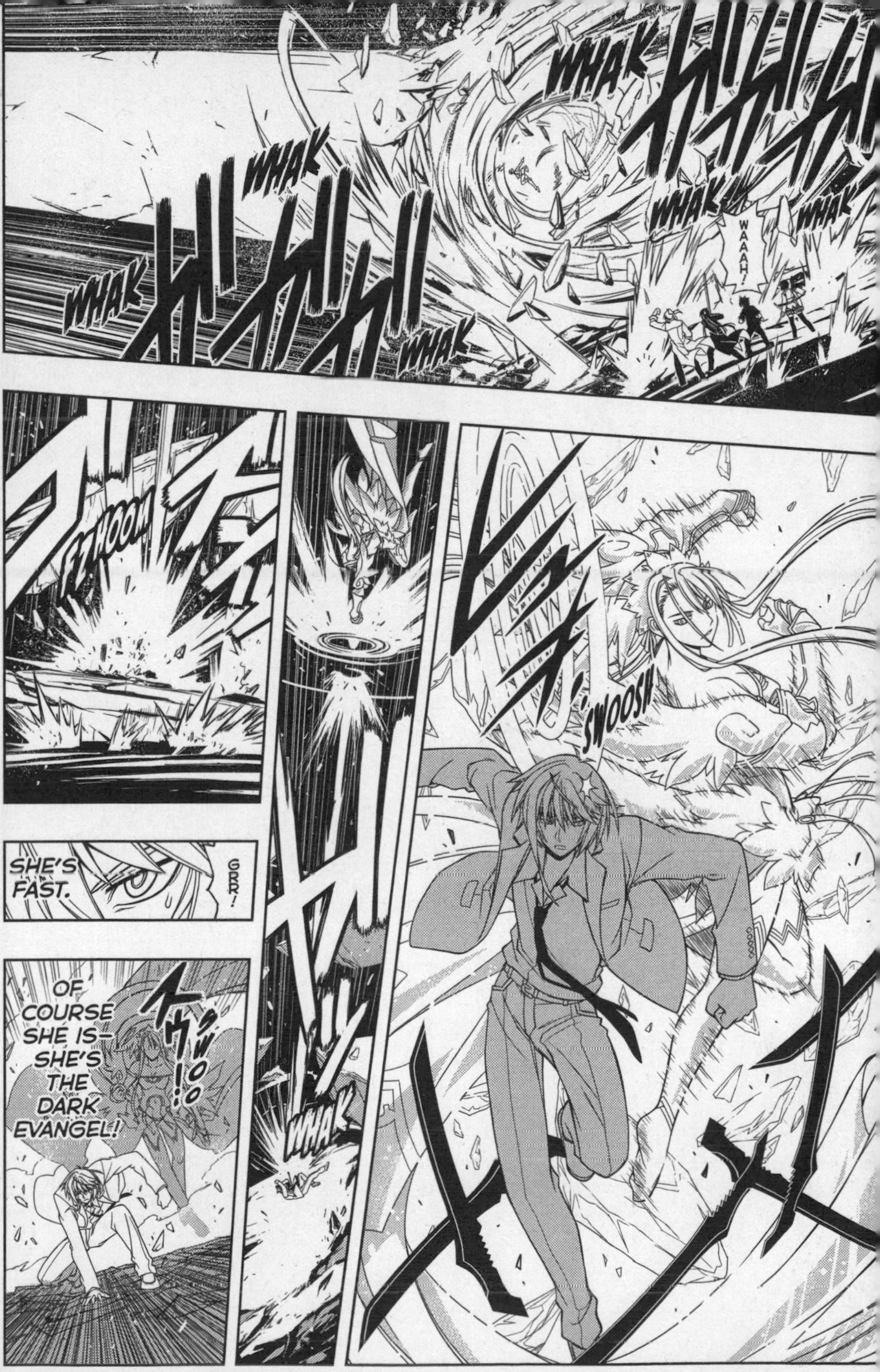
WHAK
WHAK
WHAK
WAAAH!
WHAK
WHAK
WHAK
SWOOSH
WHAK
FZHOOM
GRR!
SHE'S FAST.
OF COURSE SHE IS— SHE'S THE DARK EVANGEL!
SWOOO

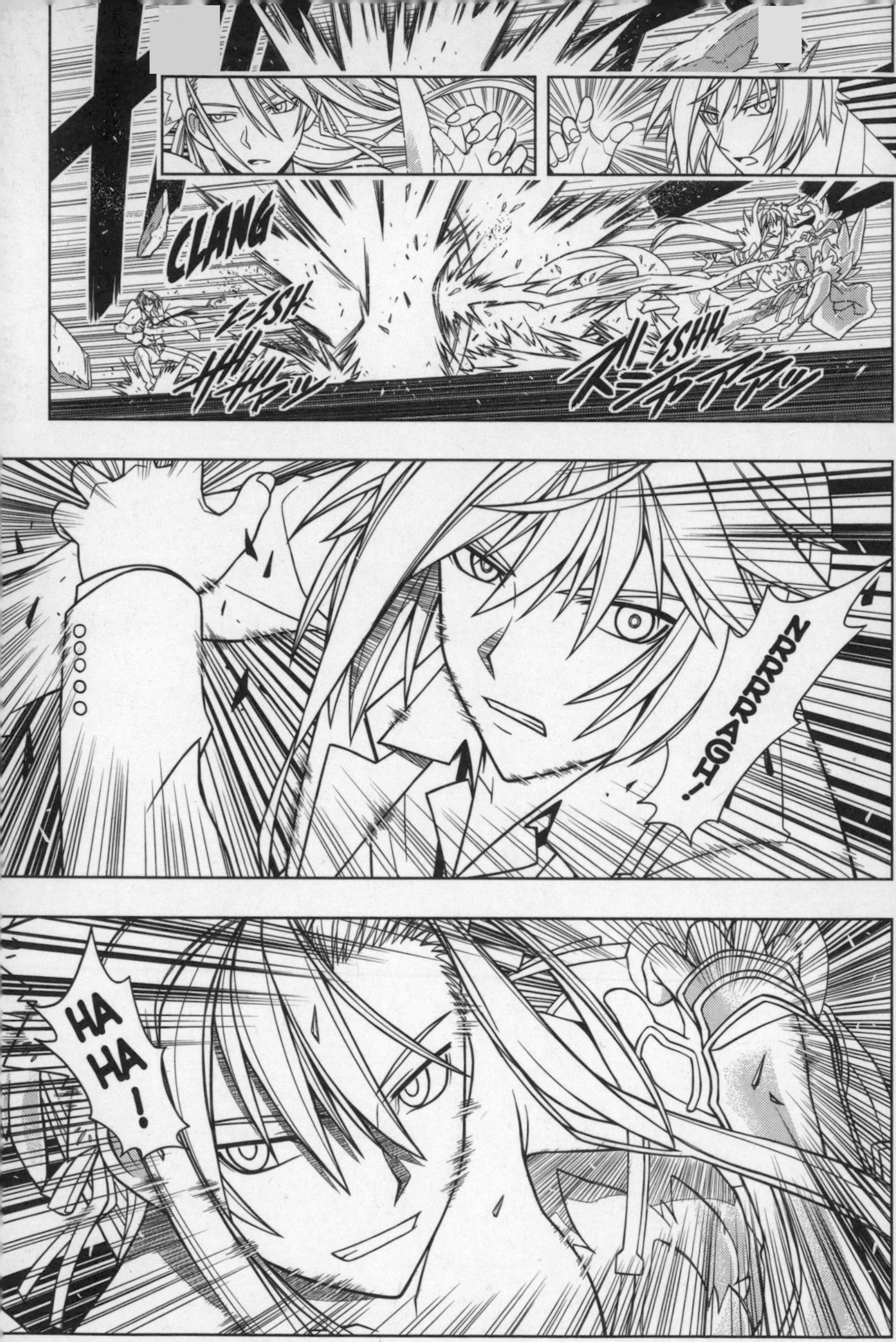
CLANG
ZSHH
Z-ZSH
ZRRRRAGH!
HA HA!

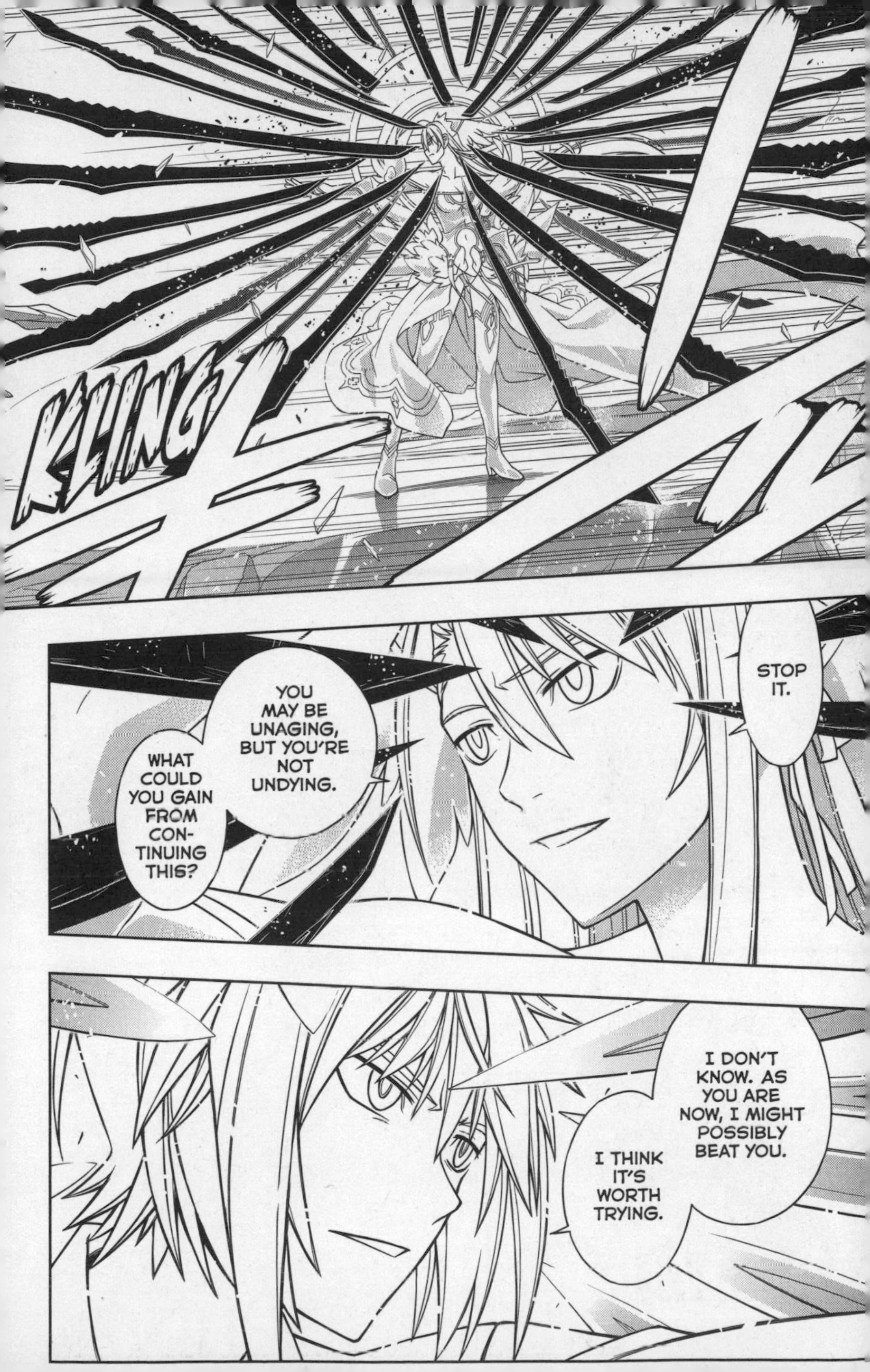
KLING
STOP IT.
YOU MAY BE UNAGING, BUT YOU'RE NOT UNDYING.
WHAT COULD YOU GAIN FROM CON-TINUING THIS?
I DON'T KNOW. AS YOU ARE NOW, I MIGHT POSSIBLY BEAT YOU.
I THINK IT'S WORTH TRYING.

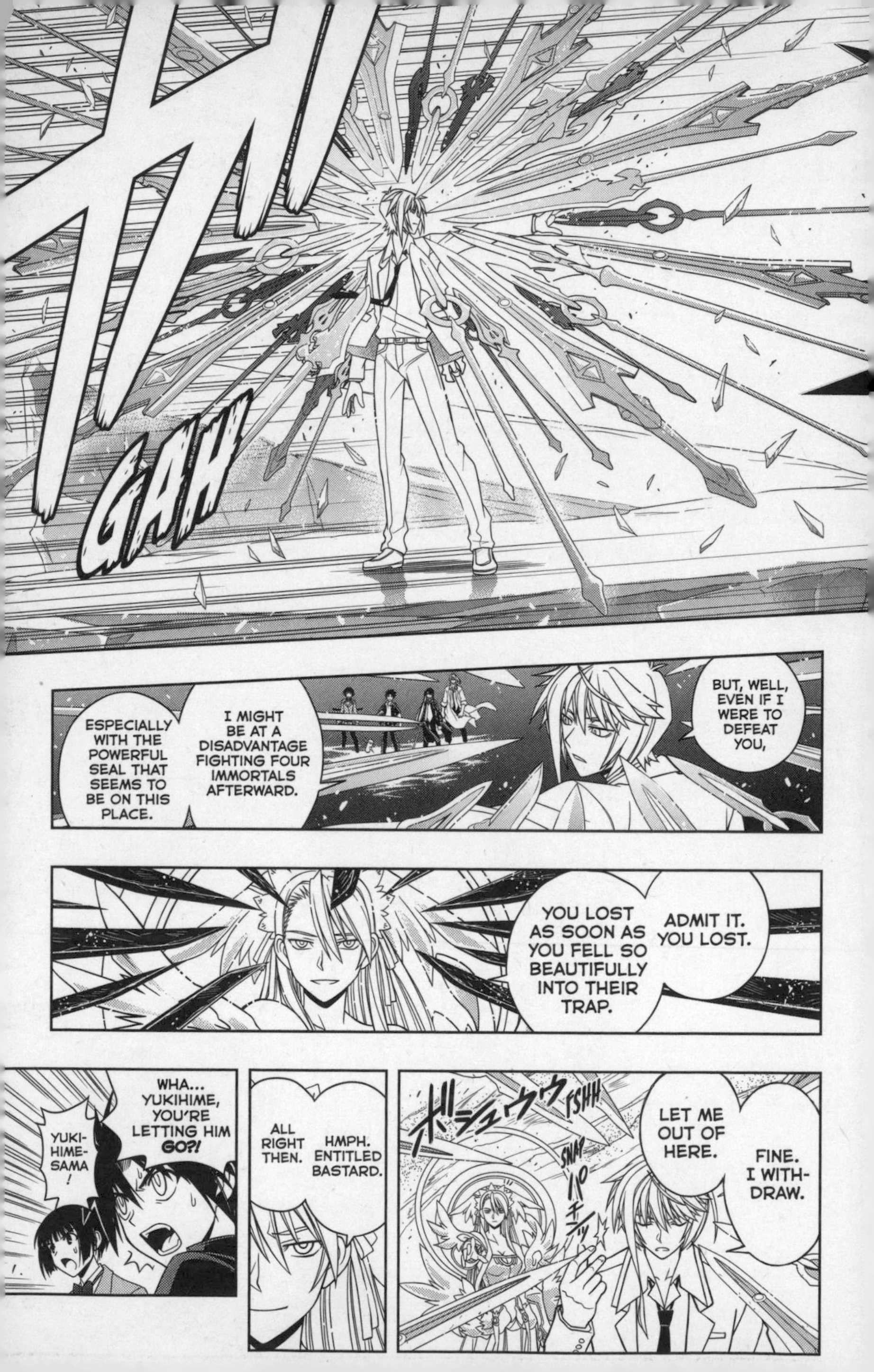
GAH
BUT, WELL, EVEN IF I WERE TO DEFEAT YOU,
I MIGHT BE AT A DISADVANTAGE FIGHTING FOUR IMMORTALS AFTERWARD.
ESPECIALLY WITH THE POWERFUL SEAL THAT SEEMS TO BE ON THIS PLACE.
ADMIT IT. YOU LOST.
YOU LOST AS SOON AS YOU FELL SO BEAUTIFULLY INTO THEIR TRAP.
FINE. I WITH-DRAW.
LET ME OUT OF HERE.
FSHH
SNAP
HMPH. ENTITLED BASTARD.
ALL RIGHT THEN.
WHA... YUKIHIME, YOU'RE LETTING HIM GO?!
YUKI-HIME-SAMA!

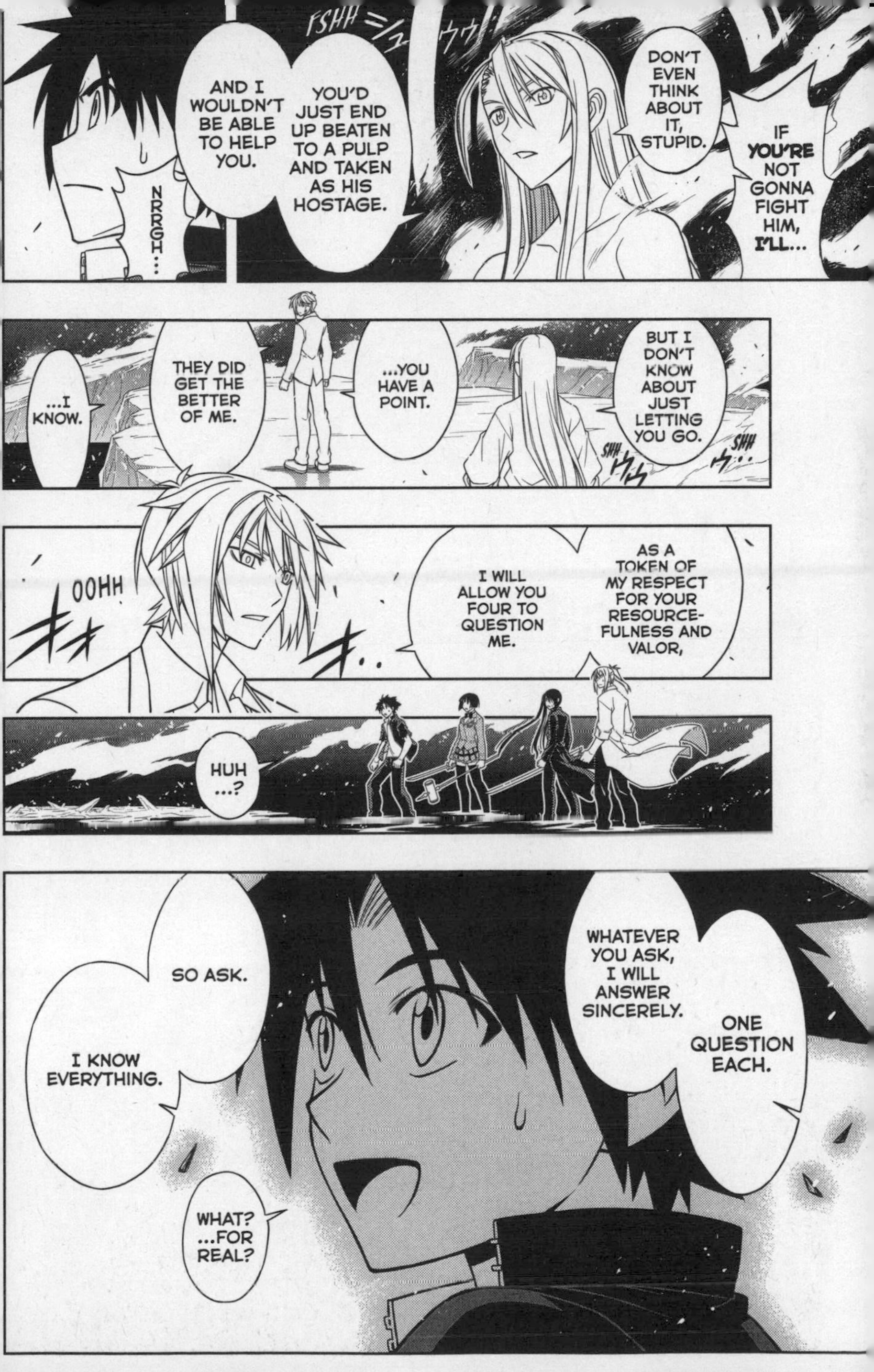
IF YOU'RE NOT GONNA FIGHT HIM, I'LL...
DON'T EVEN THINK ABOUT IT, STUPID.
FSHH
YOU'D JUST END UP BEATEN TO A PULP AND TAKEN AS HIS HOSTAGE.
AND I WOULDN'T BE ABLE TO HELP YOU.
NRRGH...
BUT I DON'T KNOW ABOUT JUST LETTING YOU GO.
SHH
SHH
...YOU HAVE A POINT.
THEY DID GET THE BETTER OF ME.
...I KNOW.
AS A TOKEN OF MY RESPECT FOR YOUR RESOURCE-FULNESS AND VALOR,
I WILL ALLOW YOU FOUR TO QUESTION ME.
OOHH
HUH ...?
ONE QUESTION EACH.
WHATEVER YOU ASK, I WILL ANSWER SINCERELY.
SO ASK.
I KNOW EVERYTHING.
WHAT? ...FOR REAL?

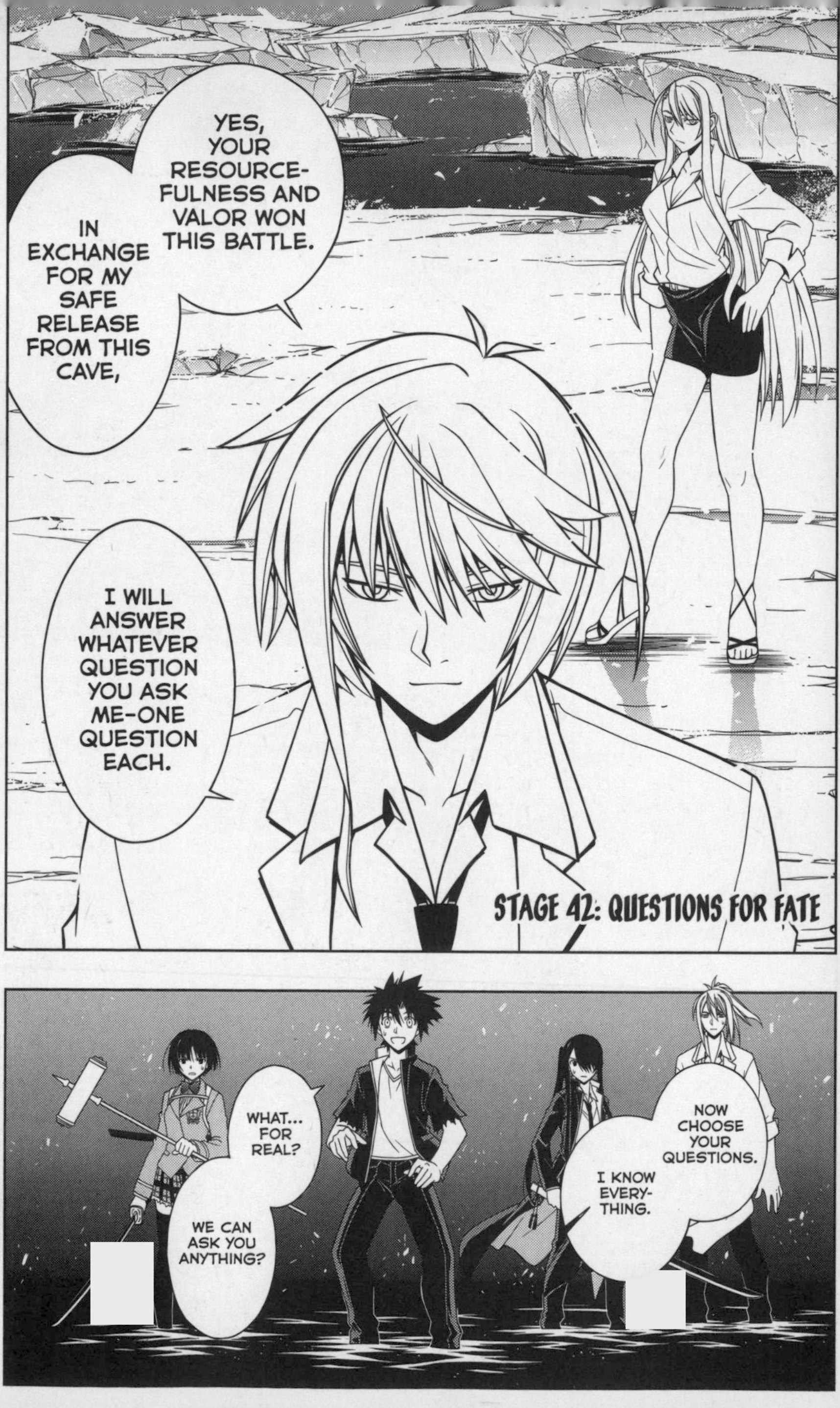
YES, YOUR RESOURCE-FULNESS AND VALOR WON THIS BATTLE.
IN EXCHANGE FOR MY SAFE RELEASE FROM THIS CAVE,
I WILL ANSWER WHATEVER QUESTION YOU ASK ME-ONE QUESTION EACH.
STAGE 42: QUESTIONS FOR FATE
NOW CHOOSE YOUR QUESTIONS.
I KNOW EVERY-THING.
WHAT... FOR REAL?
WE CAN ASK YOU ANYTHING?

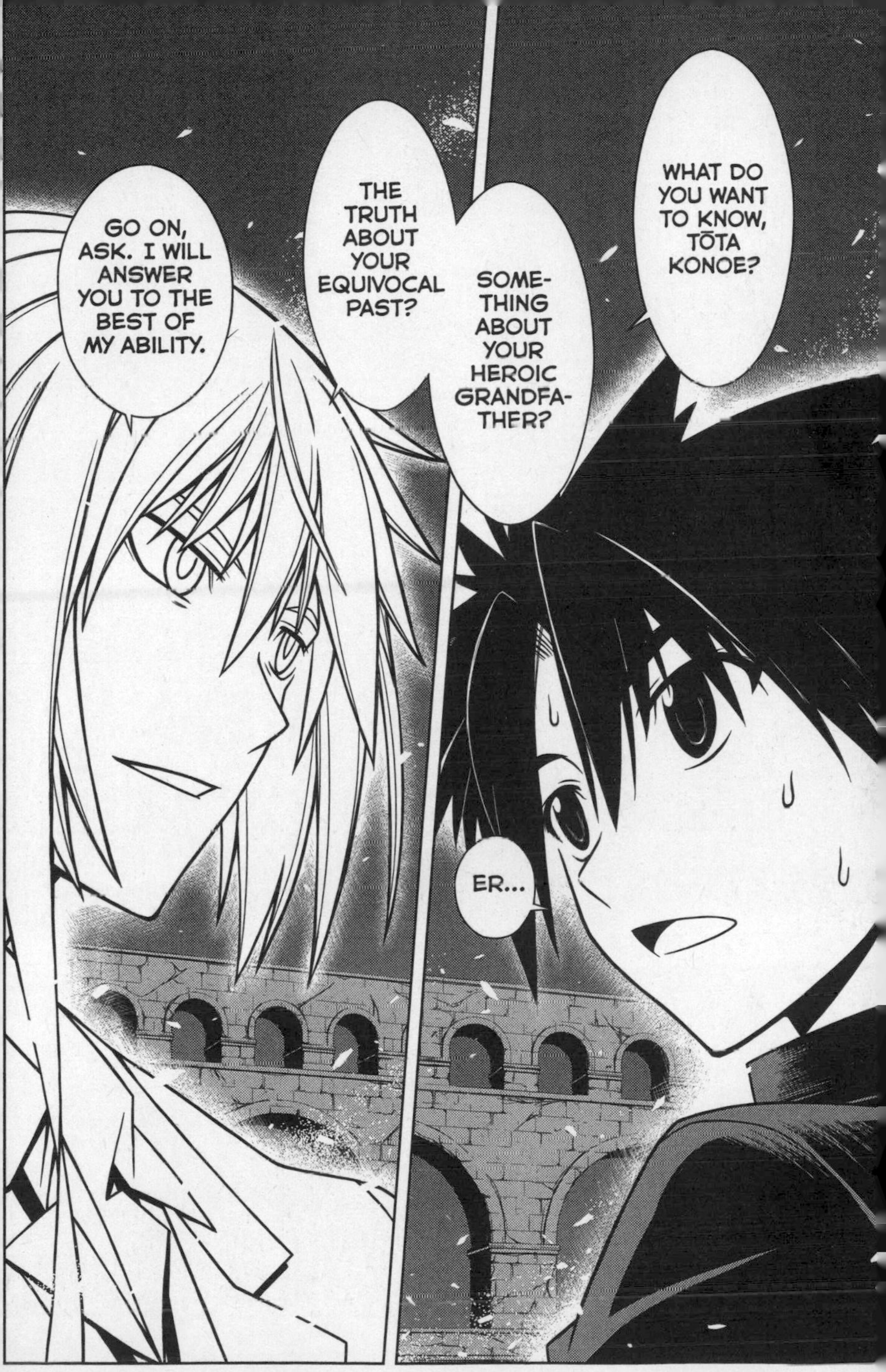
WHAT DO YOU WANT TO KNOW, TŌTA KONOE?
SOMETHING ABOUT YOUR HEROIC GRANDFATHER?
ER...
THE TRUTH ABOUT YOUR EQUIVOCAL PAST?
GO ON, ASK. I WILL ANSWER YOU TO THE BEST OF MY ABILITY.

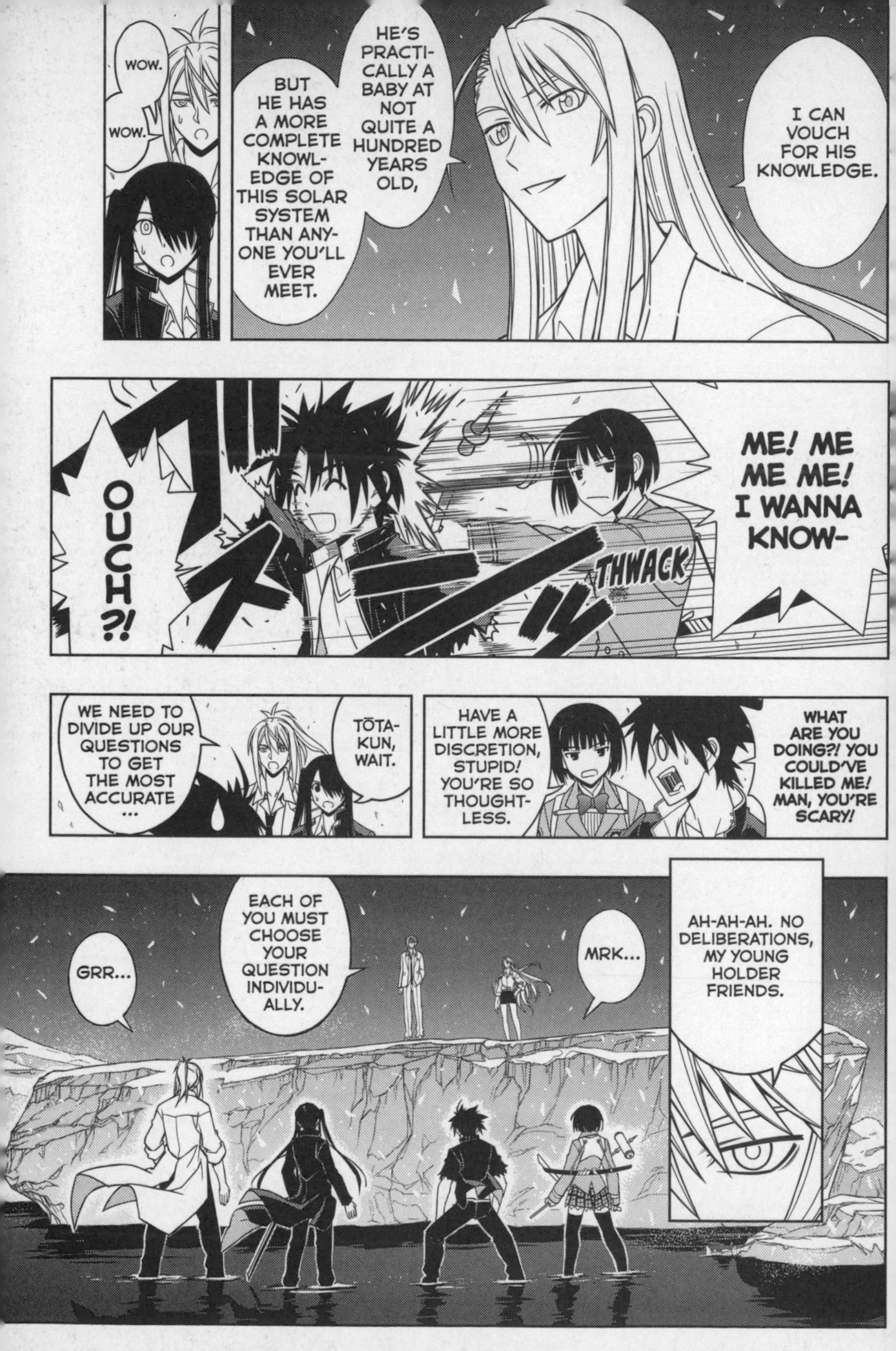
I CAN VOUCH FOR HIS KNOWLEDGE.
HE'S PRACTICALLY A BABY AT NOT QUITE A HUNDRED YEARS OLD,
BUT HE HAS A MORE COMPLETE KNOWLEDGE OF THIS SOLAR SYSTEM THAN ANYONE YOU'LL EVER MEET.
WOW.
WOW.
ME! ME ME ME! I WANNA KNOW-
THWACK
OUCH?!
WHAT ARE YOU DOING?! YOU COULD'VE KILLED ME! MAN, YOU'RE SCARY!
HAVE A LITTLE MORE DISCRETION, STUPID! YOU'RE SO THOUGHTLESS.
TŌTA-KUN, WAIT.
WE NEED TO DIVIDE UP OUR QUESTIONS TO GET THE MOST ACCURATE ...
AH-AH-AH. NO DELIBERATIONS, MY YOUNG HOLDER FRIENDS.
MRK...
EACH OF YOU MUST CHOOSE YOUR QUESTION INDIVIDUALLY.
GRR...

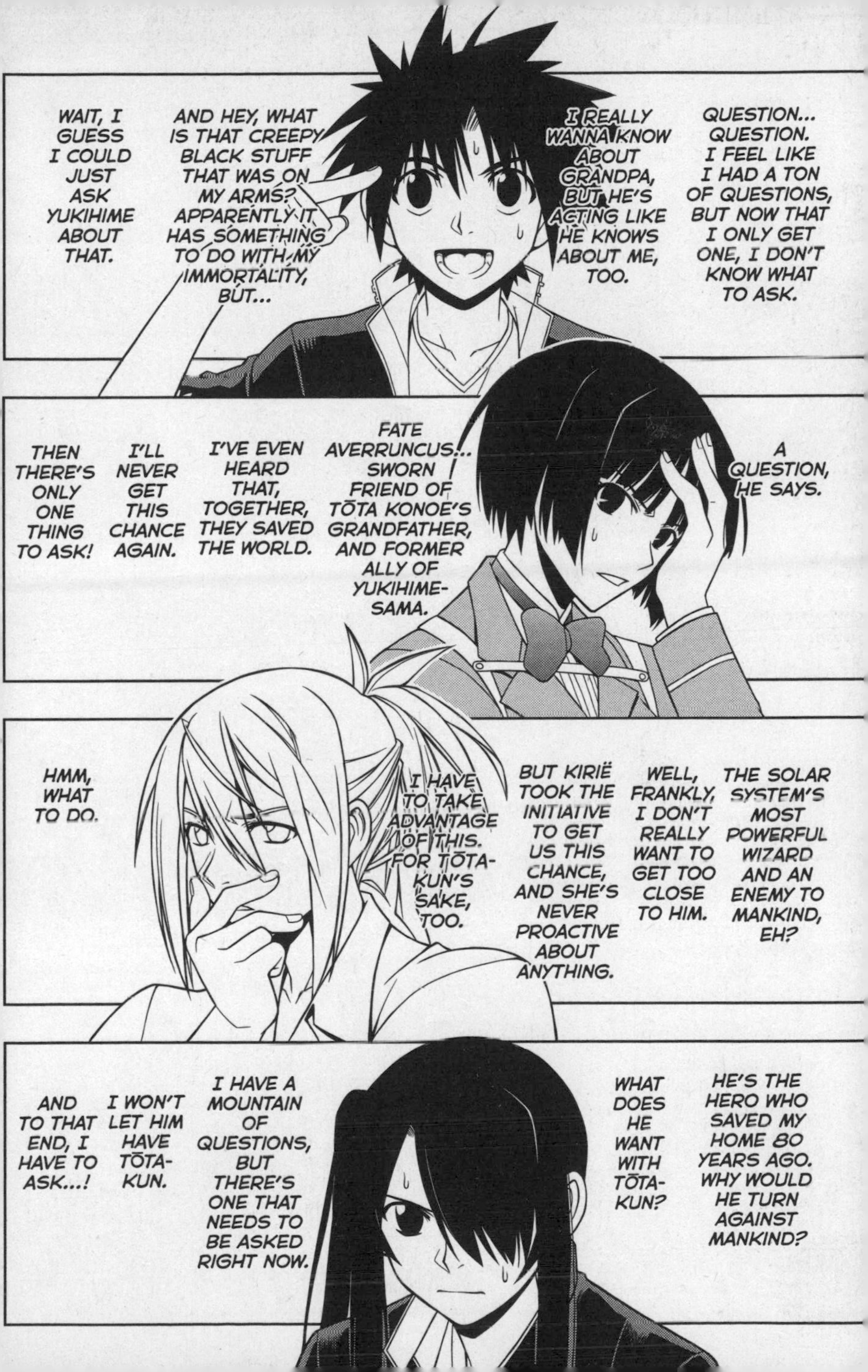
QUESTION... QUESTION. I FEEL LIKE I HAD A TON OF QUESTIONS, BUT NOW THAT I ONLY GET ONE, I DON'T KNOW WHAT TO ASK.
I REALLY WANNA KNOW ABOUT GRANDPA, BUT HE'S ACTING LIKE HE KNOWS ABOUT ME, TOO.
AND HEY, WHAT IS THAT CREEPY BLACK STUFF THAT WAS ON MY ARMS? APPARENTLY IT HAS SOMETHING TO DO WITH MY IMMORTALITY, BUT...
WAIT, I GUESS I COULD JUST ASK YUKIHIME ABOUT THAT.
A QUESTION, HE SAYS.
FATE AVERRUNCUS... SWORN FRIEND OF TŌTA KONOE'S GRANDFATHER, AND FORMER ALLY OF YUKIHIME-SAMA.
I'VE EVEN HEARD THAT, TOGETHER, THEY SAVED THE WORLD.
I'LL NEVER GET THIS CHANCE AGAIN.
THEN THERE'S ONLY ONE THING TO ASK!
THE SOLAR SYSTEM'S MOST POWERFUL WIZARD AND AN ENEMY TO MANKIND, EH?
WELL, FRANKLY, I DON'T REALLY WANT TO GET TOO CLOSE TO HIM.
BUT KIRIË TOOK THE INITIATIVE TO GET US THIS CHANCE, AND SHE'S NEVER PROACTIVE ABOUT ANYTHING.
I HAVE TO TAKE ADVANTAGE OF THIS. FOR TŌTA-KUN'S SAKE, TOO.
HMM, WHAT TO DO.
HE'S THE HERO WHO SAVED MY HOME 80 YEARS AGO. WHY WOULD HE TURN AGAINST MANKIND?
WHAT DOES HE WANT WITH TŌTA-KUN?
I HAVE A MOUNTAIN OF QUESTIONS, BUT THERE'S ONE THAT NEEDS TO BE ASKED RIGHT NOW.
I WON'T LET HIM HAVE TŌTA-KUN.
AND TO THAT END, I HAVE TO ASK...!

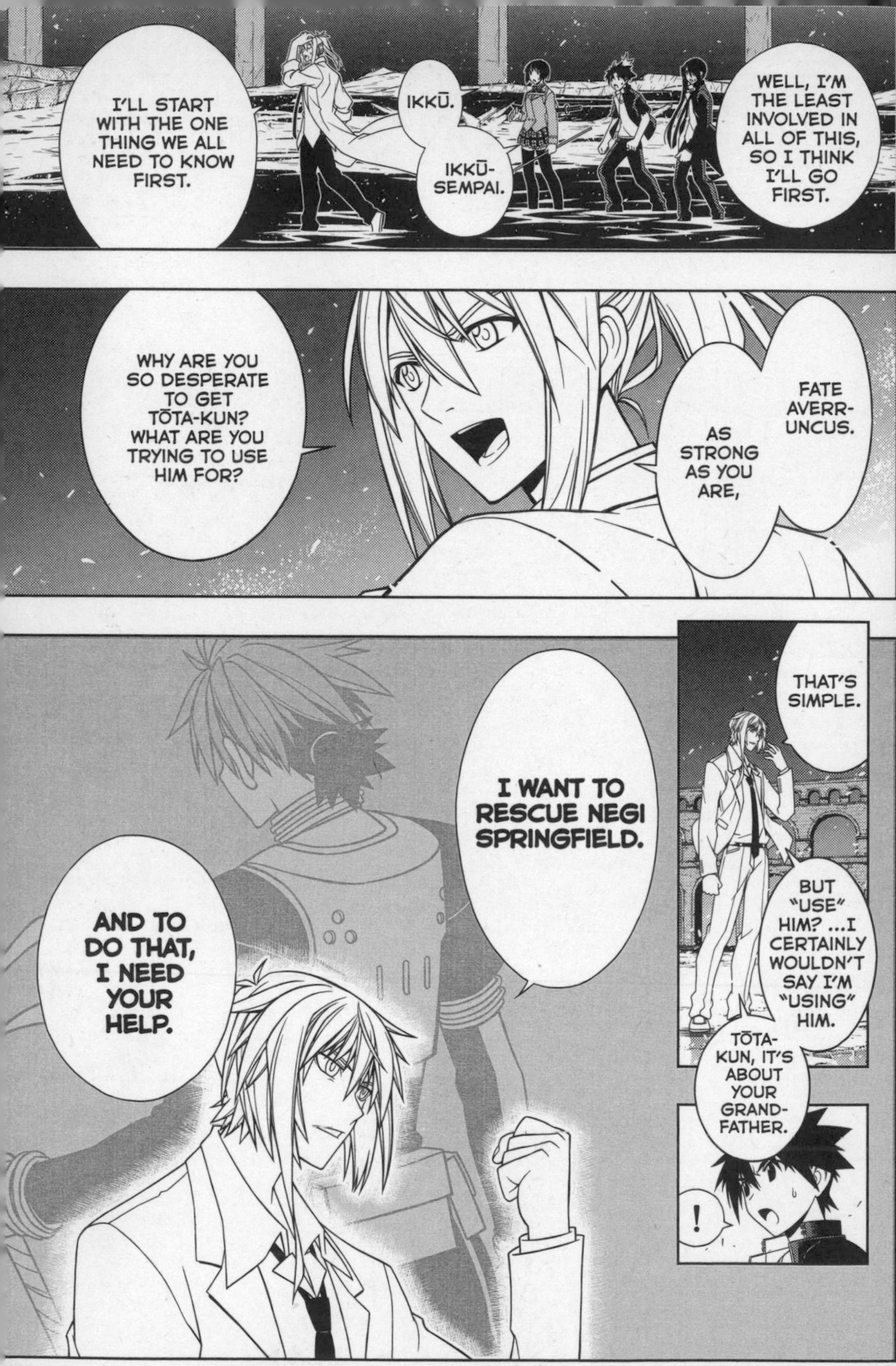
WELL, I'M THE LEAST INVOLVED IN ALL OF THIS, SO I THINK I'LL GO FIRST.
IKKŪ.
IKKŪ-SEMPAI.
I'LL START WITH THE ONE THING WE ALL NEED TO KNOW FIRST.
FATE AVERR-UNCUS.
AS STRONG AS YOU ARE,
WHY ARE YOU SO DESPERATE TO GET TŌTA-KUN? WHAT ARE YOU TRYING TO USE HIM FOR?
THAT'S SIMPLE.
BUT "USE" HIM? ...I CERTAINLY WOULDN'T SAY I'M "USING" HIM.
TŌTA-KUN, IT'S ABOUT YOUR GRAND-FATHER.
!
I WANT TO RESCUE NEGI SPRINGFIELD.
AND TO DO THAT, I NEED YOUR HELP.

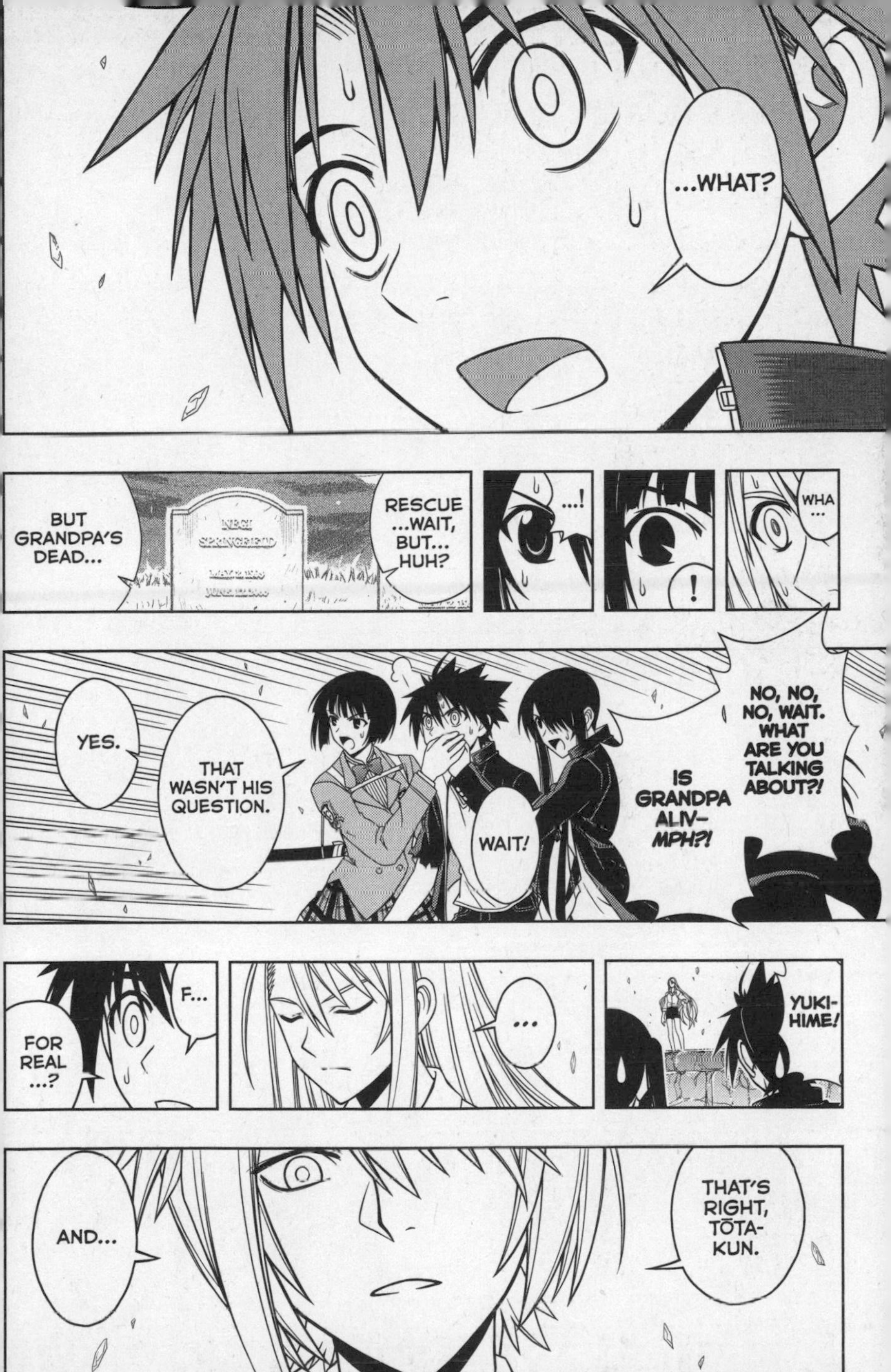
...WHAT?
WHA...
!
...!
RESCUE ...WAIT, BUT... HUH?
BUT GRANDPA'S DEAD...
NO, NO, NO, WAIT. WHAT ARE YOU TALKING ABOUT?!
IS GRANDPA ALIV-MPH?!
WAIT!
THAT WASN'T HIS QUESTION.
YES.
YUKI-HIME!
...
F...
FOR REAL ...?
THAT'S RIGHT, TŌTA-KUN.
AND...

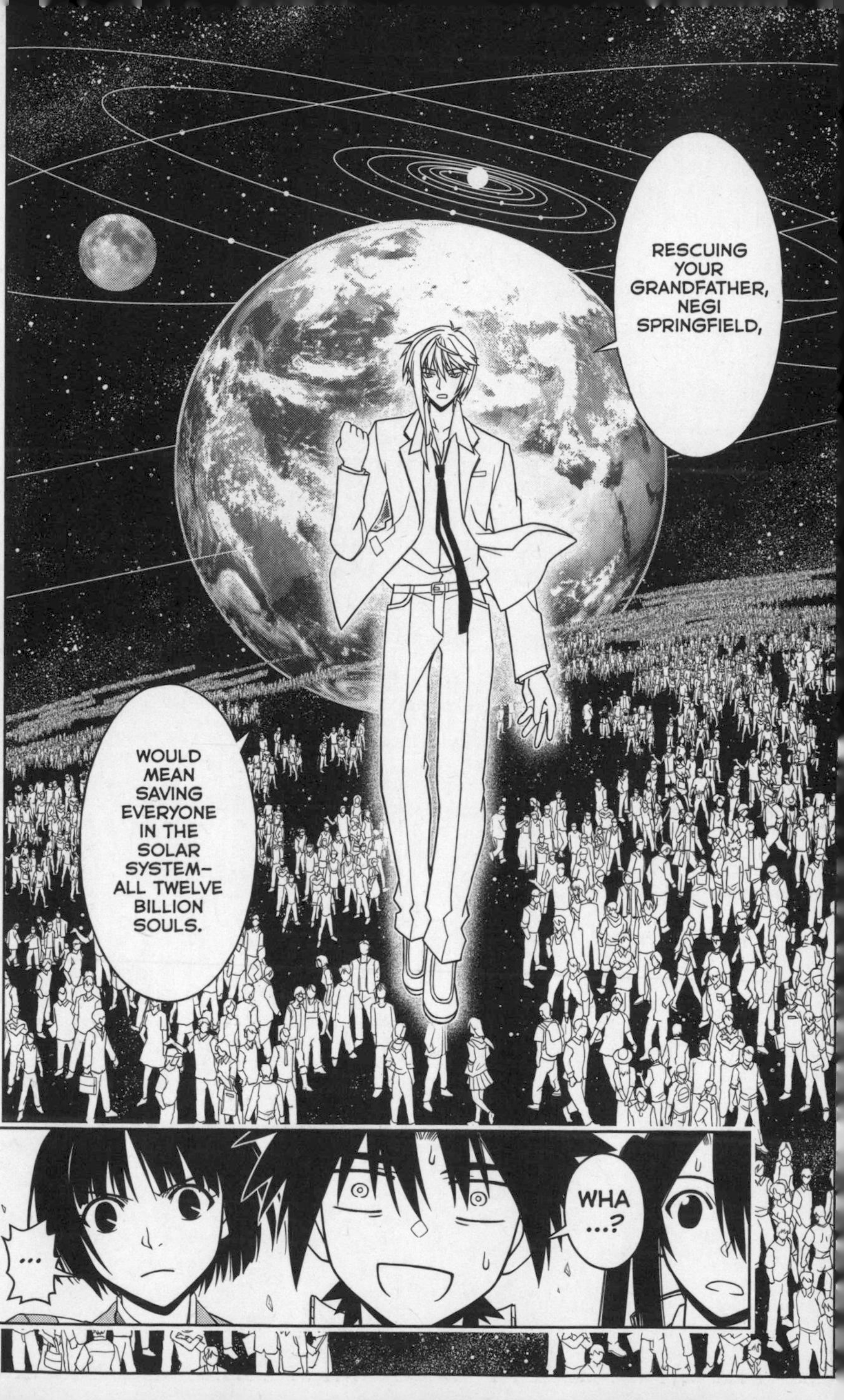
RESCUING YOUR GRANDFATHER, NEGI SPRINGFIELD,
WOULD MEAN SAVING EVERYONE IN THE SOLAR SYSTEM—ALL TWELVE BILLION SOULS.
WHA ...?
...

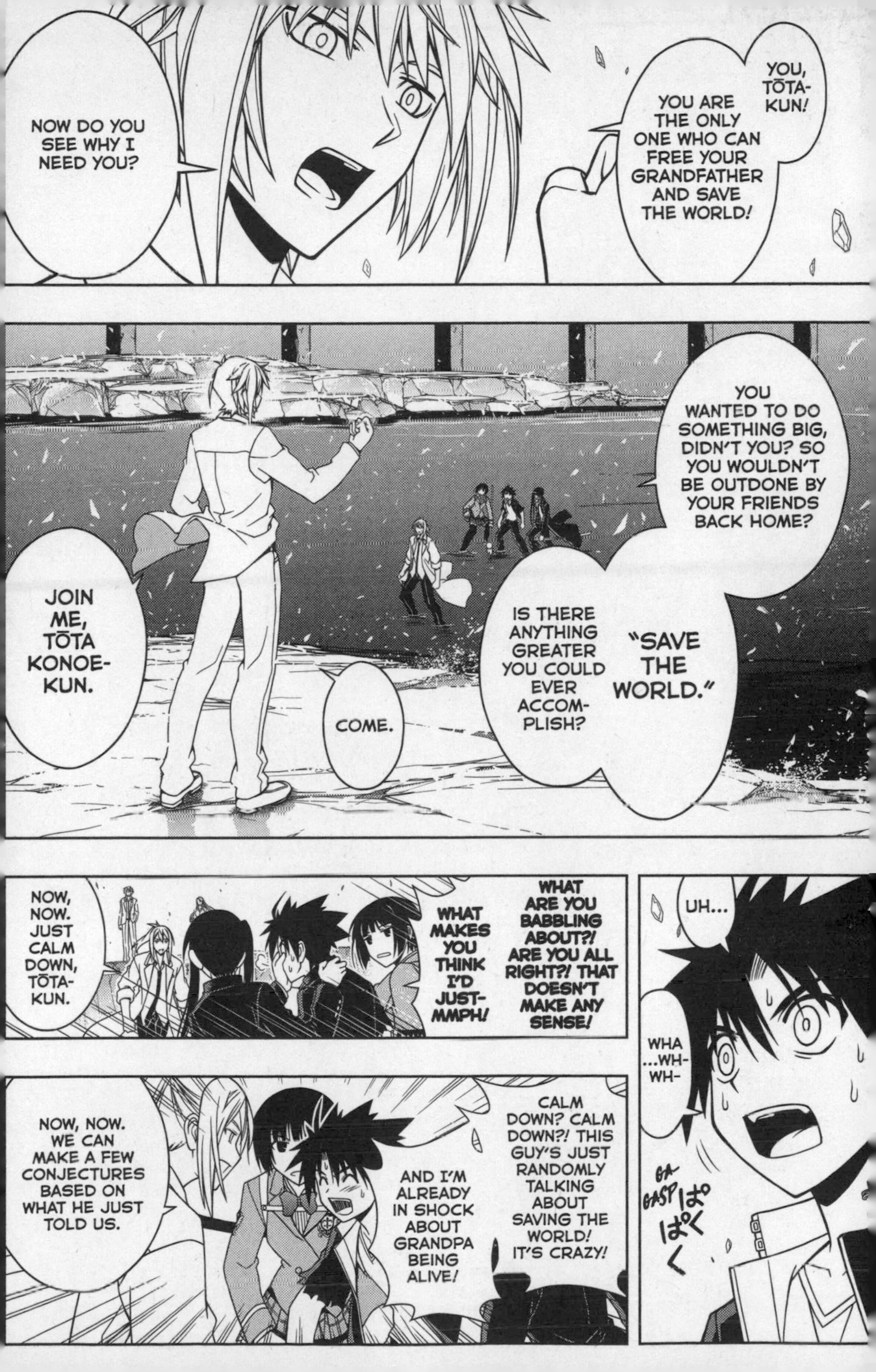
YOU, TŌTA-KUN!
YOU ARE THE ONLY ONE WHO CAN FREE YOUR GRANDFATHER AND SAVE THE WORLD!
NOW DO YOU SEE WHY I NEED YOU?
YOU WANTED TO DO SOMETHING BIG, DIDN'T YOU? SO YOU WOULDN'T BE OUTDONE BY YOUR FRIENDS BACK HOME?
"SAVE THE WORLD."
IS THERE ANYTHING GREATER YOU COULD EVER ACCOMPLISH?
COME.
JOIN ME, TŌTA KONOE-KUN.
UH...
WHA...WH-WH-
GA GASP ぱくぱく
WHAT ARE YOU BABBLING ABOUT?! ARE YOU ALL RIGHT?! THAT DOESN'T MAKE ANY SENSE!
WHAT MAKES YOU THINK I'D JUST-MMPH!
NOW, NOW. JUST CALM DOWN, TŌTA-KUN.
CALM DOWN? CALM DOWN?! THIS GUY'S JUST RANDOMLY TALKING ABOUT SAVING THE WORLD! IT'S CRAZY!
AND I'M ALREADY IN SHOCK ABOUT GRANDPA BEING ALIVE!
NOW, NOW. WE CAN MAKE A FEW CONJECTURES BASED ON WHAT HE JUST TOLD US.

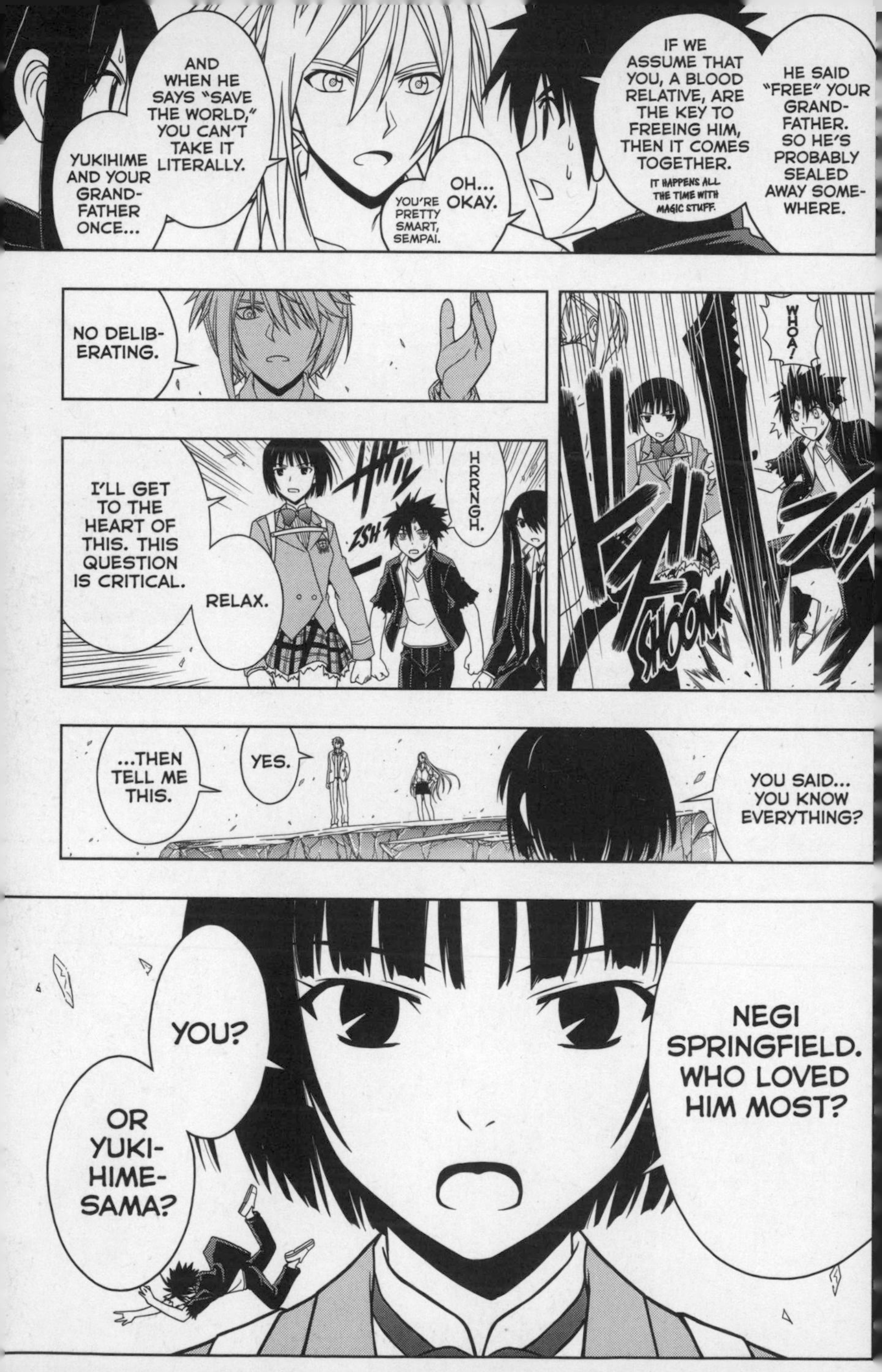
HE SAID "FREE" YOUR GRANDFATHER. SO HE'S PROBABLY SEALED AWAY SOMEWHERE.
IF WE ASSUME THAT YOU, A BLOOD RELATIVE, ARE THE KEY TO FREEING HIM, THEN IT COMES TOGETHER.
IT HAPPENS ALL THE TIME WITH MAGIC STUFF.
OH... OKAY.
YOU'RE PRETTY SMART, SEMPAI.
AND WHEN HE SAYS "SAVE THE WORLD," YOU CAN'T TAKE IT LITERALLY.
YUKIHIME AND YOUR GRANDFATHER ONCE...
WHOA!
SHOONK
NO DELIBERATING.
HRRNGH.
ZSH
I'LL GET TO THE HEART OF THIS. THIS QUESTION IS CRITICAL.
RELAX.
YOU SAID... YOU KNOW EVERYTHING?
YES.
...THEN TELL ME THIS.
NEGI SPRINGFIELD. WHO LOVED HIM MOST?
YOU?
OR YUKI-HIME-SAMA?

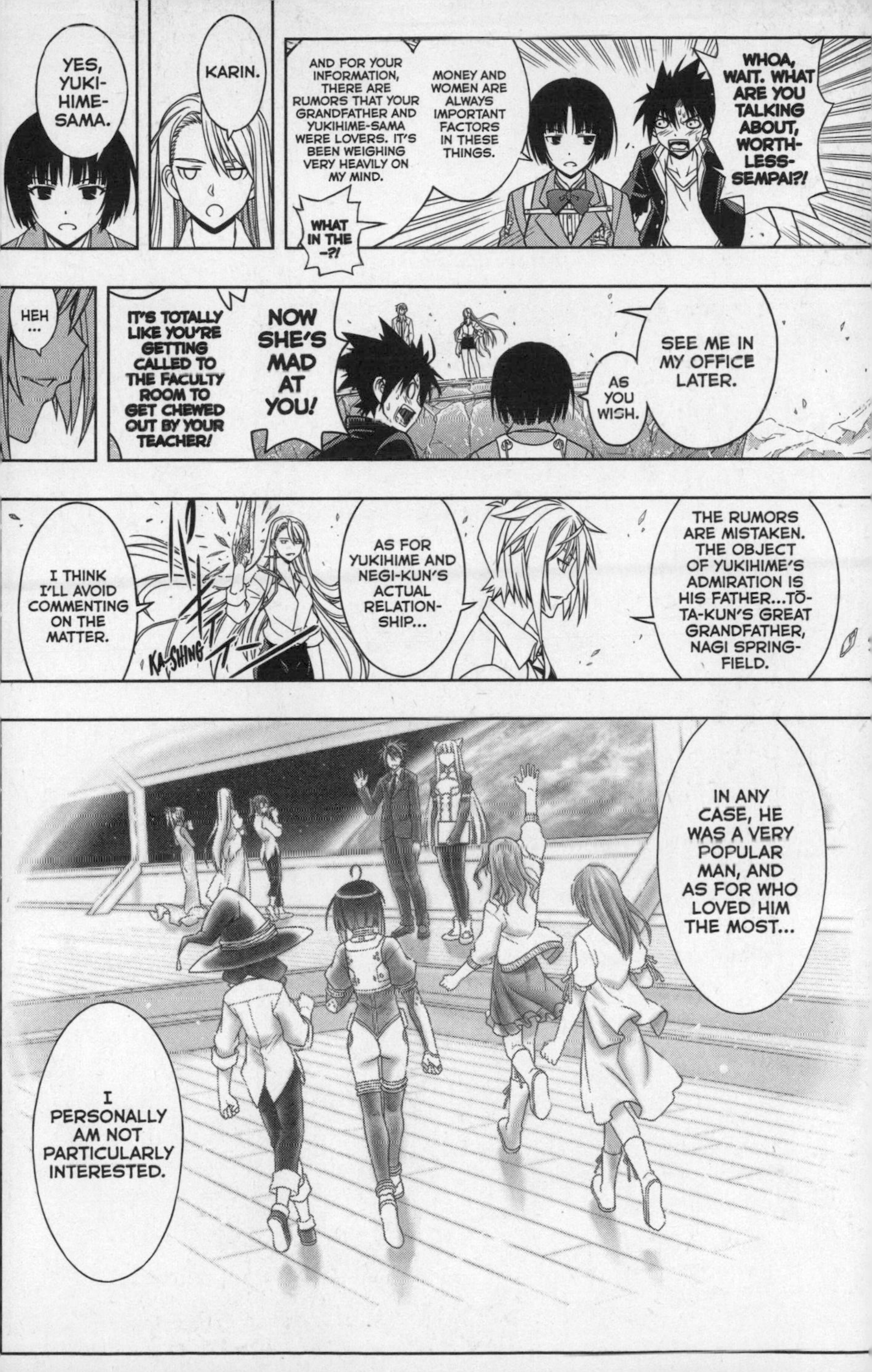
WHOA, WAIT. WHAT ARE YOU TALKING ABOUT, WORTHLESS-SEMPAI?!
MONEY AND WOMEN ARE ALWAYS IMPORTANT FACTORS IN THESE THINGS.
AND FOR YOUR INFORMATION, THERE ARE RUMORS THAT YOUR GRANDFATHER AND YUKIHIME-SAMA WERE LOVERS. IT'S BEEN WEIGHING VERY HEAVILY ON MY MIND.
WHAT IN THE--?!
KARIN.
YES, YUKIHIME-SAMA.
SEE ME IN MY OFFICE LATER.
AS YOU WISH.
NOW SHE'S MAD AT YOU!
IT'S TOTALLY LIKE YOU'RE GETTING CALLED TO THE FACULTY ROOM TO GET CHEWED OUT BY YOUR TEACHER!
HEH...
THE RUMORS ARE MISTAKEN. THE OBJECT OF YUKIHIME'S ADMIRATION IS HIS FATHER...TŌTA-KUN'S GREAT GRANDFATHER, NAGI SPRINGFIELD.
AS FOR YUKIHIME AND NEGI-KUN'S ACTUAL RELATIONSHIP...
KA-SHING
I THINK I'LL AVOID COMMENTING ON THE MATTER.
IN ANY CASE, HE WAS A VERY POPULAR MAN, AND AS FOR WHO LOVED HIM THE MOST...
I PERSONALLY AM NOT PARTICULARLY INTERESTED.

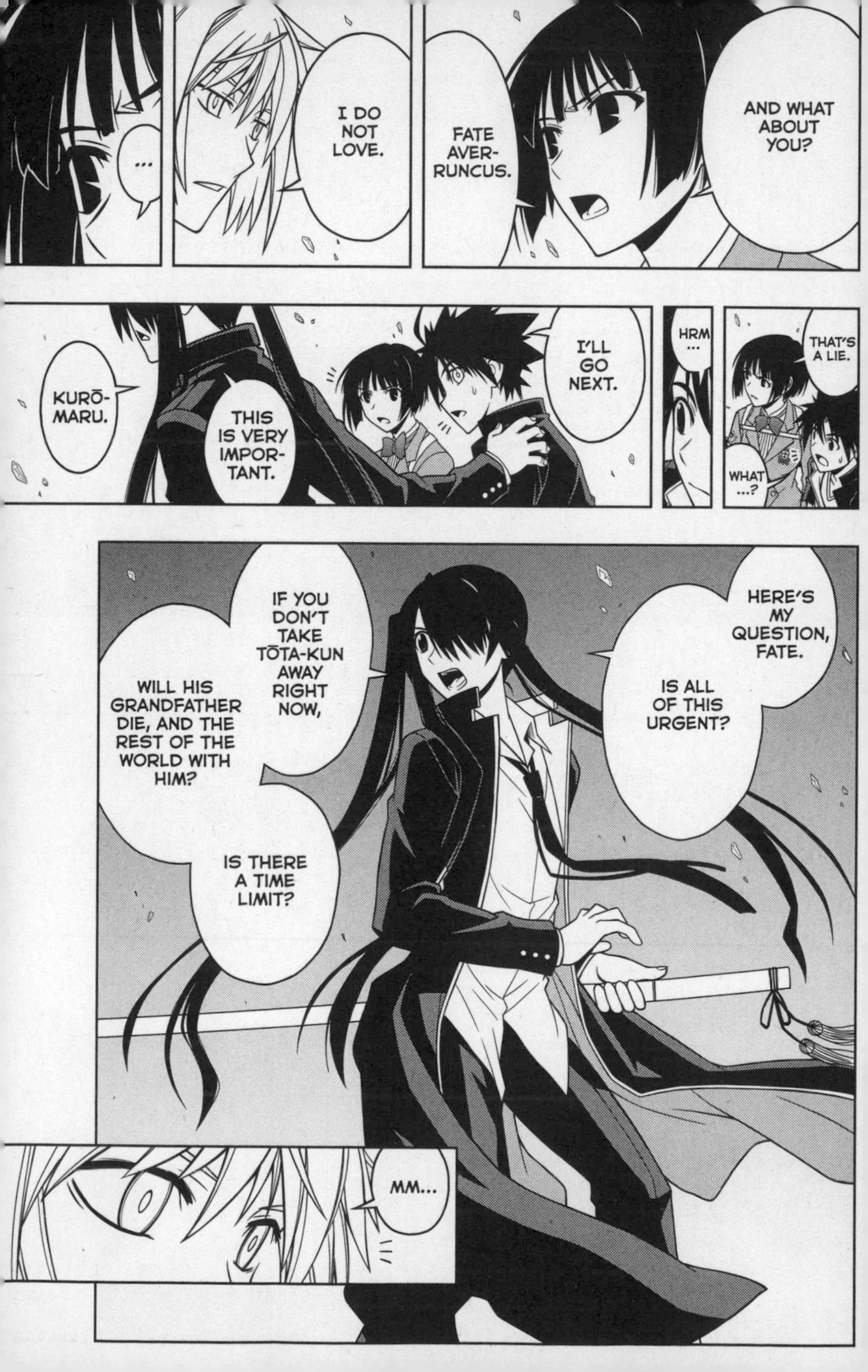
AND WHAT ABOUT YOU?
FATE AVER-RUNCUS.
I DO NOT LOVE.
...
THAT'S A LIE.
WHAT ...?
HRM ...
I'LL GO NEXT.
KURŌ-MARU.
THIS IS VERY IMPORTANT.
HERE'S MY QUESTION, FATE.
IS ALL OF THIS URGENT?
IF YOU DON'T TAKE TŌTA-KUN AWAY RIGHT NOW,
WILL HIS GRANDFATHER DIE, AND THE REST OF THE WORLD WITH HIM?
IS THERE A TIME LIMIT?
MM...

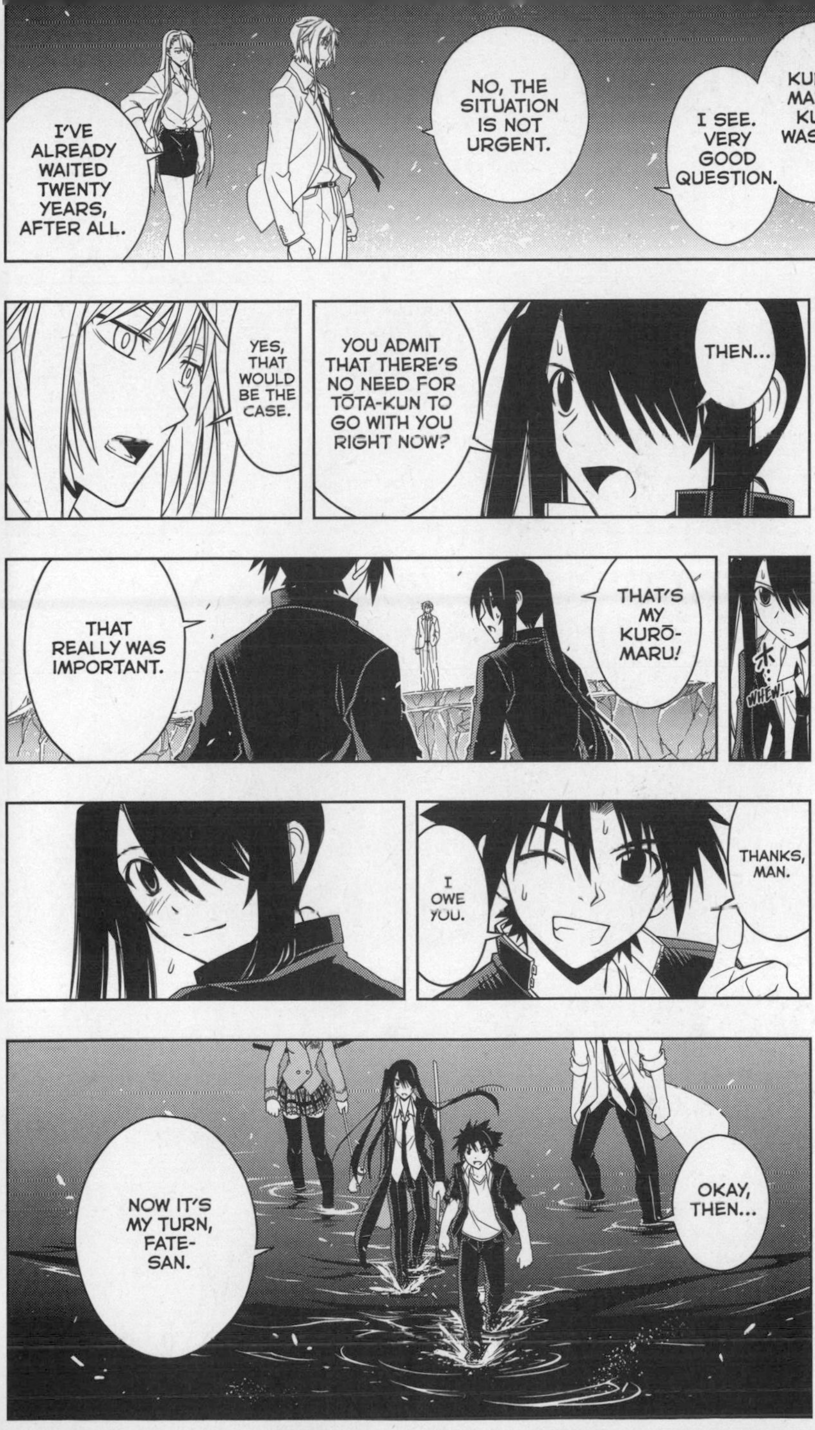
KURŌ-MARU-KUN, WAS IT?
I SEE. VERY GOOD QUESTION.
NO, THE SITUATION IS NOT URGENT.
I'VE ALREADY WAITED TWENTY YEARS, AFTER ALL.
THEN...
YOU ADMIT THAT THERE'S NO NEED FOR TŌTA-KUN TO GO WITH YOU RIGHT NOW?
YES, THAT WOULD BE THE CASE.
WHEW...
THAT'S MY KURŌ-MARU!
THAT REALLY WAS IMPORTANT.
THANKS, MAN.
I OWE YOU.
OKAY, THEN...
NOW IT'S MY TURN, FATE-SAN.

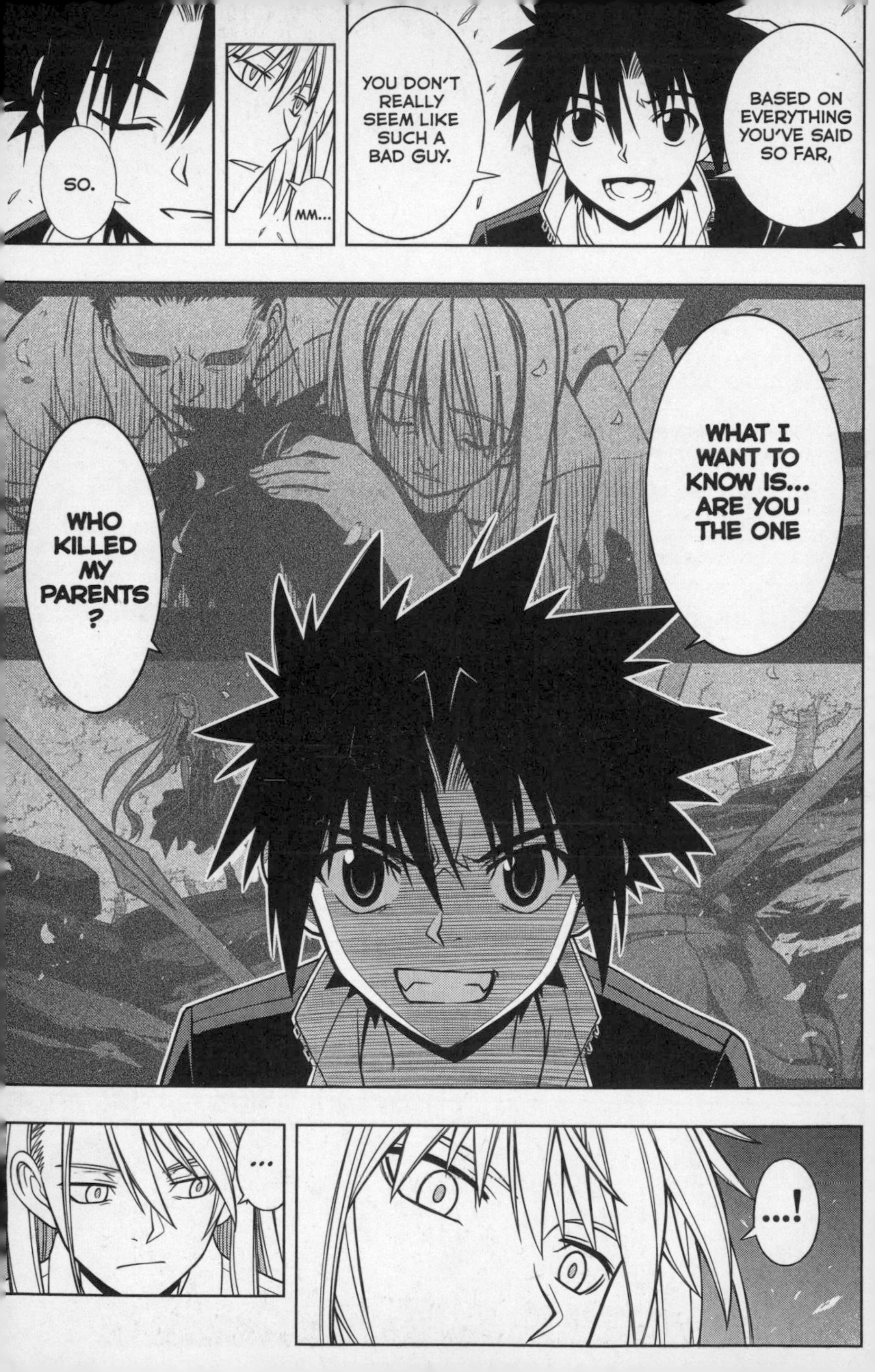
BASED ON EVERYTHING YOU'VE SAID SO FAR,
YOU DON'T REALLY SEEM LIKE SUCH A BAD GUY.
MM...
SO.
WHAT I WANT TO KNOW IS... ARE YOU THE ONE
WHO KILLED MY PARENTS?
...!
...

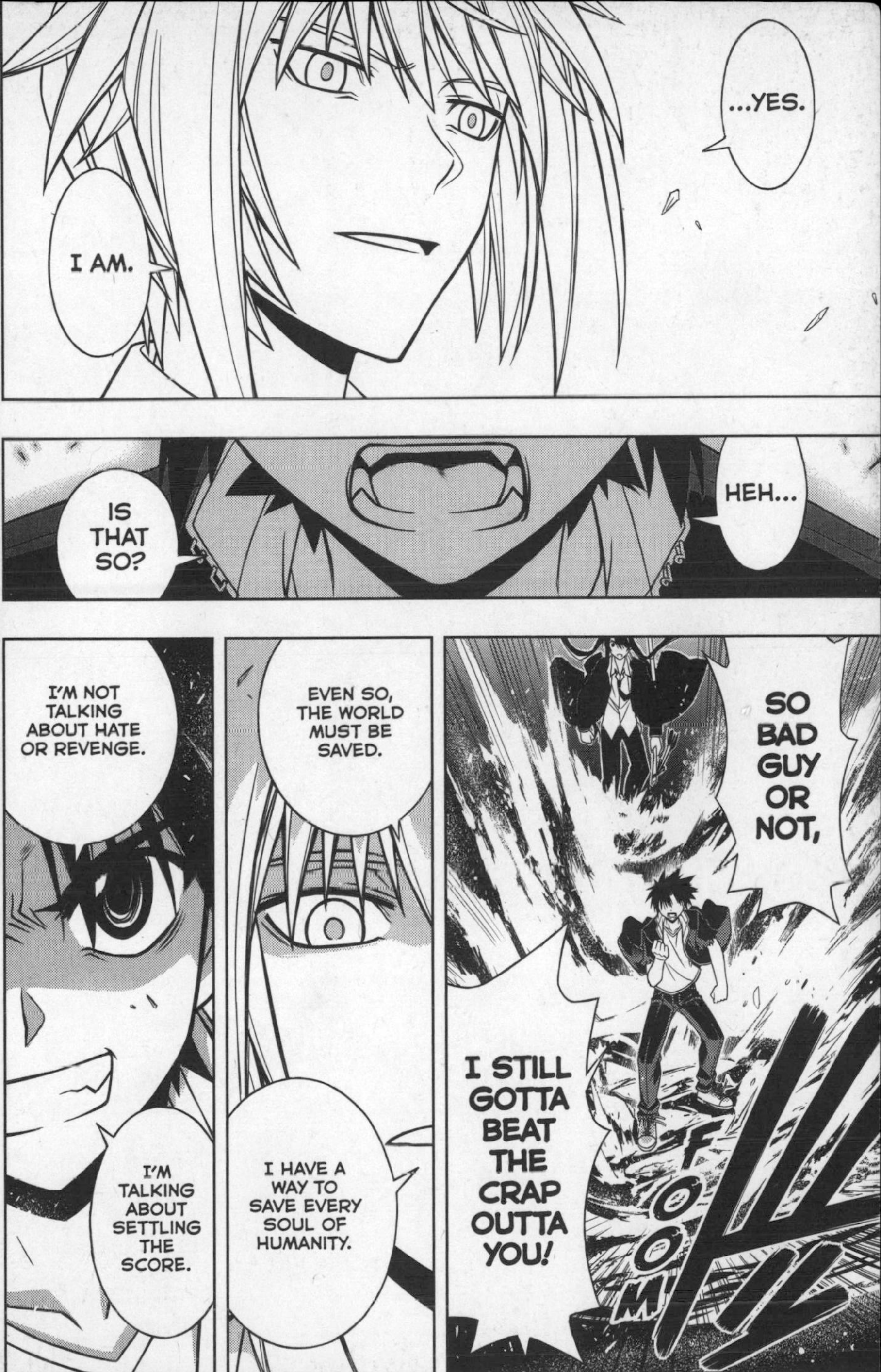
...YES.
I AM.
HEH...
IS THAT SO?
SO BAD GUY OR NOT,
I STILL GOTTA BEAT THE CRAP OUTTA YOU!
FOOM
EVEN SO, THE WORLD MUST BE SAVED.
I HAVE A WAY TO SAVE EVERY SOUL OF HUMANITY.
I'M NOT TALKING ABOUT HATE OR REVENGE.
I'M TALKING ABOUT SETTLING THE SCORE.

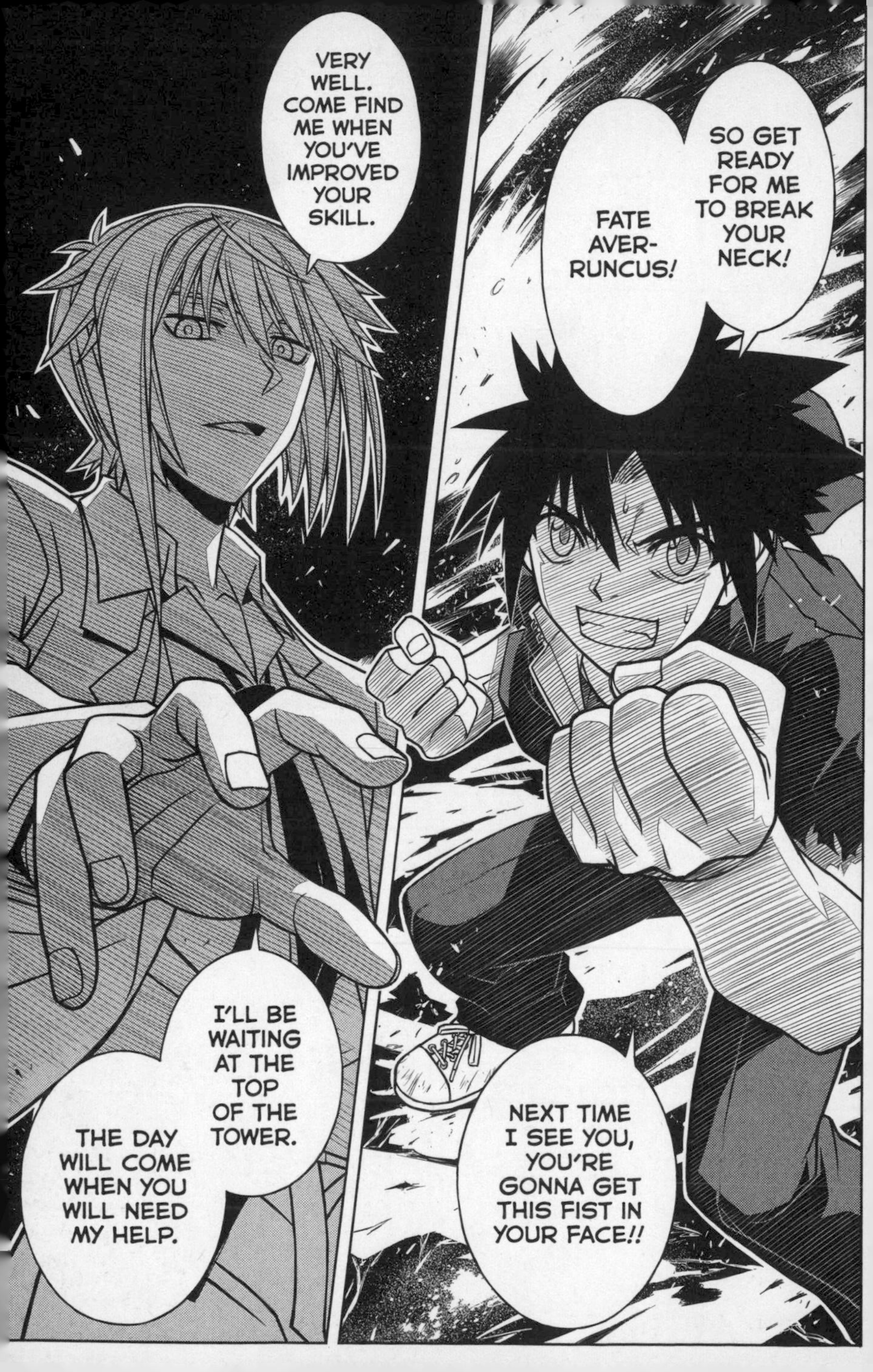
SO GET READY FOR ME TO BREAK YOUR NECK!
FATE AVER-RUNCUS!
NEXT TIME I SEE YOU, YOU'RE GONNA GET THIS FIST IN YOUR FACE!!
VERY WELL. COME FIND ME WHEN YOU'VE IMPROVED YOUR SKILL.
I'LL BE WAITING AT THE TOP OF THE TOWER.
THE DAY WILL COME WHEN YOU WILL NEED MY HELP.

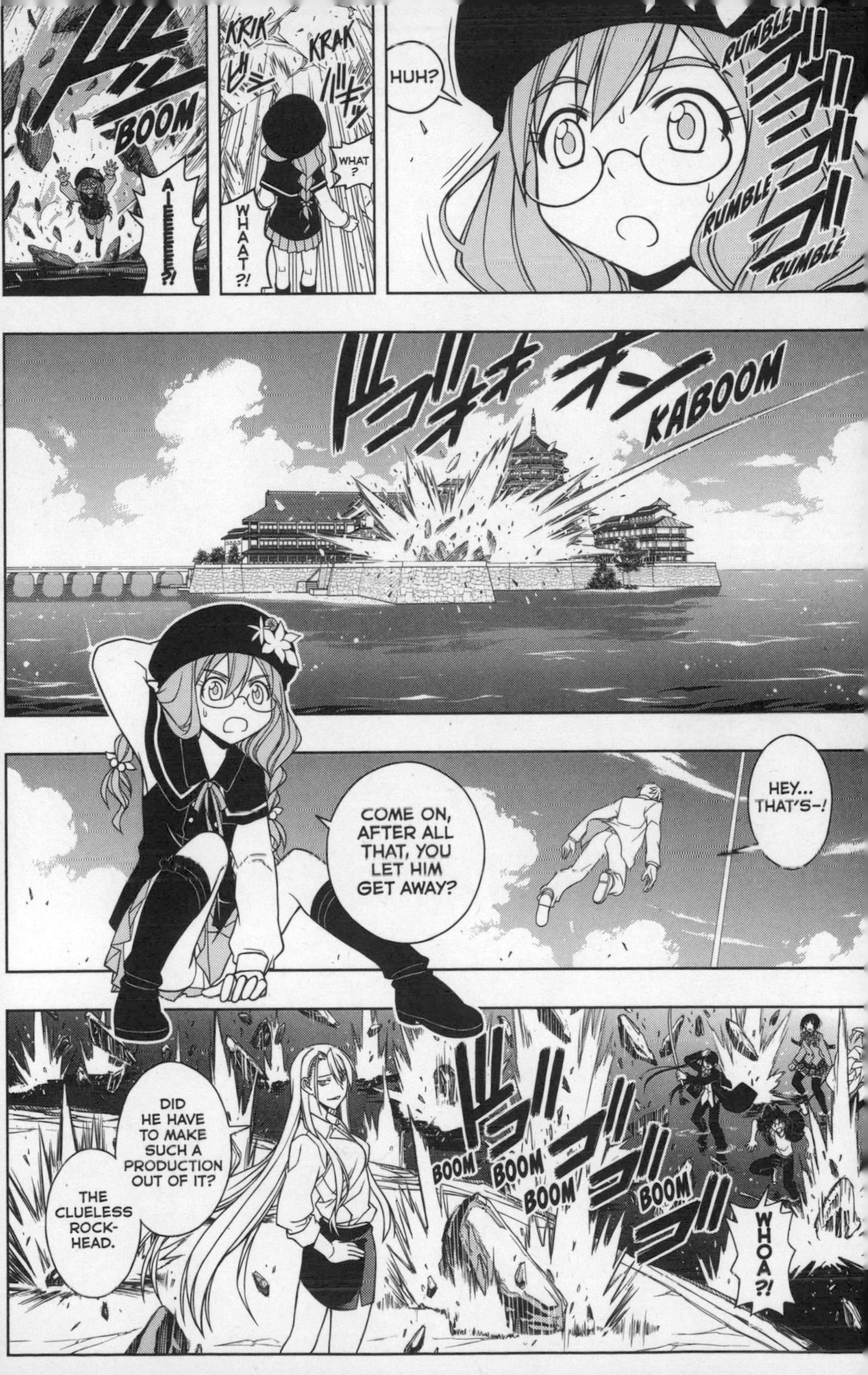
RUMBLE
RUMBLE
RUMBLE
HUH?
KRIK
KRAK
WHAT?
WHAAT?!
BOOM
AIEEEEEEEEEE?!
KABOOM
HEY... THAT'S-!
COME ON, AFTER ALL THAT, YOU LET HIM GET AWAY?
WHOA?!
BOOM
BOOM
BOOM
BOOM
DID HE HAVE TO MAKE SUCH A PRODUCTION OUT OF IT?
THE CLUELESS ROCK-HEAD.

UQ HOLDER!

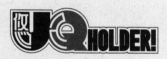

UQ HOLDER!

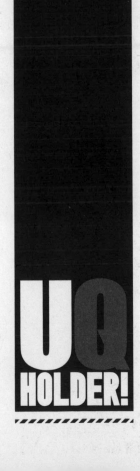

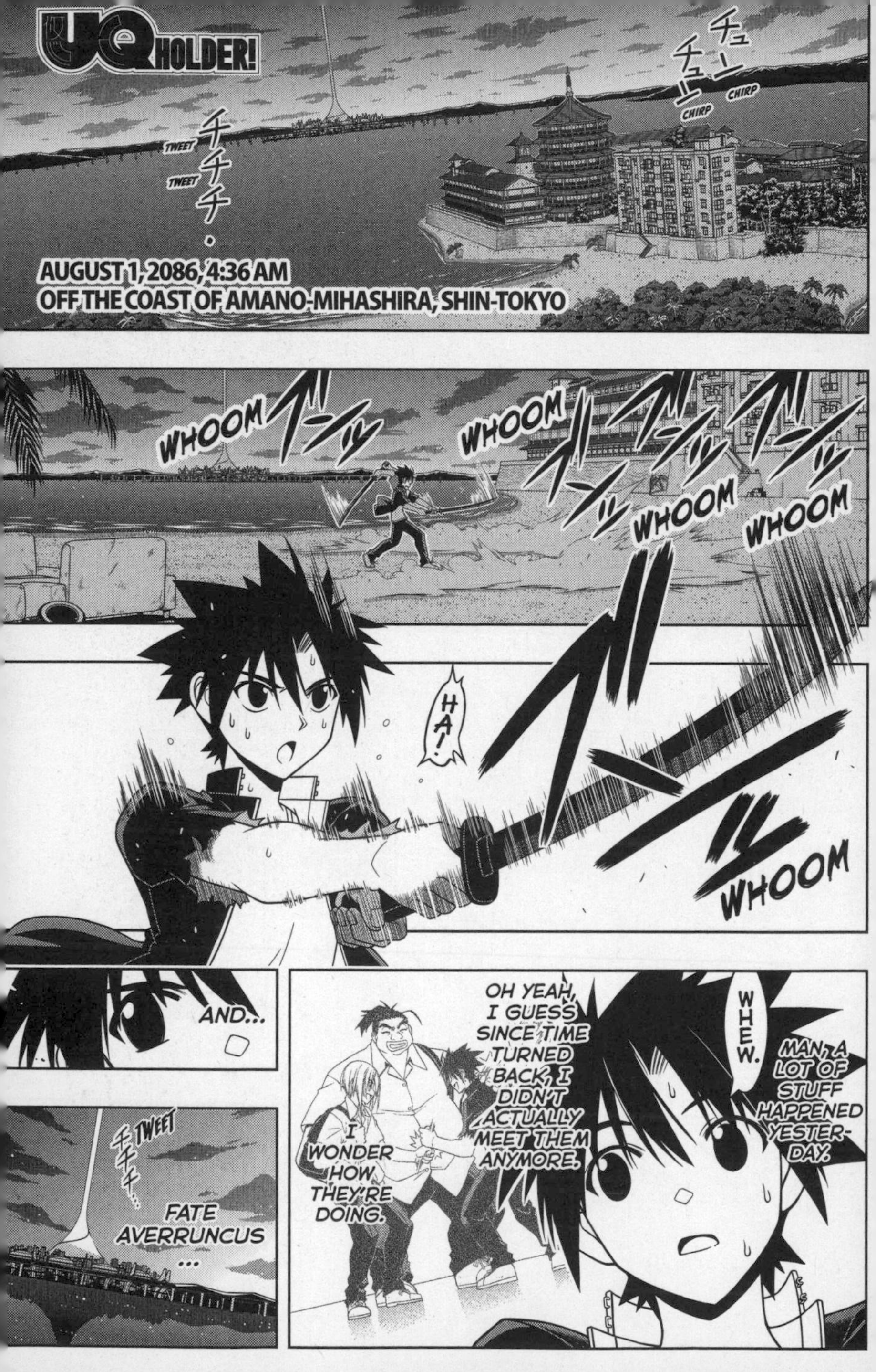
CHIRP
CHIRP
チチチ・
TWEET
TWEET
AUGUST 1, 2086, 4:36 AM
OFF THE COAST OF AMANO-MIHASHIRA, SHIN-TOKYO
WHOOM
WHOOM
WHOOM
WHOOM
WHOOM
HA!
WHOOM
WHEW.
MAN, A LOT OF STUFF HAPPENED YESTERDAY.
OH YEAH, I GUESS SINCE TIME TURNED BACK, I DIDN'T ACTUALLY MEET THEM ANYMORE.
I WONDER HOW THEY'RE DOING.
AND...
チチチ…
TWEET
FATE AVERRUNCUS...

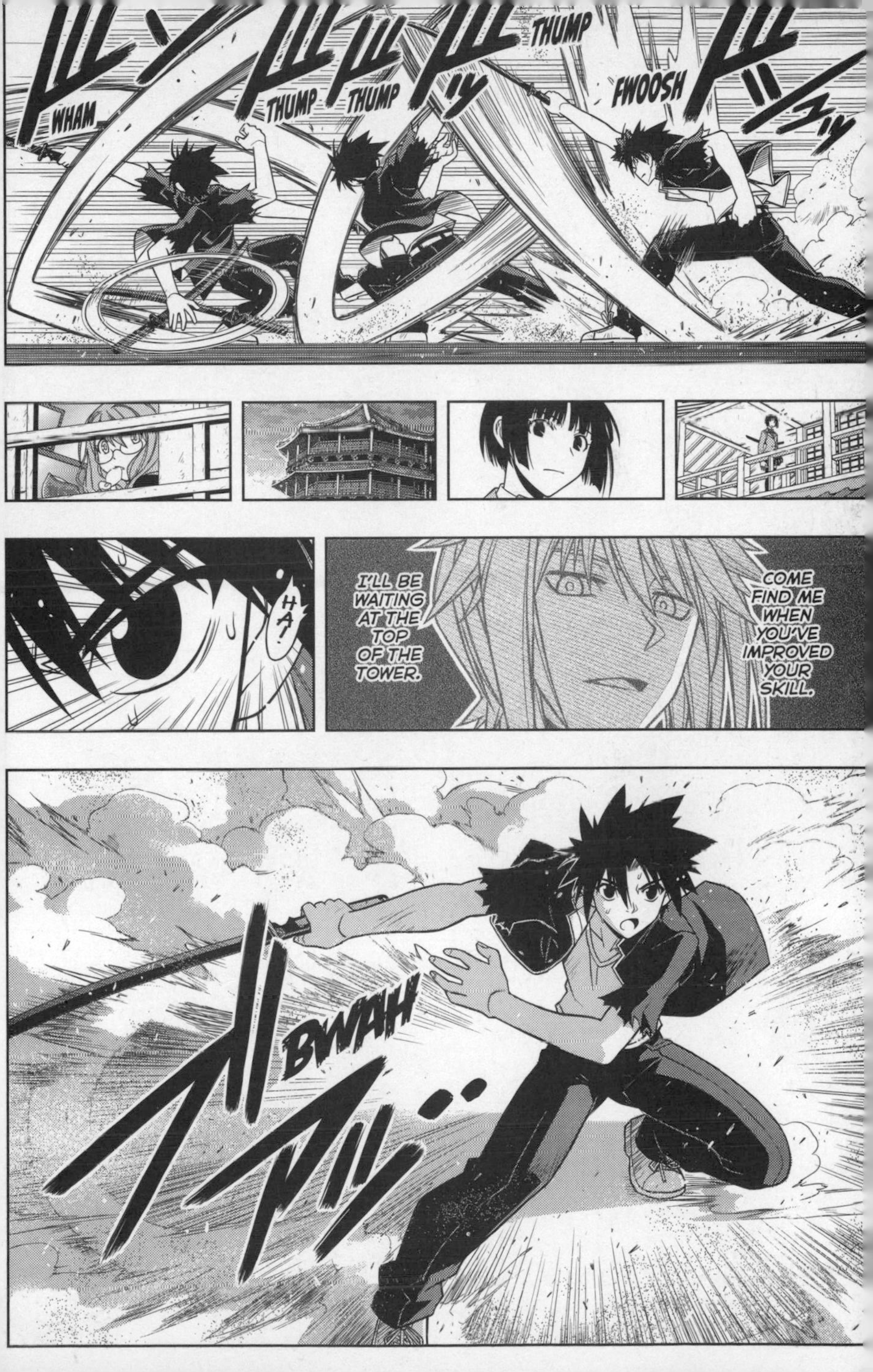
FWOOSH
THUMP
THUMP
THUMP
WHAM
COME FIND ME WHEN YOU'VE IMPROVED YOUR SKILL.
I'LL BE WAITING AT THE TOP OF THE TOWER.
HA!
BWAH

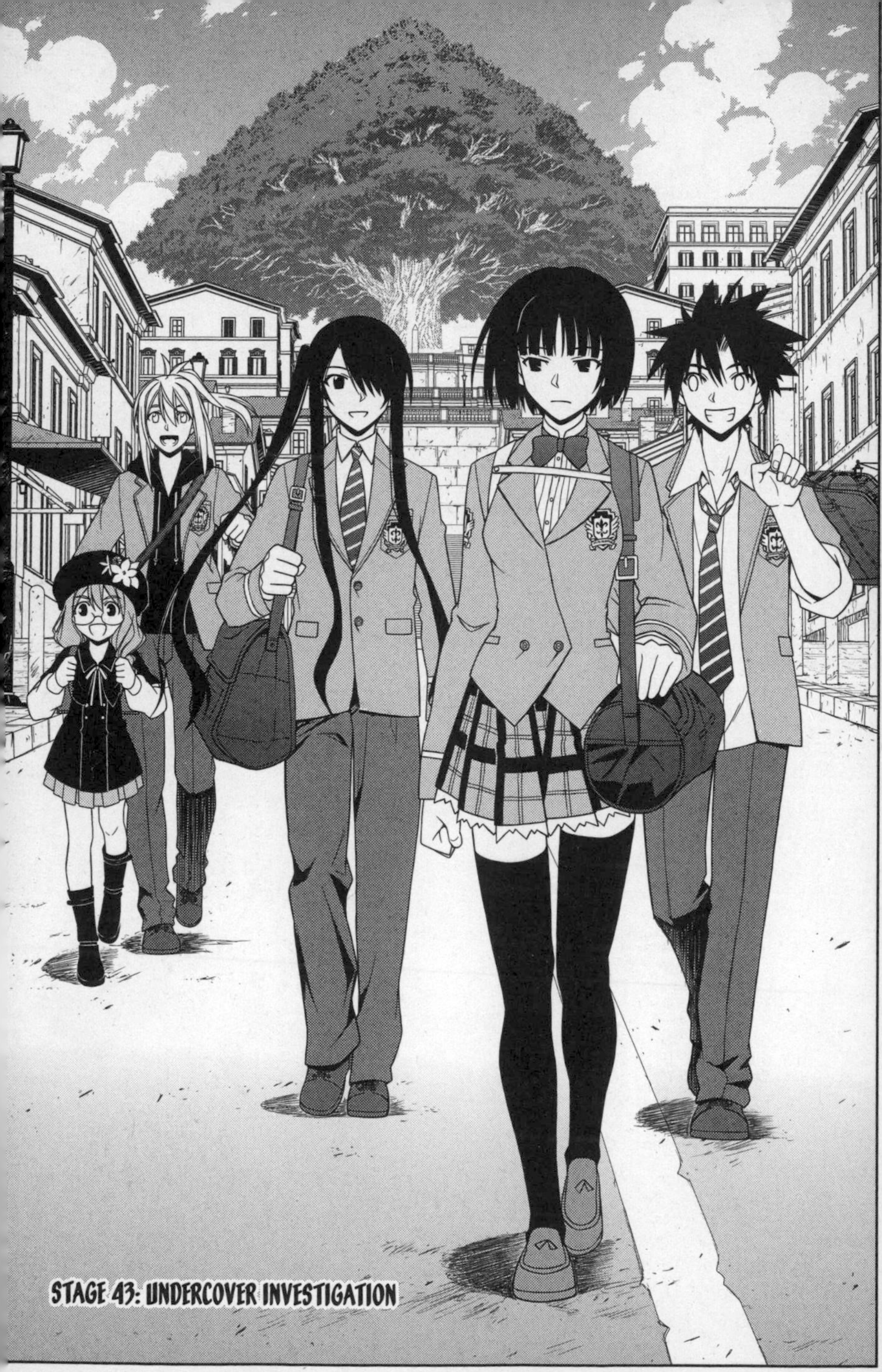
STAGE 43: UNDERCOVER INVESTIGATION

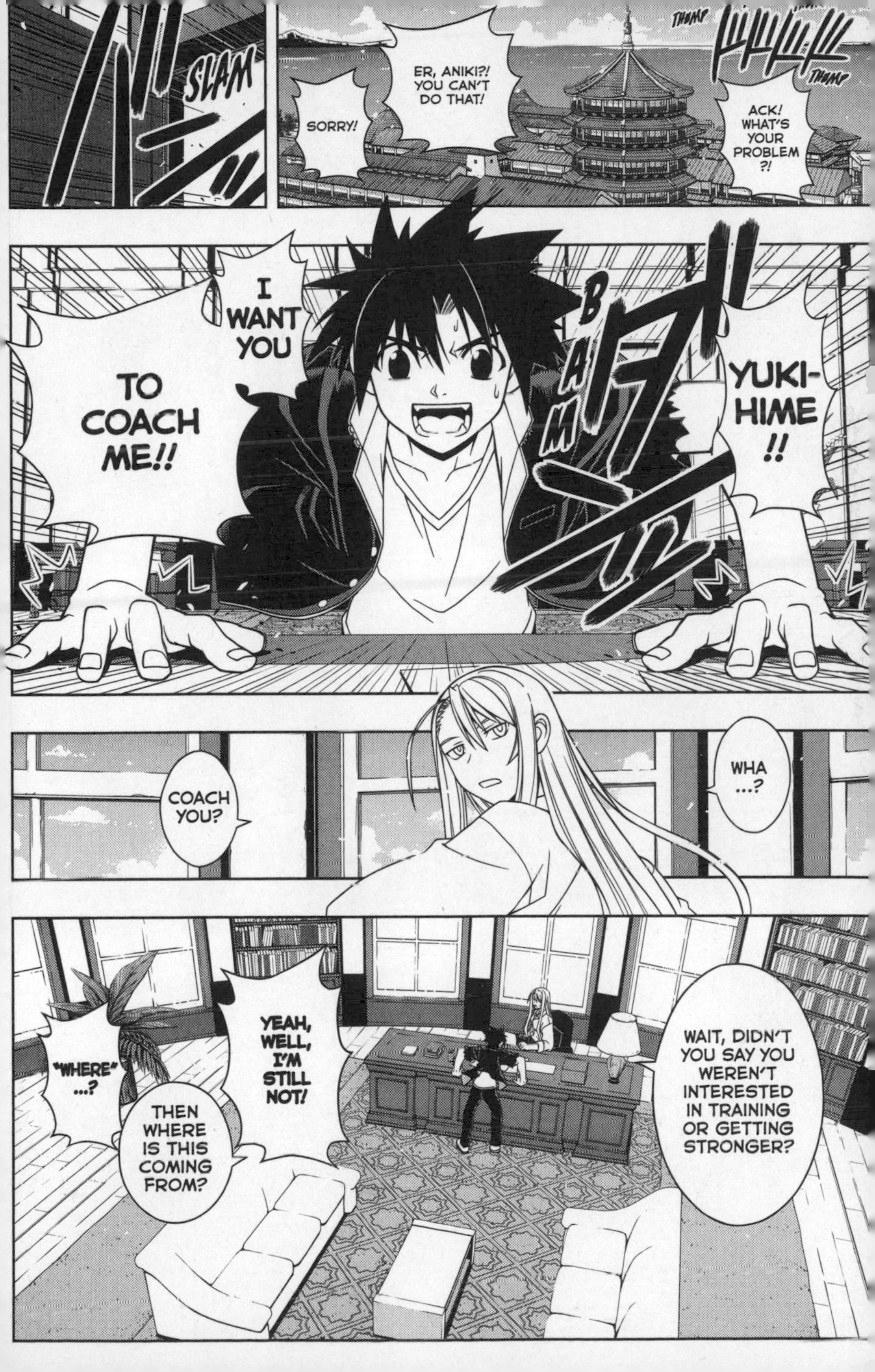
THUMP
THUMP
ACK! WHAT'S YOUR PROBLEM ?!
ER, ANIKI?! YOU CAN'T DO THAT!
SORRY!
SLAM
YUKI-HIME !!
BAM
I WANT YOU
TO COACH ME!!
WHA ...?
COACH YOU?
WAIT, DIDN'T YOU SAY YOU WEREN'T INTERESTED IN TRAINING OR GETTING STRONGER?
YEAH, WELL, I'M STILL NOT!
THEN WHERE IS THIS COMING FROM?
"WHERE" ...?

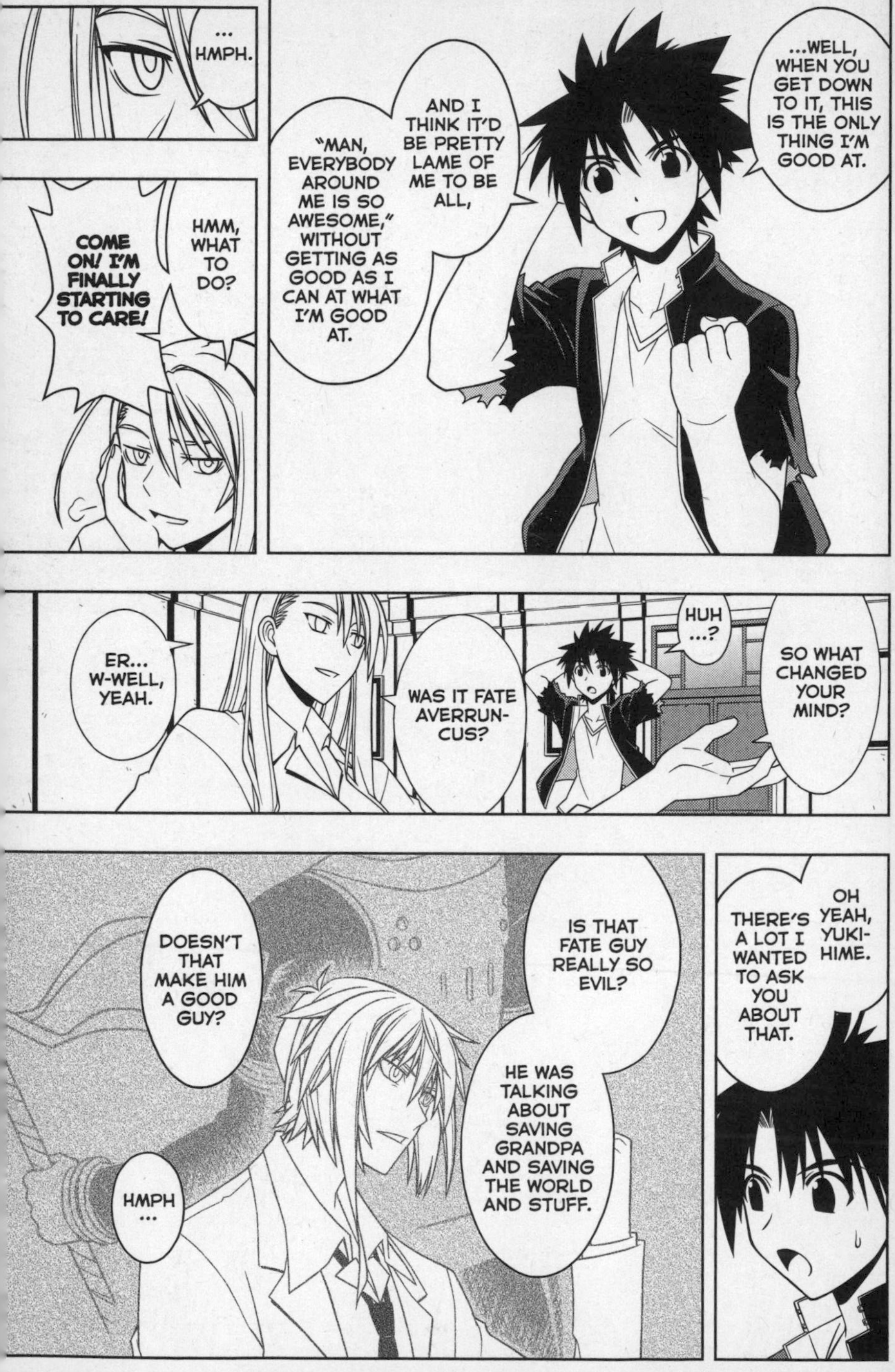
...WELL, WHEN YOU GET DOWN TO IT, THIS IS THE ONLY THING I'M GOOD AT.
AND I THINK IT'D BE PRETTY LAME OF ME TO BE ALL,
"MAN, EVERYBODY AROUND ME IS SO AWESOME," WITHOUT GETTING AS GOOD AS I CAN AT WHAT I'M GOOD AT.
... HMPH.
HMM, WHAT TO DO?
COME ON! I'M FINALLY STARTING TO CARE!
SO WHAT CHANGED YOUR MIND?
HUH ...?
WAS IT FATE AVERRUN-CUS?
ER... W-WELL, YEAH.
OH YEAH, YUKI-HIME.
THERE'S A LOT I WANTED TO ASK YOU ABOUT THAT.
IS THAT FATE GUY REALLY SO EVIL?
HE WAS TALKING ABOUT SAVING GRANDPA AND SAVING THE WORLD AND STUFF.
DOESN'T THAT MAKE HIM A GOOD GUY?
HMPH ...

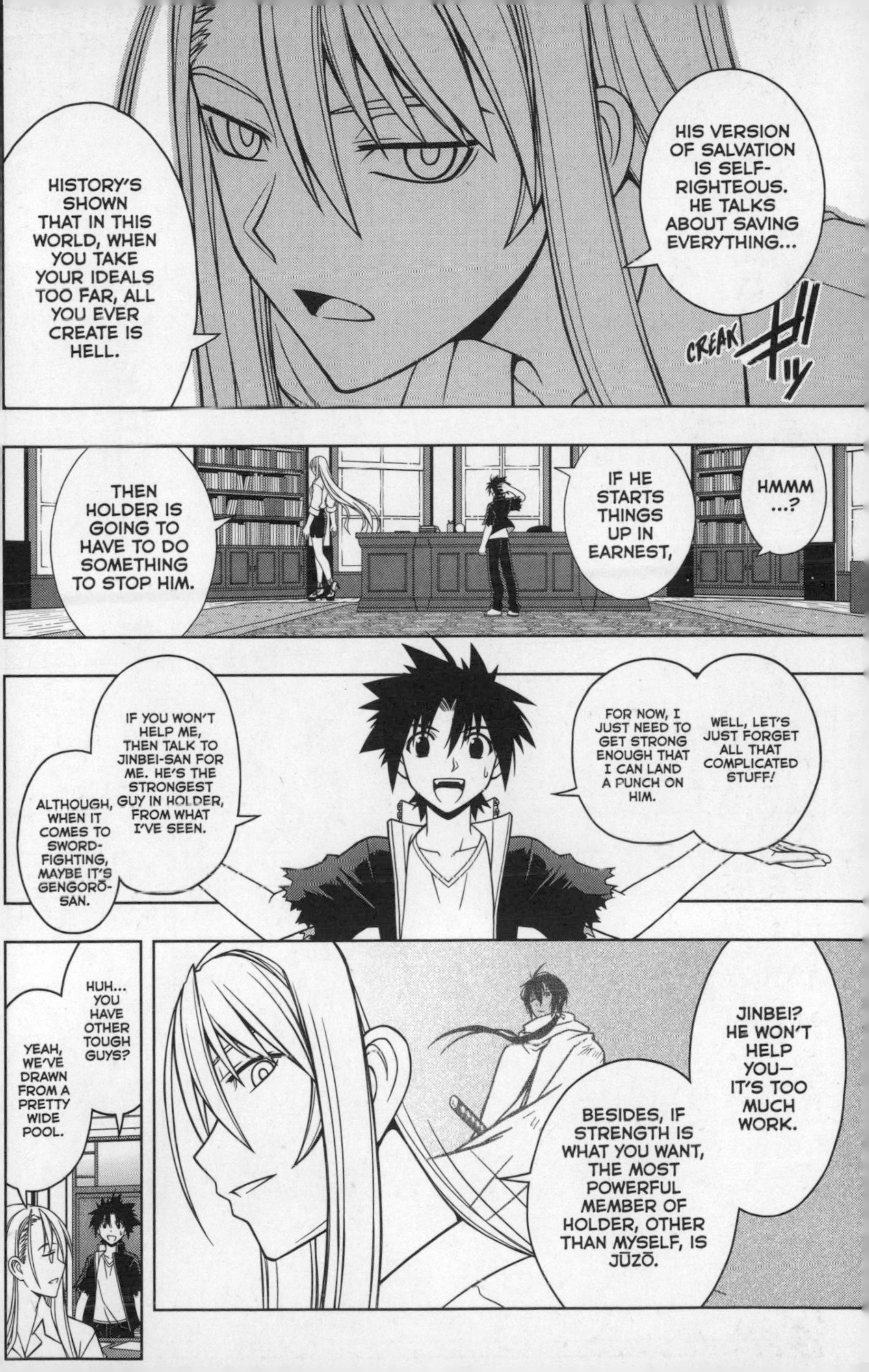

HIS VERSION OF SALVATION IS SELF-RIGHTEOUS. HE TALKS ABOUT SAVING EVERYTHING...
HISTORY'S SHOWN THAT IN THIS WORLD, WHEN YOU TAKE YOUR IDEALS TOO FAR, ALL YOU EVER CREATE IS HELL.
CREAK
HMMM ...?
IF HE STARTS THINGS UP IN EARNEST,
THEN HOLDER IS GOING TO HAVE TO DO SOMETHING TO STOP HIM.
WELL, LET'S JUST FORGET ALL THAT COMPLICATED STUFF!
FOR NOW, I JUST NEED TO GET STRONG ENOUGH THAT I CAN LAND A PUNCH ON HIM.
IF YOU WON'T HELP ME, THEN TALK TO JINBEI-SAN FOR ME. HE'S THE STRONGEST GUY IN HOLDER, FROM WHAT I'VE SEEN.
ALTHOUGH, WHEN IT COMES TO SWORD-FIGHTING, MAYBE IT'S GENGORŌ-SAN.
JINBEI? HE WON'T HELP YOU— IT'S TOO MUCH WORK.
BESIDES, IF STRENGTH IS WHAT YOU WANT, THE MOST POWERFUL MEMBER OF HOLDER, OTHER THAN MYSELF, IS JŪZŌ.
HUH... YOU HAVE OTHER TOUGH GUYS?
YEAH, WE'VE DRAWN FROM A PRETTY WIDE POOL.

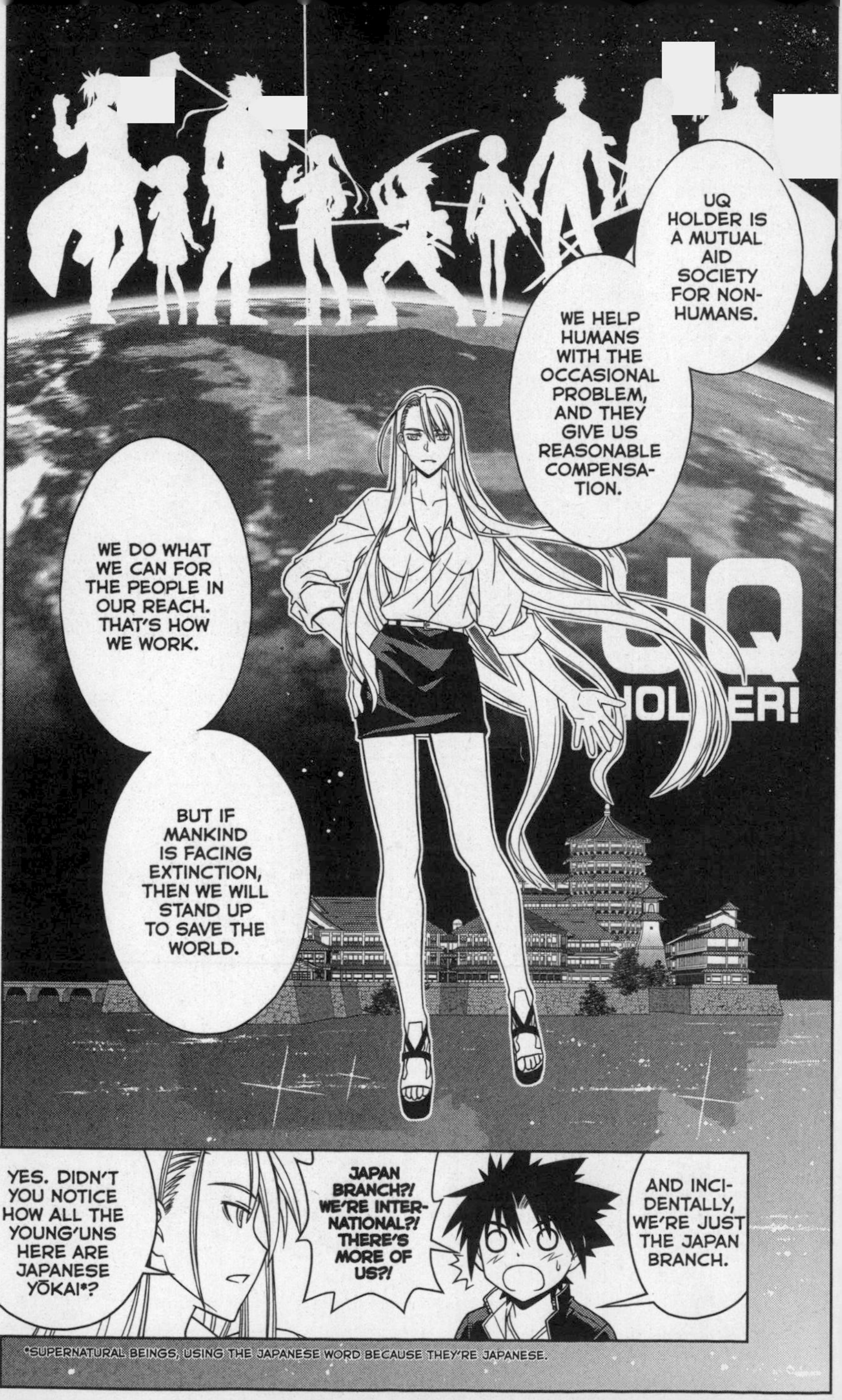
UQ HOLDER IS A MUTUAL AID SOCIETY FOR NON-HUMANS.
WE HELP HUMANS WITH THE OCCASIONAL PROBLEM, AND THEY GIVE US REASONABLE COMPENSA-TION.
WE DO WHAT WE CAN FOR THE PEOPLE IN OUR REACH. THAT'S HOW WE WORK.
BUT IF MANKIND IS FACING EXTINCTION, THEN WE WILL STAND UP TO SAVE THE WORLD.
AND INCI-DENTALLY, WE'RE JUST THE JAPAN BRANCH.
JAPAN BRANCH?! WE'RE INTER-NATIONAL?! THERE'S MORE OF US?!
YES. DIDN'T YOU NOTICE HOW ALL THE YOUNG'UNS HERE ARE JAPANESE YŌKAI*?

*SUPERNATURAL BEINGS, USING THE JAPANESE WORD BECAUSE THEY'RE JAPANESE.

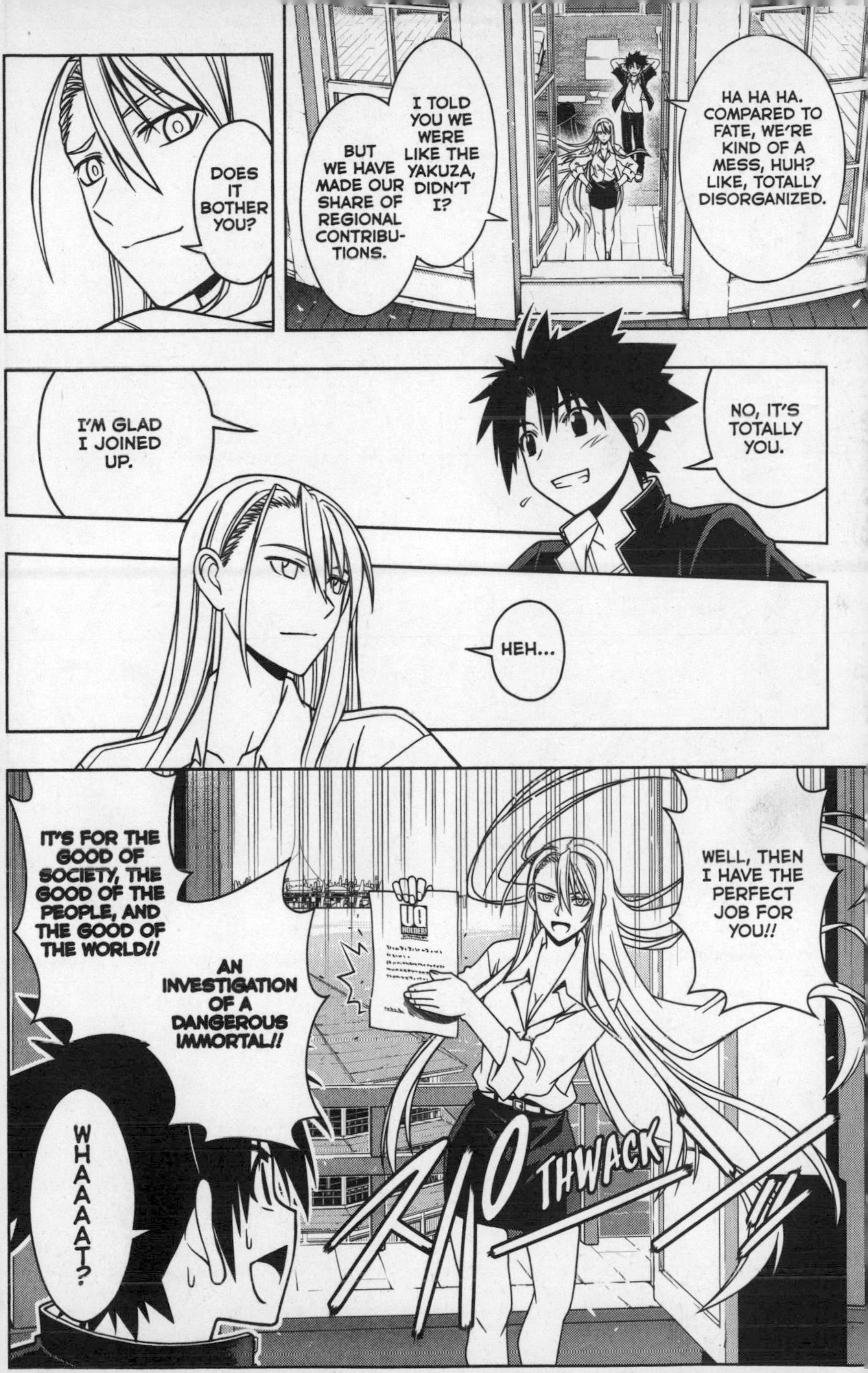
HA HA HA. COMPARED TO FATE, WE'RE KIND OF A MESS, HUH? LIKE, TOTALLY DISORGANIZED.
I TOLD YOU WE WERE LIKE THE YAKUZA, DIDN'T I?
BUT WE HAVE MADE OUR SHARE OF REGIONAL CONTRIBU-TIONS.
DOES IT BOTHER YOU?
NO, IT'S TOTALLY YOU.
I'M GLAD I JOINED UP.
HEH...
WELL, THEN I HAVE THE PERFECT JOB FOR YOU!!
UQ HOLDER!
AN INVESTIGATION OF A DANGEROUS IMMORTAL!!
IT'S FOR THE GOOD OF SOCIETY, THE GOOD OF THE PEOPLE, AND THE GOOD OF THE WORLD!!
THWACK
WHAAAAT?

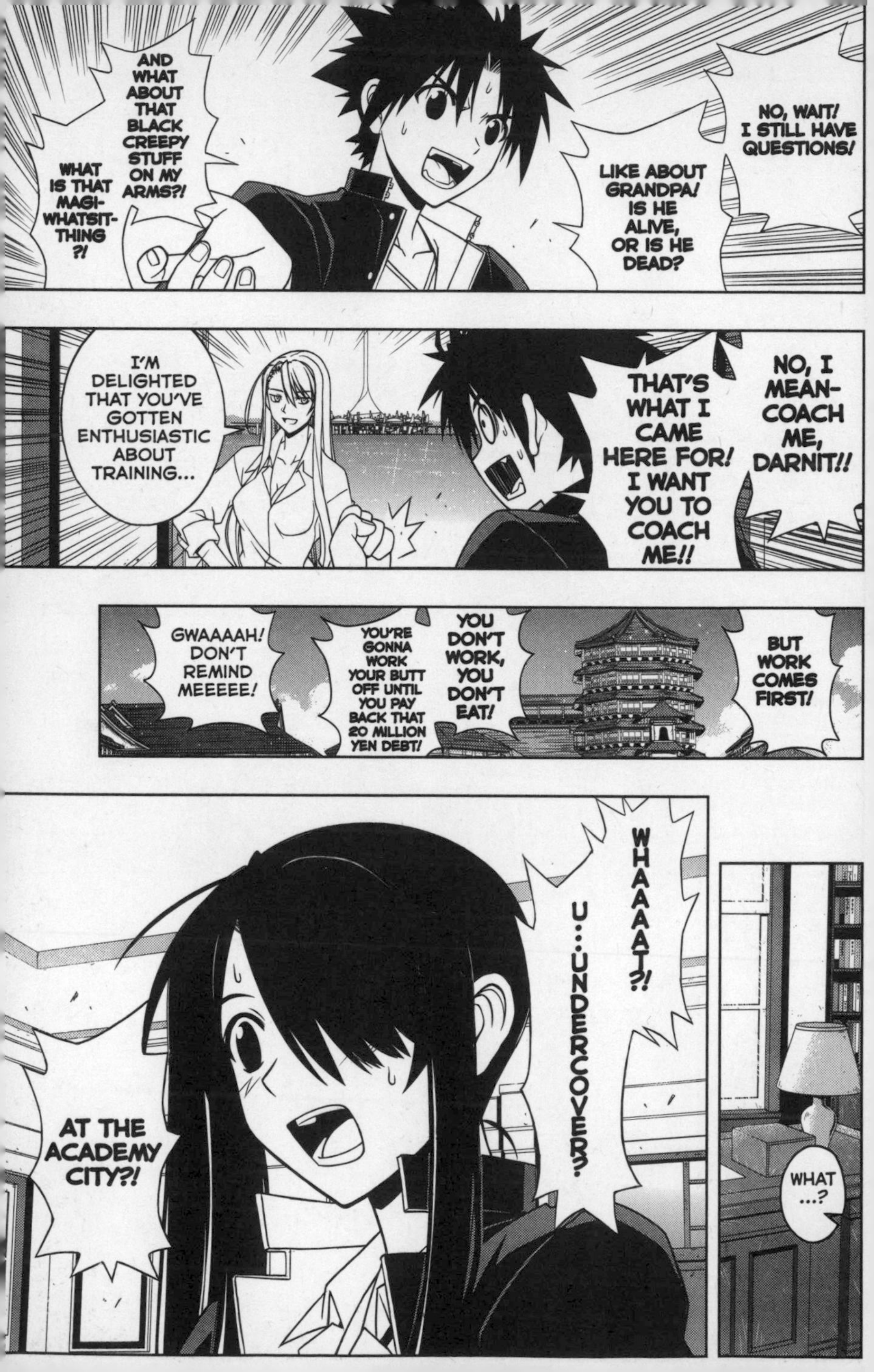
NO, WAIT! I STILL HAVE QUESTIONS!
LIKE ABOUT GRANDPA! IS HE ALIVE, OR IS HE DEAD?
AND WHAT ABOUT THAT BLACK CREEPY STUFF ON MY ARMS?!
WHAT IS THAT MAGI-WHATSIT-THING?!
NO, I MEAN-COACH ME, DARNIT!!
THAT'S WHAT I CAME HERE FOR! I WANT YOU TO COACH ME!!
I'M DELIGHTED THAT YOU'VE GOTTEN ENTHUSIASTIC ABOUT TRAINING...
BUT WORK COMES FIRST!
YOU DON'T WORK, YOU DON'T EAT!
YOU'RE GONNA WORK YOUR BUTT OFF UNTIL YOU PAY BACK THAT 20 MILLION YEN DEBT!
GWAAAAH! DON'T REMIND MEEEEE!
WHAT ...?
WHAAAAT?!
U...UNDERCOVER?
AT THE ACADEMY CITY?!

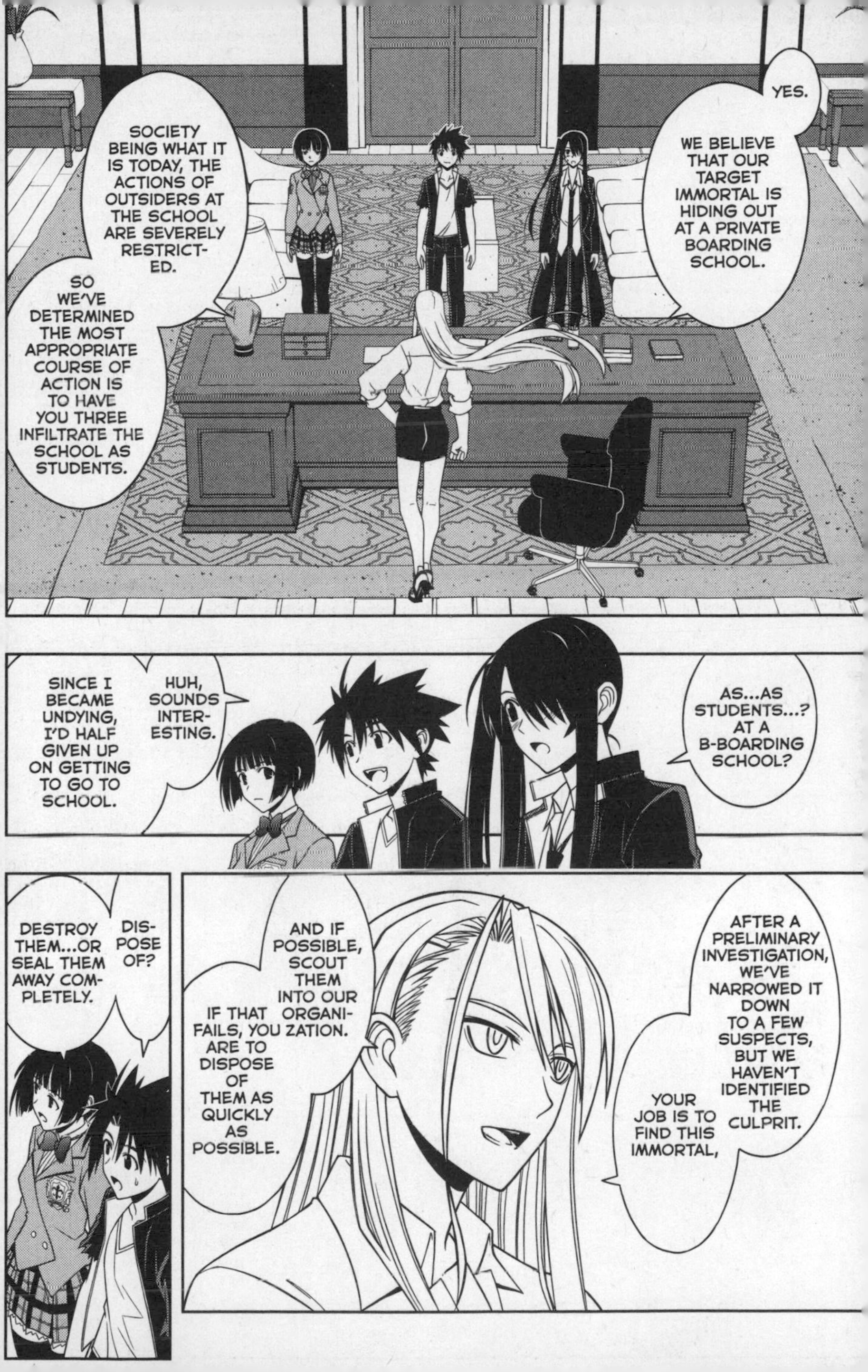
YES.
WE BELIEVE THAT OUR TARGET IMMORTAL IS HIDING OUT AT A PRIVATE BOARDING SCHOOL.
SOCIETY BEING WHAT IT IS TODAY, THE ACTIONS OF OUTSIDERS AT THE SCHOOL ARE SEVERELY RESTRICT-ED.
SO WE'VE DETERMINED THE MOST APPROPRIATE COURSE OF ACTION IS TO HAVE YOU THREE INFILTRATE THE SCHOOL AS STUDENTS.
AS...AS STUDENTS...? AT A B-BOARDING SCHOOL?
HUH, SOUNDS INTER-ESTING.
SINCE I BECAME UNDYING, I'D HALF GIVEN UP ON GETTING TO GO TO SCHOOL.
AFTER A PRELIMINARY INVESTIGATION, WE'VE NARROWED IT DOWN TO A FEW SUSPECTS, BUT WE HAVEN'T IDENTIFIED THE CULPRIT.
YOUR JOB IS TO FIND THIS IMMORTAL,
AND IF POSSIBLE, SCOUT THEM INTO OUR ORGANI-ZATION.
IF THAT FAILS, YOU ARE TO DISPOSE OF THEM AS QUICKLY AS POSSIBLE.
DIS-POSE OF?
DESTROY THEM...OR SEAL THEM AWAY COM-PLETELY.

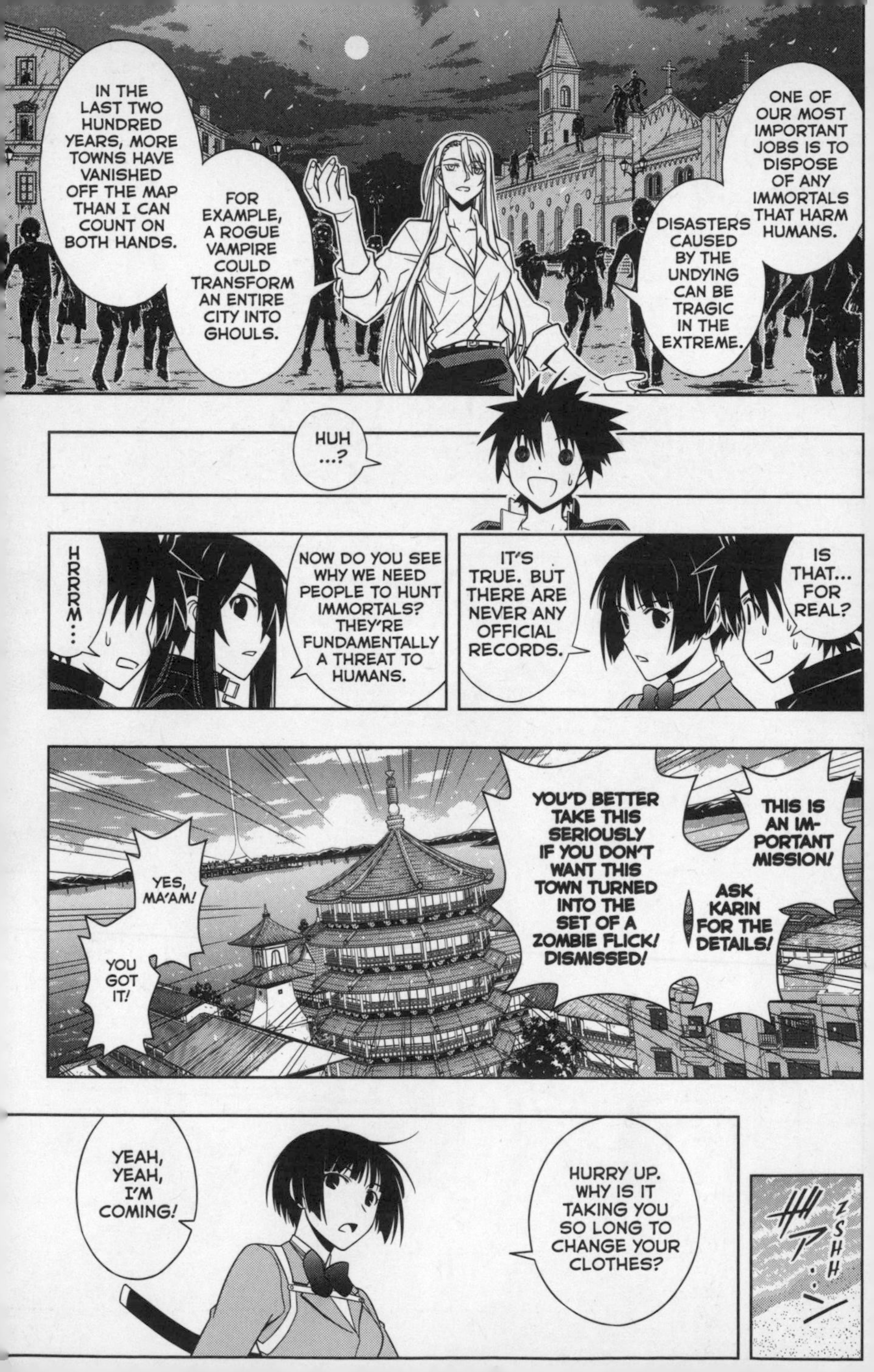
ONE OF OUR MOST IMPORTANT JOBS IS TO DISPOSE OF ANY IMMORTALS THAT HARM HUMANS.
DISASTERS CAUSED BY THE UNDYING CAN BE TRAGIC IN THE EXTREME.
IN THE LAST TWO HUNDRED YEARS, MORE TOWNS HAVE VANISHED OFF THE MAP THAN I CAN COUNT ON BOTH HANDS.
FOR EXAMPLE, A ROGUE VAMPIRE COULD TRANSFORM AN ENTIRE CITY INTO GHOULS.
HUH ...?
IS THAT... FOR REAL?
IT'S TRUE. BUT THERE ARE NEVER ANY OFFICIAL RECORDS.
NOW DO YOU SEE WHY WE NEED PEOPLE TO HUNT IMMORTALS? THEY'RE FUNDAMENTALLY A THREAT TO HUMANS.
HRRRM...
THIS IS AN IM-PORTANT MISSION!
ASK KARIN FOR THE DETAILS!
YOU'D BETTER TAKE THIS SERIOUSLY IF YOU DON'T WANT THIS TOWN TURNED INTO THE SET OF A ZOMBIE FLICK! DISMISSED!
YES, MA'AM!
YOU GOT IT!
ZSHH
HURRY UP. WHY IS IT TAKING YOU SO LONG TO CHANGE YOUR CLOTHES?
YEAH, YEAH, I'M COMING!

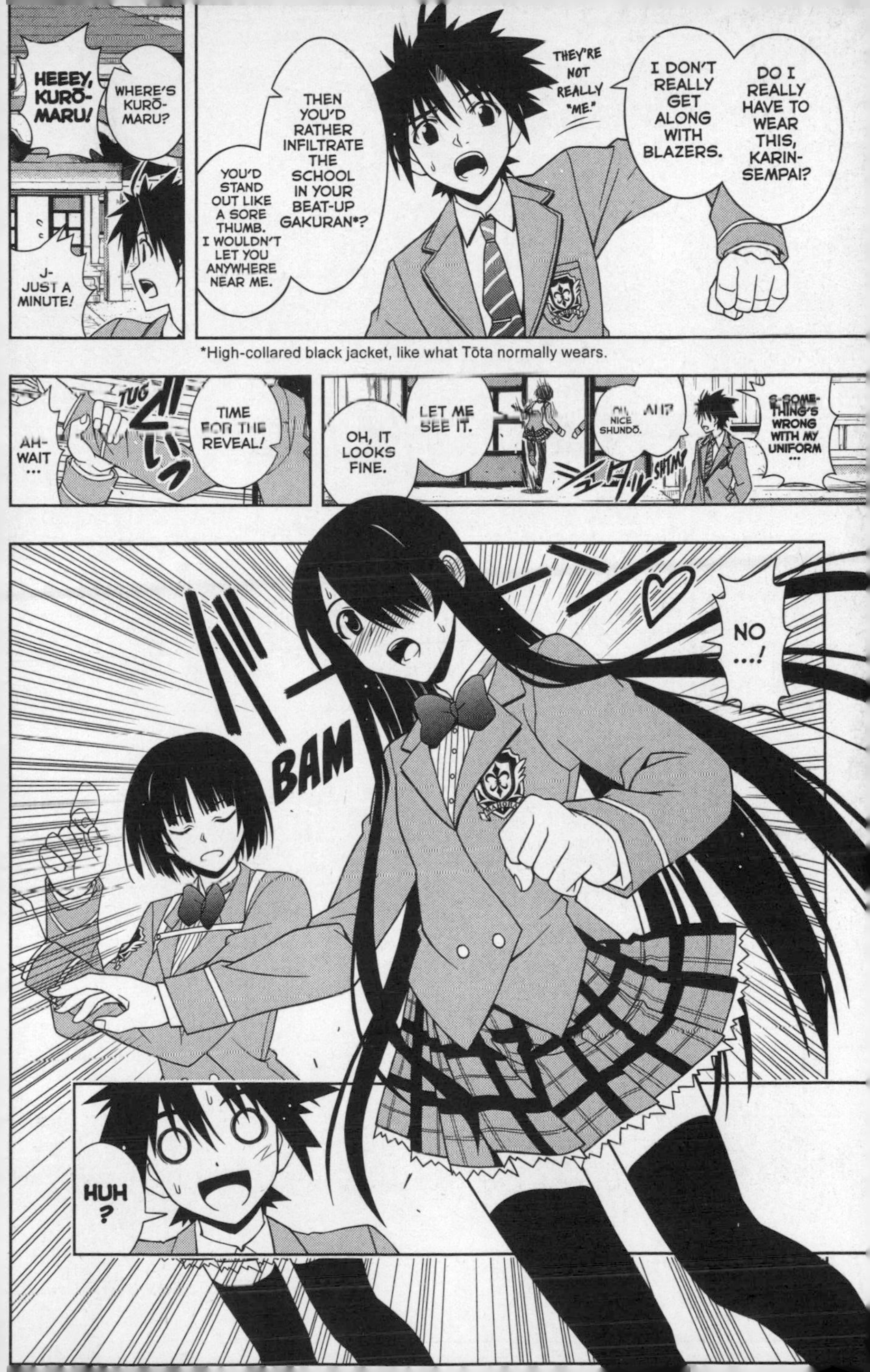
DO I REALLY HAVE TO WEAR THIS, KARIN-SEMPAI?
I DON'T REALLY GET ALONG WITH BLAZERS.
THEY'RE NOT REALLY "ME."
THEN YOU'D RATHER INFILTRATE THE SCHOOL IN YOUR BEAT-UP GAKURAN*?
YOU'D STAND OUT LIKE A SORE THUMB. I WOULDN'T LET YOU ANYWHERE NEAR ME.
HEEEY, KURŌ-MARU!
WHERE'S KURŌ-MARU?
J-JUST A MINUTE!
*High-collared black jacket, like what Tōta normally wears.
S-SOMETHING'S WRONG WITH MY UNIFORM ...
AH!?
OH, NICE SHUNDŌ.
SHIM
LET ME SEE IT.
OH, IT LOOKS FINE.
TIME FOR THE REVEAL!
TUG
AH-WAIT ...
NO ...!
BAM
HUH ?

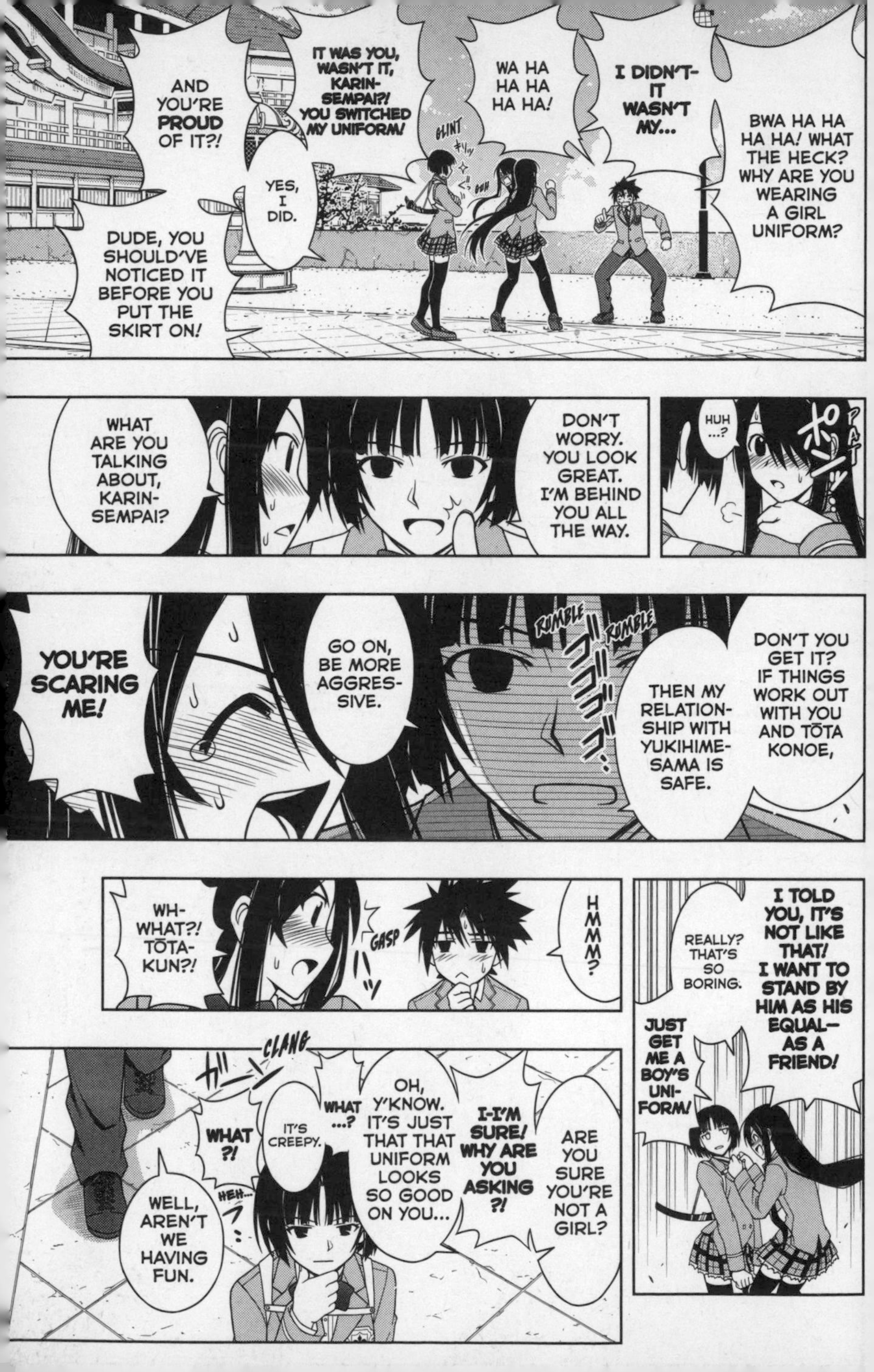
BWA HA HA HA HA! WHAT THE HECK? WHY ARE YOU WEARING A GIRL UNIFORM?
I DIDN'T- IT WASN'T MY...
WA HA HA HA HA HA!
IT WAS YOU, WASN'T IT, KARIN-SEMPAI?! YOU SWITCHED MY UNIFORM!
GLINT
YES, I DID.
AND YOU'RE PROUD OF IT?!
DUDE, YOU SHOULD'VE NOTICED IT BEFORE YOU PUT THE SKIRT ON!
PAT
HUH ...?
DON'T WORRY. YOU LOOK GREAT. I'M BEHIND YOU ALL THE WAY.
WHAT ARE YOU TALKING ABOUT, KARIN-SEMPAI?
DON'T YOU GET IT? IF THINGS WORK OUT WITH YOU AND TŌTA KONOE,
THEN MY RELATIONSHIP WITH YUKIHIME-SAMA IS SAFE.
RUMBLE RUMBLE
GO ON, BE MORE AGGRESSIVE.
YOU'RE SCARING ME!
I TOLD YOU, IT'S NOT LIKE THAT! I WANT TO STAND BY HIM AS HIS EQUAL—AS A FRIEND!
REALLY? THAT'S SO BORING.
JUST GET ME A BOY'S UNIFORM!
HMMM?
GASP
WH-WHAT?! TŌTA-KUN?!
ARE YOU SURE YOU'RE NOT A GIRL?
I-I'M SURE! WHY ARE YOU ASKING?!
OH, Y'KNOW. IT'S JUST THAT THAT UNIFORM LOOKS SO GOOD ON YOU...
WHAT ...?
CLANG
IT'S CREEPY.
WHAT ?!
HEH...
WELL, AREN'T WE HAVING FUN.

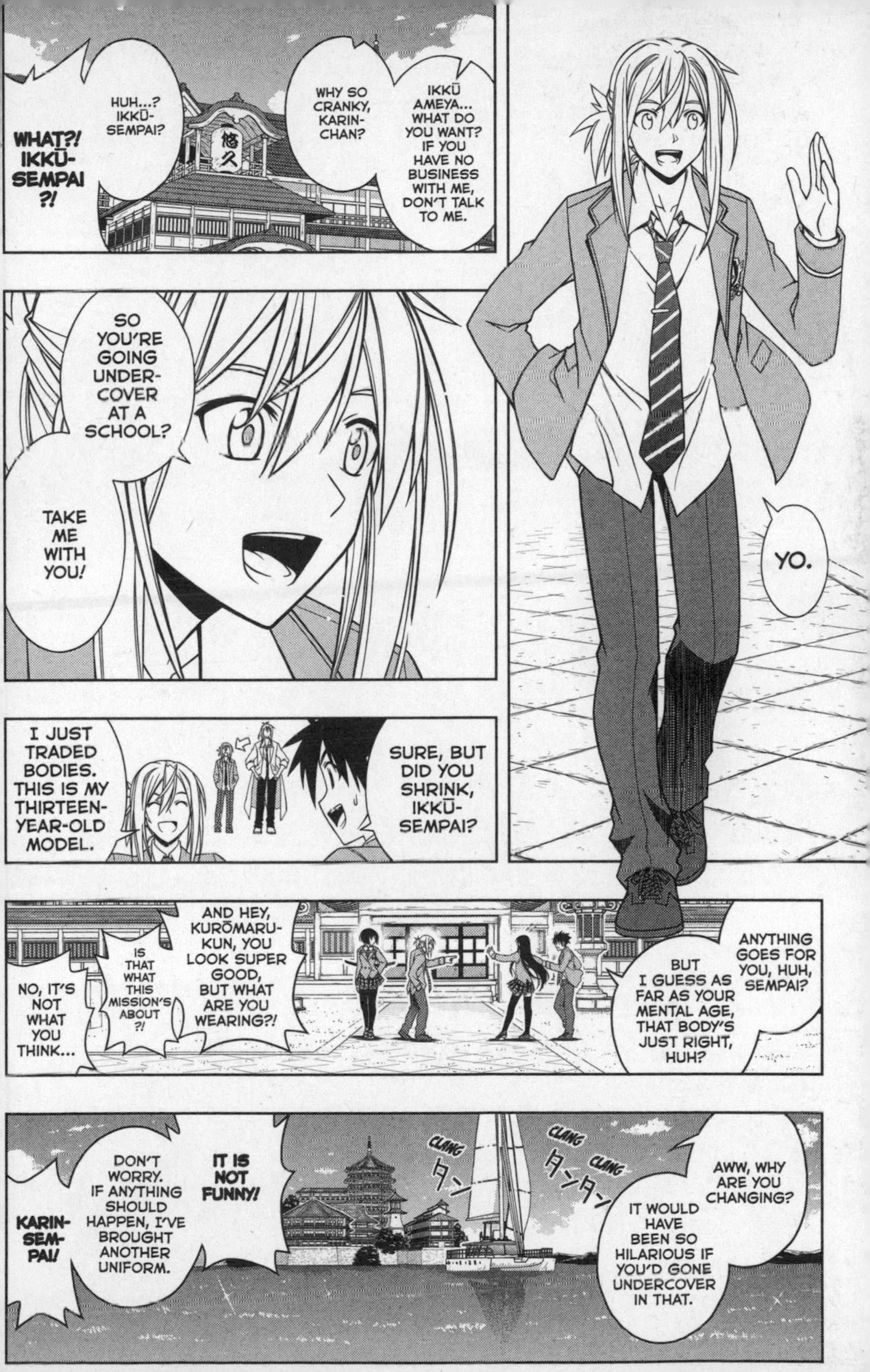
YO.
IKKŪ AMEYA... WHAT DO YOU WANT? IF YOU HAVE NO BUSINESS WITH ME, DON'T TALK TO ME.
WHY SO CRANKY, KARIN-CHAN?
悠久
HUH...? IKKŪ-SEMPAI?
WHAT?! IKKŪ-SEMPAI?!
SO YOU'RE GOING UNDERCOVER AT A SCHOOL?
TAKE ME WITH YOU!
SURE, BUT DID YOU SHRINK, IKKŪ-SEMPAI?
I JUST TRADED BODIES. THIS IS MY THIRTEEN-YEAR-OLD MODEL.
ANYTHING GOES FOR YOU, HUH, SEMPAI?
BUT I GUESS AS FAR AS YOUR MENTAL AGE, THAT BODY'S JUST RIGHT, HUH?
AND HEY, KURŌMARU-KUN, YOU LOOK SUPER GOOD, BUT WHAT ARE YOU WEARING?!
IS THAT WHAT THIS MISSION'S ABOUT?!
NO, IT'S NOT WHAT YOU THINK...
AWW, WHY ARE YOU CHANGING?
IT WOULD HAVE BEEN SO HILARIOUS IF YOU'D GONE UNDERCOVER IN THAT.
CLANG CLANG
タンタン
CLANG
タン
IT IS NOT FUNNY!
DON'T WORRY. IF ANYTHING SHOULD HAPPEN, I'VE BROUGHT ANOTHER UNIFORM.
KARIN-SEMPAI!

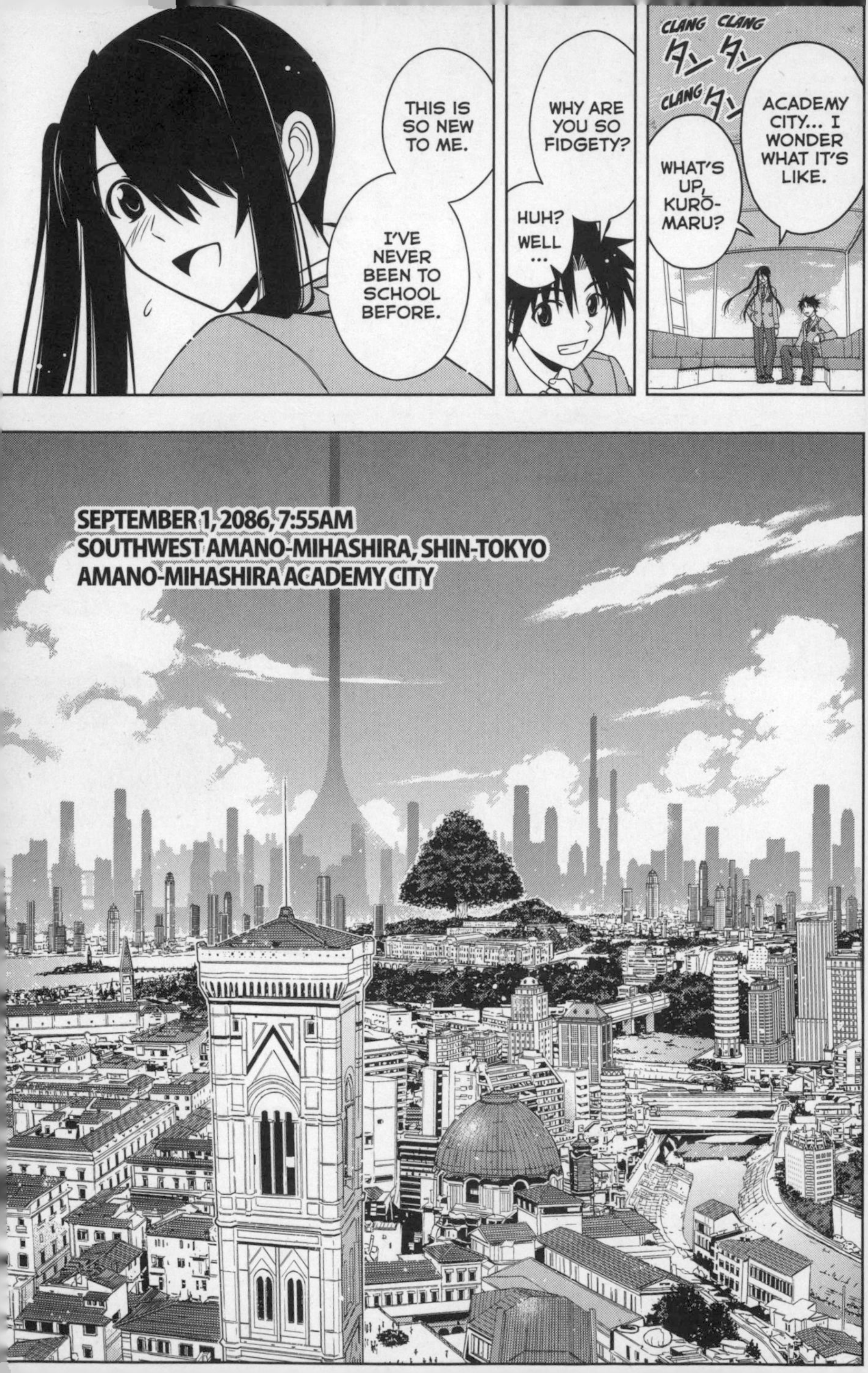
CLANG CLANG
タン タン
CLANG タン
ACADEMY CITY... I WONDER WHAT IT'S LIKE.
WHAT'S UP, KURO-MARU?
WHY ARE YOU SO FIDGETY?
HUH? WELL ...
THIS IS SO NEW TO ME.
I'VE NEVER BEEN TO SCHOOL BEFORE.
SEPTEMBER 1, 2086, 7:55AM
SOUTHWEST AMANO-MIHASHIRA, SHIN-TOKYO
AMANO-MIHASHIRA ACADEMY CITY

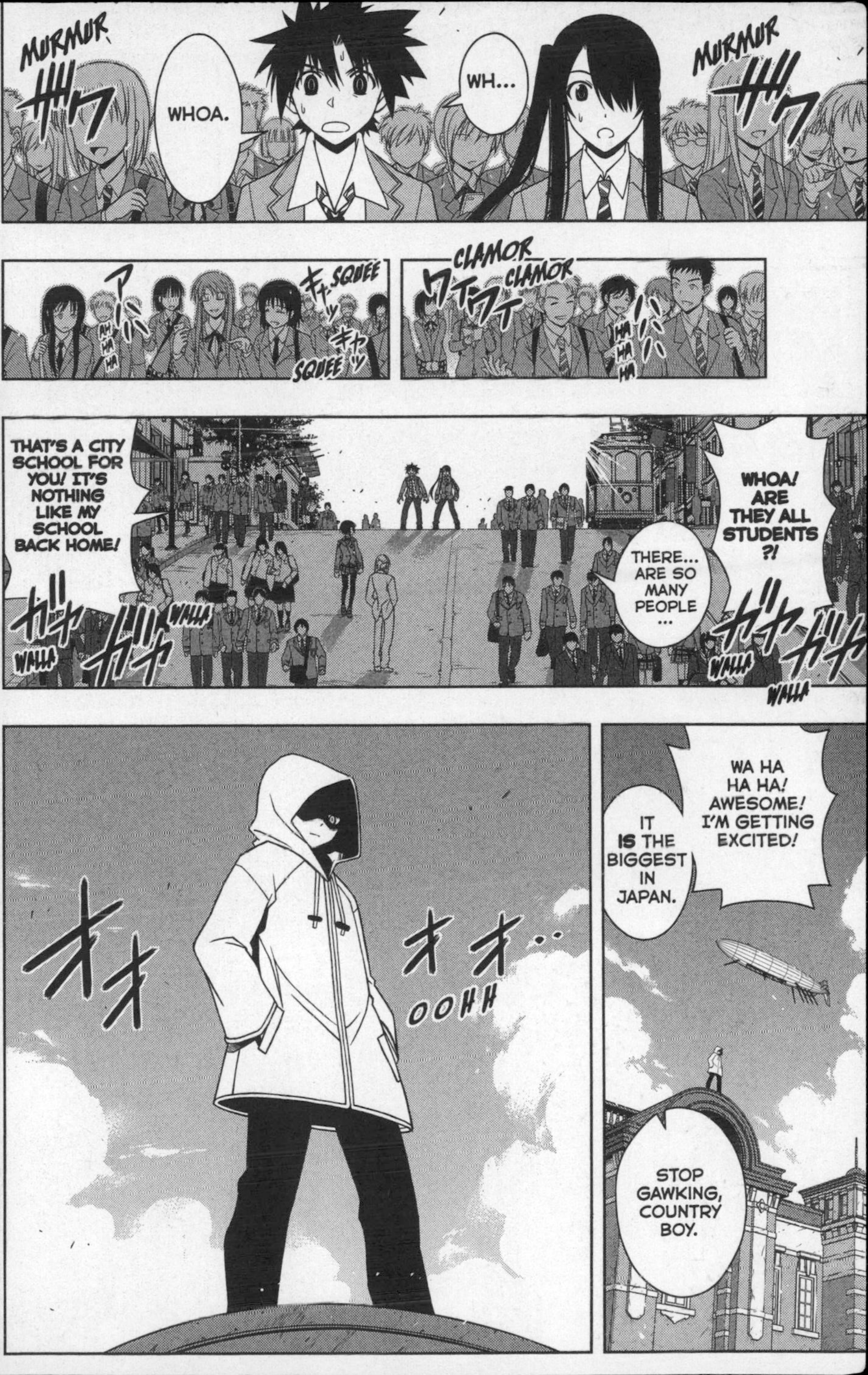
MURMUR
WH...
WHOA.
MURMUR
CLAMOR
CLAMOR
HA HA HA
SQUEE
SQUEE
AH HA HA
WHOA! ARE THEY ALL STUDENTS?!
THERE... ARE SO MANY PEOPLE...
THAT'S A CITY SCHOOL FOR YOU! IT'S NOTHING LIKE MY SCHOOL BACK HOME!
WALLA
WALLA
WALLA
WALLA
WA HA HA HA! AWESOME! I'M GETTING EXCITED!
IT IS THE BIGGEST IN JAPAN.
STOP GAWKING, COUNTRY BOY.
OOHH

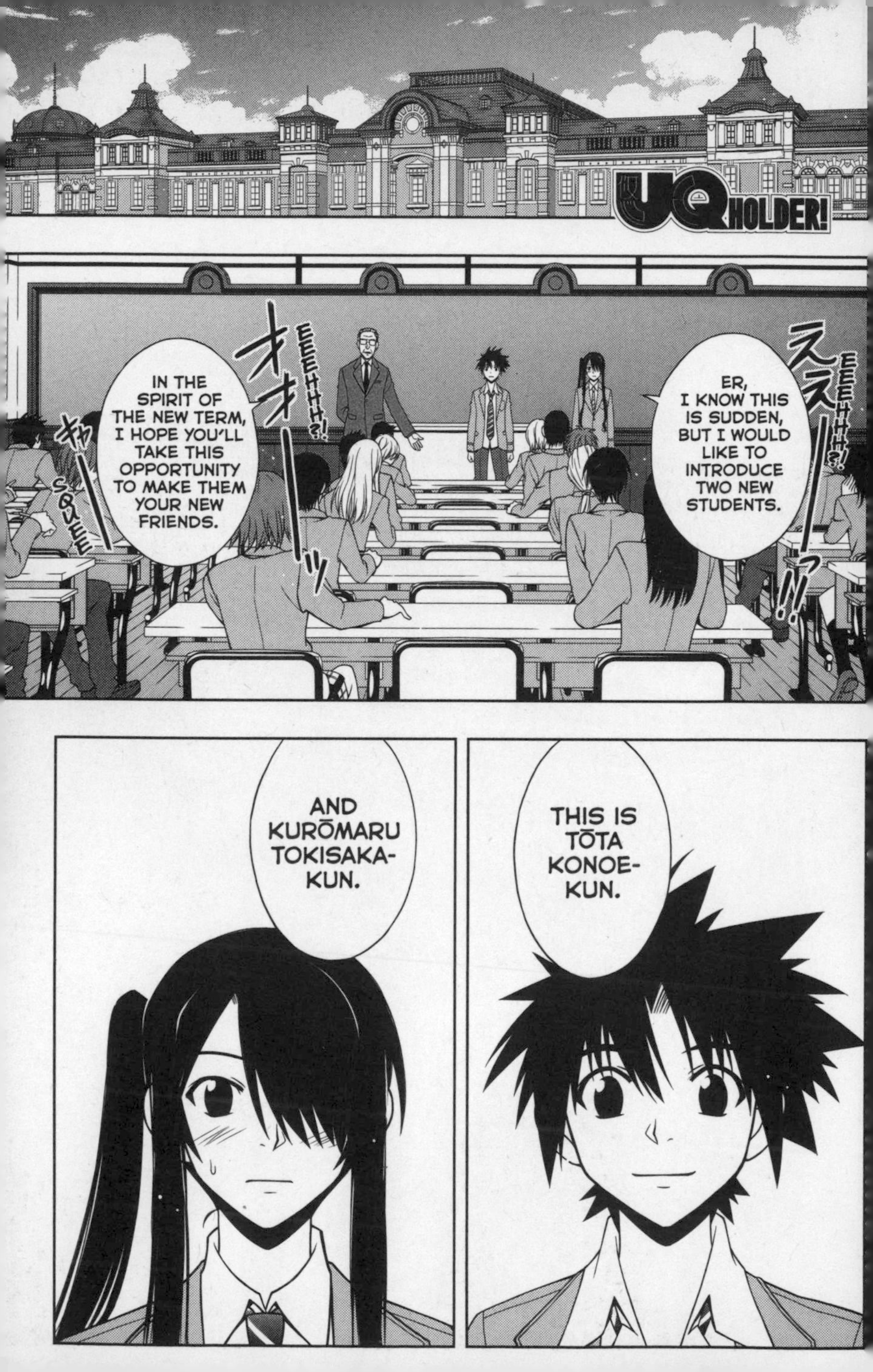
UQ HOLDER!
ER, I KNOW THIS IS SUDDEN, BUT I WOULD LIKE TO INTRODUCE TWO NEW STUDENTS.
EEEHHHH?!
IN THE SPIRIT OF THE NEW TERM, I HOPE YOU'LL TAKE THIS OPPORTUNITY TO MAKE THEM YOUR NEW FRIENDS.
EEEHHHH?!
SQUEE
THIS IS TŌTA KONOE-KUN.
AND KURŌMARU TOKISAKA-KUN.

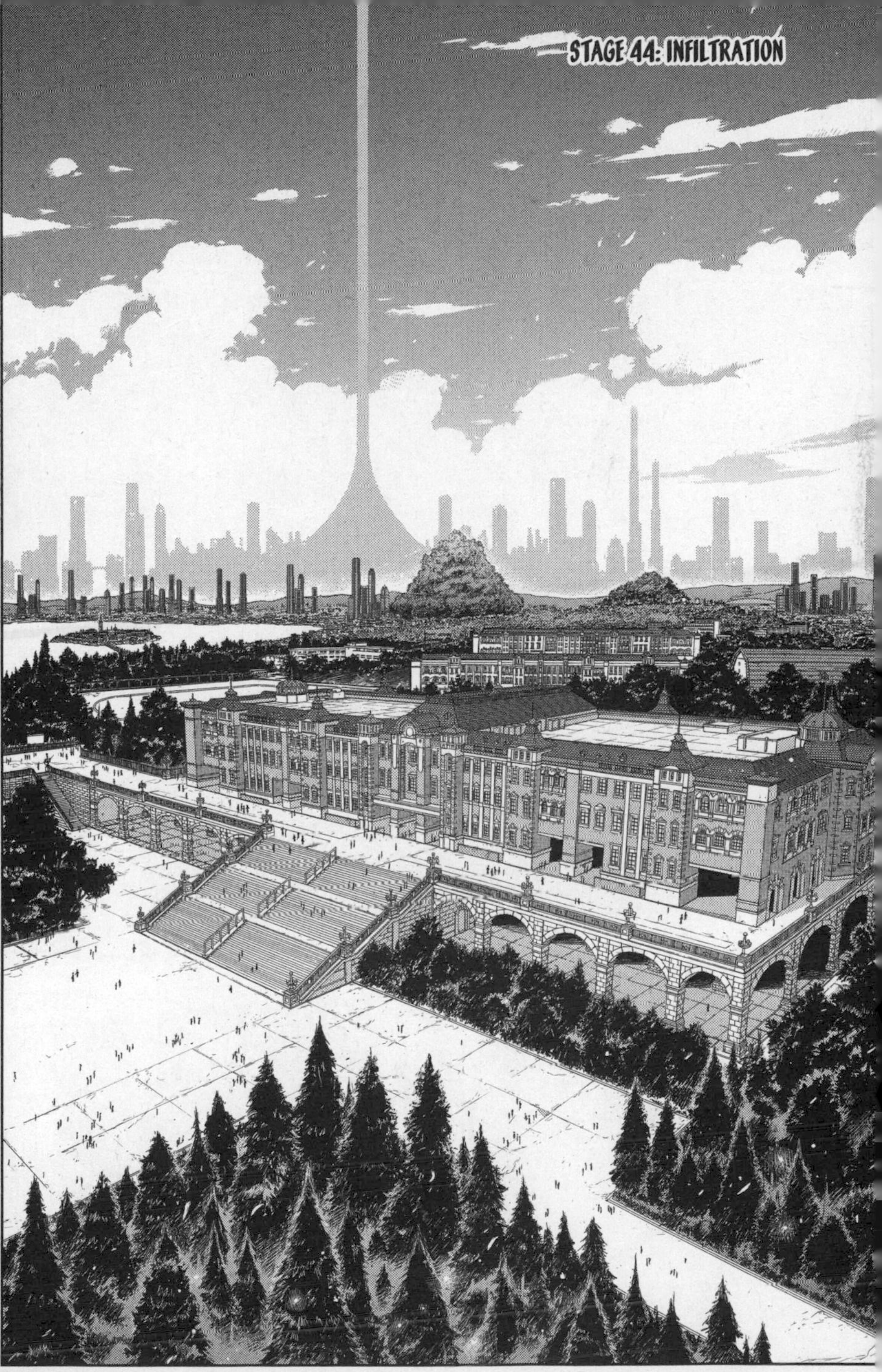
STAGE 44: INFILTRATION

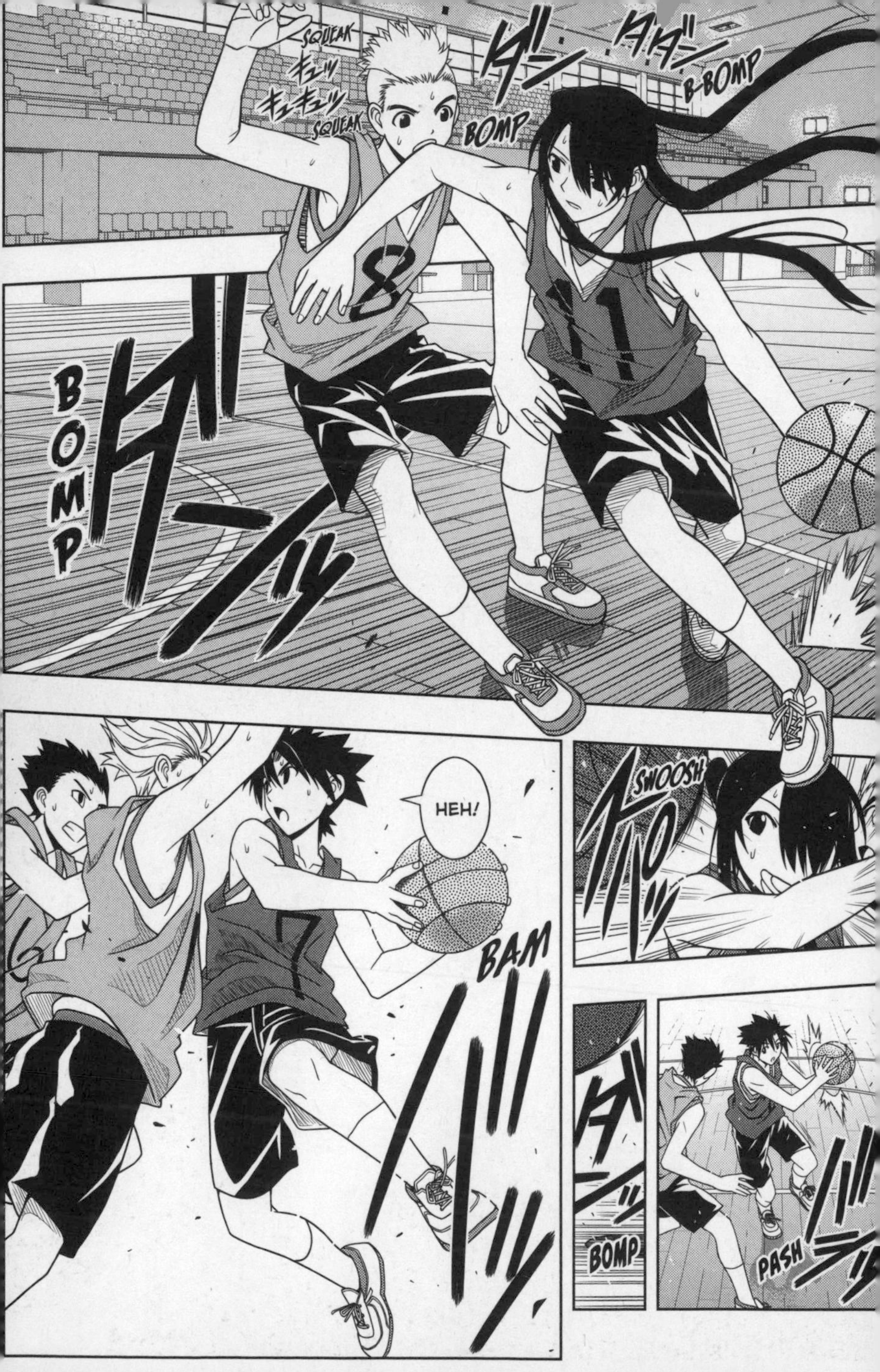
B-BOMP
BOMP
SQUEAK
キュッ
キュキュッ
SQUEAK
BOMP
BOMP
SWOOSH
HEH!
BAM
PASH
BOMP

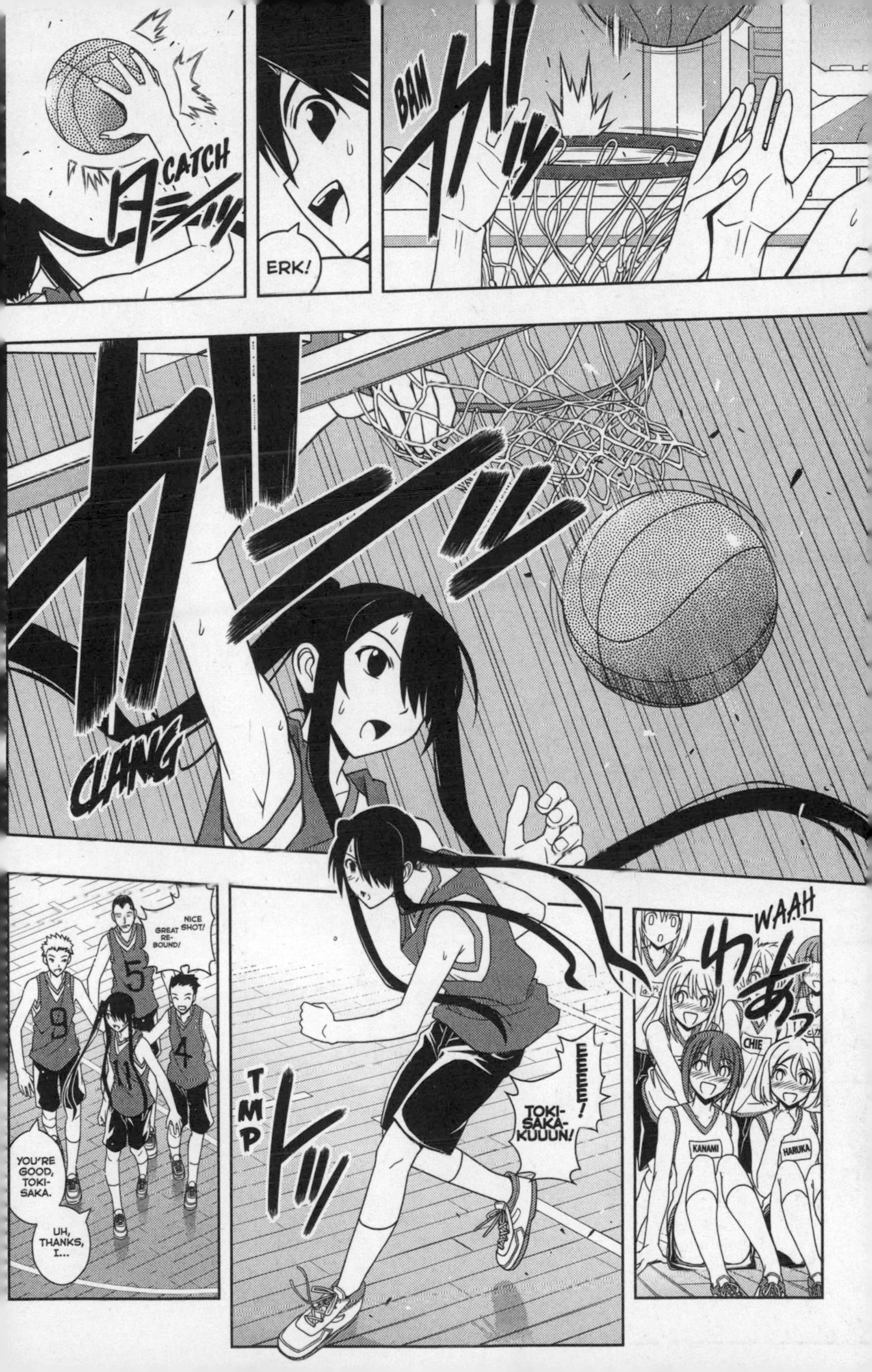
BAM
ERK!
CATCH
CLANG
WAAH
CHIE
KANAMI
HARUKA
EEEE!
TOKI-SAKA-KUUUN!
TMP
NICE SHOT!
GREAT RE-BOUND!
YOU'RE GOOD, TOKI-SAKA.
UH, THANKS, I...

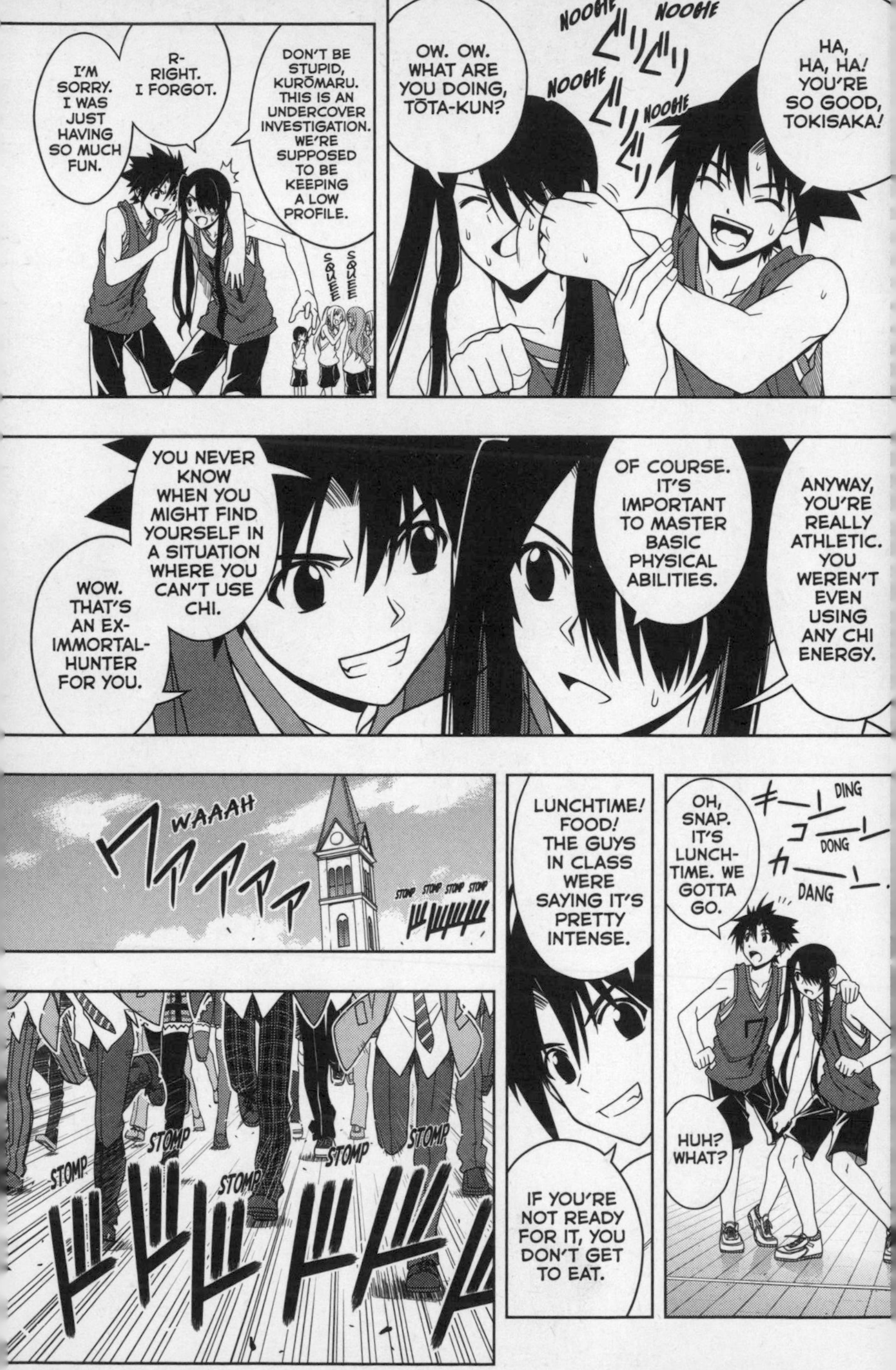
NOOGIE NOOGIE NOOGIE NOOGIE
HA, HA, HA! YOU'RE SO GOOD, TOKISAKA!
OW. OW. WHAT ARE YOU DOING, TŌTA-KUN?
DON'T BE STUPID, KURŌMARU. THIS IS AN UNDERCOVER INVESTIGATION. WE'RE SUPPOSED TO BE KEEPING A LOW PROFILE.
R-RIGHT. I FORGOT.
I'M SORRY. I WAS JUST HAVING SO MUCH FUN.
SQUEE SQUEE
ANYWAY, YOU'RE REALLY ATHLETIC. YOU WEREN'T EVEN USING ANY CHI ENERGY.
OF COURSE. IT'S IMPORTANT TO MASTER BASIC PHYSICAL ABILITIES.
YOU NEVER KNOW WHEN YOU MIGHT FIND YOURSELF IN A SITUATION WHERE YOU CAN'T USE CHI.
WOW. THAT'S AN EX-IMMORTAL-HUNTER FOR YOU.
DING DONG DANG
OH, SNAP. IT'S LUNCH-TIME. WE GOTTA GO.
HUH? WHAT?
LUNCHTIME! FOOD! THE GUYS IN CLASS WERE SAYING IT'S PRETTY INTENSE.
IF YOU'RE NOT READY FOR IT, YOU DON'T GET TO EAT.
WAAAH
STOMP STOMP STOMP STOMP
STOMP STOMP STOMP STOMP STOMP

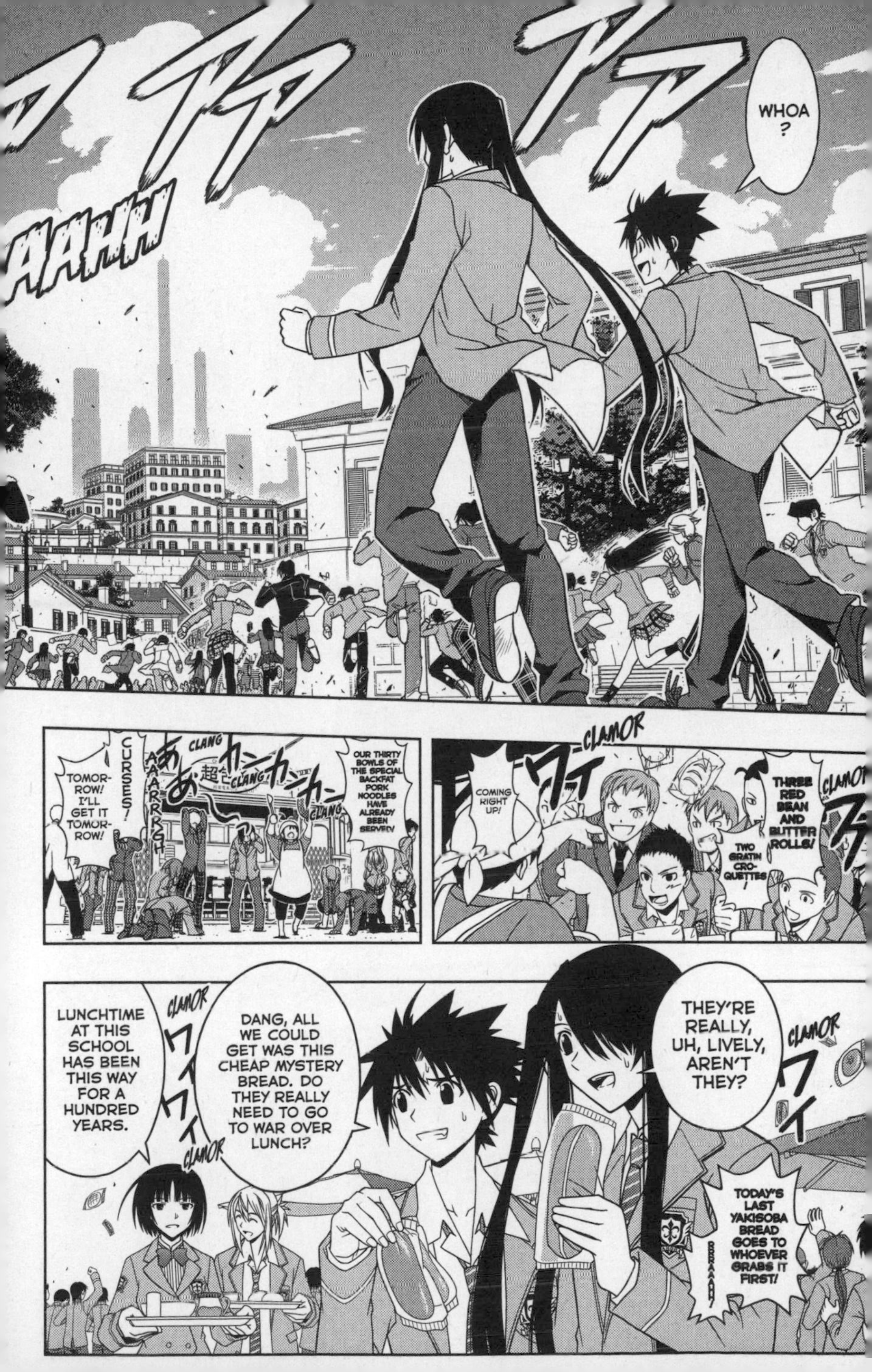
WHOA?
AAHH
CLAMOR
THREE RED BEAN AND BUTTER ROLLS!
CLAMOR
COMING RIGHT UP!
TWO GRATIN CROQUETTES!
OUR THIRTY BOWLS OF THE SPECIAL BACKFAT PORK NOODLES HAVE ALREADY BEEN SERVED!
CLANG
CLANG
CLANG
AAARRRGH
CURSES!
TOMORROW! I'LL GET IT TOMORROW!
THEY'RE REALLY, UH, LIVELY, AREN'T THEY?
CLAMOR
DANG, ALL WE COULD GET WAS THIS CHEAP MYSTERY BREAD. DO THEY REALLY NEED TO GO TO WAR OVER LUNCH?
CLAMOR
LUNCHTIME AT THIS SCHOOL HAS BEEN THIS WAY FOR A HUNDRED YEARS.
CLAMOR
TODAY'S LAST YAKISOBA BREAD GOES TO WHOEVER GRABS IT FIRST!

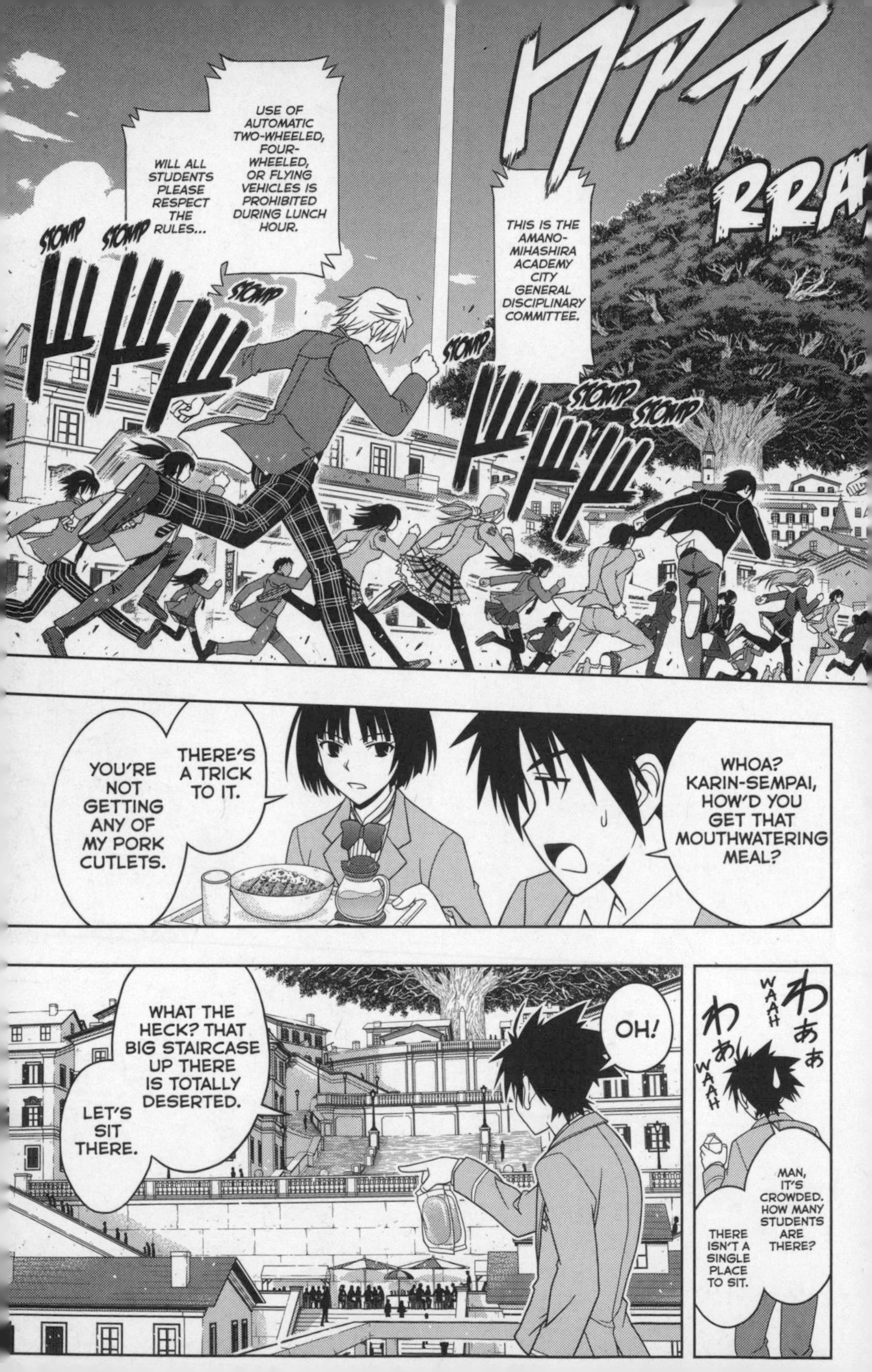
RRA
THIS IS THE AMANO-MIHASHIRA ACADEMY CITY GENERAL DISCIPLINARY COMMITTEE.
USE OF AUTOMATIC TWO-WHEELED, FOUR-WHEELED, OR FLYING VEHICLES IS PROHIBITED DURING LUNCH HOUR.
WILL ALL STUDENTS PLEASE RESPECT THE RULES...
STOMP STOMP STOMP STOMP STOMP STOMP
WHOA? KARIN-SEMPAI, HOW'D YOU GET THAT MOUTHWATERING MEAL?
THERE'S A TRICK TO IT.
YOU'RE NOT GETTING ANY OF MY PORK CUTLETS.
わぁぁ WAAH
わあ WAAH
MAN, IT'S CROWDED. HOW MANY STUDENTS ARE THERE?
THERE ISN'T A SINGLE PLACE TO SIT.
OH!
WHAT THE HECK? THAT BIG STAIRCASE UP THERE IS TOTALLY DESERTED.
LET'S SIT THERE.

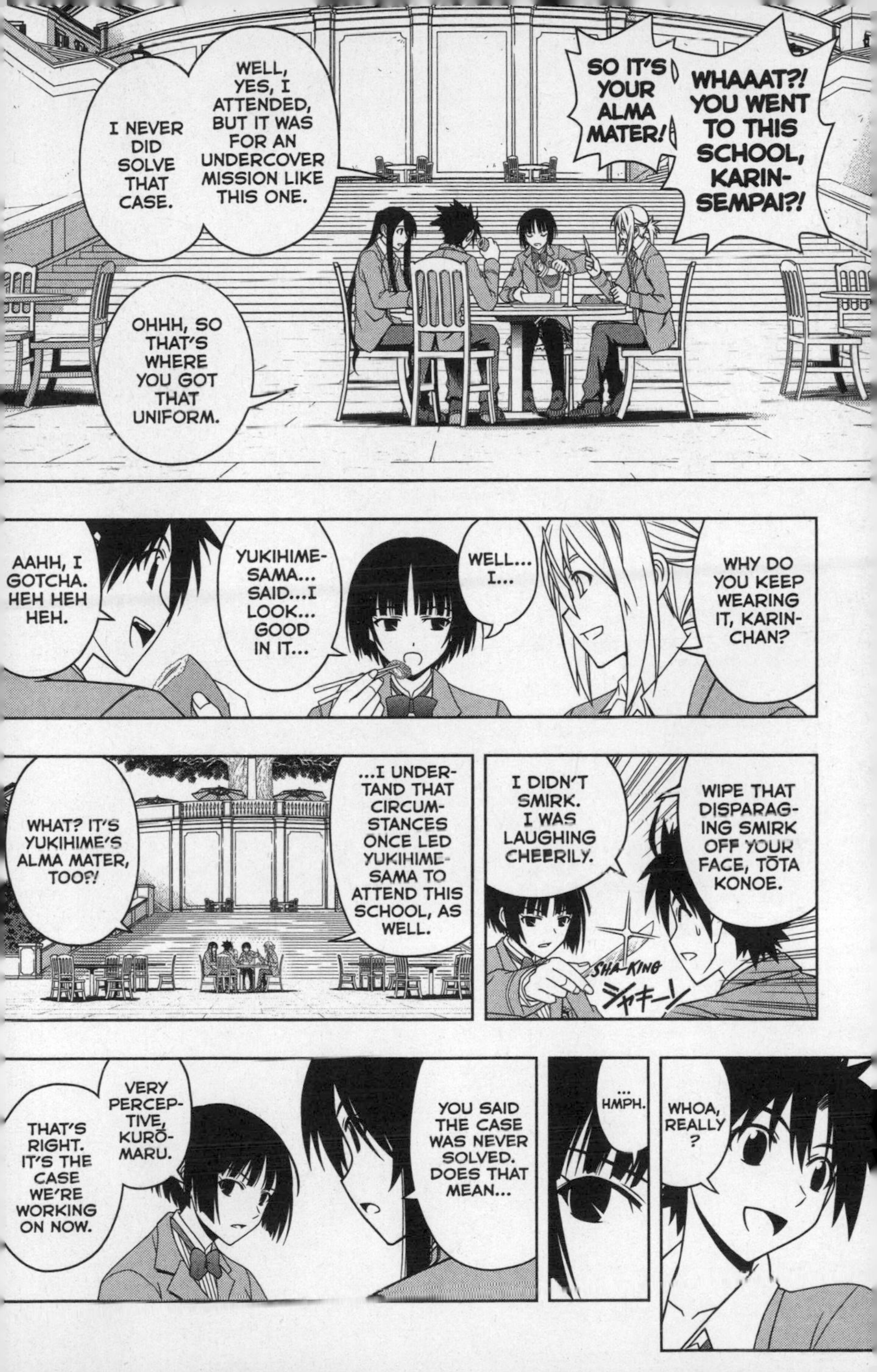
WHAAAT?! YOU WENT TO THIS SCHOOL, KARIN-SEMPAI?!
SO IT'S YOUR ALMA MATER!
WELL, YES, I ATTENDED, BUT IT WAS FOR AN UNDERCOVER MISSION LIKE THIS ONE.
I NEVER DID SOLVE THAT CASE.
OHHH, SO THAT'S WHERE YOU GOT THAT UNIFORM.
WHY DO YOU KEEP WEARING IT, KARIN-CHAN?
WELL... I...
YUKIHIME-SAMA... SAID...I LOOK... GOOD IN IT...
AAHH, I GOTCHA. HEH HEH HEH.
WIPE THAT DISPARAGING SMIRK OFF YOUR FACE, TŌTA KONOE.
I DIDN'T SMIRK. I WAS LAUGHING CHEERILY.
SHA-KING
シャキーン
...I UNDERTAND THAT CIRCUMSTANCES ONCE LED YUKIHIME-SAMA TO ATTEND THIS SCHOOL, AS WELL.
WHAT? IT'S YUKIHIME'S ALMA MATER, TOO?!
WHOA, REALLY?
...HMPH.
YOU SAID THE CASE WAS NEVER SOLVED. DOES THAT MEAN...
VERY PERCEPTIVE, KURŌMARU.
THAT'S RIGHT. IT'S THE CASE WE'RE WORKING ON NOW.

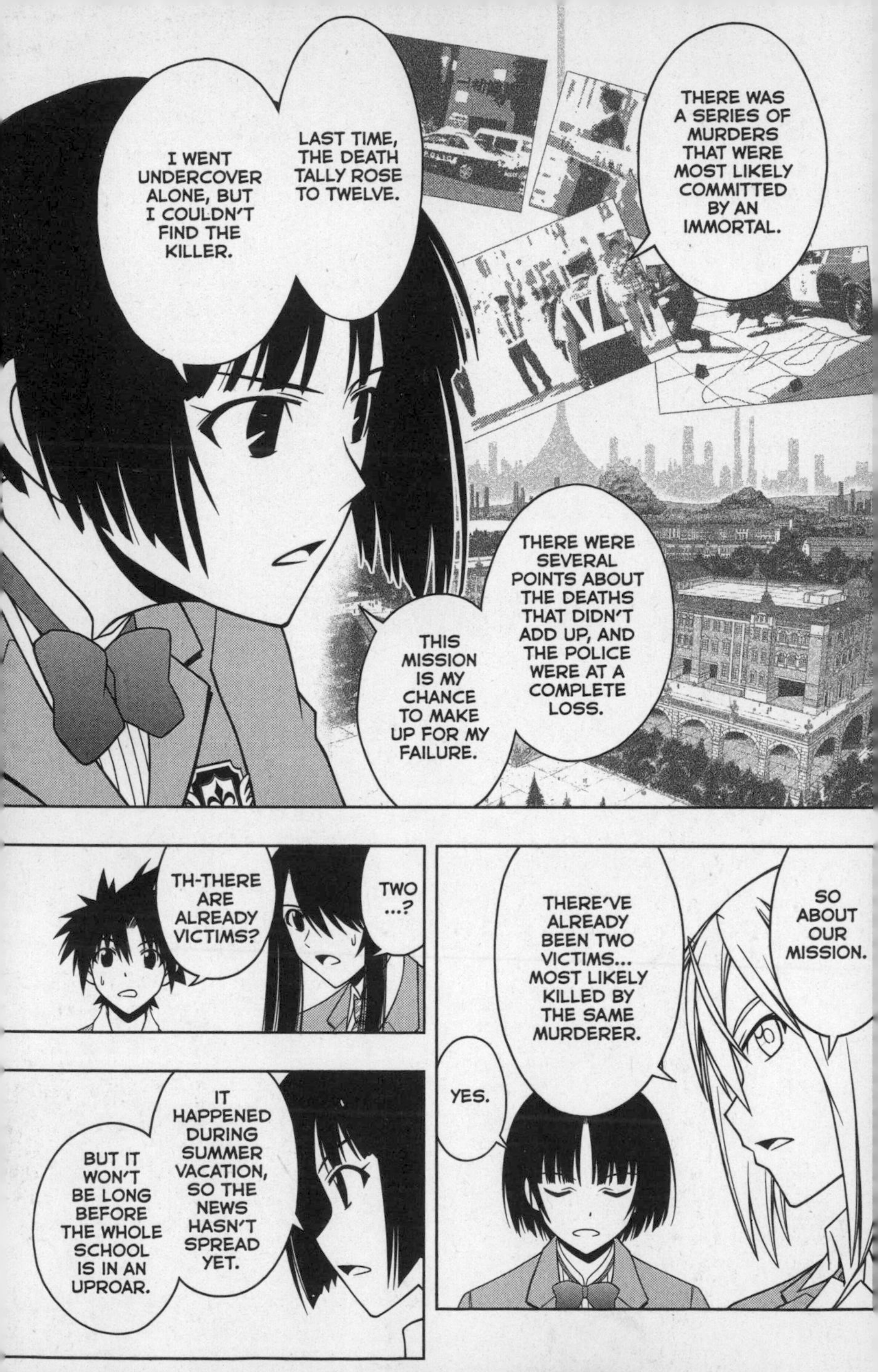
THERE WAS A SERIES OF MURDERS THAT WERE MOST LIKELY COMMITTED BY AN IMMORTAL.
LAST TIME, THE DEATH TALLY ROSE TO TWELVE.
I WENT UNDERCOVER ALONE, BUT I COULDN'T FIND THE KILLER.
THERE WERE SEVERAL POINTS ABOUT THE DEATHS THAT DIDN'T ADD UP, AND THE POLICE WERE AT A COMPLETE LOSS.
THIS MISSION IS MY CHANCE TO MAKE UP FOR MY FAILURE.
SO ABOUT OUR MISSION.
THERE'VE ALREADY BEEN TWO VICTIMS... MOST LIKELY KILLED BY THE SAME MURDERER.
YES.
TWO ...?
TH-THERE ARE ALREADY VICTIMS?
IT HAPPENED DURING SUMMER VACATION, SO THE NEWS HASN'T SPREAD YET.
BUT IT WON'T BE LONG BEFORE THE WHOLE SCHOOL IS IN AN UPROAR.

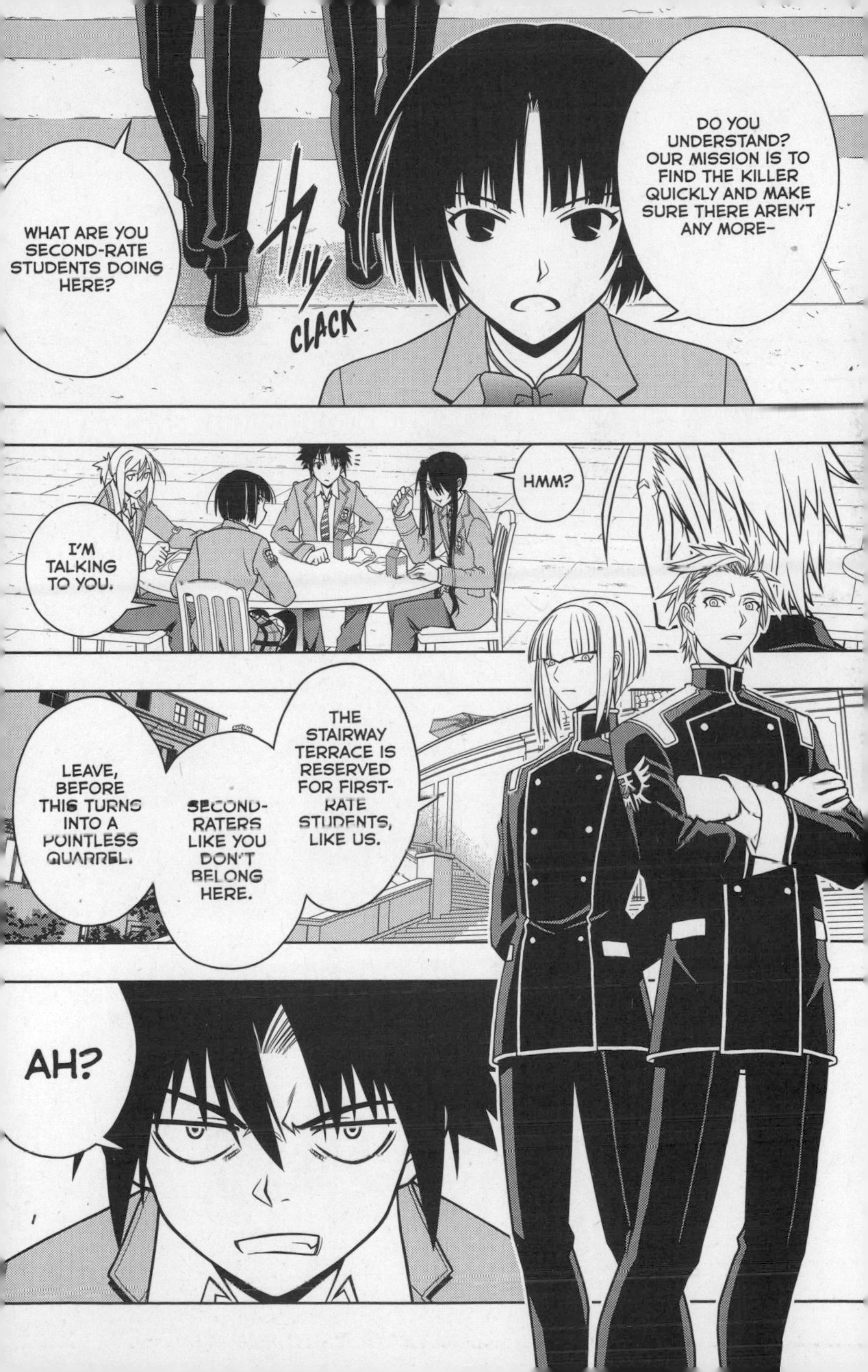
DO YOU UNDERSTAND? OUR MISSION IS TO FIND THE KILLER QUICKLY AND MAKE SURE THERE AREN'T ANY MORE-
CLACK
WHAT ARE YOU SECOND-RATE STUDENTS DOING HERE?
HMM?
I'M TALKING TO YOU.
THE STAIRWAY TERRACE IS RESERVED FOR FIRST-RATE STUDENTS, LIKE US.
SECOND-RATERS LIKE YOU DON'T BELONG HERE.
LEAVE, BEFORE THIS TURNS INTO A POINTLESS QUARREL.
AH?

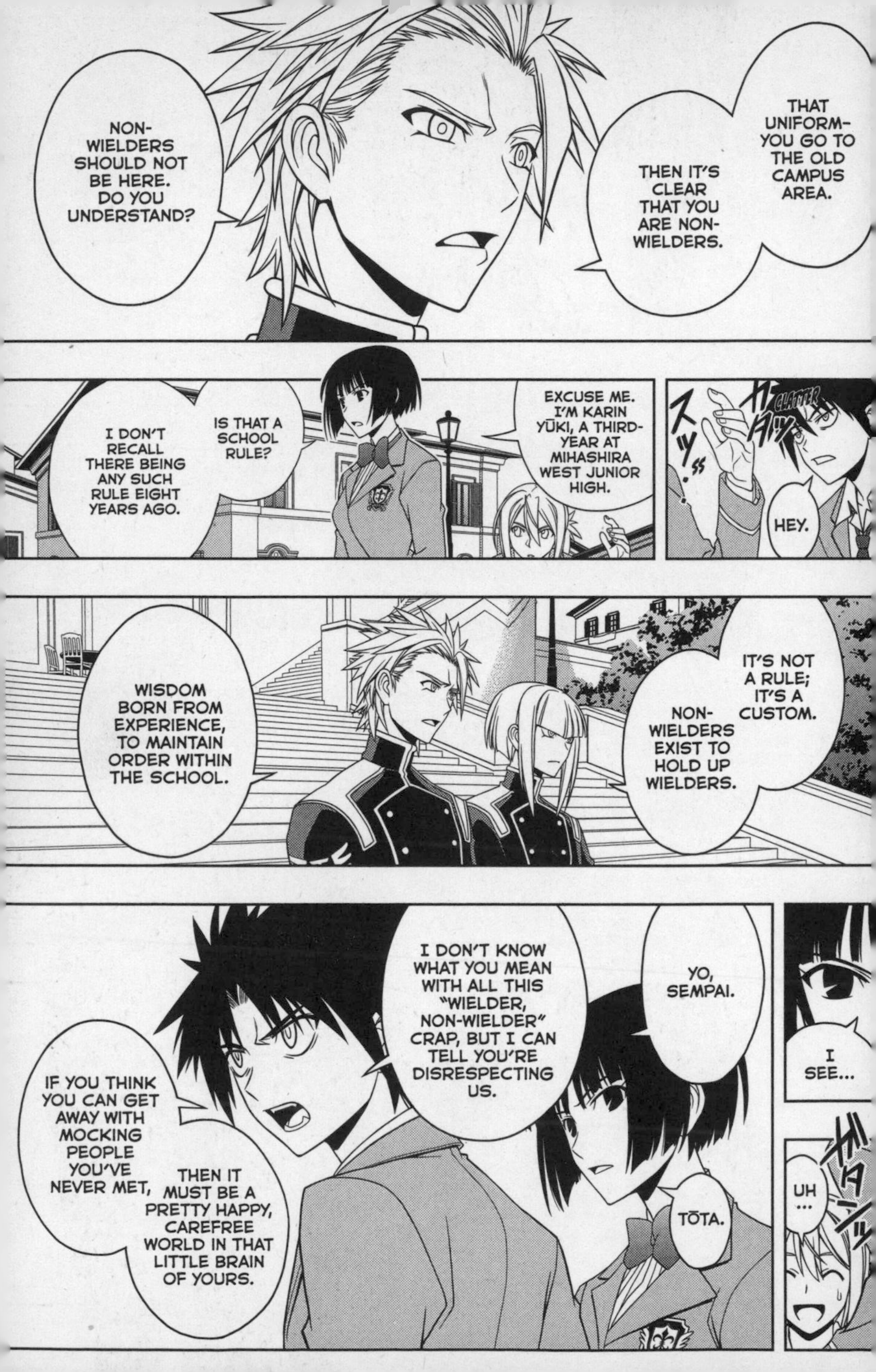
THAT UNIFORM— YOU GO TO THE OLD CAMPUS AREA.
THEN IT'S CLEAR THAT YOU ARE NON-WIELDERS.
NON-WIELDERS SHOULD NOT BE HERE. DO YOU UNDERSTAND?
CLATTER
HEY.
EXCUSE ME. I'M KARIN YŪKI, A THIRD-YEAR AT MIHASHIRA WEST JUNIOR HIGH.
IS THAT A SCHOOL RULE?
I DON'T RECALL THERE BEING ANY SUCH RULE EIGHT YEARS AGO.
IT'S NOT A RULE; IT'S A CUSTOM.
NON-WIELDERS EXIST TO HOLD UP WIELDERS.
WISDOM BORN FROM EXPERIENCE, TO MAINTAIN ORDER WITHIN THE SCHOOL.
I SEE...
UH ...
YO, SEMPAI.
I DON'T KNOW WHAT YOU MEAN WITH ALL THIS "WIELDER, NON-WIELDER" CRAP, BUT I CAN TELL YOU'RE DISRESPECTING US.
TŌTA.
IF YOU THINK YOU CAN GET AWAY WITH MOCKING PEOPLE YOU'VE NEVER MET,
THEN IT MUST BE A PRETTY HAPPY, CAREFREE WORLD IN THAT LITTLE BRAIN OF YOURS.

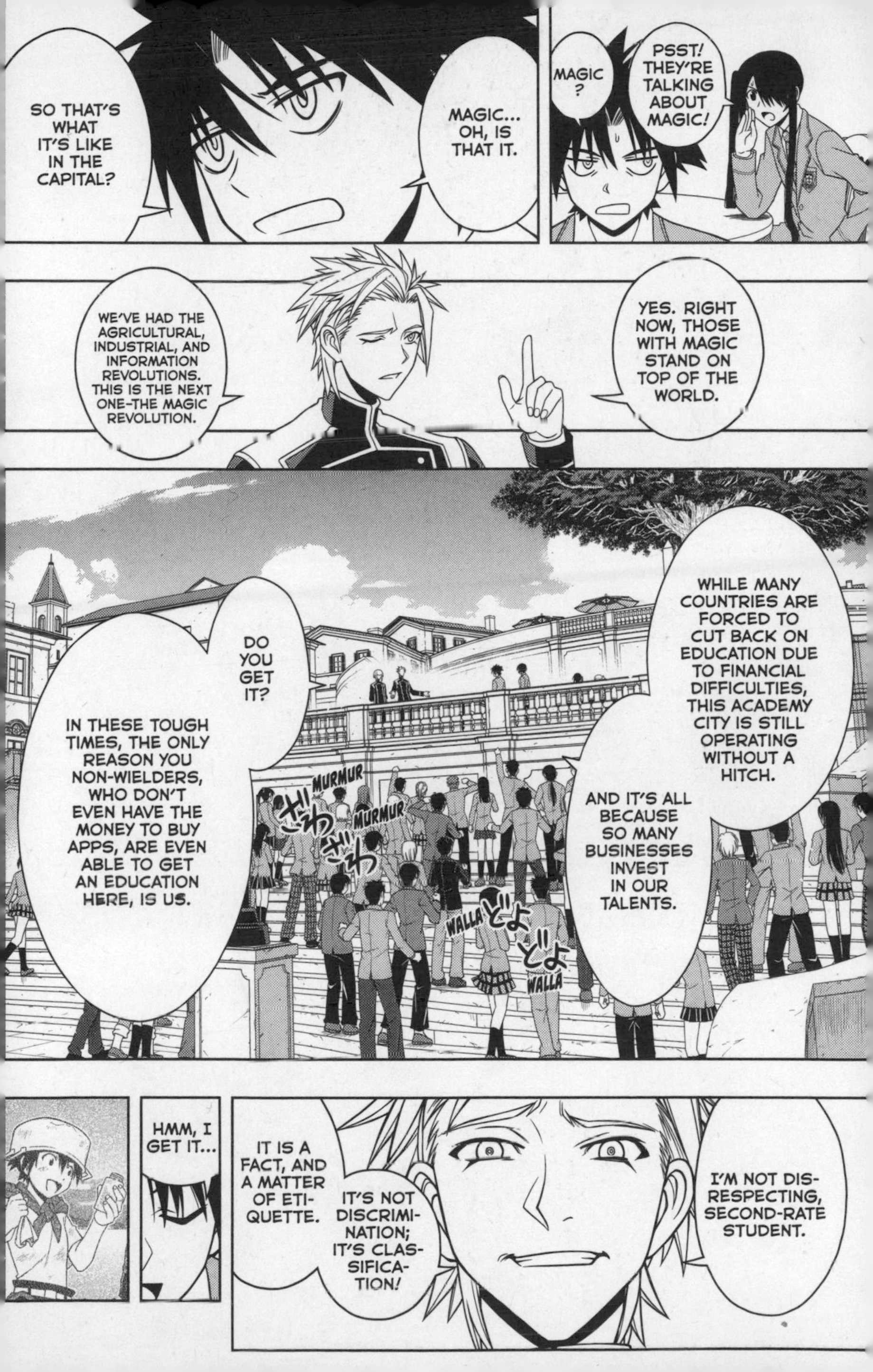
PSST! THEY'RE TALKING ABOUT MAGIC!
MAGIC ?
MAGIC... OH, IS THAT IT.
SO THAT'S WHAT IT'S LIKE IN THE CAPITAL?
YES. RIGHT NOW, THOSE WITH MAGIC STAND ON TOP OF THE WORLD.
WE'VE HAD THE AGRICULTURAL, INDUSTRIAL, AND INFORMATION REVOLUTIONS. THIS IS THE NEXT ONE–THE MAGIC REVOLUTION.
WHILE MANY COUNTRIES ARE FORCED TO CUT BACK ON EDUCATION DUE TO FINANCIAL DIFFICULTIES, THIS ACADEMY CITY IS STILL OPERATING WITHOUT A HITCH.
AND IT'S ALL BECAUSE SO MANY BUSINESSES INVEST IN OUR TALENTS.
DO YOU GET IT?
IN THESE TOUGH TIMES, THE ONLY REASON YOU NON-WIELDERS, WHO DON'T EVEN HAVE THE MONEY TO BUY APPS, ARE EVEN ABLE TO GET AN EDUCATION HERE, IS US.
MURMUR
MURMUR
WALLA
WALLA
I'M NOT DIS-RESPECTING, SECOND-RATE STUDENT.
IT'S NOT DISCRIMI-NATION; IT'S CLAS-SIFICA-TION!
IT IS A FACT, AND A MATTER OF ETI-QUETTE.
HMM, I GET IT...

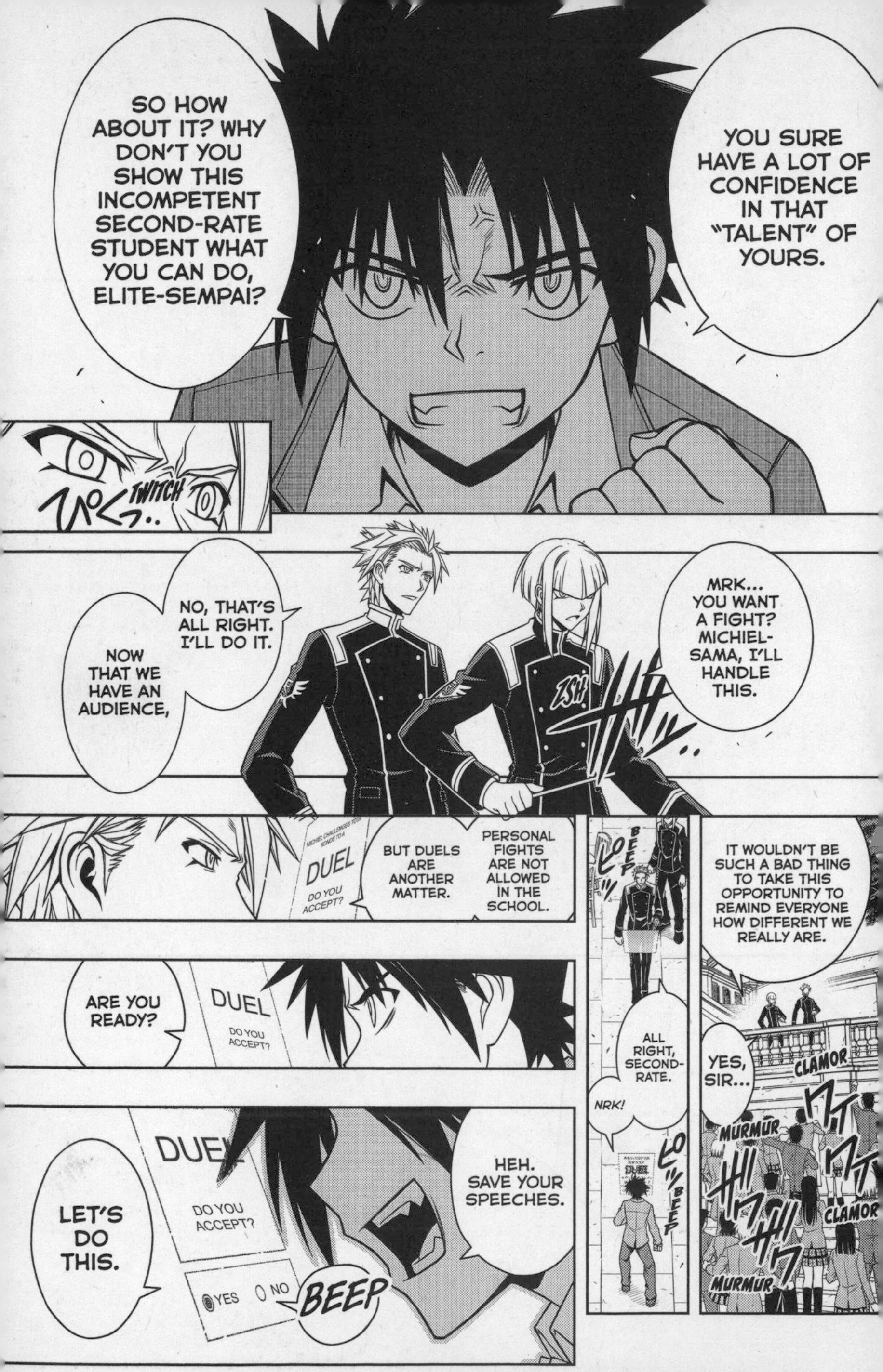
YOU SURE HAVE A LOT OF CONFIDENCE IN THAT "TALENT" OF YOURS.
SO HOW ABOUT IT? WHY DON'T YOU SHOW THIS INCOMPETENT SECOND-RATE STUDENT WHAT YOU CAN DO, ELITE-SEMPAI?
TWITCH
MRK... YOU WANT A FIGHT? MICHIEL-SAMA, I'LL HANDLE THIS.
NO, THAT'S ALL RIGHT. I'LL DO IT.
NOW THAT WE HAVE AN AUDIENCE,
IT WOULDN'T BE SUCH A BAD THING TO TAKE THIS OPPORTUNITY TO REMIND EVERYONE HOW DIFFERENT WE REALLY ARE.
YES, SIR...
CLAMOR
MURMUR
CLAMOR
MURMUR
BEEP
ALL RIGHT, SECOND-RATE.
NRK!
BEEP
PERSONAL FIGHTS ARE NOT ALLOWED IN THE SCHOOL.
BUT DUELS ARE ANOTHER MATTER.
DUEL
DO YOU ACCEPT?
ARE YOU READY?
DUEL
DO YOU ACCEPT?
HEH. SAVE YOUR SPEECHES.
LET'S DO THIS.
DUEL
DO YOU ACCEPT?
YES
NO
BEEP

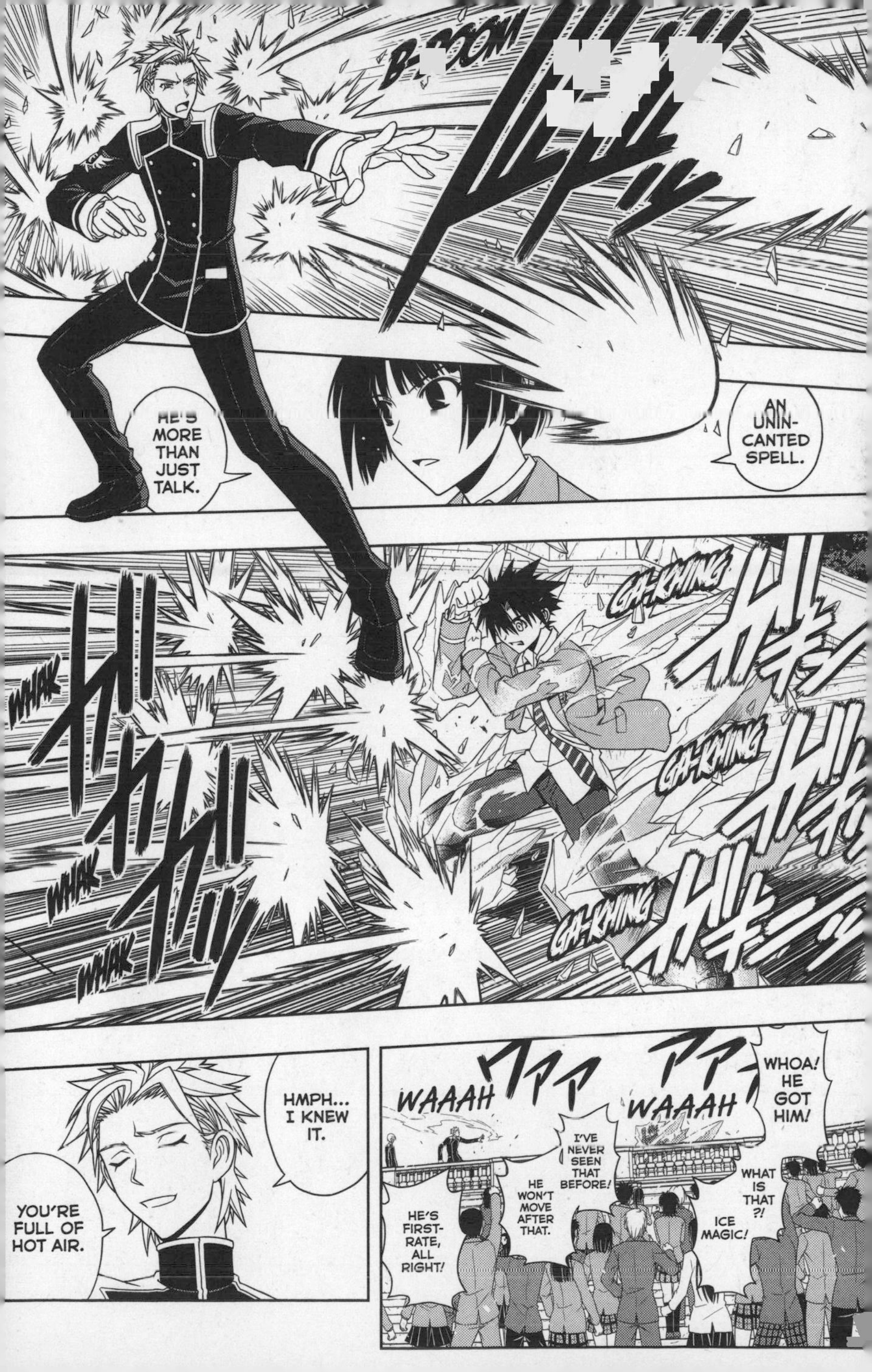
AN UNIN-CANTED SPELL.
HE'S MORE THAN JUST TALK.
GA-KHING
GA-KHING
GA-KHING
WHAK
WHAK
WHAK
WHOA! HE GOT HIM!
WAAAH
WAAAH
WHAT IS THAT?!
ICE MAGIC!
I'VE NEVER SEEN THAT BEFORE!
HE WON'T MOVE AFTER THAT.
HE'S FIRST-RATE, ALL RIGHT!
HMPH... I KNEW IT.
YOU'RE FULL OF HOT AIR.

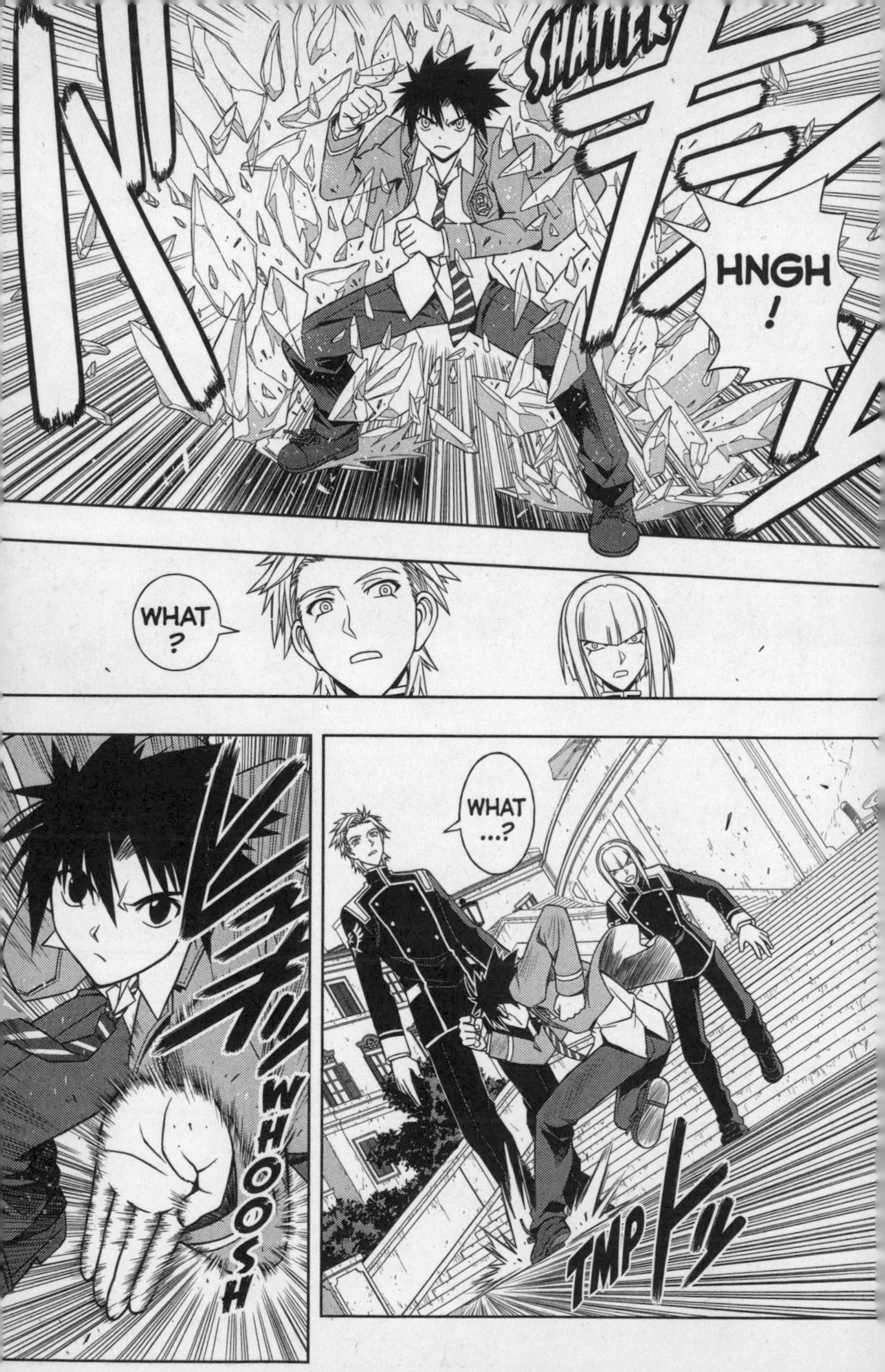
SHATTERS
HNGH!
WHAT?
WHAT...?
TMP
WHOOSH

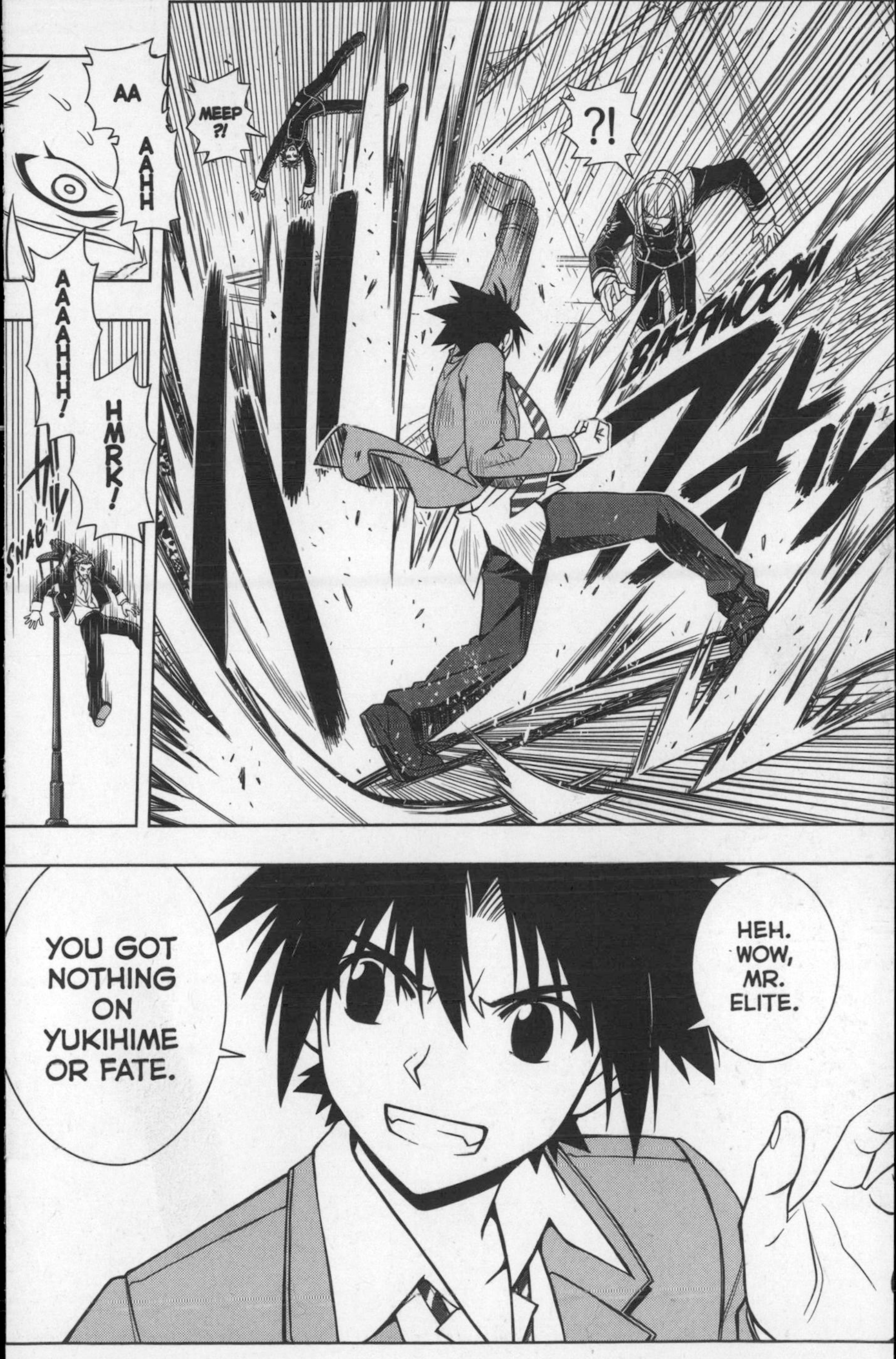
?!
MEEP ?!
BA-FWOOM
AA AAHH
AAAAHHH!
HMRK!
SNAG
HEH. WOW, MR. ELITE.
YOU GOT NOTHING ON YUKIHIME OR FATE.

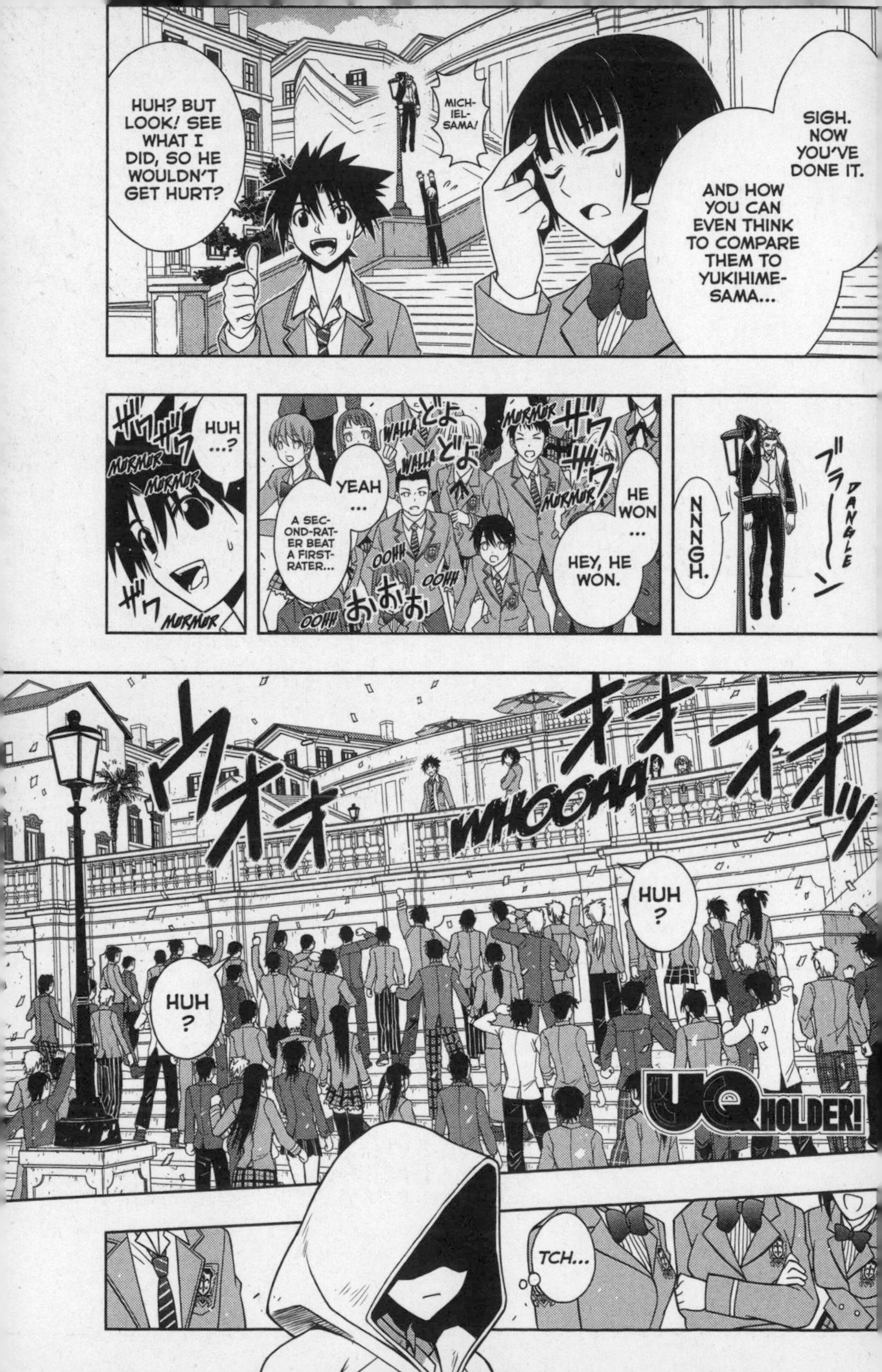
SIGH. NOW YOU'VE DONE IT.
AND HOW YOU CAN EVEN THINK TO COMPARE THEM TO YUKIHIME-SAMA...
MICHIEL-SAMA!
HUH? BUT LOOK! SEE WHAT I DID, SO HE WOULDN'T GET HURT?
ブラーン
DANGLE
NNNGH.
ザワ ザワ
MURMUR
HE WON...
HEY, HE WON.
どよ どよ
WALLA WALLA
YEAH...
A SECOND-RATER BEAT A FIRST-RATER...
おおお
OOHH OOHH OOHH
ザワ ザワ
MURMUR MURMUR
HUH...?
ザワ
MURMUR
オオオッ
WHOOAA
ウオオ
HUH ?
HUH ?
TCH...

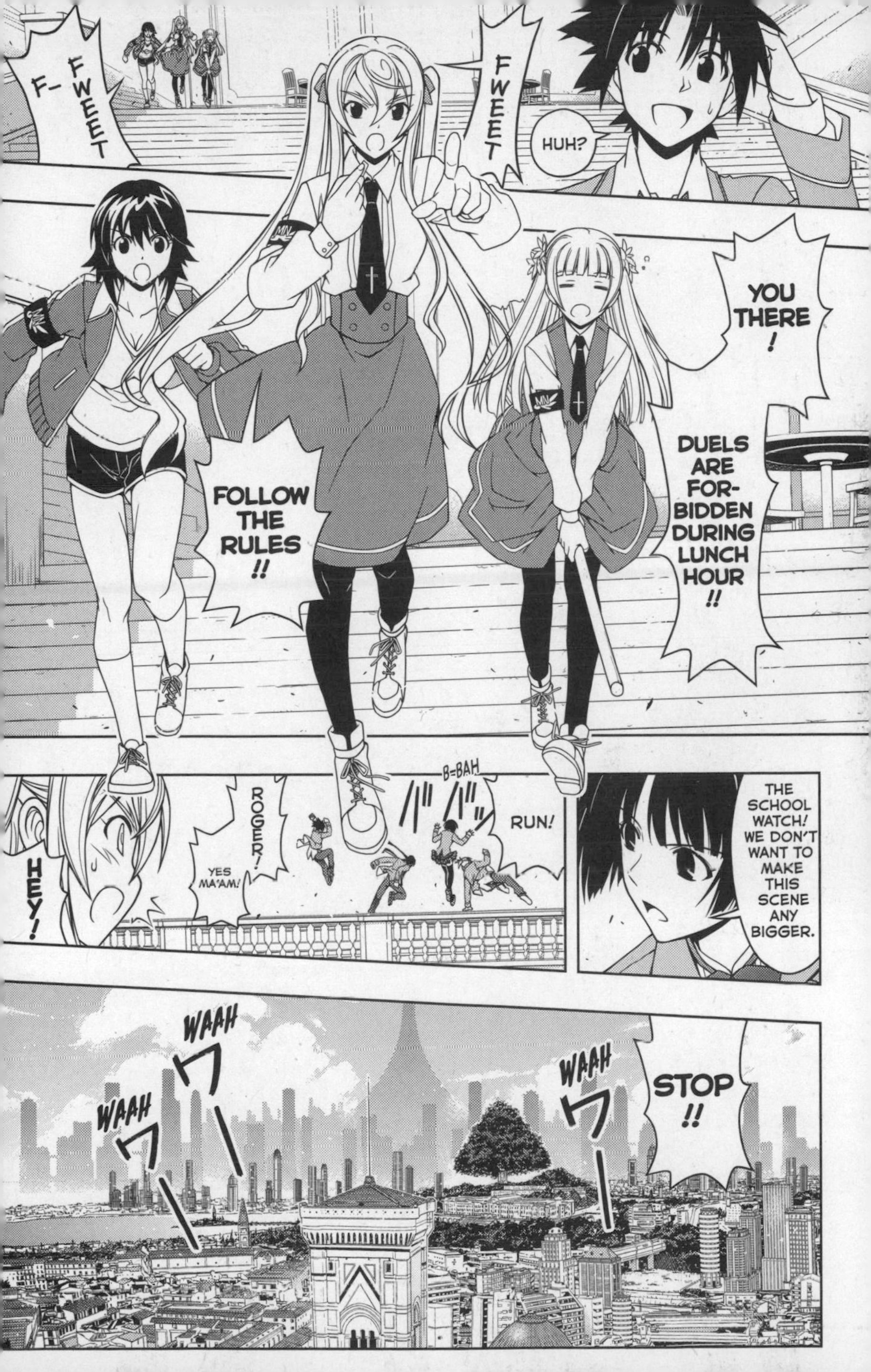
HUH?
FWEET
F- FWEET
YOU THERE!
DUELS ARE FOR-BIDDEN DURING LUNCH HOUR!!
FOLLOW THE RULES!!
THE SCHOOL WATCH! WE DON'T WANT TO MAKE THIS SCENE ANY BIGGER.
RUN!
B=BAH
ROGER!
YES MA'AM!
HEY!
STOP!!
WAAH
WAAH
WAAH

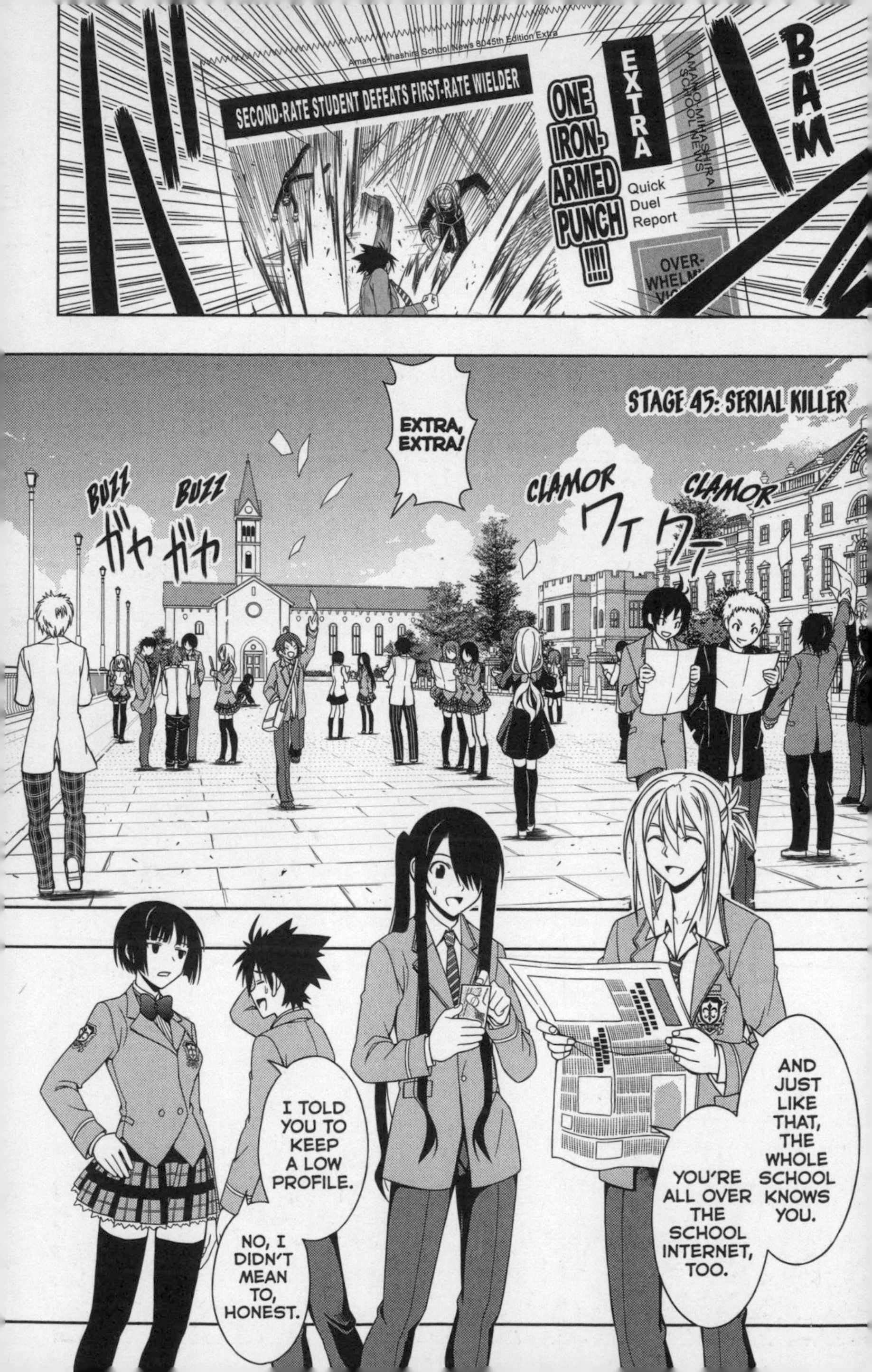
BAM
AMANO-MIHASHIRA SCHOOL NEWS
EXTRA
Quick Duel Report
OVER-
ONE IRON-ARMED PUNCH !!!!
Amano-Mihashira School News 8045th Edition Extra
SECOND-RATE STUDENT DEFEATS FIRST-RATE WIELDER
STAGE 45: SERIAL KILLER
EXTRA, EXTRA!
CLAMOR CLAMOR
ワイワイ
BUZZ BUZZ
ガヤガヤ
AND JUST LIKE THAT, THE WHOLE SCHOOL KNOWS YOU.
YOU'RE ALL OVER THE SCHOOL INTERNET, TOO.
I TOLD YOU TO KEEP A LOW PROFILE.
NO, I DIDN'T MEAN TO, HONEST.

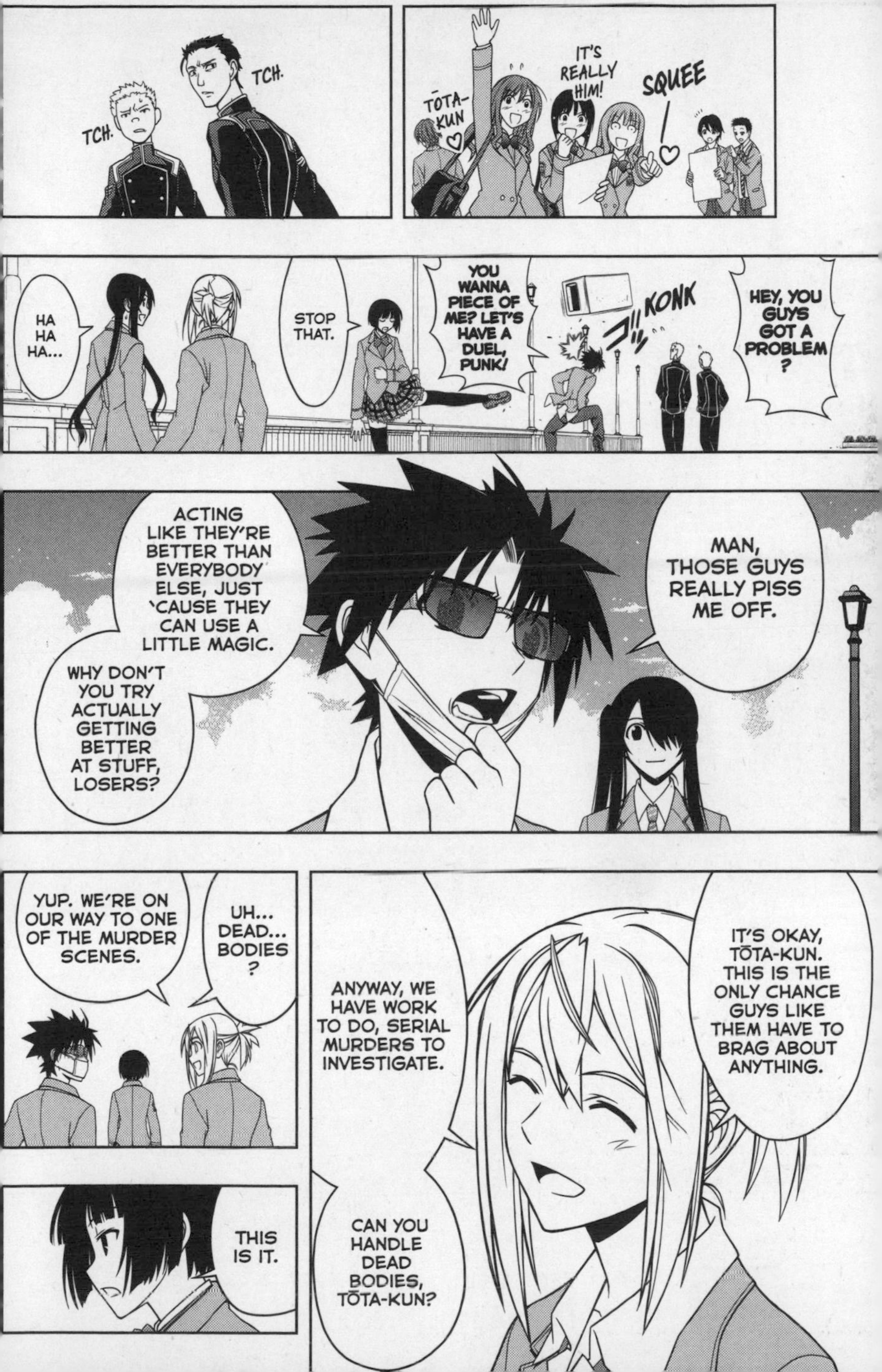
SQUEE
IT'S REALLY HIM!
TŌTA-KUN
TCH.
TCH.
HEY, YOU GUYS GOT A PROBLEM?
KONK
YOU WANNA PIECE OF ME? LET'S HAVE A DUEL, PUNK!
STOP THAT.
HA HA HA...
MAN, THOSE GUYS REALLY PISS ME OFF.
ACTING LIKE THEY'RE BETTER THAN EVERYBODY ELSE, JUST 'CAUSE THEY CAN USE A LITTLE MAGIC.
WHY DON'T YOU TRY ACTUALLY GETTING BETTER AT STUFF, LOSERS?
IT'S OKAY, TŌTA-KUN. THIS IS THE ONLY CHANCE GUYS LIKE THEM HAVE TO BRAG ABOUT ANYTHING.
ANYWAY, WE HAVE WORK TO DO, SERIAL MURDERS TO INVESTIGATE.
CAN YOU HANDLE DEAD BODIES, TŌTA-KUN?
UH... DEAD... BODIES?
YUP. WE'RE ON OUR WAY TO ONE OF THE MURDER SCENES.
THIS IS IT.

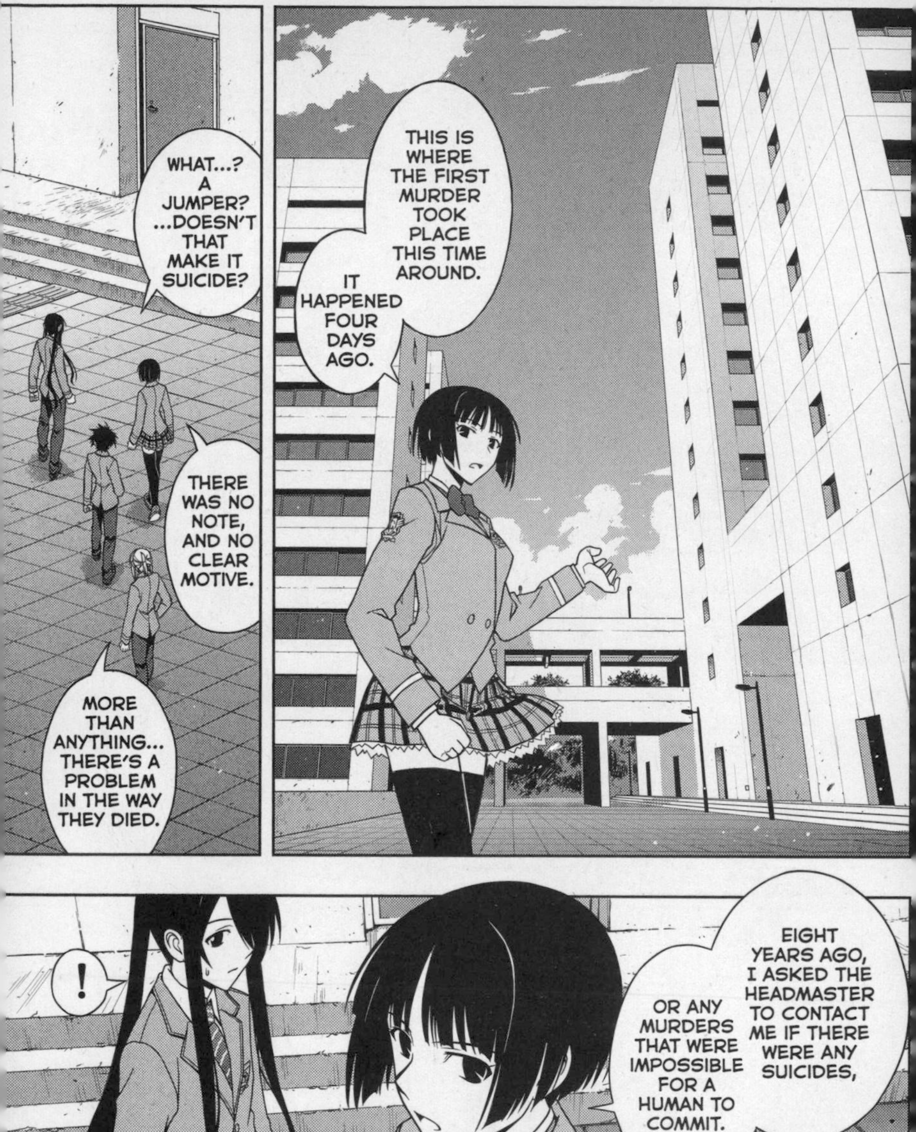
THIS IS WHERE THE FIRST MURDER TOOK PLACE THIS TIME AROUND.
IT HAPPENED FOUR DAYS AGO.
WHAT...? A JUMPER? ...DOESN'T THAT MAKE IT SUICIDE?
THERE WAS NO NOTE, AND NO CLEAR MOTIVE.
MORE THAN ANYTHING... THERE'S A PROBLEM IN THE WAY THEY DIED.
EIGHT YEARS AGO, I ASKED THE HEADMASTER TO CONTACT ME IF THERE WERE ANY SUICIDES,
OR ANY MURDERS THAT WERE IMPOSSIBLE FOR A HUMAN TO COMMIT.
!

Augmented Reality. At this stage, it will be projected on Tōta's sunglasses, while the others have apps that display the images on their retinas.

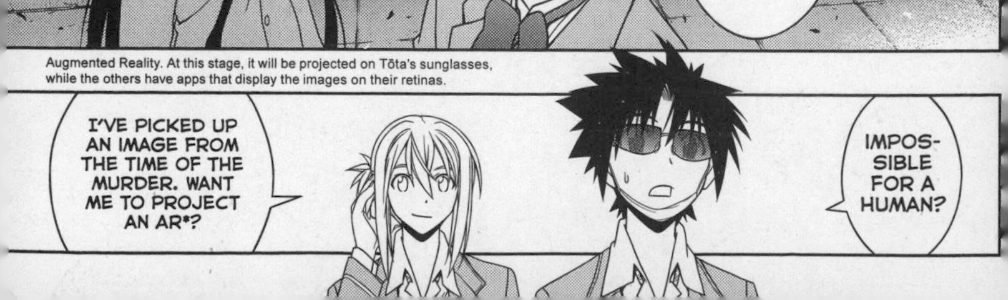
IMPOS-SIBLE FOR A HUMAN?
I'VE PICKED UP AN IMAGE FROM THE TIME OF THE MURDER. WANT ME TO PROJECT AN AR*?

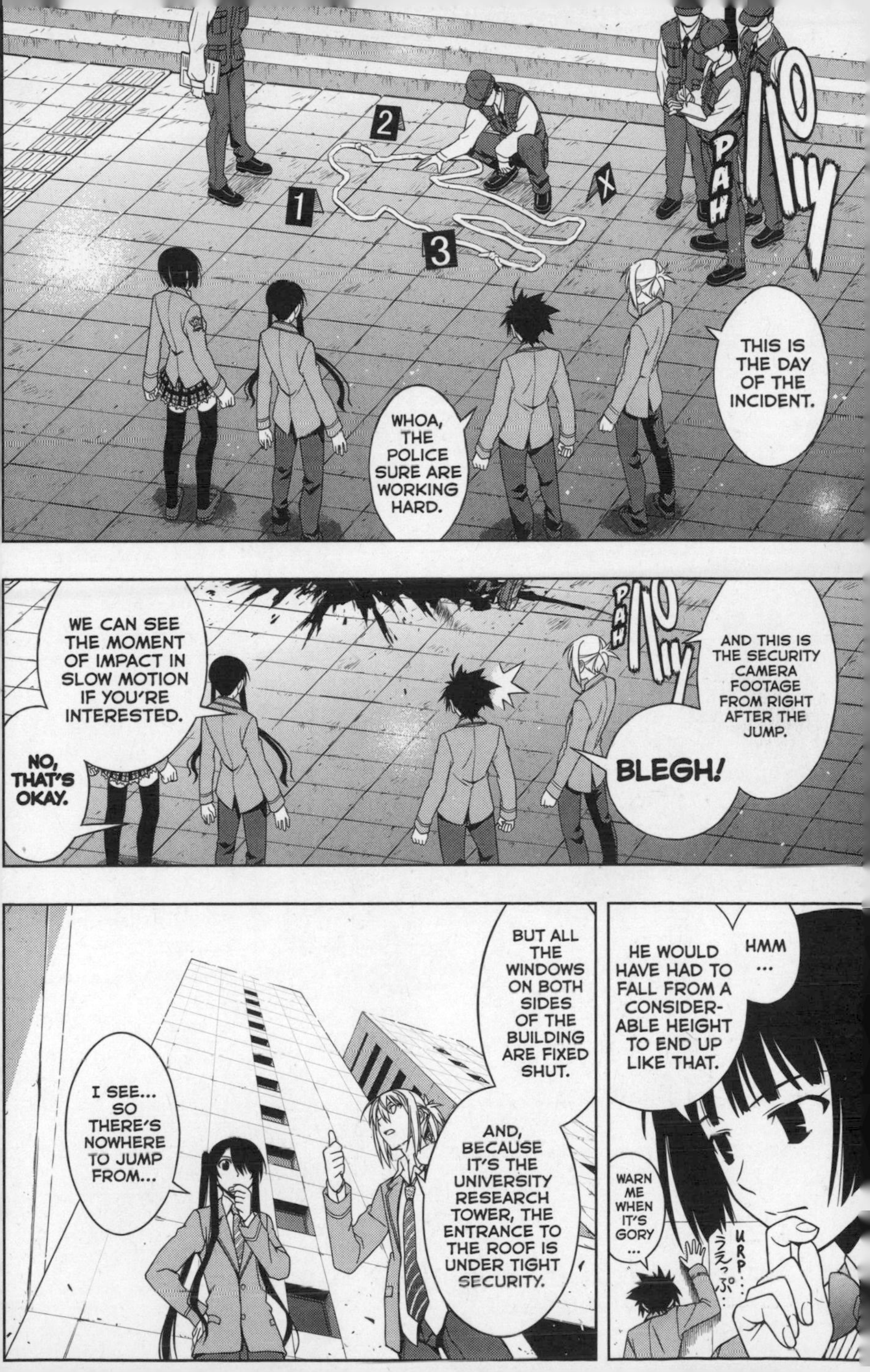
PAH
THIS IS THE DAY OF THE INCIDENT.
WHOA, THE POLICE SURE ARE WORKING HARD.
PAH
AND THIS IS THE SECURITY CAMERA FOOTAGE FROM RIGHT AFTER THE JUMP.
BLEGH!
WE CAN SEE THE MOMENT OF IMPACT IN SLOW MOTION IF YOU'RE INTERESTED.
NO, THAT'S OKAY.
HMM ...
HE WOULD HAVE HAD TO FALL FROM A CONSIDER-ABLE HEIGHT TO END UP LIKE THAT.
WARN ME WHEN IT'S GORY ...
URP...
うえっぷ…
BUT ALL THE WINDOWS ON BOTH SIDES OF THE BUILDING ARE FIXED SHUT.
AND, BECAUSE IT'S THE UNIVERSITY RESEARCH TOWER, THE ENTRANCE TO THE ROOF IS UNDER TIGHT SECURITY.
I SEE... SO THERE'S NOWHERE TO JUMP FROM...

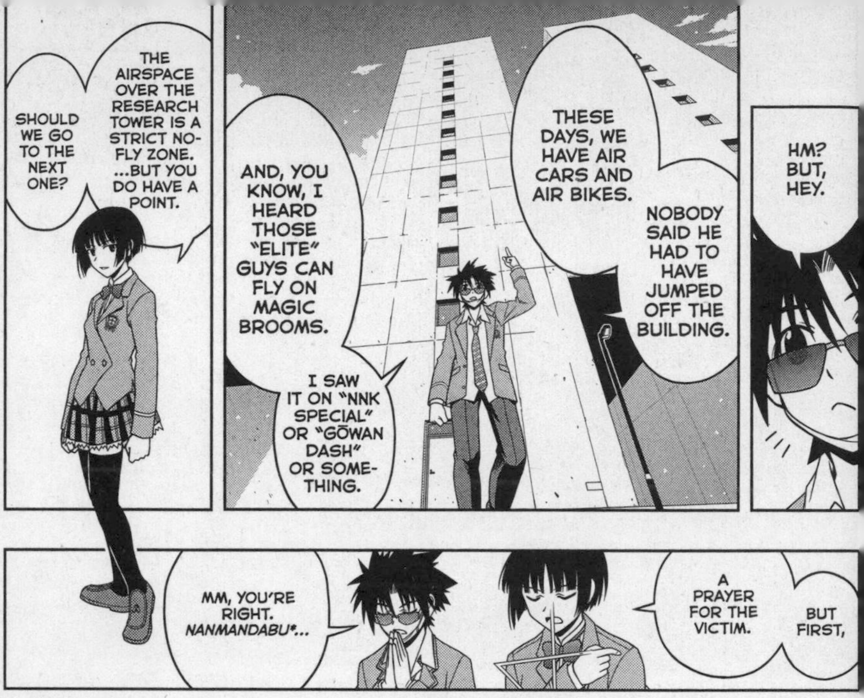
HM? BUT, HEY.
THESE DAYS, WE HAVE AIR CARS AND AIR BIKES.
NOBODY SAID HE HAD TO HAVE JUMPED OFF THE BUILDING.
AND, YOU KNOW, I HEARD THOSE "ELITE" GUYS CAN FLY ON MAGIC BROOMS.
I SAW IT ON "NNK SPECIAL" OR "GŌWAN DASH" OR SOMETHING.
THE AIRSPACE OVER THE RESEARCH TOWER IS A STRICT NO-FLY ZONE. ...BUT YOU DO HAVE A POINT.
SHOULD WE GO TO THE NEXT ONE?
BUT FIRST,
A PRAYER FOR THE VICTIM.
MM, YOU'RE RIGHT. *NANMANDABU**...

*A Buddhist prayer

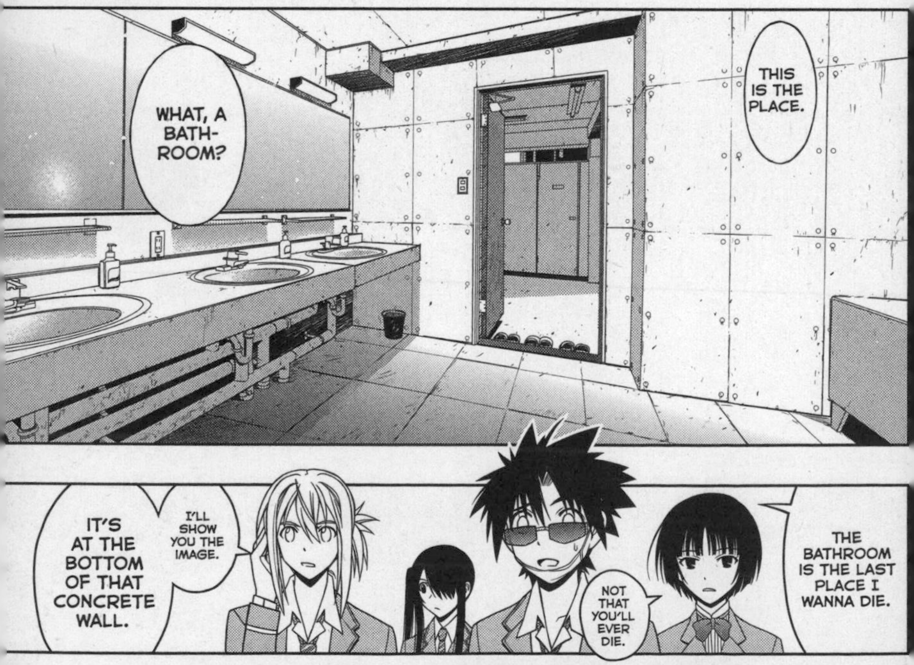
THIS IS THE PLACE.
WHAT, A BATHROOM?
THE BATHROOM IS THE LAST PLACE I WANNA DIE.
NOT THAT YOU'LL EVER DIE.
I'LL SHOW YOU THE IMAGE.
IT'S AT THE BOTTOM OF THAT CONCRETE WALL.

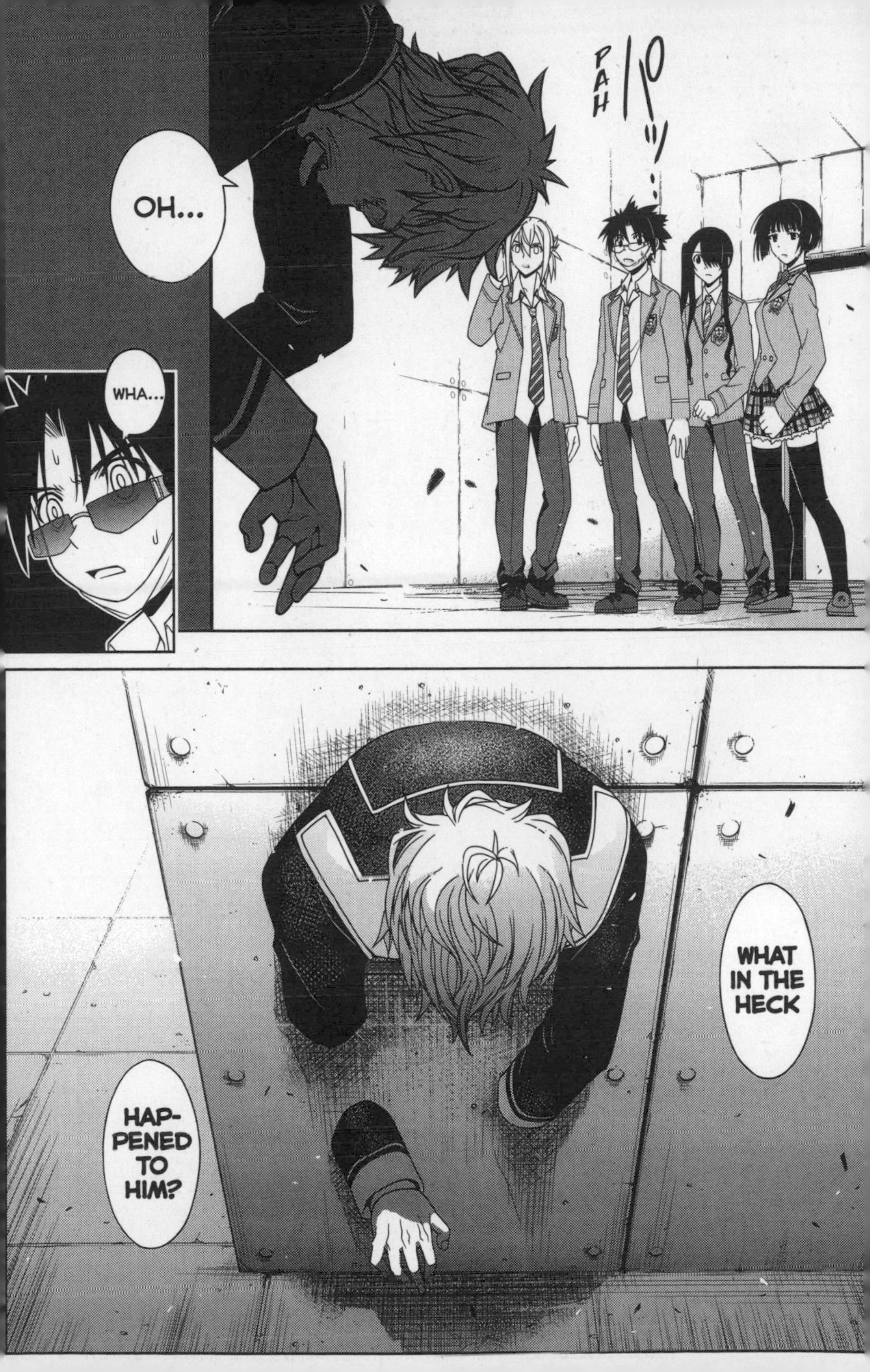
PAH
パッ…
OH...
WHA...
WHAT IN THE HECK
HAP-PENED TO HIM?

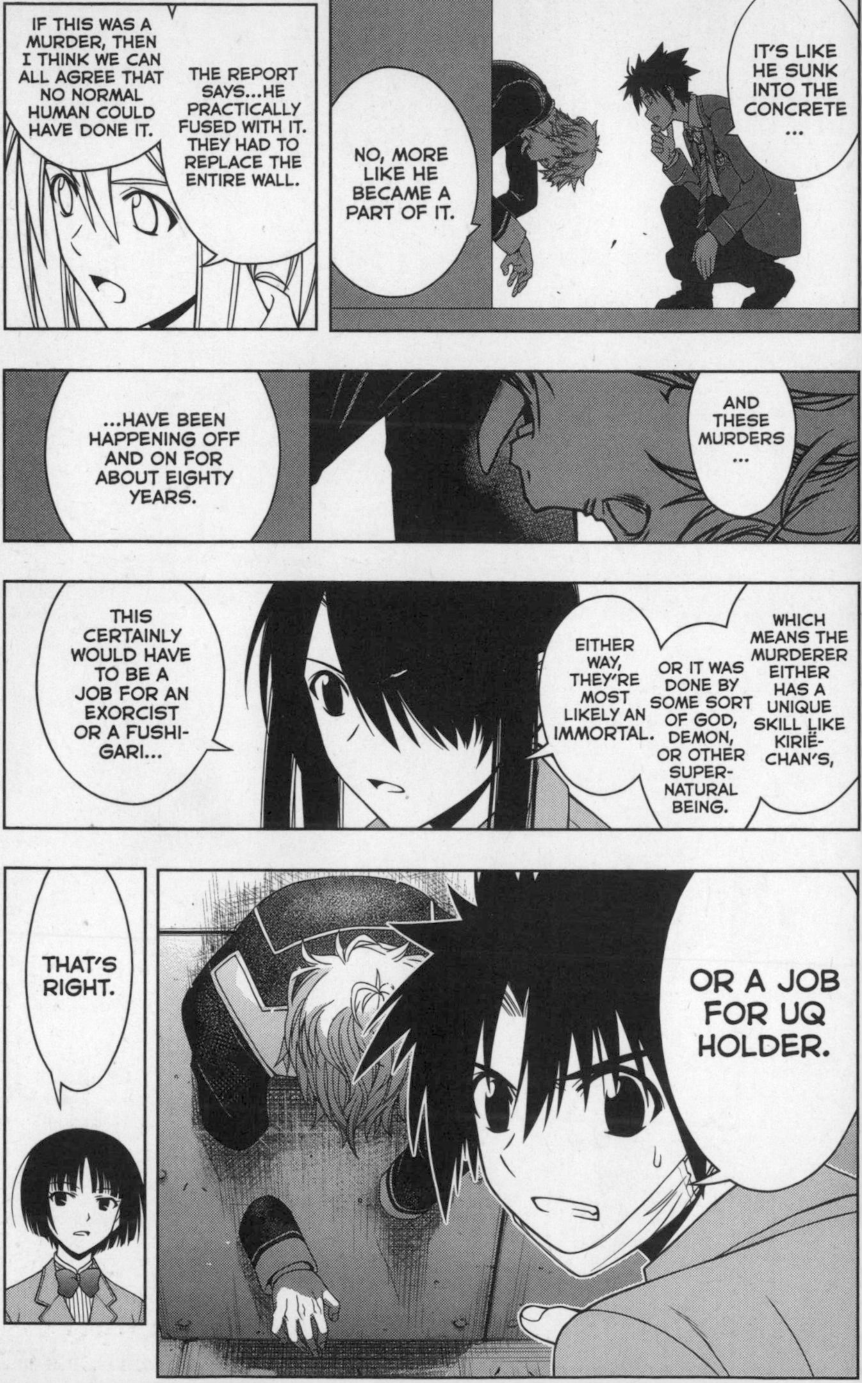
IT'S LIKE HE SUNK INTO THE CONCRETE ...
NO, MORE LIKE HE BECAME A PART OF IT.
THE REPORT SAYS...HE PRACTICALLY FUSED WITH IT. THEY HAD TO REPLACE THE ENTIRE WALL.
IF THIS WAS A MURDER, THEN I THINK WE CAN ALL AGREE THAT NO NORMAL HUMAN COULD HAVE DONE IT.
AND THESE MURDERS ...
...HAVE BEEN HAPPENING OFF AND ON FOR ABOUT EIGHTY YEARS.
WHICH MEANS THE MURDERER EITHER HAS A UNIQUE SKILL LIKE KIRIË-CHAN'S,
OR IT WAS DONE BY SOME SORT OF GOD, DEMON, OR OTHER SUPER-NATURAL BEING.
EITHER WAY, THEY'RE MOST LIKELY AN IMMORTAL.
THIS CERTAINLY WOULD HAVE TO BE A JOB FOR AN EXORCIST OR A FUSHI-GARI...
OR A JOB FOR UQ HOLDER.
THAT'S RIGHT.

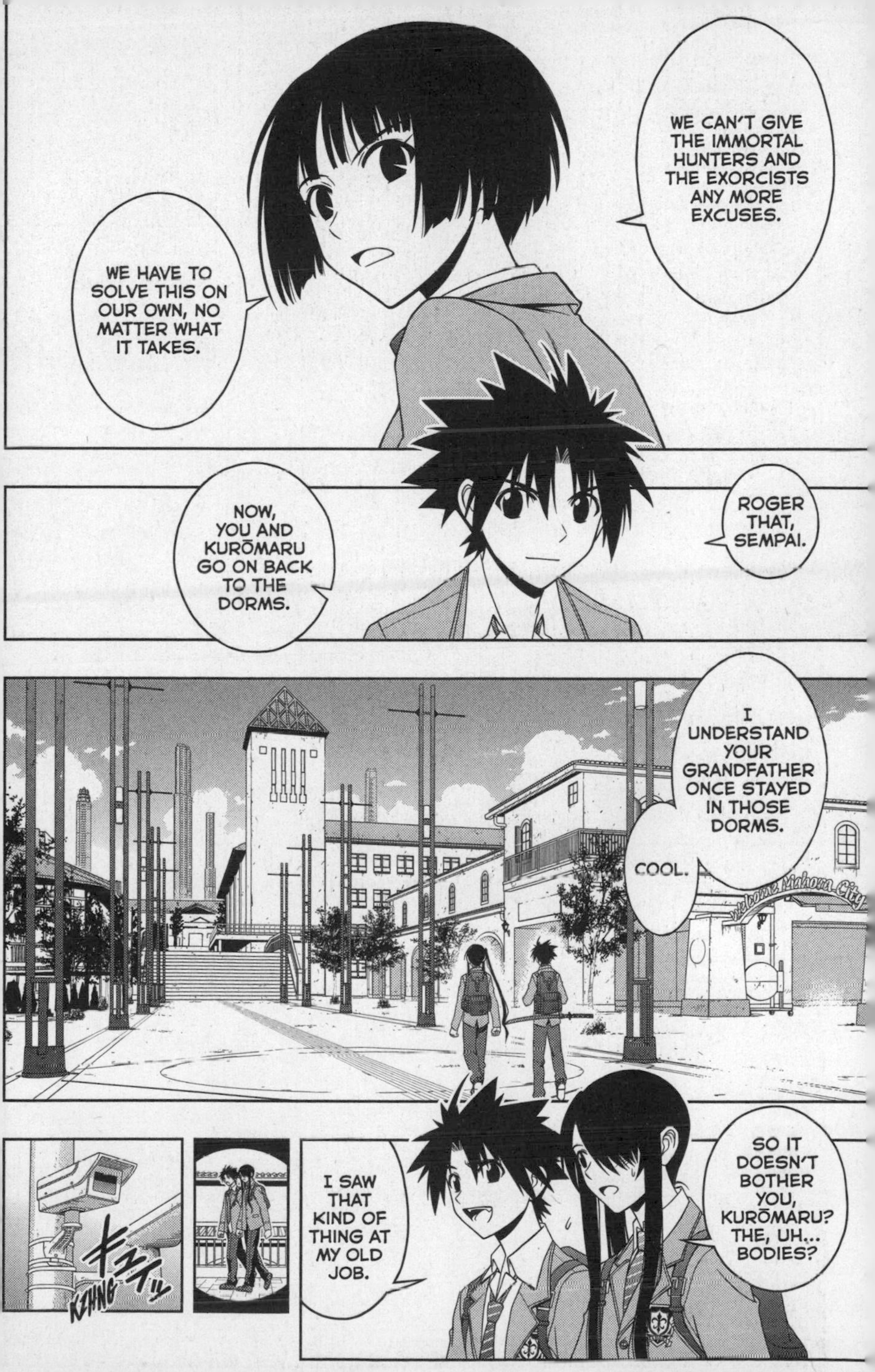
WE CAN'T GIVE THE IMMORTAL HUNTERS AND THE EXORCISTS ANY MORE EXCUSES.
WE HAVE TO SOLVE THIS ON OUR OWN, NO MATTER WHAT IT TAKES.
NOW, YOU AND KURŌMARU GO ON BACK TO THE DORMS.
ROGER THAT, SEMPAI.
I UNDERSTAND YOUR GRANDFATHER ONCE STAYED IN THOSE DORMS.
COOL.
welcome Mahora City
SO IT DOESN'T BOTHER YOU, KURŌMARU? THE, UH... BODIES?
I SAW THAT KIND OF THING AT MY OLD JOB.
キュイッ
KIHNG

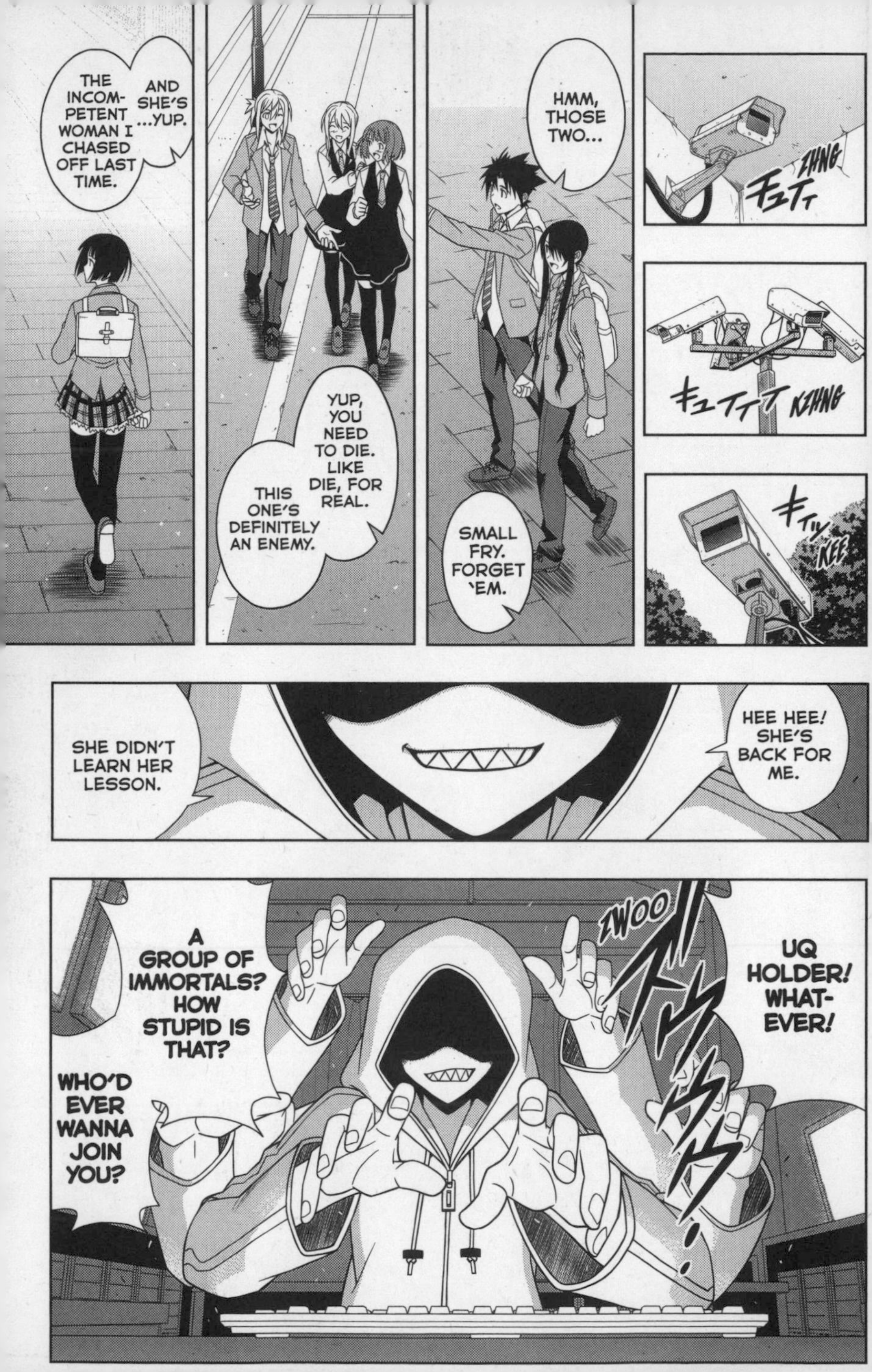
ZHNG
KZHNG
KEE
HMM, THOSE TWO...
SMALL FRY. FORGET 'EM.
YUP, YOU NEED TO DIE. LIKE DIE, FOR REAL.
THIS ONE'S DEFINITELY AN ENEMY.
THE INCOMPETENT WOMAN I CHASED OFF LAST TIME.
AND SHE'S ...YUP.
HEE HEE! SHE'S BACK FOR ME.
SHE DIDN'T LEARN HER LESSON.
UQ HOLDER! WHAT-EVER!
ZWOO
A GROUP OF IMMORTALS? HOW STUPID IS THAT?
WHO'D EVER WANNA JOIN YOU?

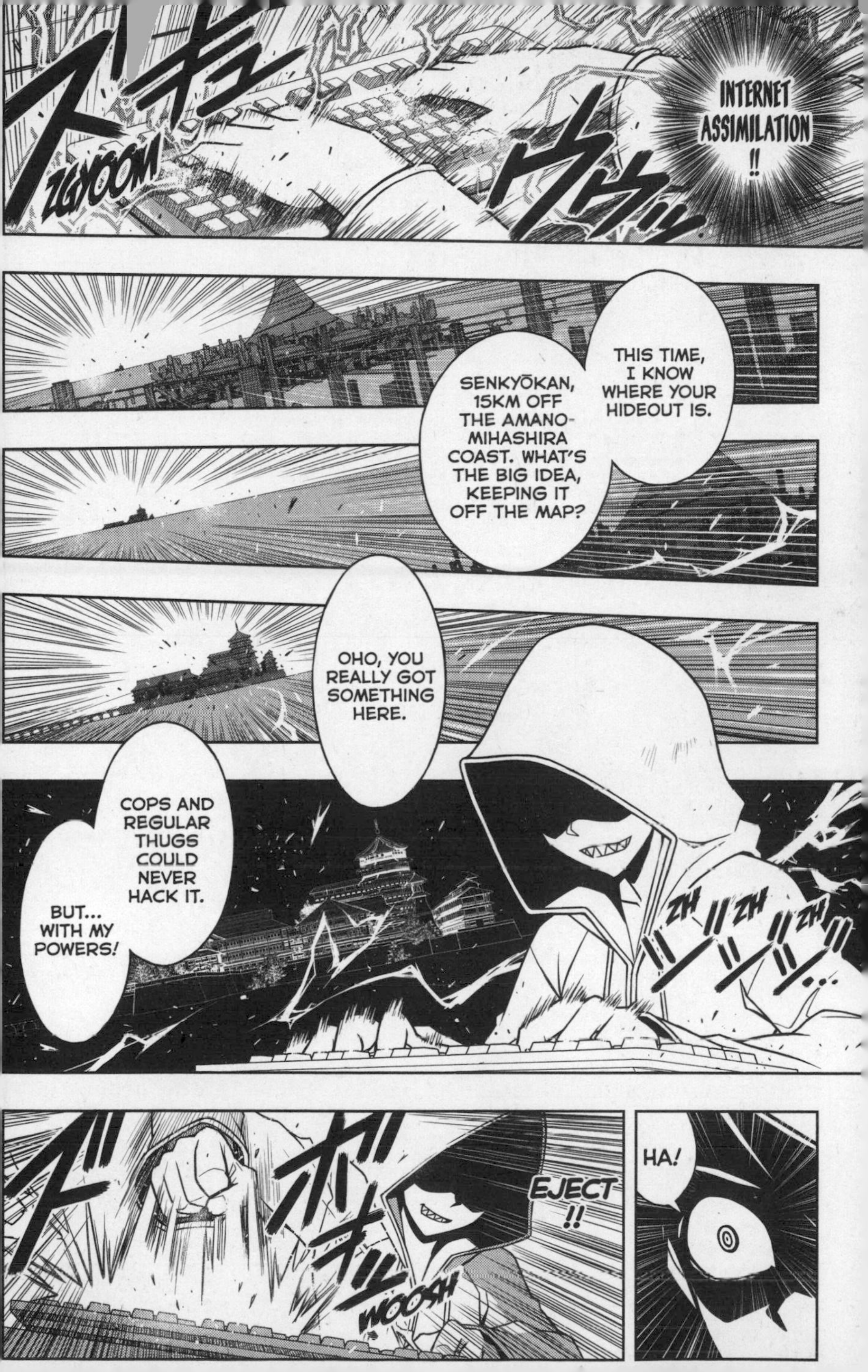
INTERNET ASSIMILATION !!
ZGYOOM
THIS TIME, I KNOW WHERE YOUR HIDEOUT IS.
SENKYŌKAN, 15KM OFF THE AMANO-MIHASHIRA COAST. WHAT'S THE BIG IDEA, KEEPING IT OFF THE MAP?
OHO, YOU REALLY GOT SOMETHING HERE.
ZH ZH ZH
COPS AND REGULAR THUGS COULD NEVER HACK IT.
BUT... WITH MY POWERS!
HA!
EJECT !!
WOOSH

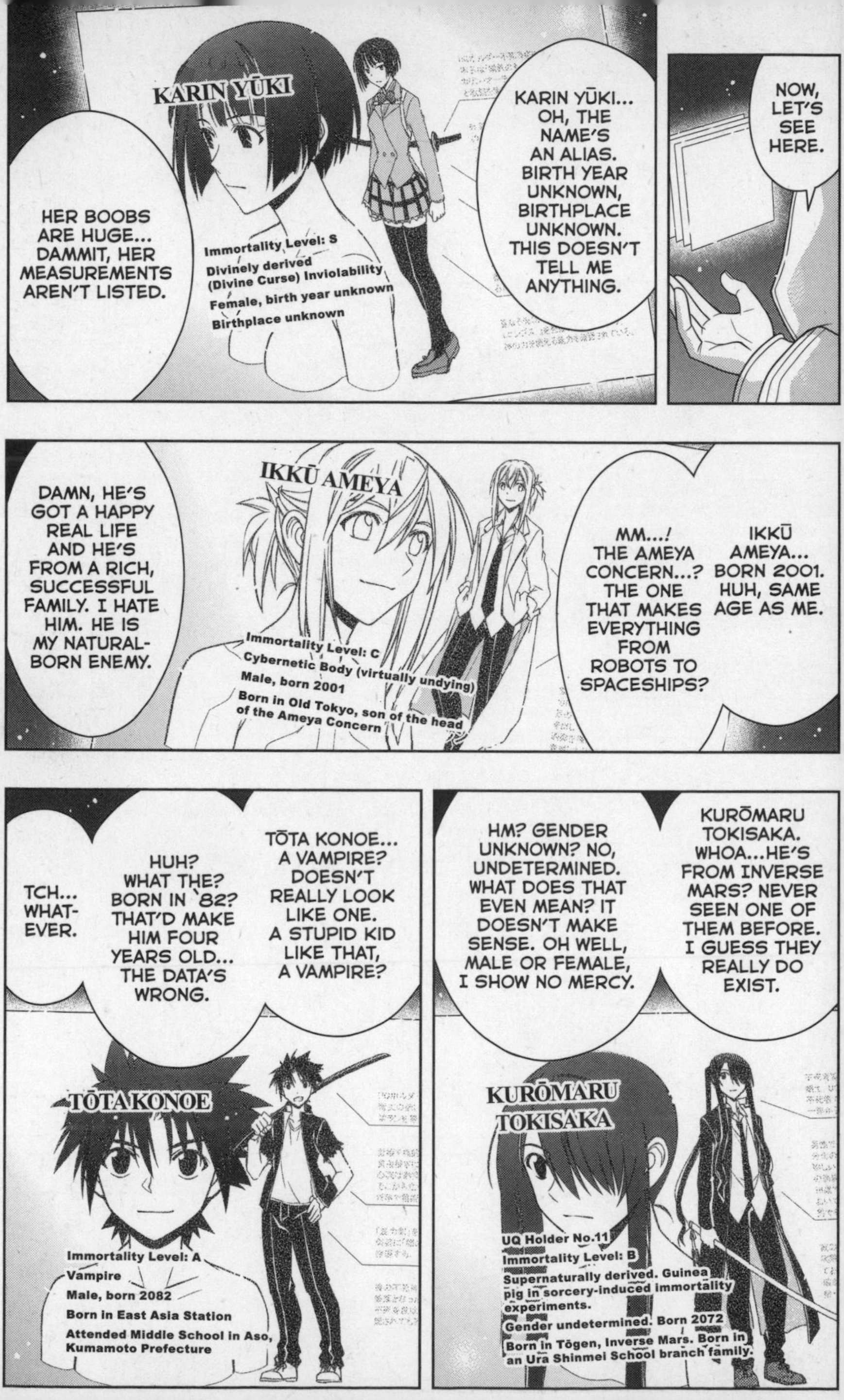
NOW, LET'S SEE HERE.
KARIN YŪKI... OH, THE NAME'S AN ALIAS. BIRTH YEAR UNKNOWN, BIRTHPLACE UNKNOWN. THIS DOESN'T TELL ME ANYTHING.
KARIN YŪKI
Immortality Level: S
Divinely derived (Divine Curse) Inviolability
Female, birth year unknown
Birthplace unknown
HER BOOBS ARE HUGE... DAMMIT, HER MEASUREMENTS AREN'T LISTED.
IKKŪ AMEYA... BORN 2001. HUH, SAME AGE AS ME.
MM...! THE AMEYA CONCERN...? THE ONE THAT MAKES EVERYTHING FROM ROBOTS TO SPACESHIPS?
IKKŪ AMEYA
Immortality Level: C
Cybernetic Body (virtually undying)
Male, born 2001
Born in Old Tokyo, son of the head of the Ameya Concern
DAMN, HE'S GOT A HAPPY REAL LIFE AND HE'S FROM A RICH, SUCCESSFUL FAMILY. I HATE HIM. HE IS MY NATURAL-BORN ENEMY.
KURŌMARU TOKISAKA. WHOA...HE'S FROM INVERSE MARS? NEVER SEEN ONE OF THEM BEFORE. I GUESS THEY REALLY DO EXIST.
HM? GENDER UNKNOWN? NO, UNDETERMINED. WHAT DOES THAT EVEN MEAN? IT DOESN'T MAKE SENSE. OH WELL, MALE OR FEMALE, I SHOW NO MERCY.
KURŌMARU TOKISAKA
UQ Holder No.11
Immortality Level: B
Supernaturally derived. Guinea pig in sorcery-induced immortality experiments.
Gender undetermined. Born 2072
Born in Tōgen, Inverse Mars. Born in an Ura Shinmei School branch family.
TŌTA KONOE... A VAMPIRE? DOESN'T REALLY LOOK LIKE ONE. A STUPID KID LIKE THAT, A VAMPIRE?
HUH? WHAT THE? BORN IN `82? THAT'D MAKE HIM FOUR YEARS OLD... THE DATA'S WRONG.
TCH... WHAT-EVER.
TŌTA KONOE
Immortality Level: A
Vampire
Male, born 2082
Born in East Asia Station
Attended Middle School in Aso, Kumamoto Prefecture

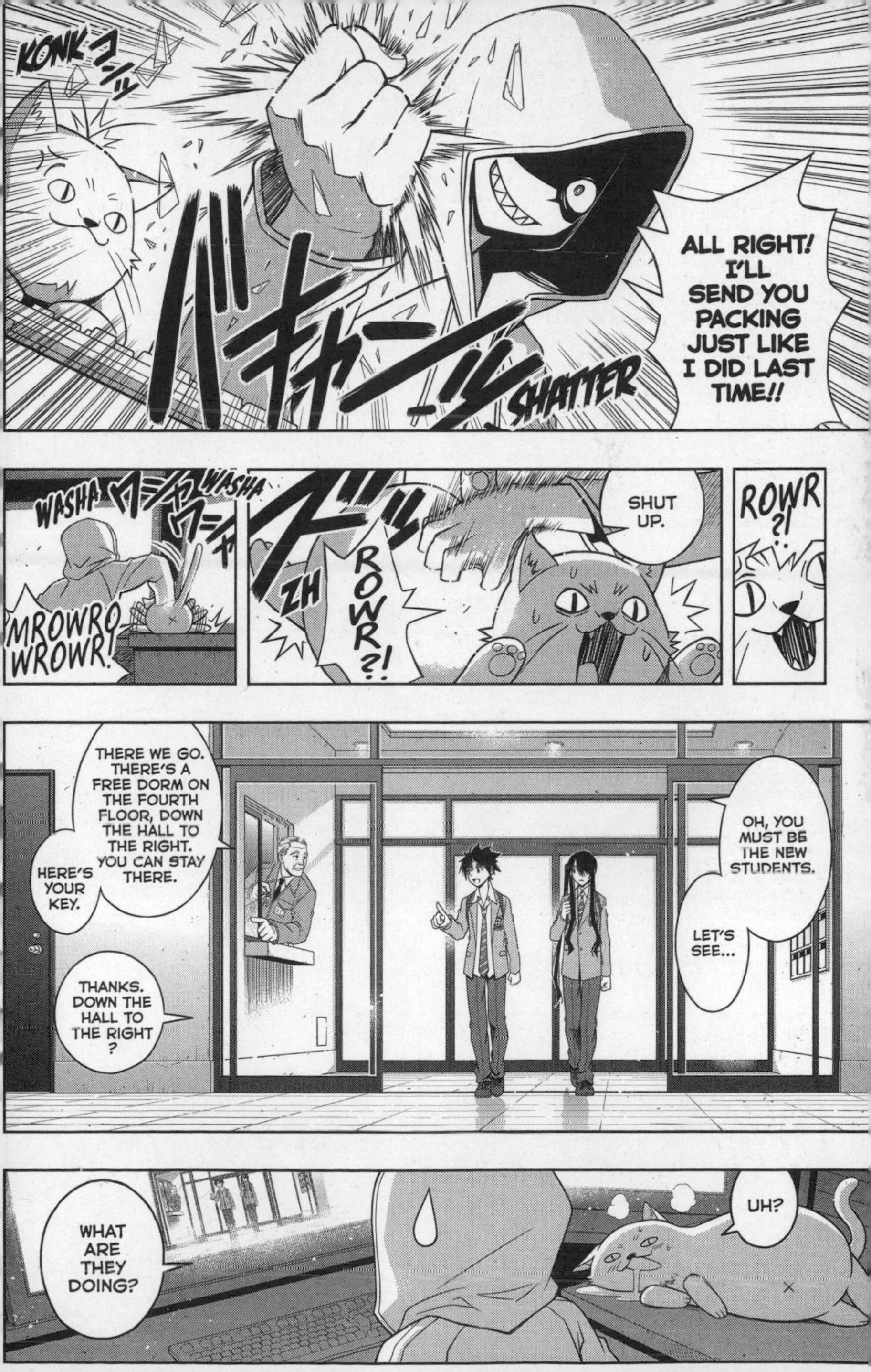
KONK
SHATTER
ALL RIGHT! I'LL SEND YOU PACKING JUST LIKE I DID LAST TIME!!
ROWR ?!
SHUT UP.
ROWR ?!
ZH
WASHA WASHA
MROWROWROWR!
OH, YOU MUST BE THE NEW STUDENTS.
LET'S SEE...
THERE WE GO. THERE'S A FREE DORM ON THE FOURTH FLOOR, DOWN THE HALL TO THE RIGHT. YOU CAN STAY THERE.
HERE'S YOUR KEY.
THANKS. DOWN THE HALL TO THE RIGHT ?
UH?
WHAT ARE THEY DOING?

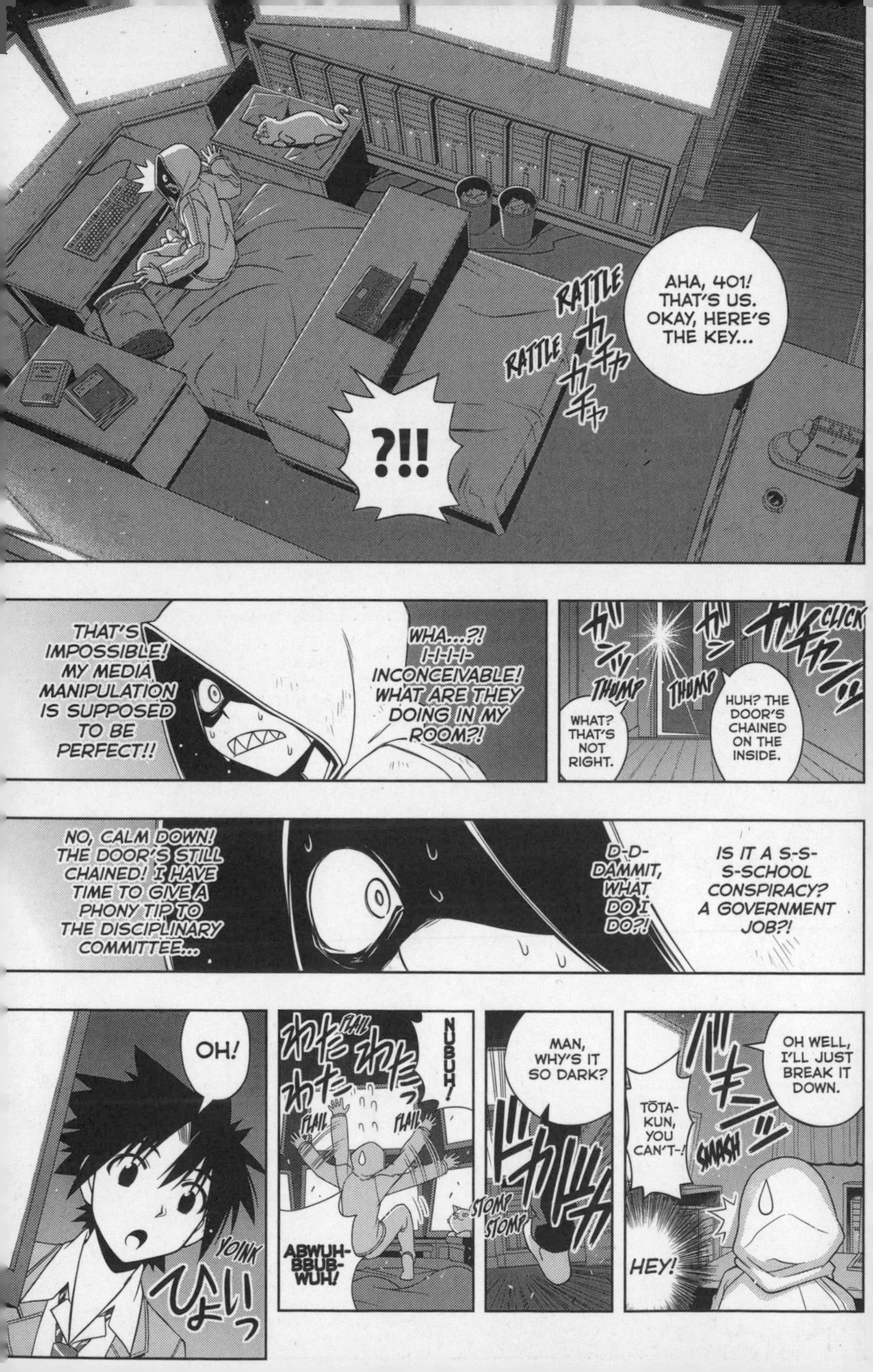
AHA, 401! THAT'S US. OKAY, HERE'S THE KEY...
RATTLE
RATTLE
カチャカチャ
?!!
CLICK
THUMP
THUMP
HUH? THE DOOR'S CHAINED ON THE INSIDE.
WHAT? THAT'S NOT RIGHT.
WHA...?! I-I-I-I-INCONCEIVABLE! WHAT ARE THEY DOING IN MY ROOM?!
THAT'S IMPOSSIBLE! MY MEDIA MANIPULATION IS SUPPOSED TO BE PERFECT!!
IS IT A S-S-S-SCHOOL CONSPIRACY? A GOVERNMENT JOB?!
D-D-DAMMIT, WHAT DO I DO?!
NO, CALM DOWN! THE DOOR'S STILL CHAINED! I HAVE TIME TO GIVE A PHONY TIP TO THE DISCIPLINARY COMMITTEE...
OH WELL, I'LL JUST BREAK IT DOWN.
SMASH
TŌTA-KUN, YOU CAN'T-!
HEY!
MAN, WHY'S IT SO DARK?
STOMP
STOMP
NUBUH!
FLAIL
FLAIL
FLAIL
ABWUH-BBUB-WUH!
OH!
YOINK
ひょいっ

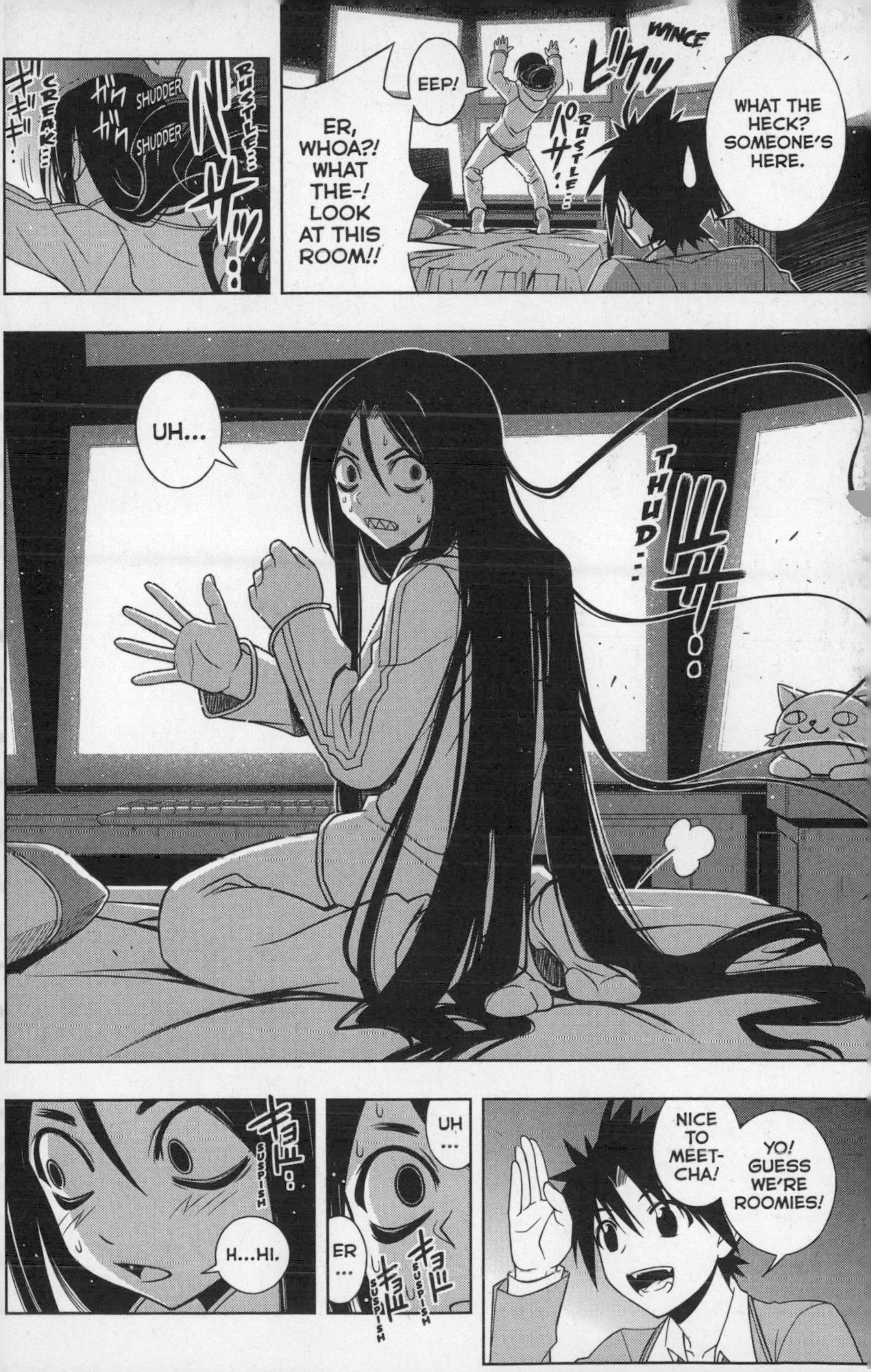
WHAT THE HECK? SOMEONE'S HERE.
WINCE
RUSTLE...
EEP!
ER, WHOA?! WHAT THE-! LOOK AT THIS ROOM!!
RUSTLE...
SHUDDER
SHUDDER
CREAK...
UH...
THUD...
YO! GUESS WE'RE ROOMIES!
NICE TO MEET-CHA!
UH...
ER...
SUSPISH
SUSPISH
SUSPISH
H...HI.

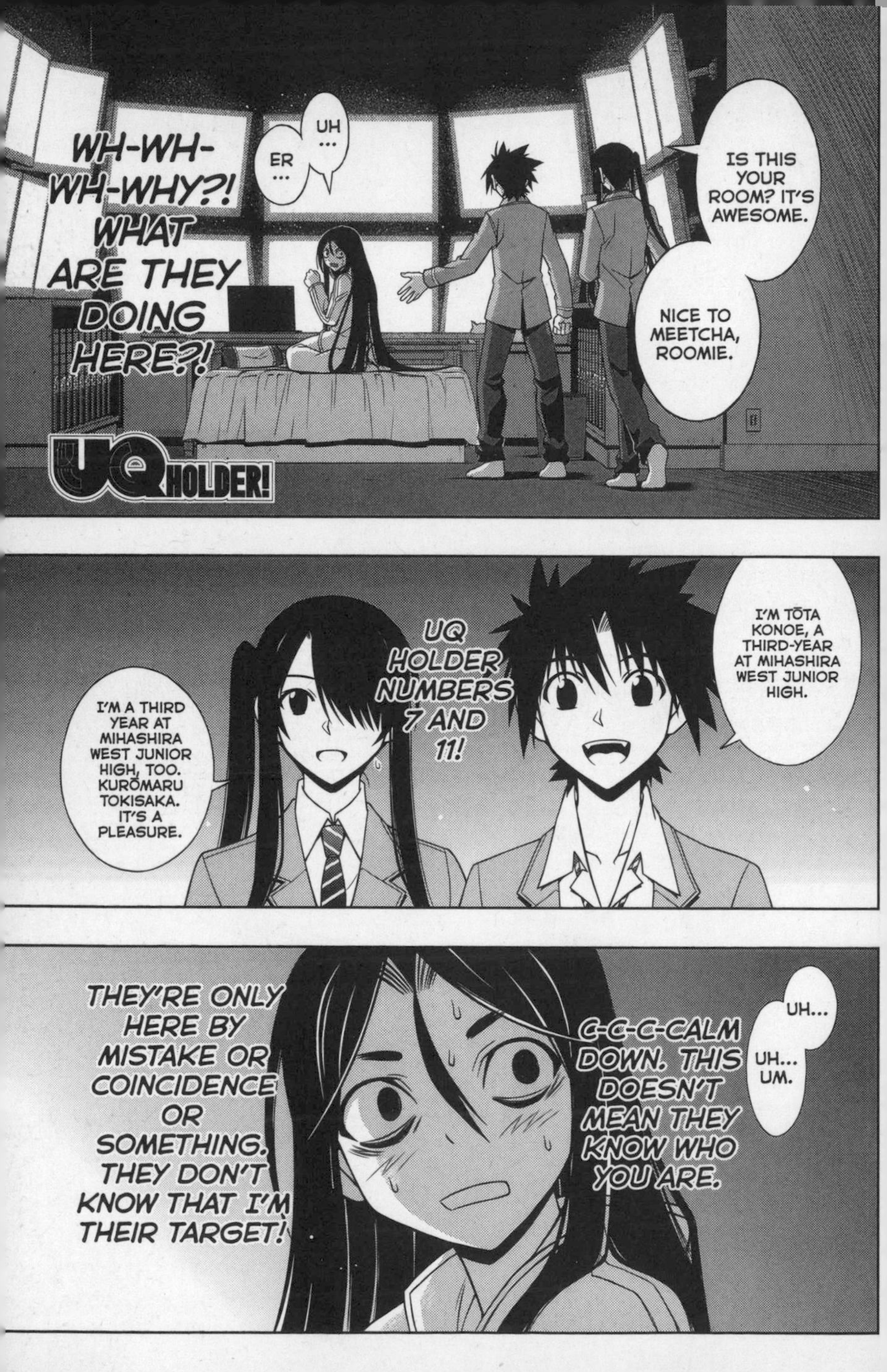
IS THIS YOUR ROOM? IT'S AWESOME.
NICE TO MEETCHA, ROOMIE.
UH ...
ER ...
WH-WH-WH-WHY?! WHAT ARE THEY DOING HERE?!
UQ HOLDER!
I'M TŌTA KONOE, A THIRD-YEAR AT MIHASHIRA WEST JUNIOR HIGH.
UQ HOLDER NUMBERS 7 AND 11!
I'M A THIRD YEAR AT MIHASHIRA WEST JUNIOR HIGH, TOO. KURŌMARU TOKISAKA. IT'S A PLEASURE.
UH...
UH... UM.
C-C-C-CALM DOWN. THIS DOESN'T MEAN THEY KNOW WHO YOU ARE.
THEY'RE ONLY HERE BY MISTAKE OR COINCIDENCE OR SOMETHING. THEY DON'T KNOW THAT I'M THEIR TARGET!

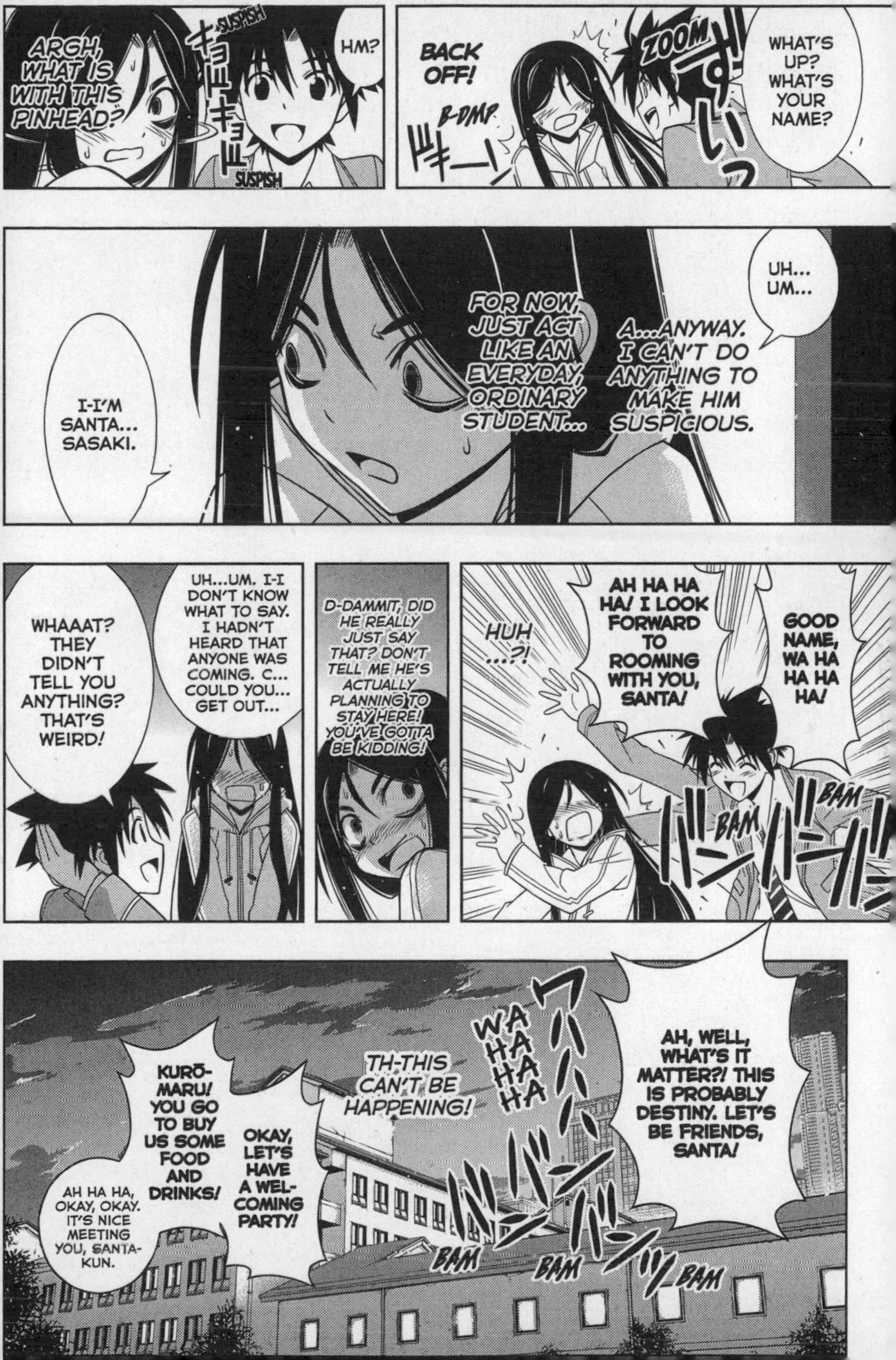
WHAT'S UP? WHAT'S YOUR NAME?
ZOOM
BACK OFF!
B-DMP
HM?
SUSPISH
ARGH, WHAT IS WITH THIS PINHEAD?
SUSPISH
UH... UM...
A...ANYWAY. I CAN'T DO ANYTHING TO MAKE HIM SUSPICIOUS.
FOR NOW, JUST ACT LIKE AN EVERYDAY, ORDINARY STUDENT...
I-I'M SANTA... SASAKI.
GOOD NAME, WA HA HA HA HA!
AH HA HA HA! I LOOK FORWARD TO ROOMING WITH YOU, SANTA!
HUH ...?!
BAM
BAM
D-DAMMIT, DID HE REALLY JUST SAY THAT? DON'T TELL ME HE'S ACTUALLY PLANNING TO STAY HERE! YOU'VE GOTTA BE KIDDING!
UH...UM. I-I DON'T KNOW WHAT TO SAY. I HADN'T HEARD THAT ANYONE WAS COMING. C... COULD YOU... GET OUT...
WHAAAT? THEY DIDN'T TELL YOU ANYTHING? THAT'S WEIRD!
AH, WELL, WHAT'S IT MATTER?! THIS IS PROBABLY DESTINY. LET'S BE FRIENDS, SANTA!
WA HA HA HA HA
BAM
BAM
BAM
TH-THIS CAN'T BE HAPPENING!
OKAY, LET'S HAVE A WEL-COMING PARTY!
KURŌ-MARU! YOU GO TO BUY US SOME FOOD AND DRINKS!
AH HA HA, OKAY, OKAY. IT'S NICE MEETING YOU, SANTA-KUN.

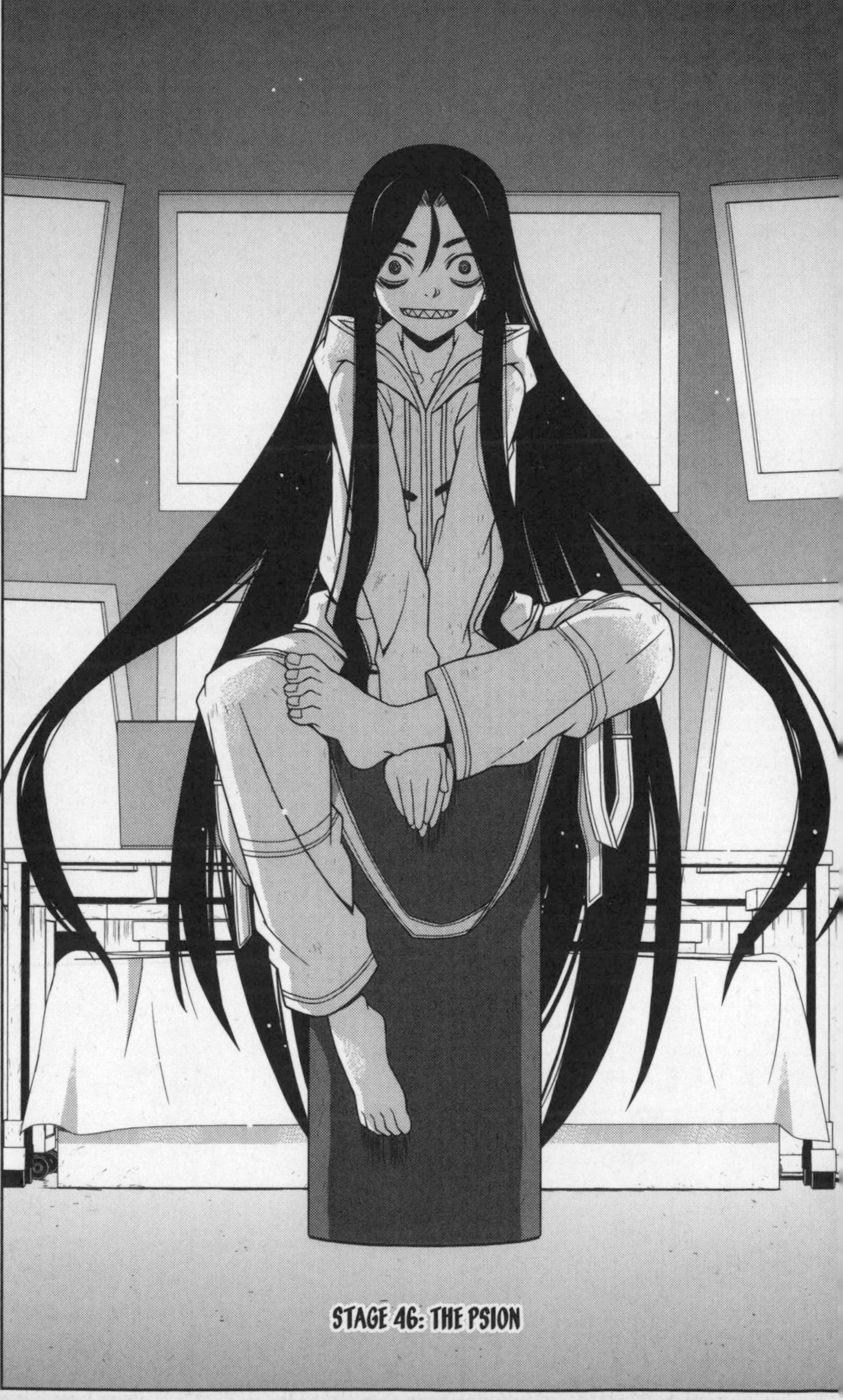
STAGE 46: THE PSION

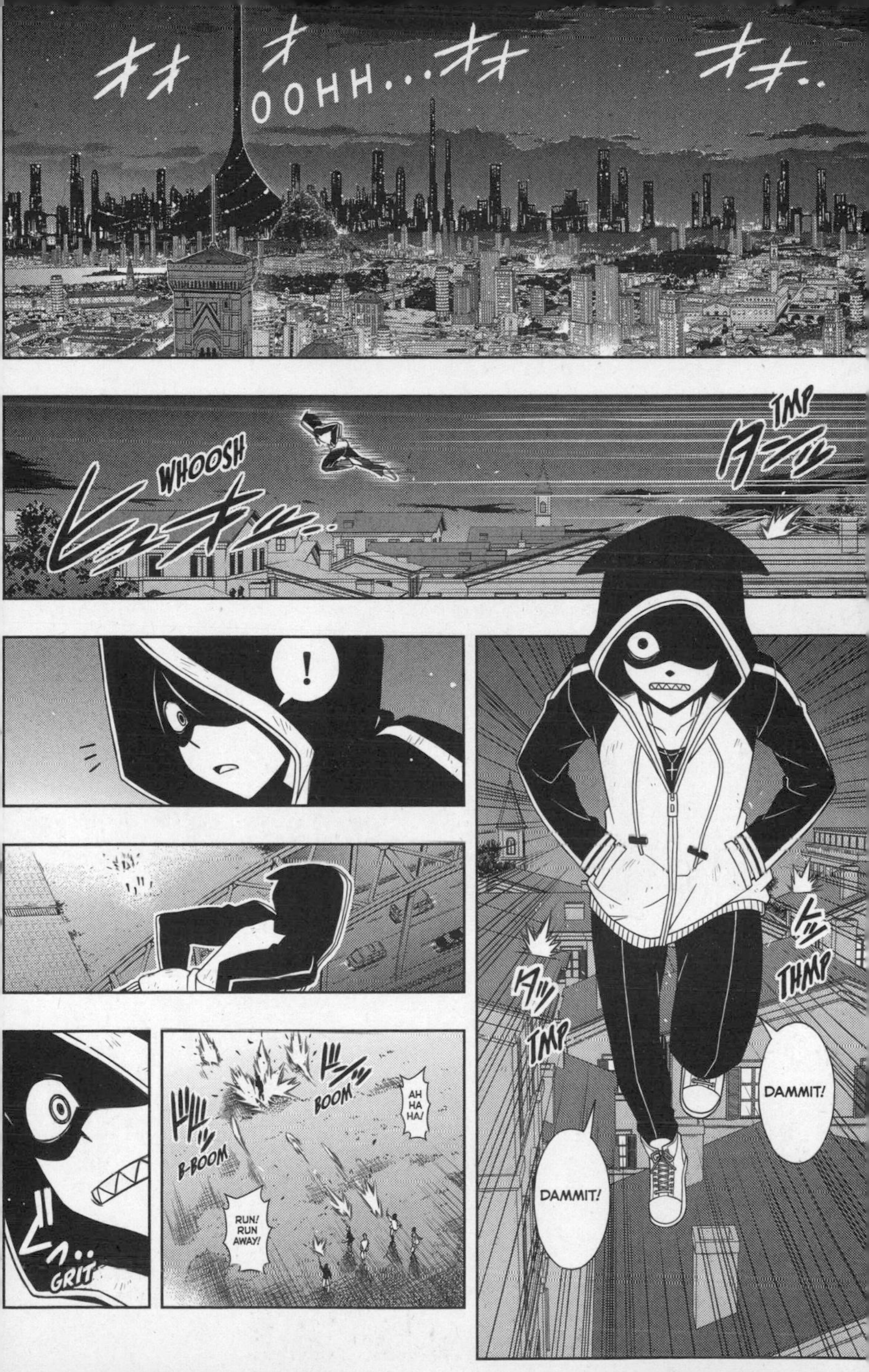

オオ
OOHH...オオ
オオ..
TMP
WHOOSH
ドッ
THMP
タッ
TMP
DAMMIT!
DAMMIT!
!
BOOM
B-BOOM
AH HA HA!
RUN! RUN AWAY!
GRIT

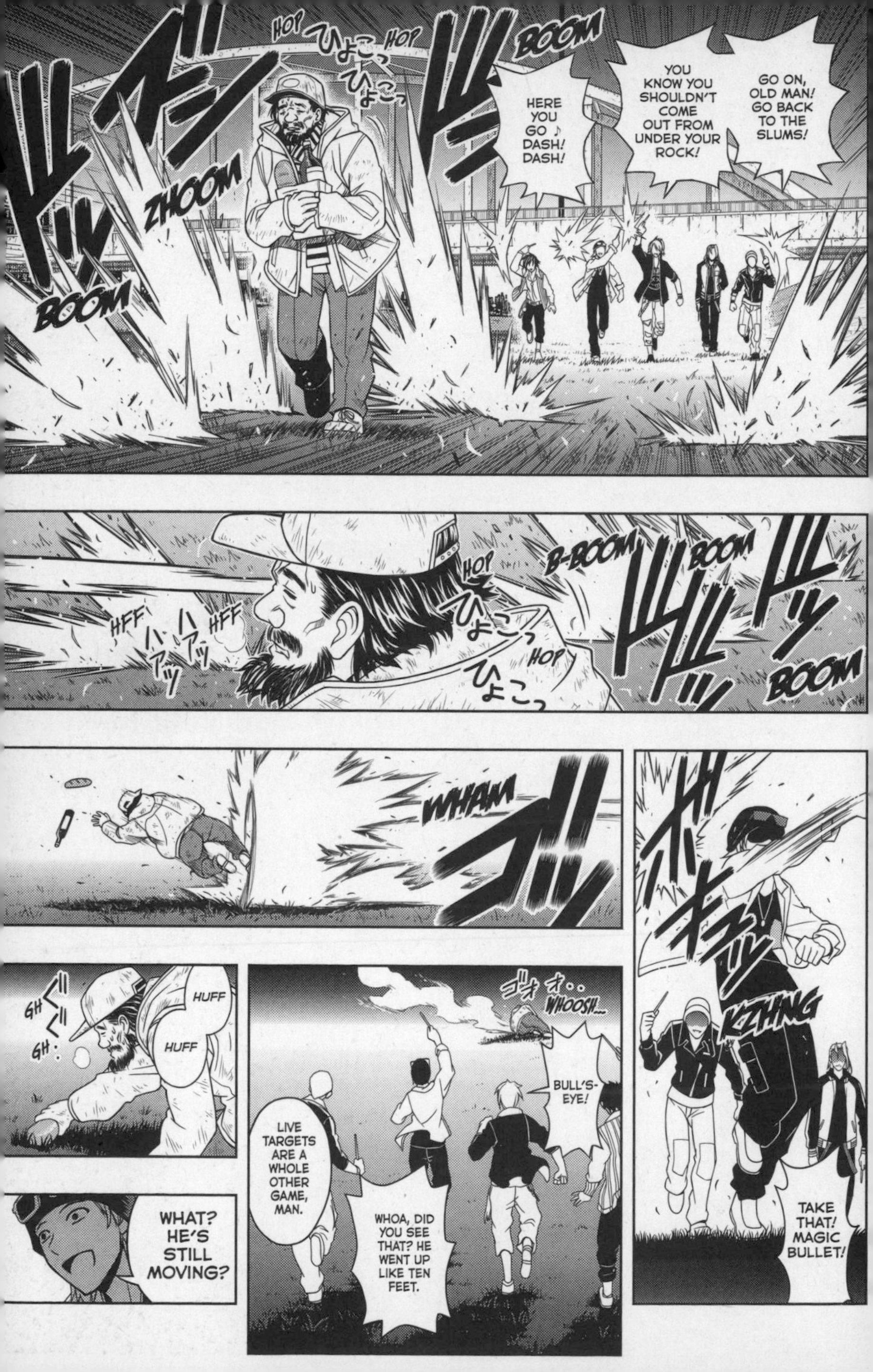
BOOM
GO ON, OLD MAN! GO BACK TO THE SLUMS!
YOU KNOW YOU SHOULDN'T COME OUT FROM UNDER YOUR ROCK!
HERE YOU GO ♪ DASH! DASH!
HOP ひょこっ HOP ひょこっ
ZHOOM
BOOM
BOOM
BOOM
B-BOOM
HOP ひょこっ
HOP ひょこっ
HFF ハアッ HFF ハアッ
KZHING
TAKE THAT! MAGIC BULLET!
WHAM
ゴオオ.. WHOOSH...
BULL'S-EYE!
WHOA, DID YOU SEE THAT? HE WENT UP LIKE TEN FEET.
LIVE TARGETS ARE A WHOLE OTHER GAME, MAN.
HUFF
HUFF
GH GH
WHAT? HE'S STILL MOVING?

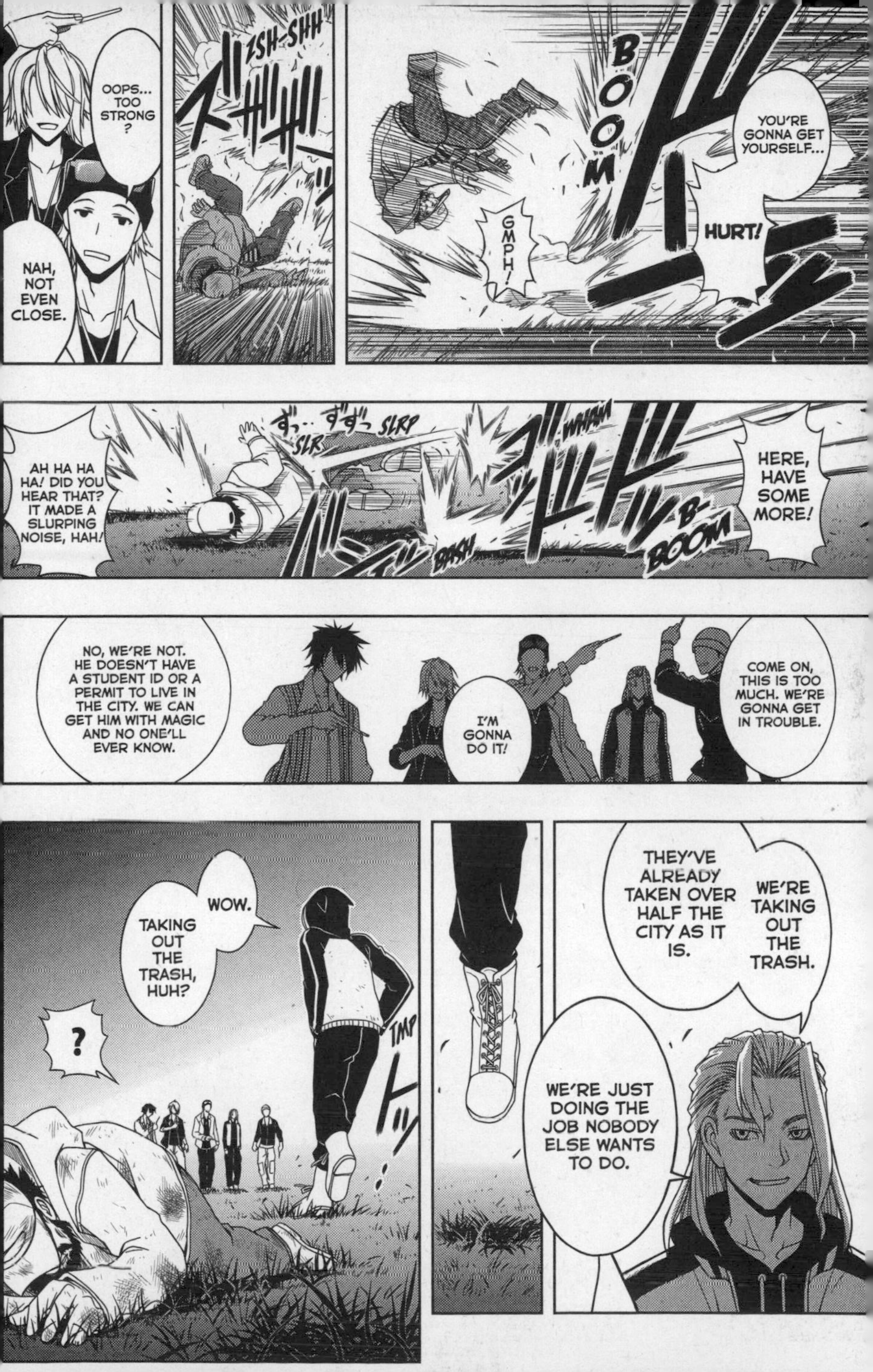

YOU'RE GONNA GET YOURSELF...
BOOM
HURT!
GMPH!
ZSH-SHH
OOPS... TOO STRONG?
NAH, NOT EVEN CLOSE.
HERE, HAVE SOME MORE!
WHAM
B-BOOM
BASH
SLRP
SLR
ずっ… ずずっ
AH HA HA HA! DID YOU HEAR THAT? IT MADE A SLURPING NOISE, HAH!
COME ON, THIS IS TOO MUCH. WE'RE GONNA GET IN TROUBLE.
I'M GONNA DO IT!
NO, WE'RE NOT. HE DOESN'T HAVE A STUDENT ID OR A PERMIT TO LIVE IN THE CITY. WE CAN GET HIM WITH MAGIC AND NO ONE'LL EVER KNOW.
WE'RE TAKING OUT THE TRASH.
THEY'VE ALREADY TAKEN OVER HALF THE CITY AS IT IS.
WE'RE JUST DOING THE JOB NOBODY ELSE WANTS TO DO.
WOW.
TAKING OUT THE TRASH, HUH?
TMP
?

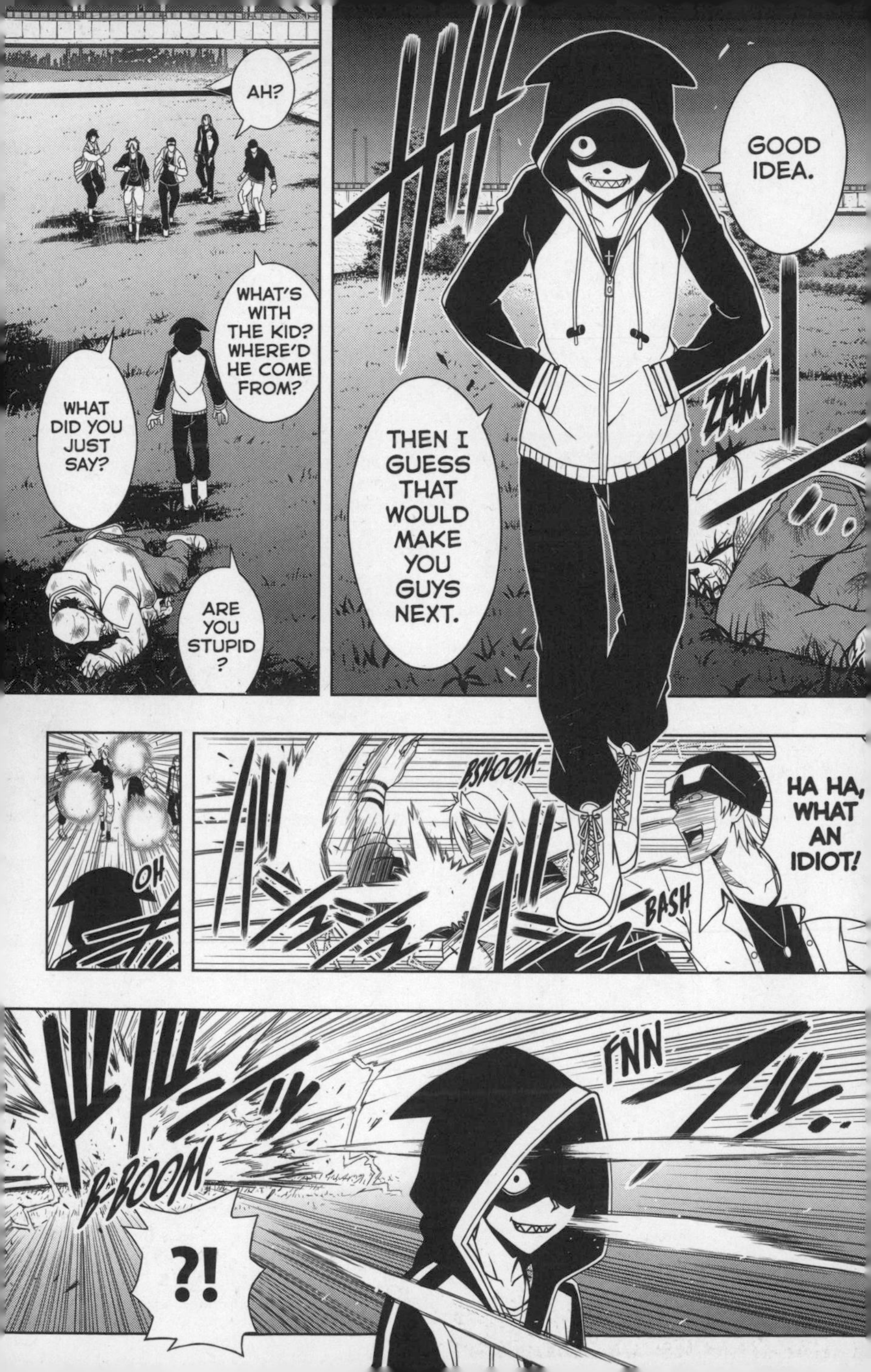
GOOD IDEA.
ZAM
THEN I GUESS THAT WOULD MAKE YOU GUYS NEXT.
AH?
WHAT'S WITH THE KID? WHERE'D HE COME FROM?
WHAT DID YOU JUST SAY?
ARE YOU STUPID?
HA HA, WHAT AN IDIOT!
BSHOOM
BASH
OH
FNN
B-BOOM
?!

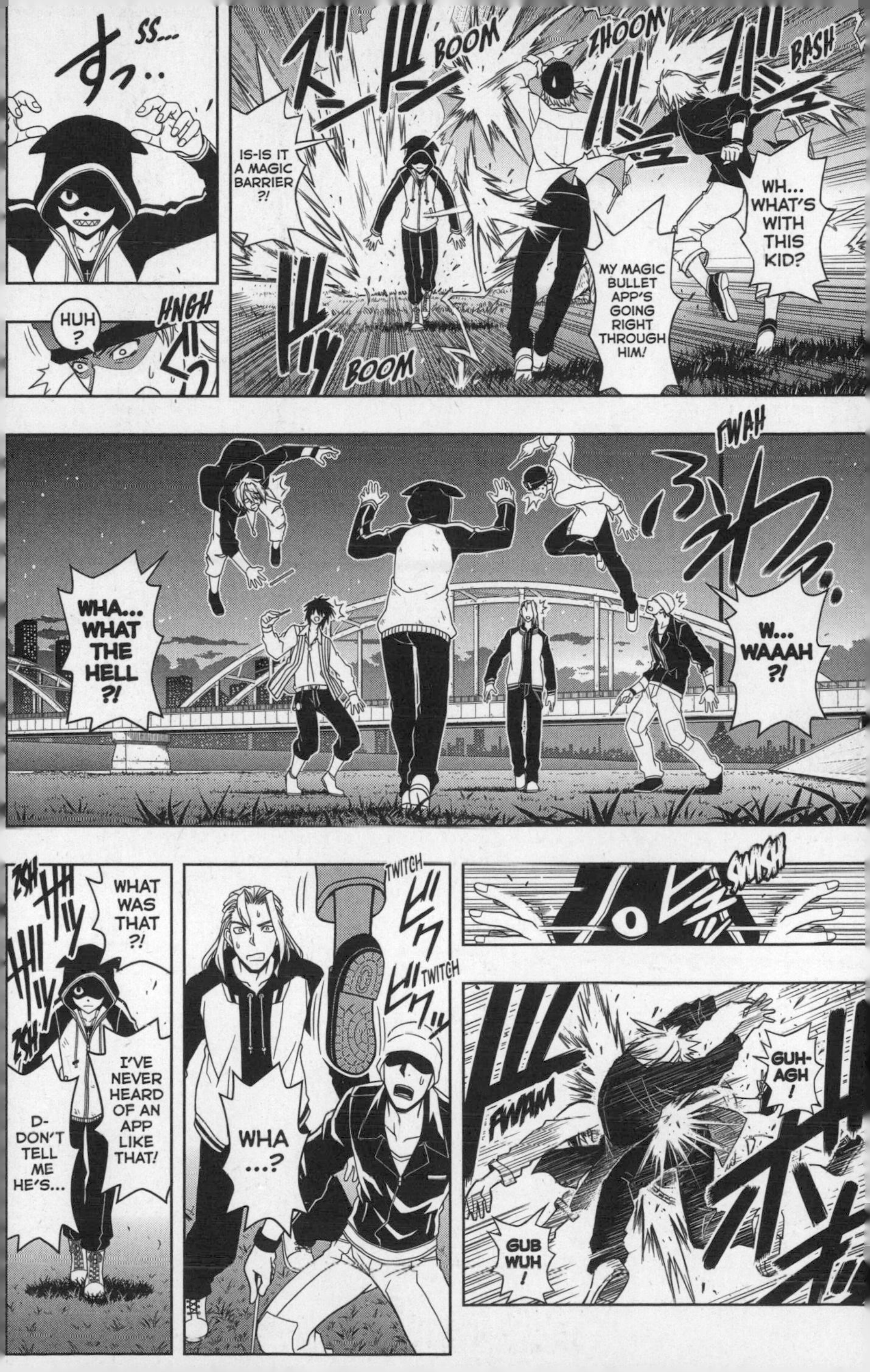
BASH
ZHOOM
BOOM
WH... WHAT'S WITH THIS KID?
MY MAGIC BULLET APP'S GOING RIGHT THROUGH HIM!
IS-IS IT A MAGIC BARRIER ?!
BOOM
SS...
HNGH
HUH ?
FWAH
W... WAAAH ?!
WHA... WHAT THE HELL ?!
SWISH
GUH-AGH !
FWAM
GUB WUH !
TWITCH
TWITCH
WHA ...?
WHAT WAS THAT ?!
ZSH
ZSH
I'VE NEVER HEARD OF AN APP LIKE THAT!
D-DON'T TELL ME HE'S...

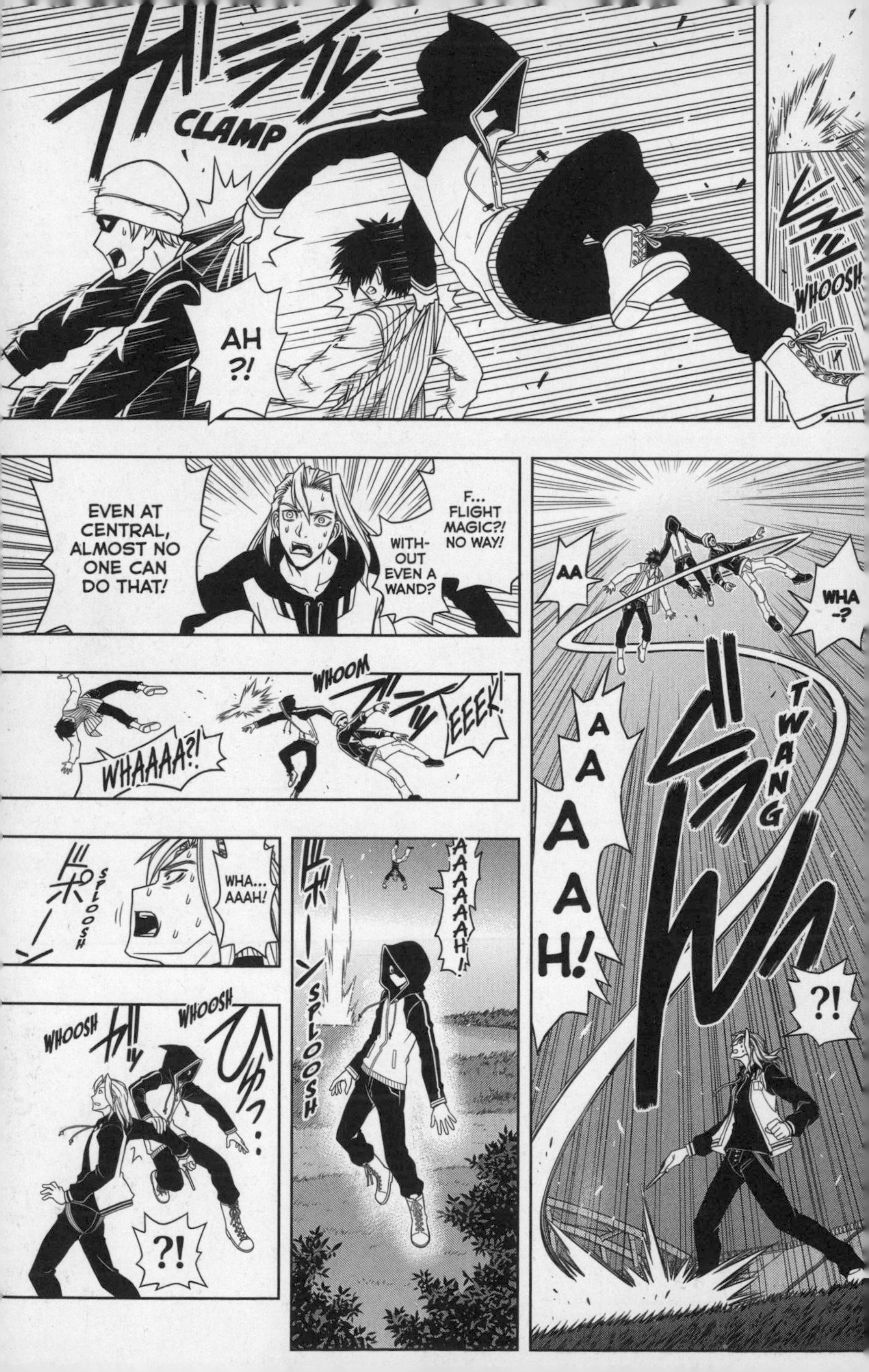
WHOOSH
CLAMP
AH ?!
AA
WHA -?
TWANG
AAAAH!
?!
F... FLIGHT MAGIC?! NO WAY!
WITH-OUT EVEN A WAND?
EVEN AT CENTRAL, ALMOST NO ONE CAN DO THAT!
WHOOM
EEEK!
WHAAAA?!
AAAAAAAAH!!
SPLOOSH
WHA... AAAH!
SPLOOSH
WHOOSH
WHOOSH
?!

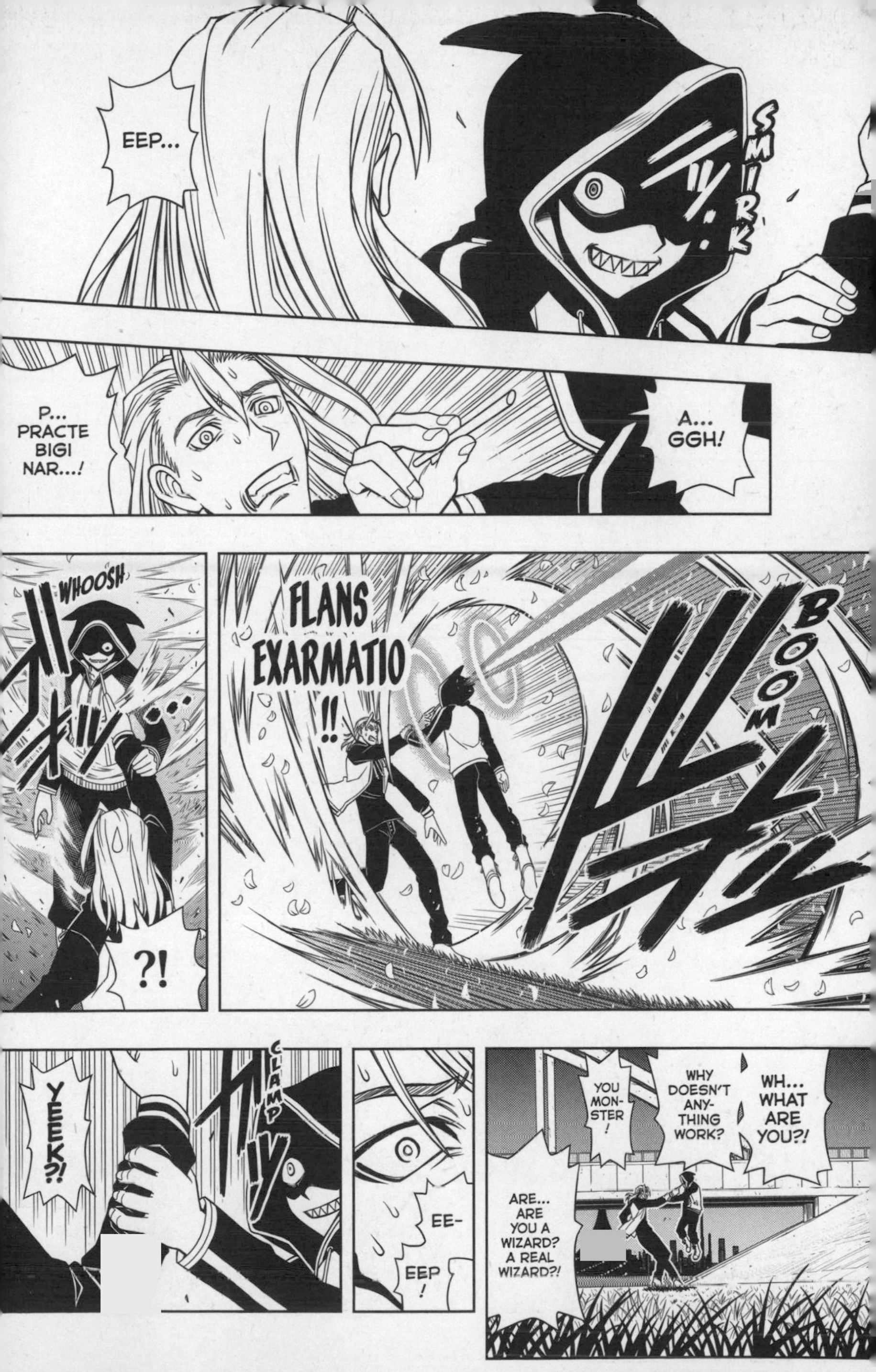
SMIRK
EEP...
A... GGH!
P... PRACTE BIGI NAR...!
BOOM
FLANS EXARMATIO!!
WHOOSH
?!
WH... WHAT ARE YOU?!
WHY DOESN'T ANY-THING WORK?
YOU MON-STER!
ARE... ARE YOU A WIZARD? A REAL WIZARD?!
EE- EEP!
CLAMP
YEEK?!

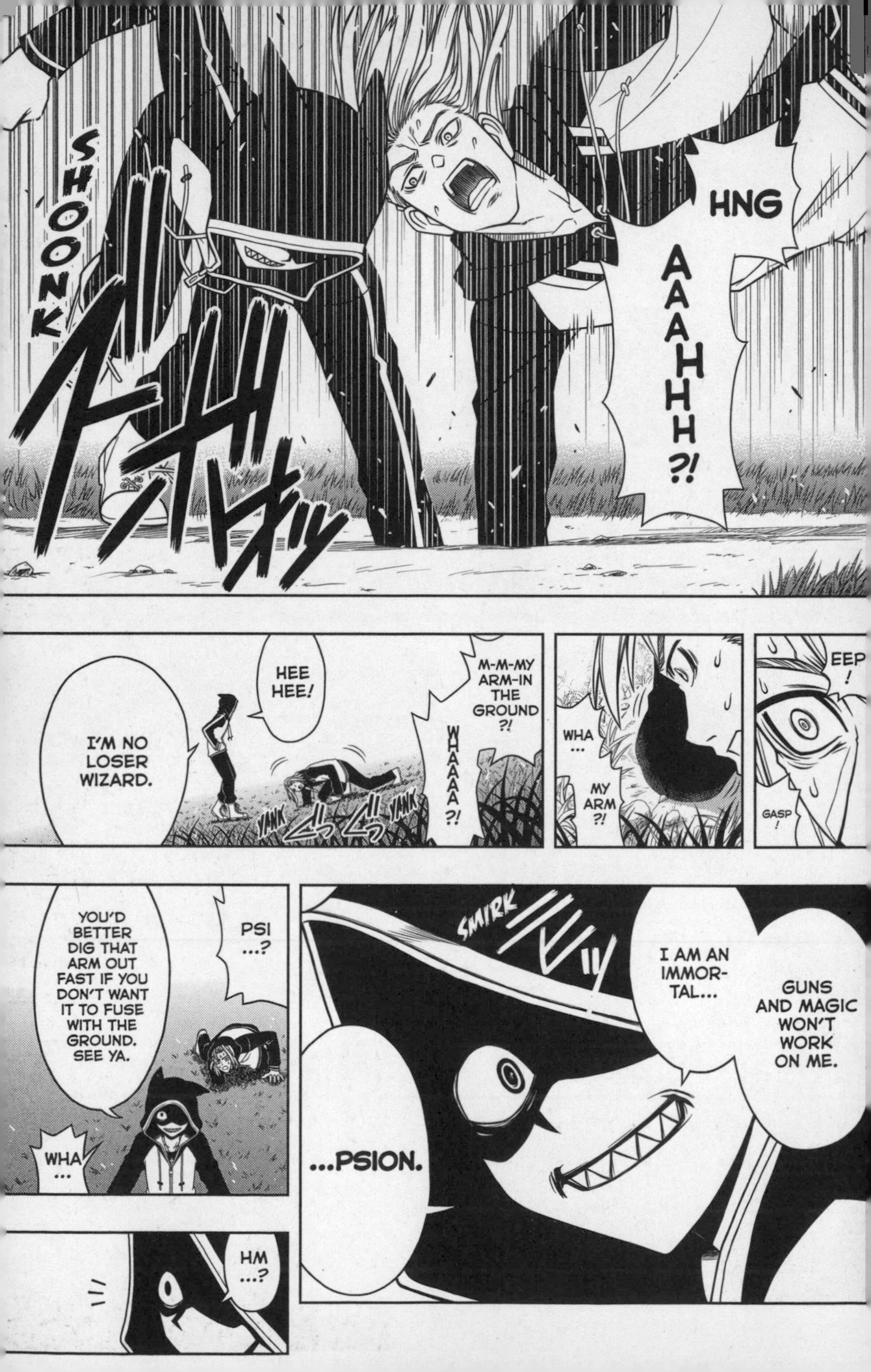
HNG
AAAHHH?!
SHOONK
EEP!
GASP!
WHA...
MY ARM?!
M-M-MY ARM-IN THE GROUND?!
WHAAAA?!
HEE HEE!
YANK
YANK
I'M NO LOSER WIZARD.
SMIRK
I AM AN IMMORTAL...
GUNS AND MAGIC WON'T WORK ON ME.
...PSION.
PSI...?
YOU'D BETTER DIG THAT ARM OUT FAST IF YOU DON'T WANT IT TO FUSE WITH THE GROUND. SEE YA.
WHA...
HM...?

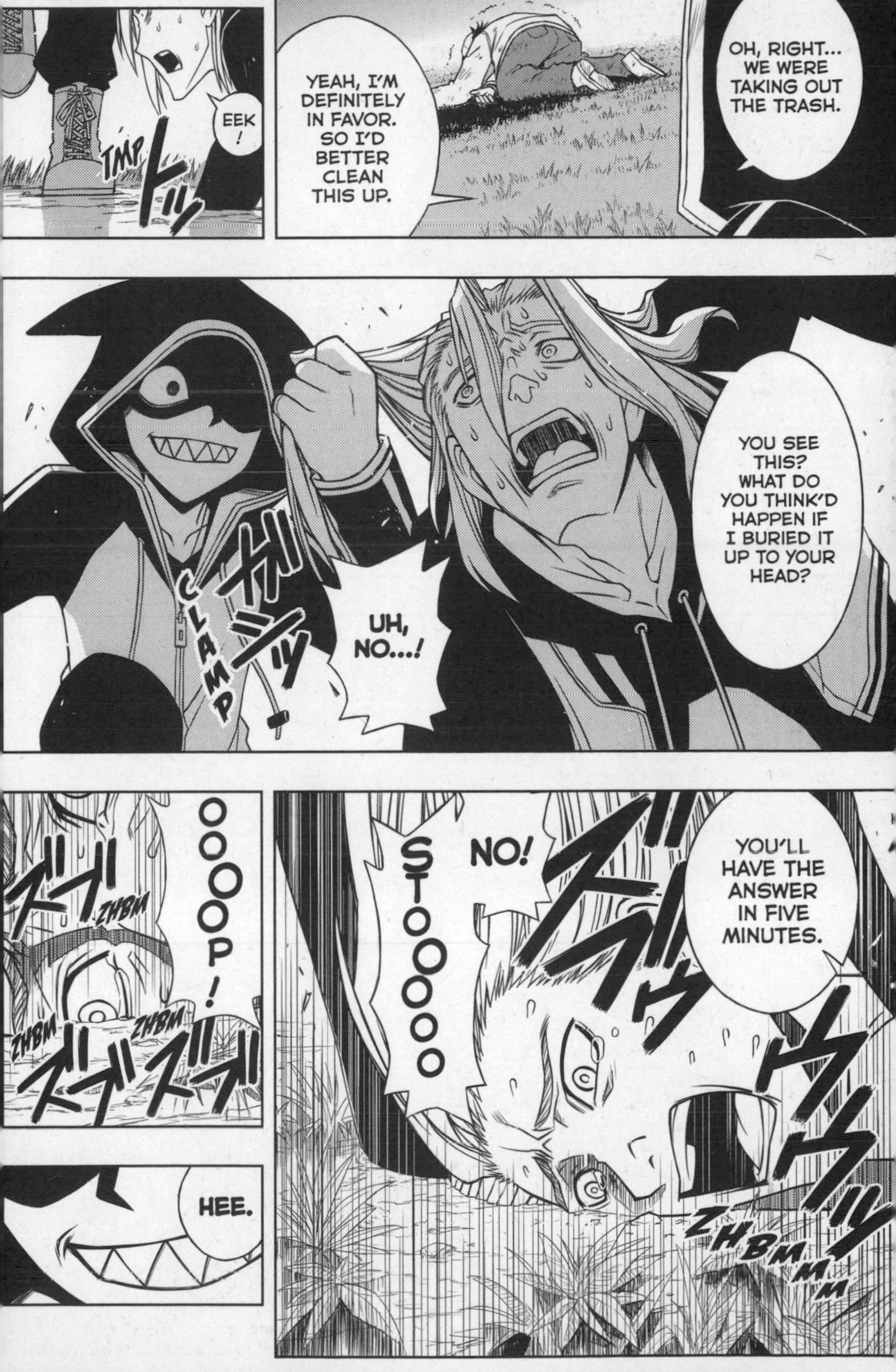
OH, RIGHT... WE WERE TAKING OUT THE TRASH.
YEAH, I'M DEFINITELY IN FAVOR. SO I'D BETTER CLEAN THIS UP.
EEK!
TMP
YOU SEE THIS? WHAT DO YOU THINK'D HAPPEN IF I BURIED IT UP TO YOUR HEAD?
UH, NO...!
CLAMP
YOU'LL HAVE THE ANSWER IN FIVE MINUTES.
NO!
STOOOOOO
ZHBMMMM
OOOOP!
ZHBM
ZHBM
ZHBM
HEE.

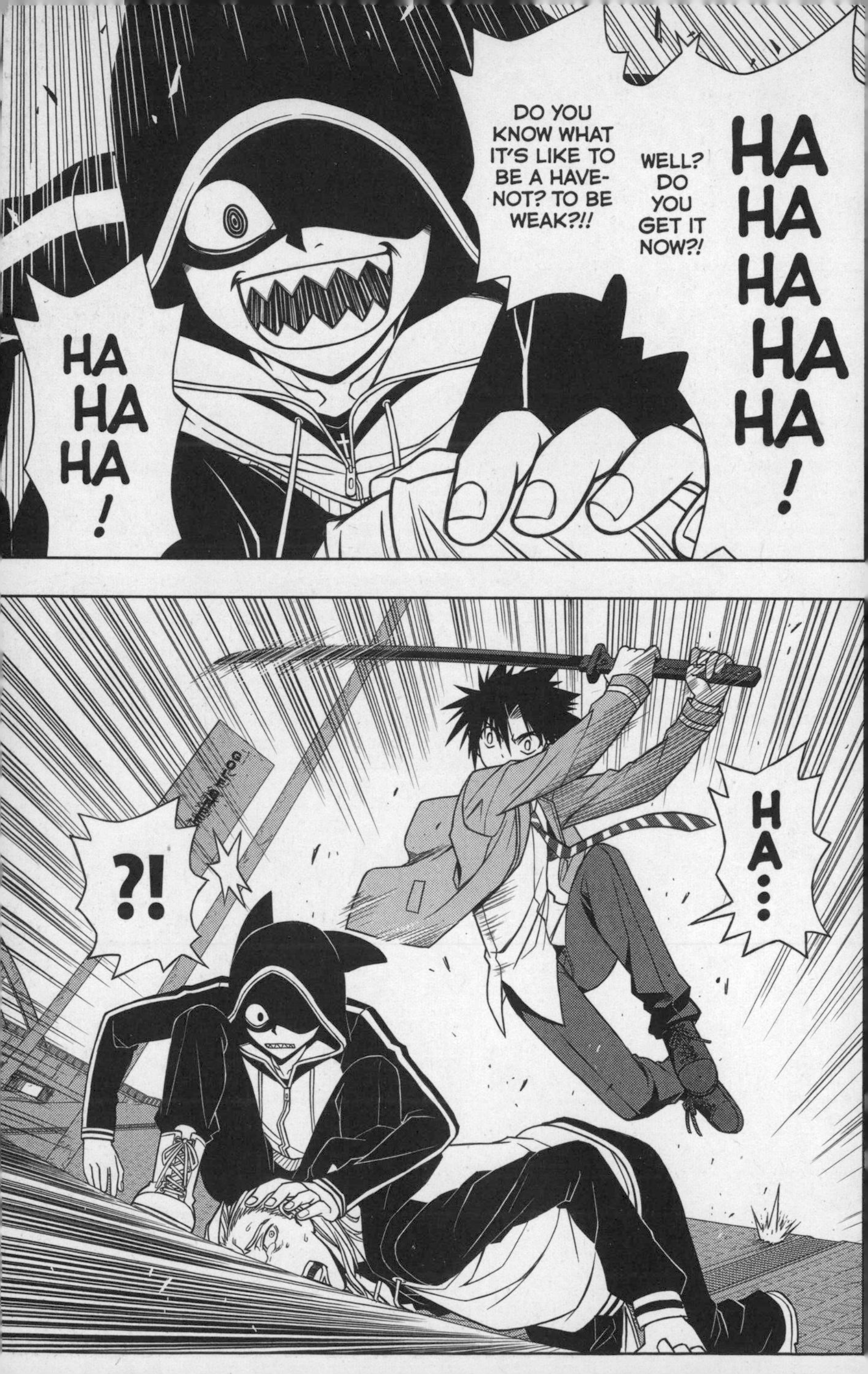
HA HA HA HA HA!
WELL? DO YOU GET IT NOW?!
DO YOU KNOW WHAT IT'S LIKE TO BE A HAVE-NOT? TO BE WEAK?!!
HA HA HA!
HA...
?!

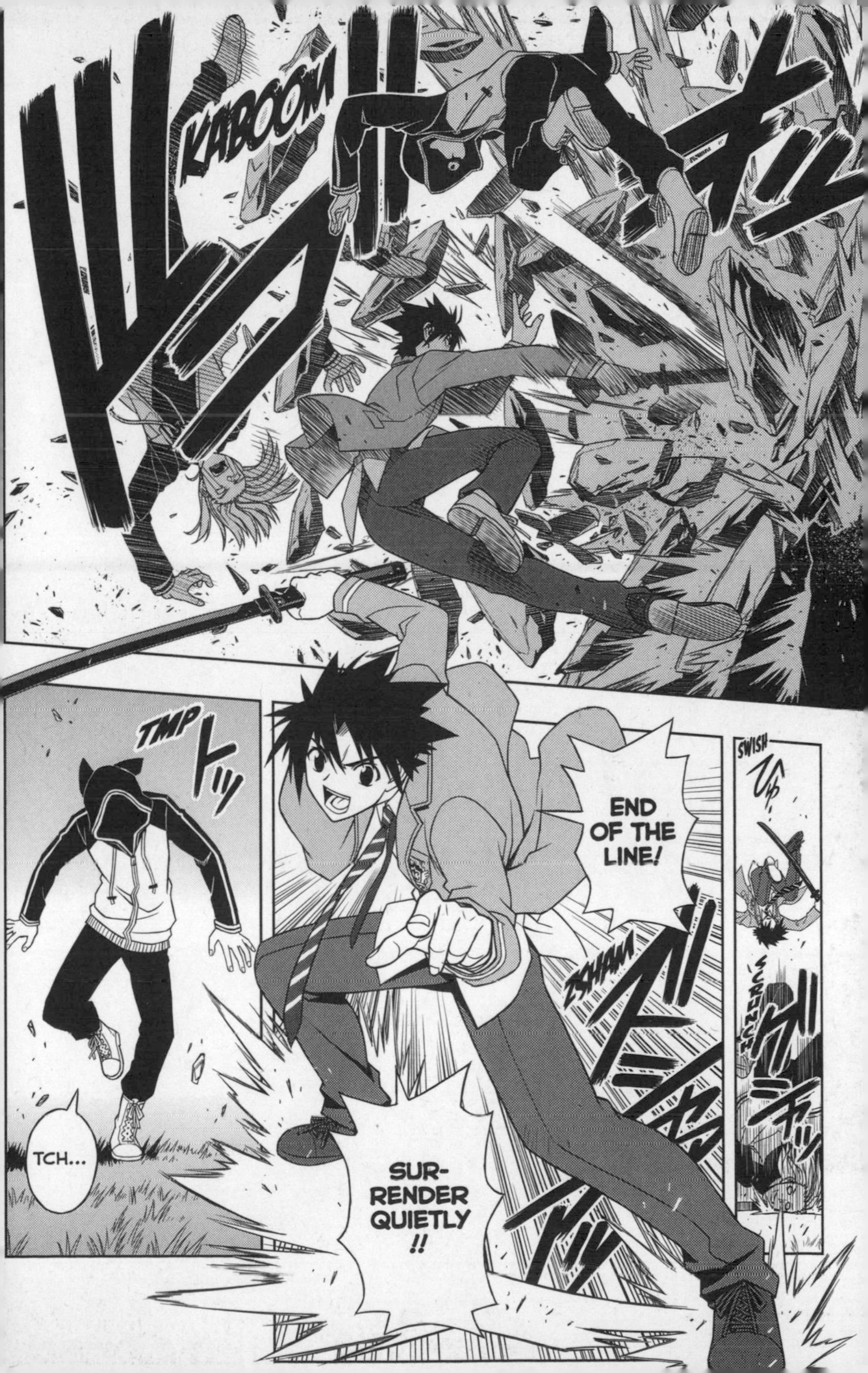
KABOOM
SWISH
SCRUNCH
END OF THE LINE!
ZSHAM
SUR-RENDER QUIETLY!!
TMP
TCH...

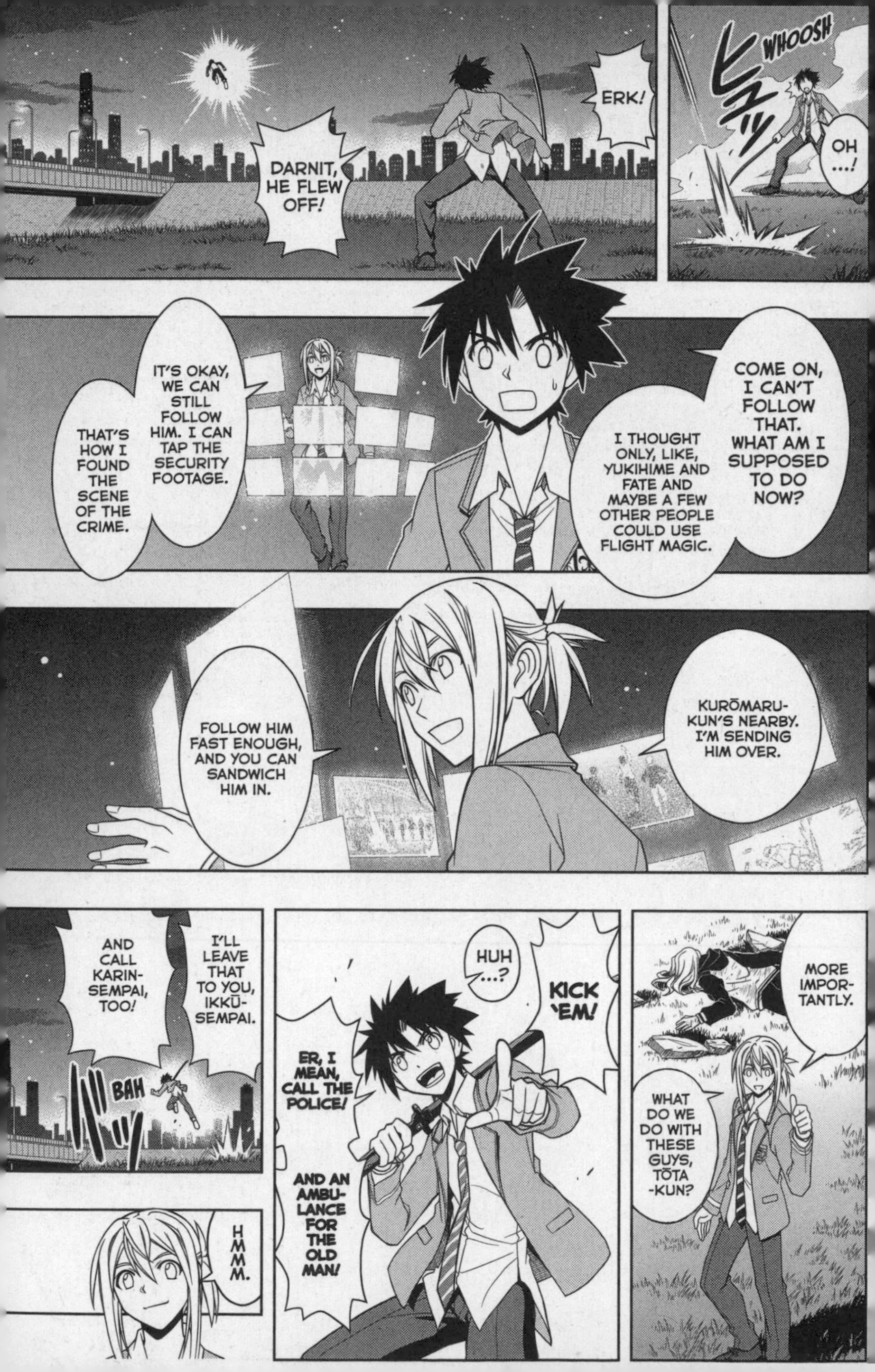
WHOOSH
OH ...!
ERK!
DARNIT, HE FLEW OFF!
COME ON, I CAN'T FOLLOW THAT. WHAT AM I SUPPOSED TO DO NOW?
I THOUGHT ONLY, LIKE, YUKIHIME AND FATE AND MAYBE A FEW OTHER PEOPLE COULD USE FLIGHT MAGIC.
IT'S OKAY, WE CAN STILL FOLLOW HIM. I CAN TAP THE SECURITY FOOTAGE.
THAT'S HOW I FOUND THE SCENE OF THE CRIME.
KURŌMARU-KUN'S NEARBY. I'M SENDING HIM OVER.
FOLLOW HIM FAST ENOUGH, AND YOU CAN SANDWICH HIM IN.
MORE IMPORTANTLY.
WHAT DO WE DO WITH THESE GUYS, TŌTA-KUN?
HUH ...?
KICK 'EM!
ER, I MEAN, CALL THE POLICE!
AND AN AMBULANCE FOR THE OLD MAN!
I'LL LEAVE THAT TO YOU, IKKŪ-SEMPAI.
AND CALL KARIN-SEMPAI, TOO!
BAH
HMMM.

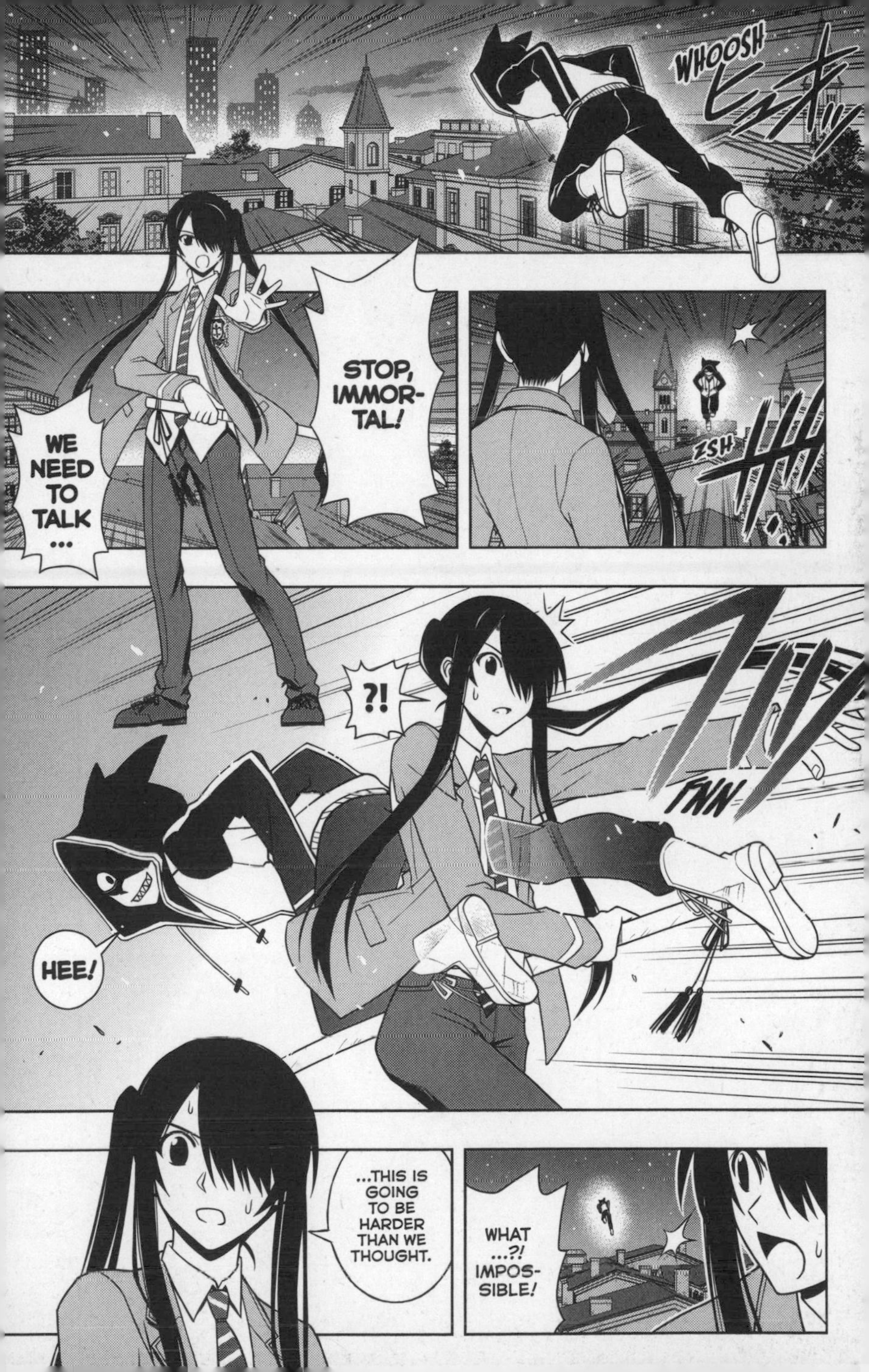
WHOOSH
ZSH
STOP, IMMORTAL!
WE NEED TO TALK...
?!
FNN
HEE!
WHAT...?! IMPOSSIBLE!
...THIS IS GOING TO BE HARDER THAN WE THOUGHT.

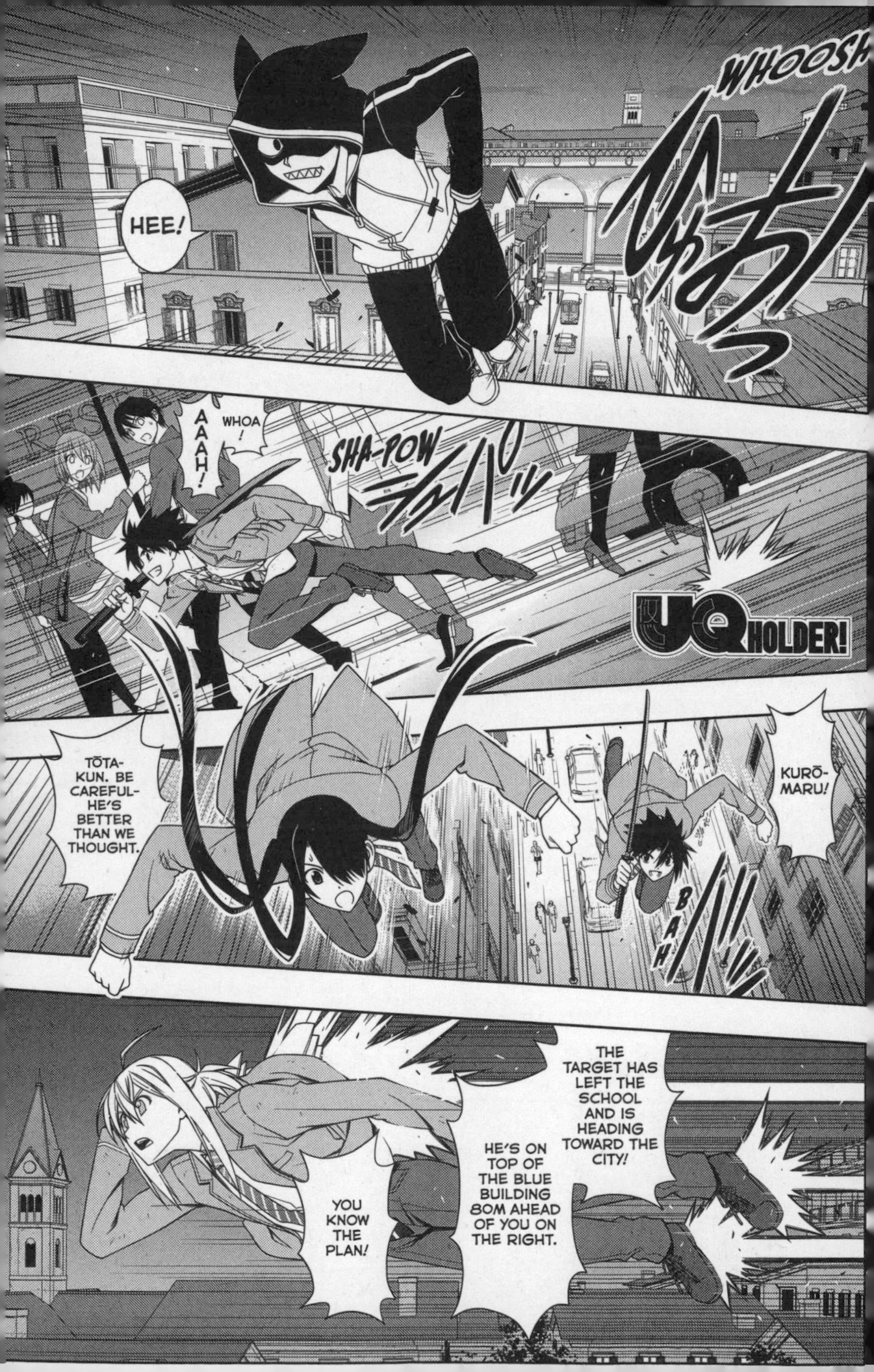
WHOOSH
HEE!
SHA-POW
WHOA!
AAAH!
UQ HOLDER!
KURŌ-MARU!
BAH
TŌTA-KUN. BE CAREFUL-HE'S BETTER THAN WE THOUGHT.
THE TARGET HAS LEFT THE SCHOOL AND IS HEADING TOWARD THE CITY!
HE'S ON TOP OF THE BLUE BUILDING 80M AHEAD OF YOU ON THE RIGHT.
YOU KNOW THE PLAN!

STAGE 47: PSION VS IMMORTALS

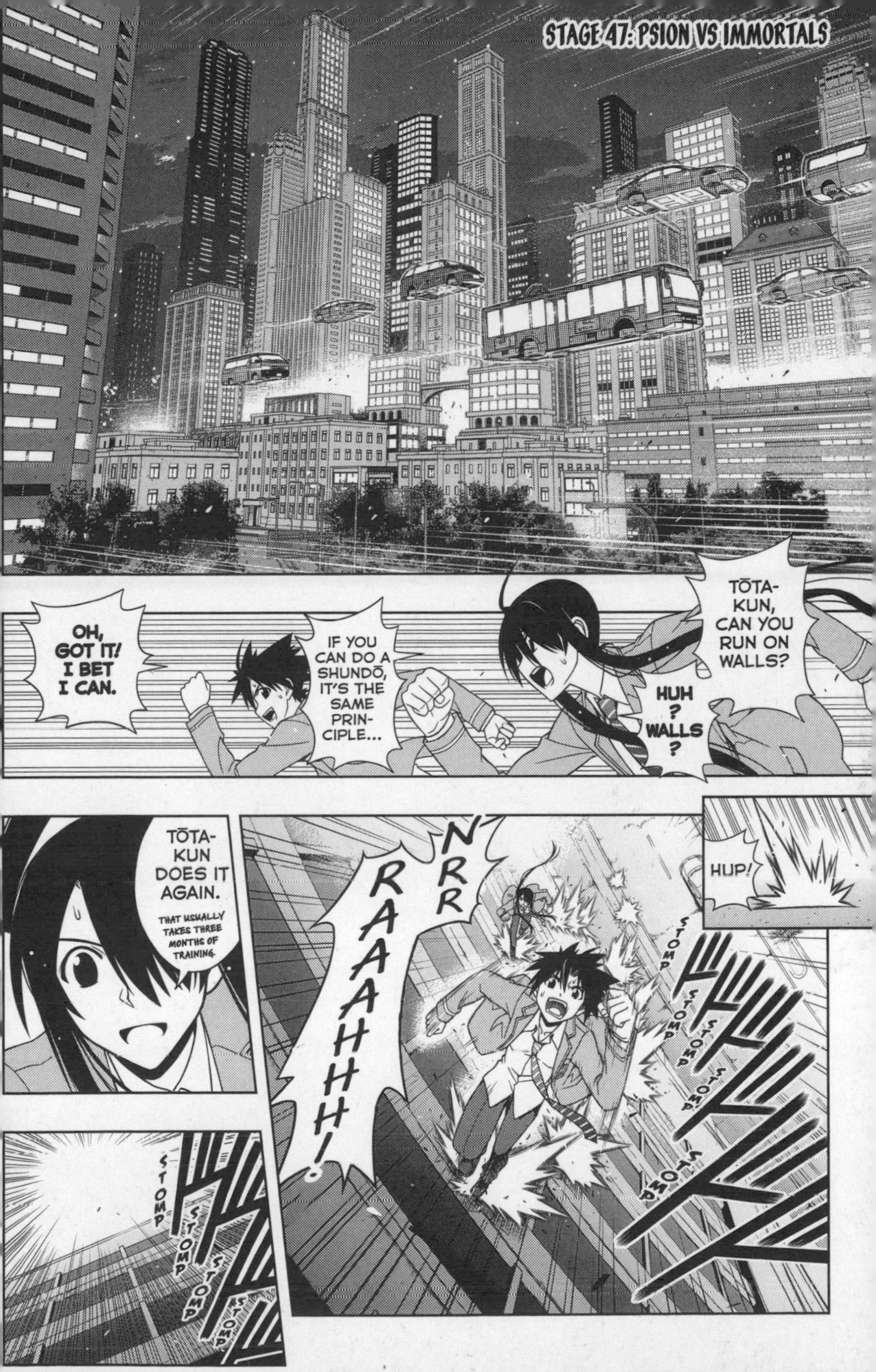
TŌTA-KUN, CAN YOU RUN ON WALLS?
HUH? WALLS?
IF YOU CAN DO A SHUNDŌ, IT'S THE SAME PRINCIPLE...
OH, GOT IT! I BET I CAN.
HUP!
NRRRAAAAHHHH!
STOMP STOMP STOMP STOMP STOMP STOMP
TŌTA-KUN DOES IT AGAIN.
THAT USUALLY TAKES THREE MONTHS OF TRAINING.
STOMP STOMP STOMP STOMP STOMP

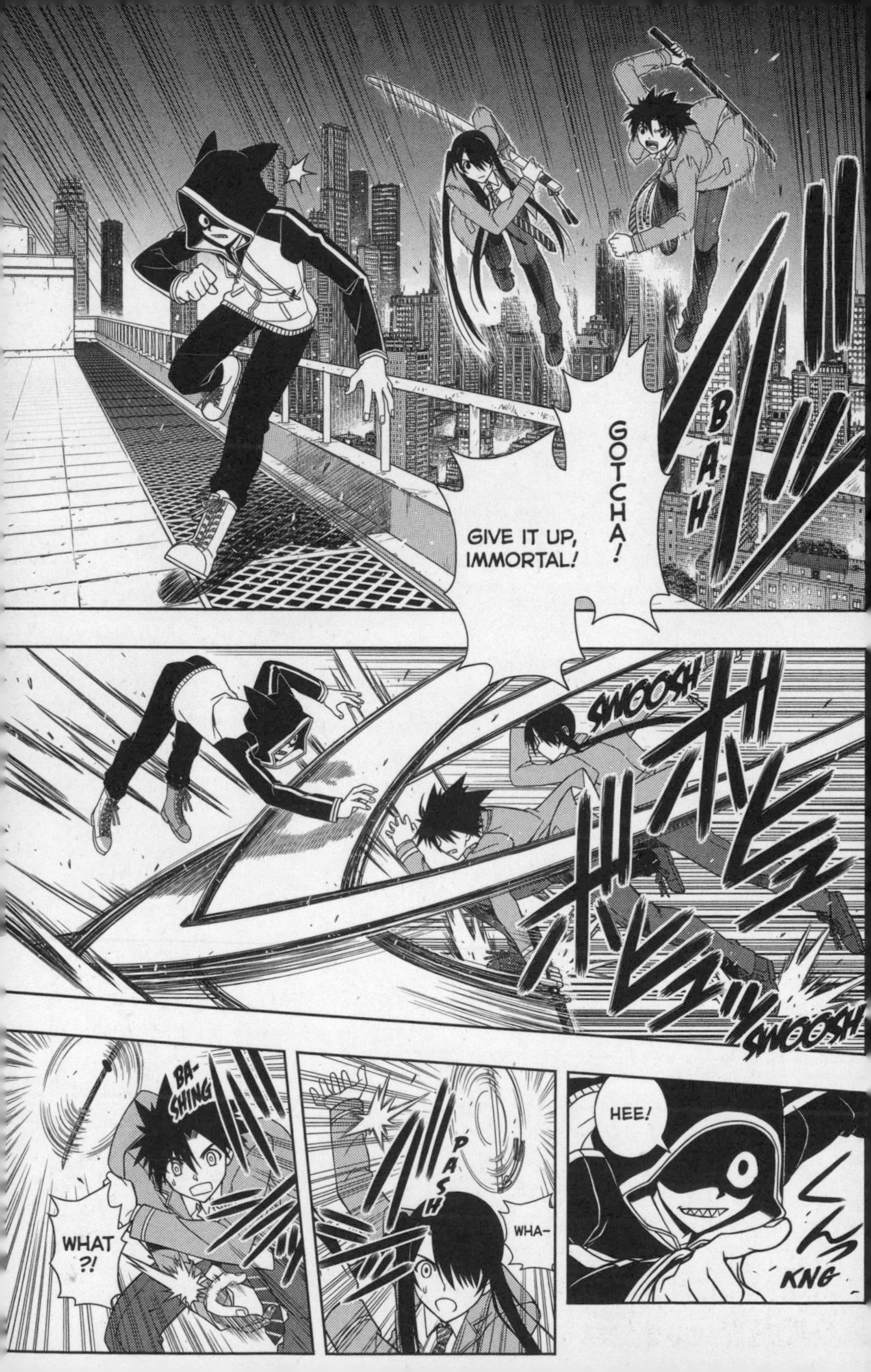
BAH
GOTCHA!
GIVE IT UP, IMMORTAL!
SWOOSH
SWOOSH
HEE!
KNG
PASH
WHA-
BA-SHING
WHAT ?!

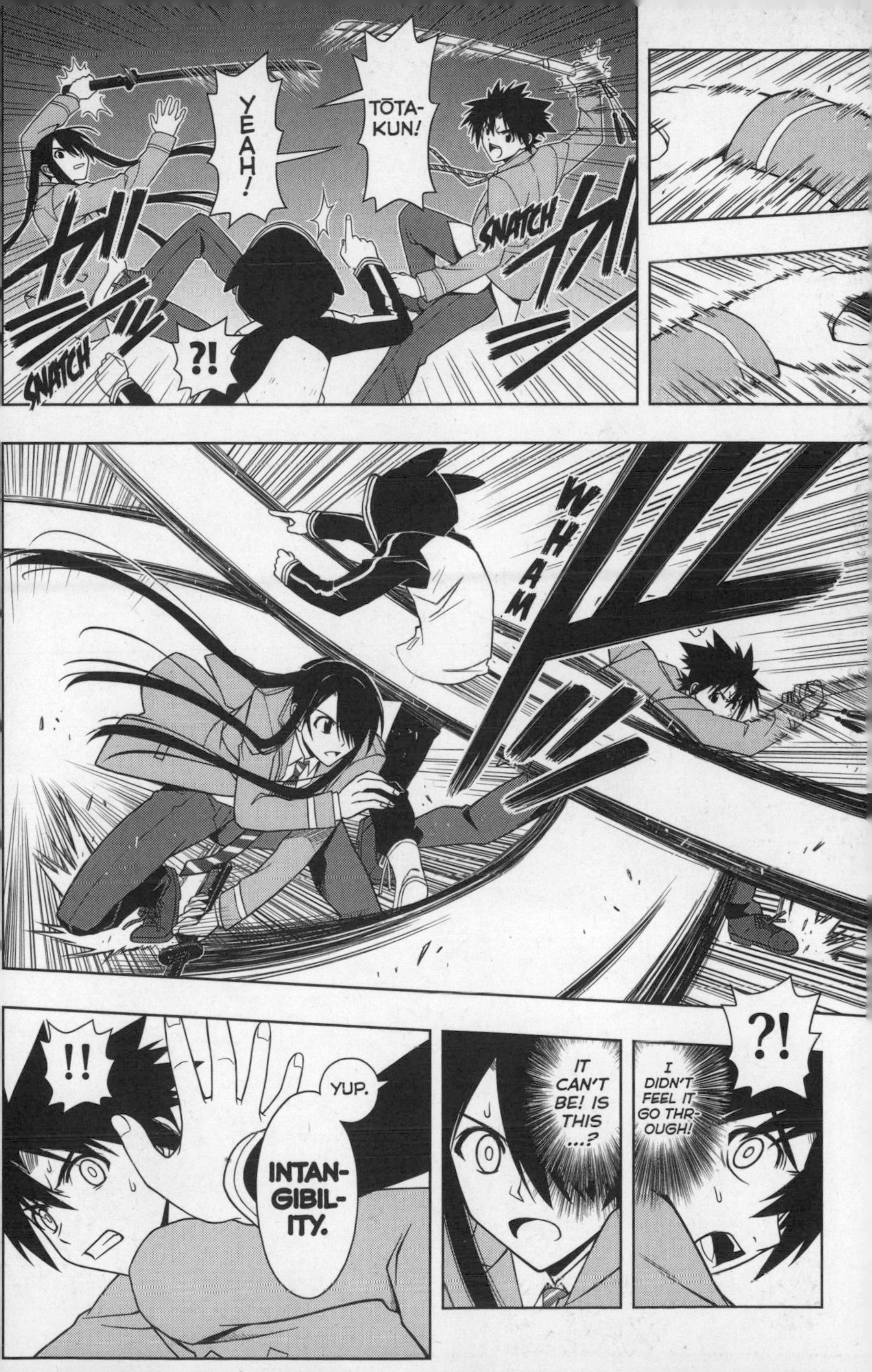

SNATCH
TŌTA-KUN!
YEAH!
SNATCH
?!
WHAM
?!
I DIDN'T FEEL IT GO THROUGH!
IT CAN'T BE! IS THIS ...?
!!
YUP.
INTANGIBILITY.

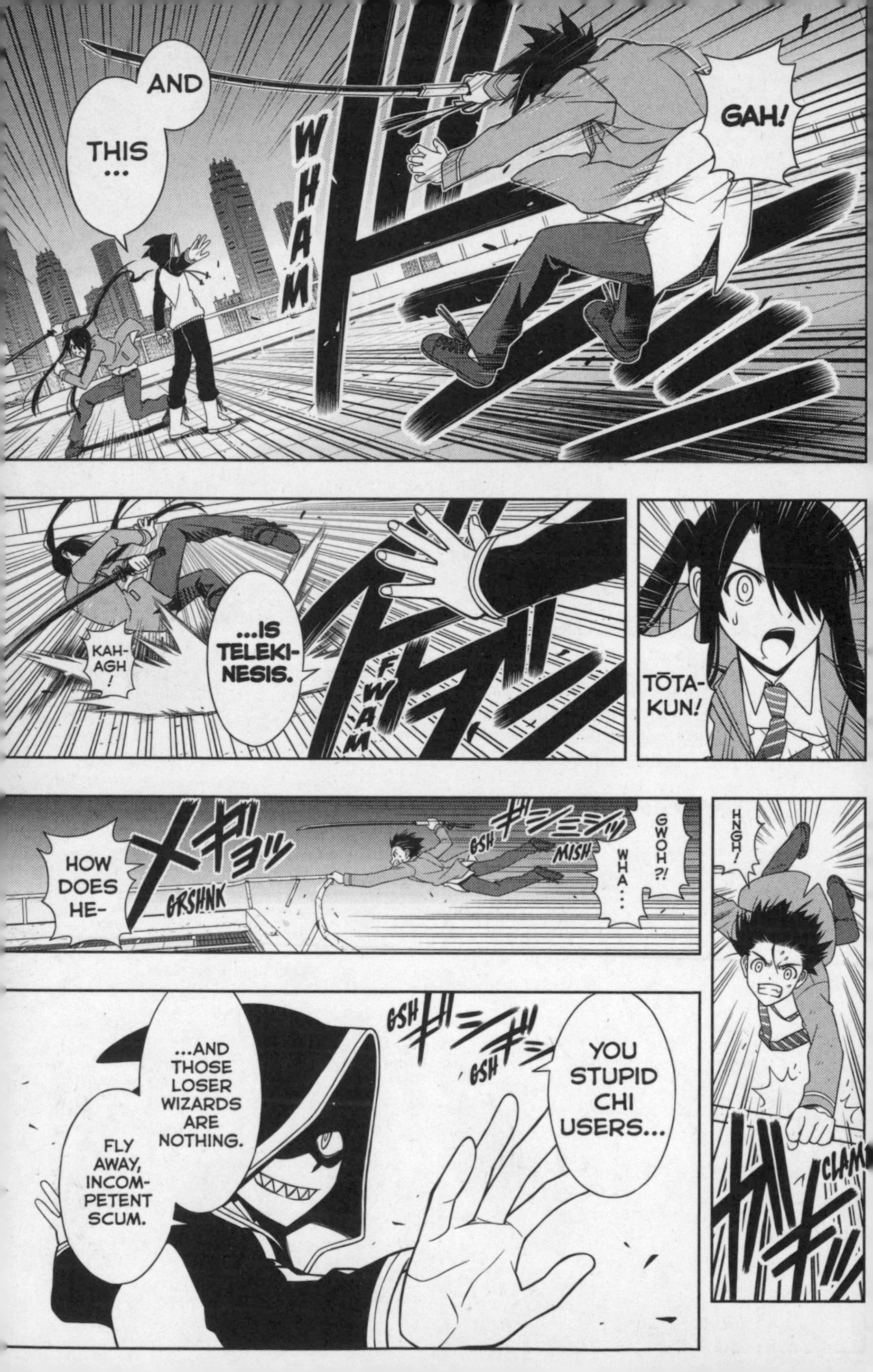
GAH!
WHAM
AND THIS...
TŌTA-KUN!
...IS TELEKINESIS.
FWAM
KAH-AGH!
HNGH!
CLAM
GWOH?!
WHA...
MISH
GSH
GRSHNK
HOW DOES HE-
YOU STUPID CHI USERS...
GSH
GSH
...AND THOSE LOSER WIZARDS ARE NOTHING.
FLY AWAY, INCOMPETENT SCUM.

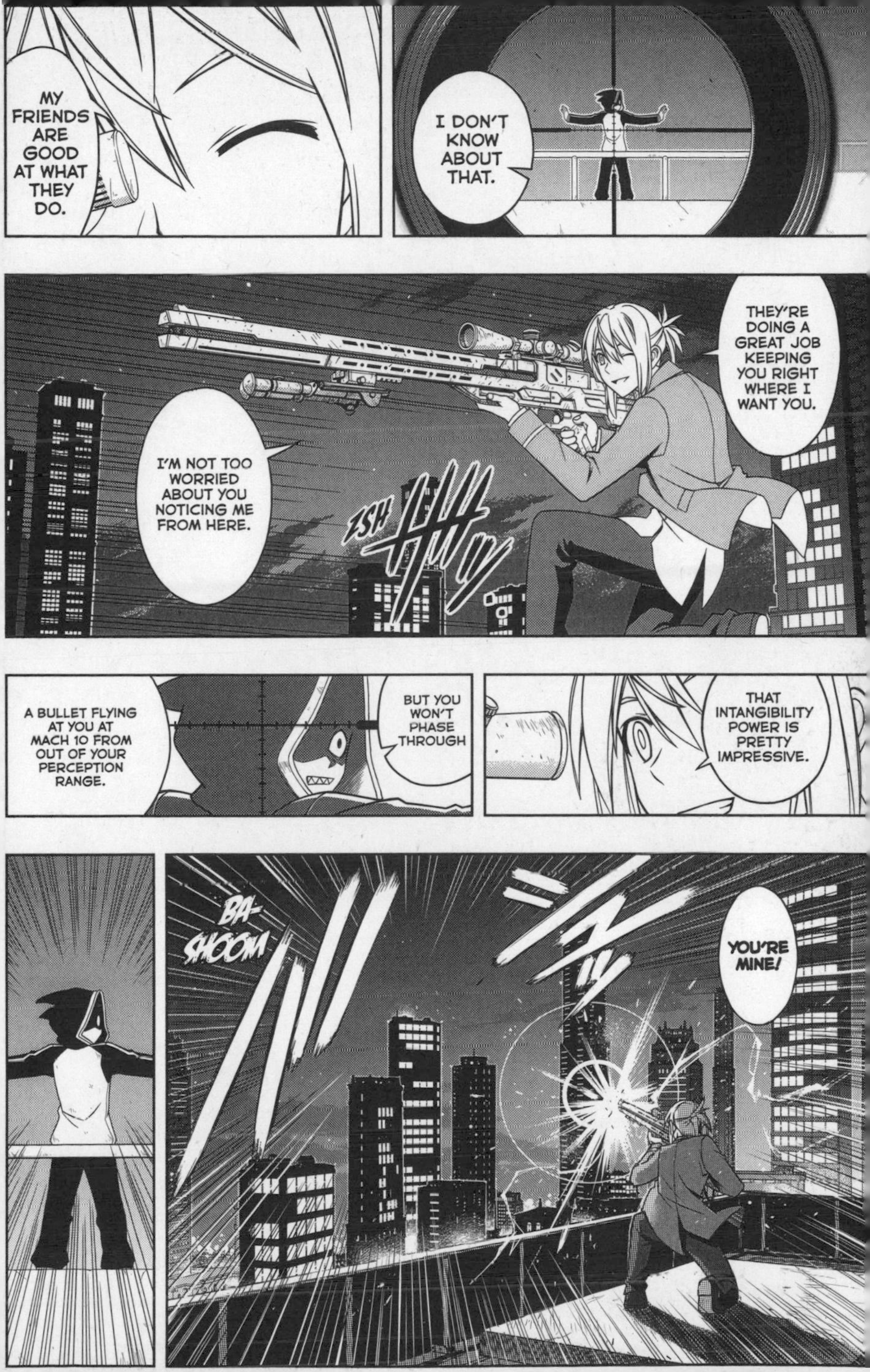

I DON'T KNOW ABOUT THAT.
MY FRIENDS ARE GOOD AT WHAT THEY DO.
THEY'RE DOING A GREAT JOB KEEPING YOU RIGHT WHERE I WANT YOU.
I'M NOT TOO WORRIED ABOUT YOU NOTICING ME FROM HERE.
ZSH
THAT INTANGIBILITY POWER IS PRETTY IMPRESSIVE.
BUT YOU WON'T PHASE THROUGH
A BULLET FLYING AT YOU AT MACH 10 FROM OUT OF YOUR PERCEPTION RANGE.
YOU'RE MINE!
BA-SHOOM

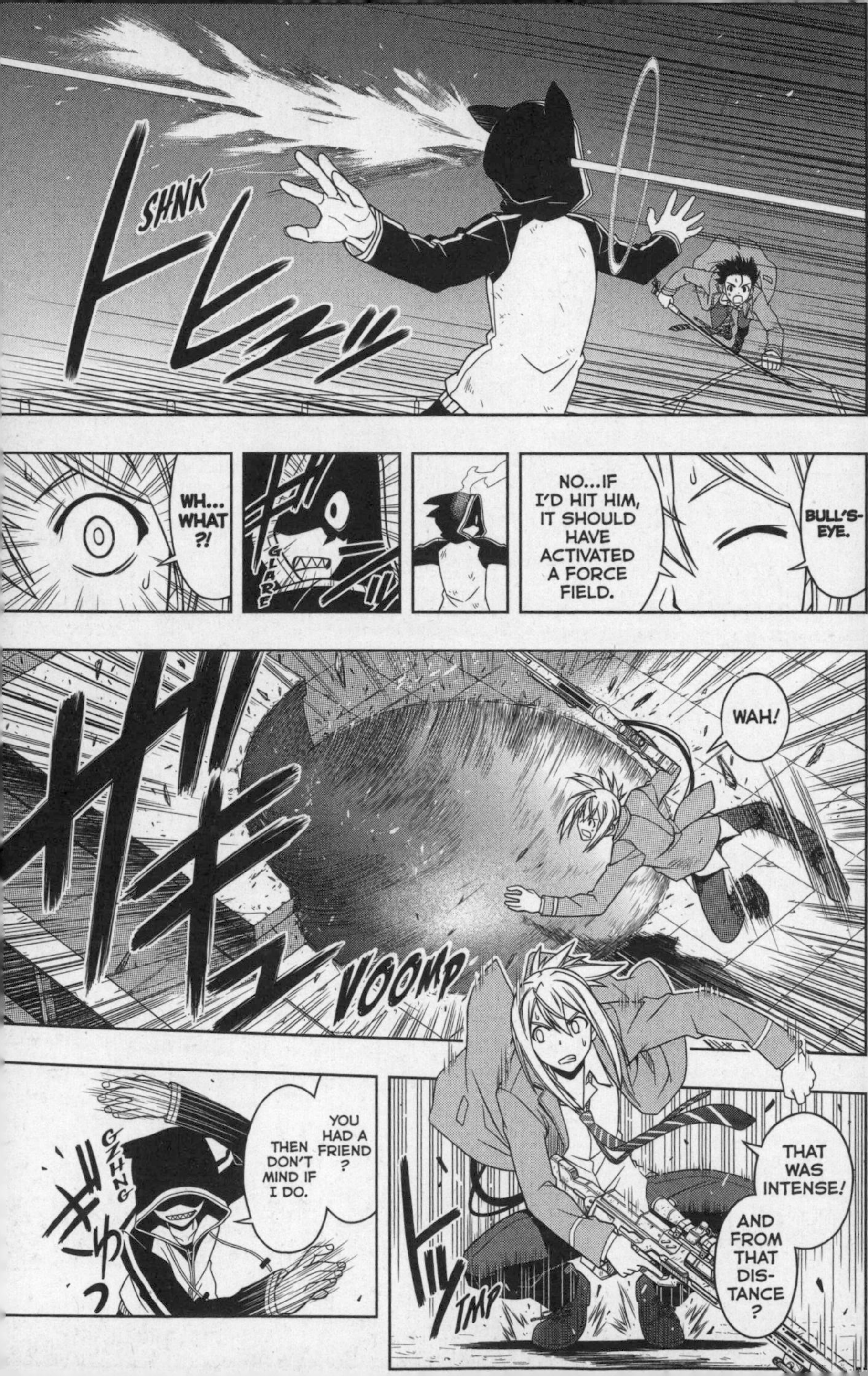
SHNK
BULL'S-EYE.
NO...IF I'D HIT HIM, IT SHOULD HAVE ACTIVATED A FORCE FIELD.
GLARE
WH... WHAT ?!
WAH!
VOOMP
THAT WAS INTENSE!
AND FROM THAT DIS-TANCE?
TMP
YOU HAD A FRIEND?
THEN DON'T MIND IF I DO.
GZHNG

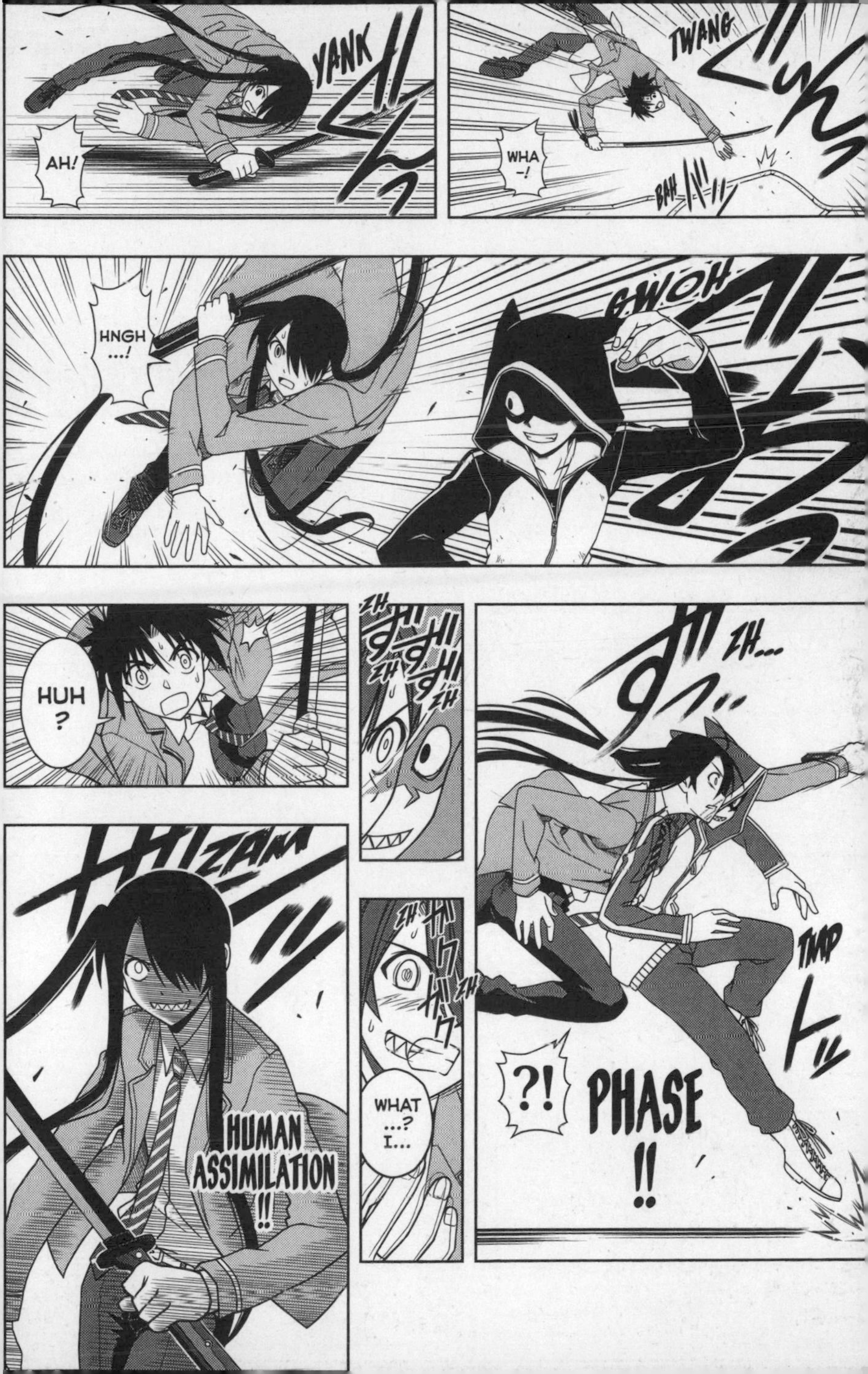
TWANG
WHA—!
BAH
YANK
AH!
GWOH
HNGH ...!
ZH...
?!
PHASE !!
TMP
ZH
ZH
ZH
ZH
ZH
WHAT ...? I...
HUH ?
ZAM
HUMAN ASSIMILATION !!

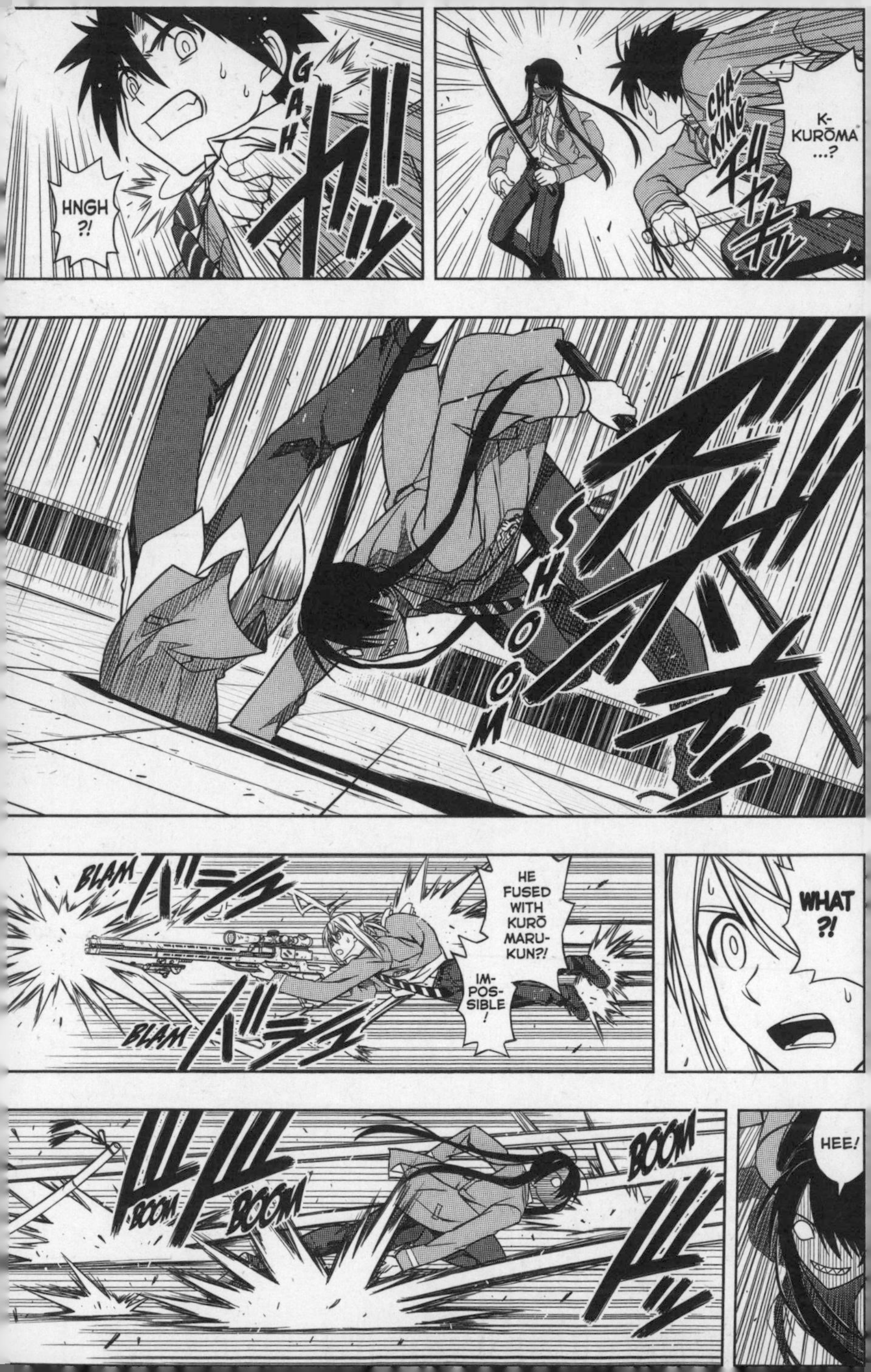
CHA-KING
K-KURŌMA...?
GAH
HNGH ?!
SHOOOM
WHAT ?!
HE FUSED WITH KURŌ MARU-KUN?!
IM-POS-SIBLE!
BLAM
BLAM
HEE!
BOOM
BOOM
BOOM

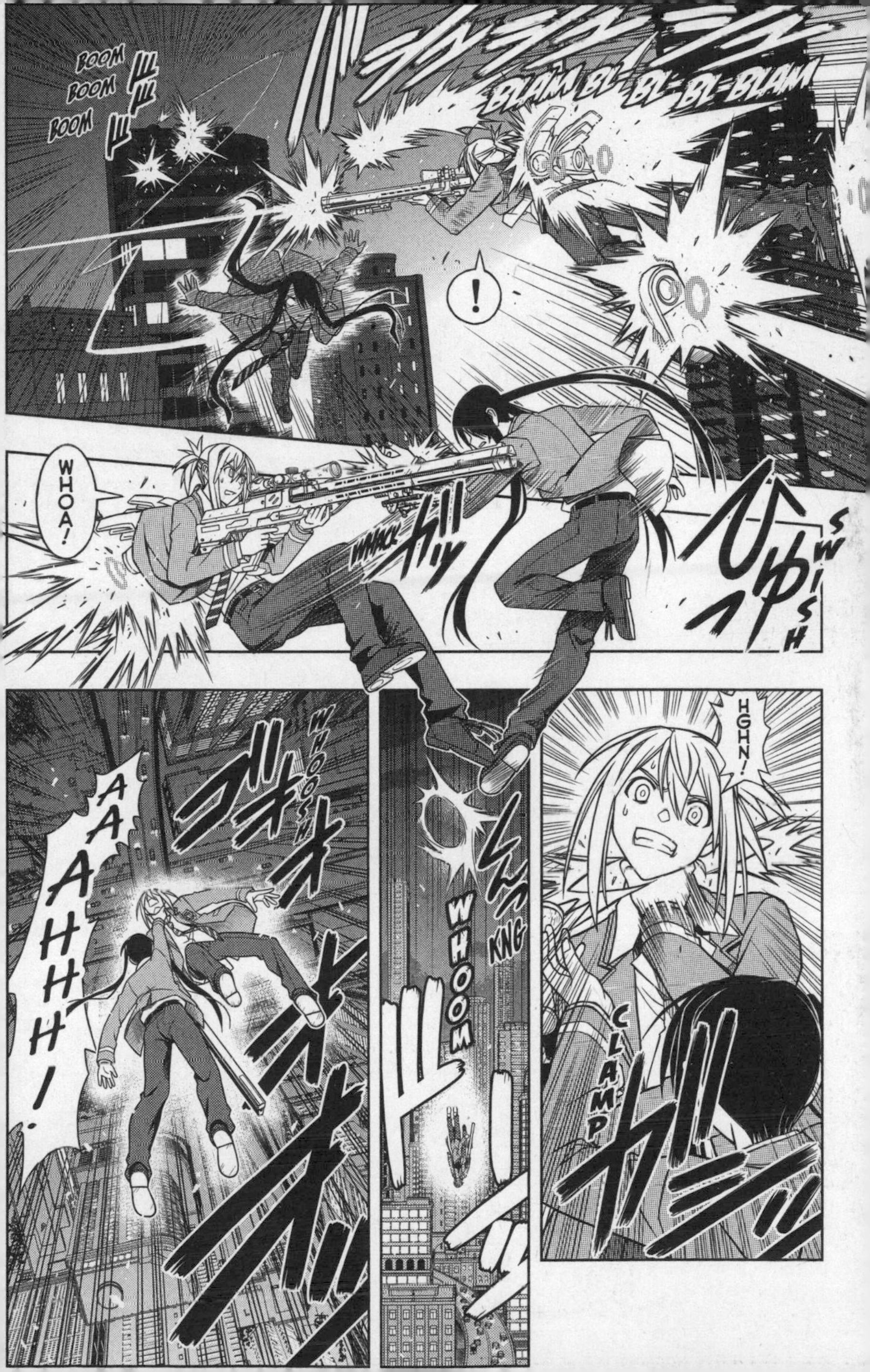
BLAM BL BL BL BLAM
BOOM BOOM BOOM
!
SWISH
WHACK
WHOA!
HGHN!
CLAMP
KNG
WHOOM
WHOOSH
AAAHHHHH!

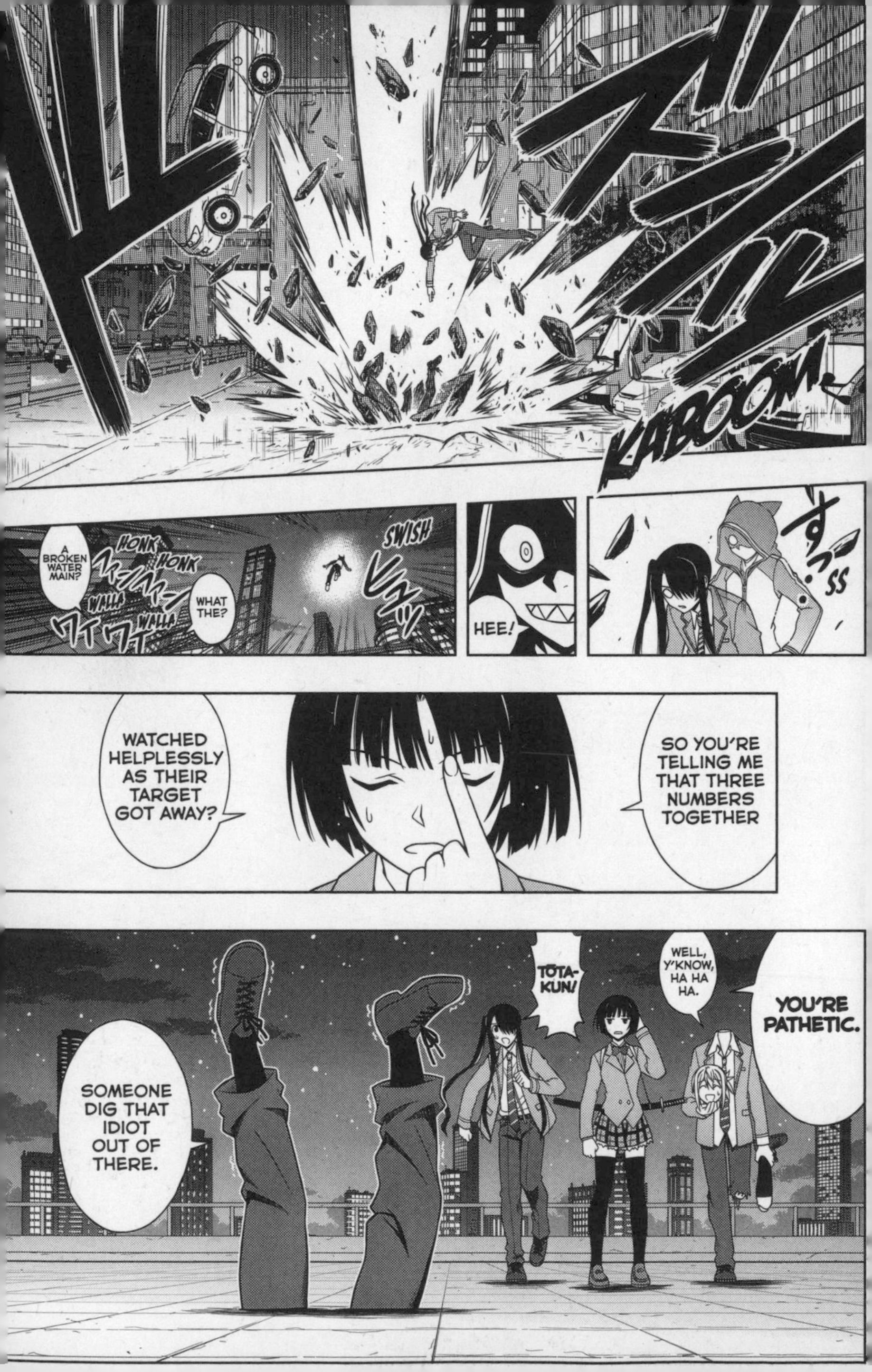
KABOOM!
すっ
SS
HEE!
SWISH
WHAT THE?
HONK HONK
WALLA WALLA
A BROKEN WATER MAIN?
SO YOU'RE TELLING ME THAT THREE NUMBERS TOGETHER
WATCHED HELPLESSLY AS THEIR TARGET GOT AWAY?
YOU'RE PATHETIC.
WELL, Y'KNOW, HA HA HA.
TŌTA-KUN!
SOMEONE DIG THAT IDIOT OUT OF THERE.

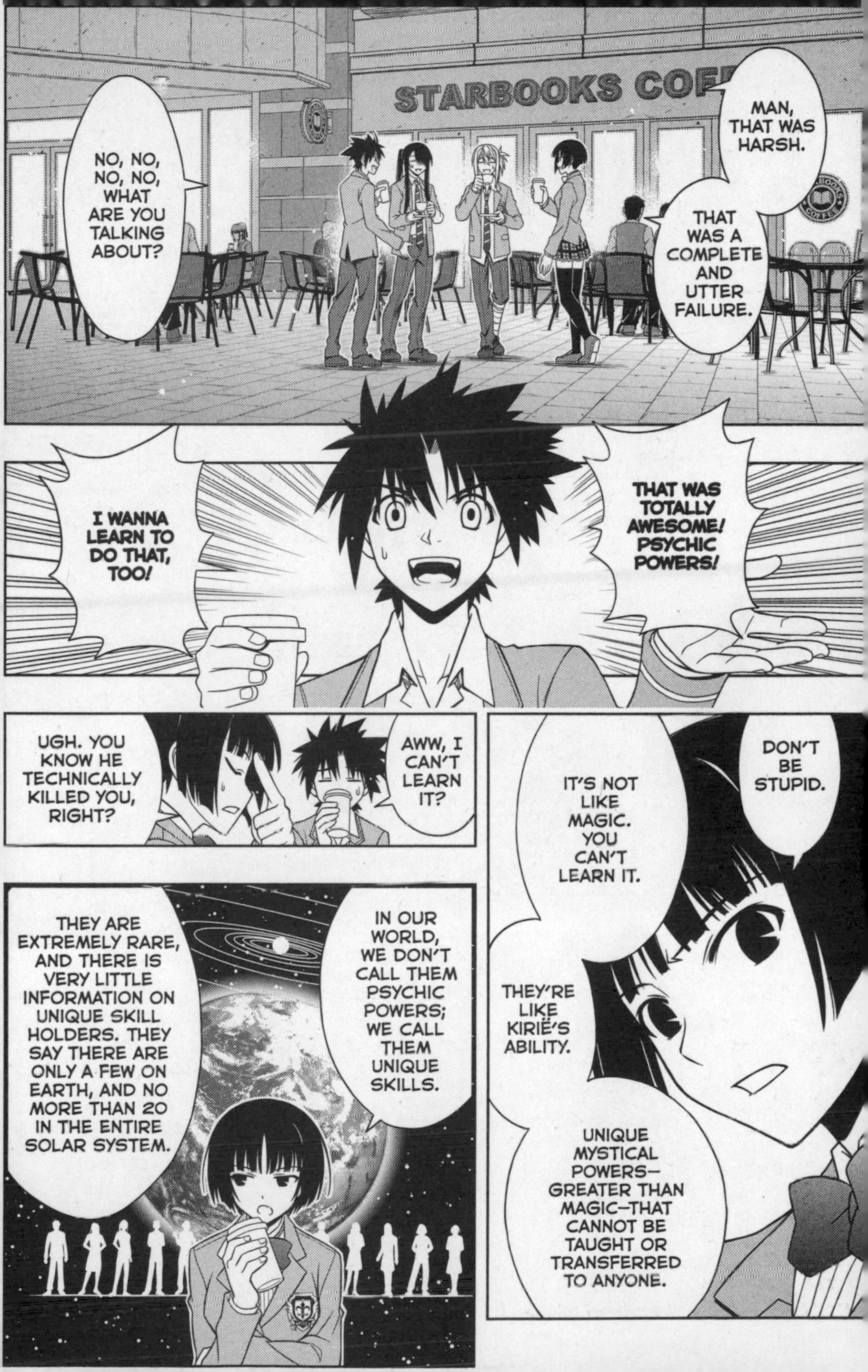
STARBOOKS COFF
MAN, THAT WAS HARSH.
THAT WAS A COMPLETE AND UTTER FAILURE.
NO, NO, NO, NO, WHAT ARE YOU TALKING ABOUT?
THAT WAS TOTALLY AWESOME! PSYCHIC POWERS!
I WANNA LEARN TO DO THAT, TOO!
DON'T BE STUPID.
IT'S NOT LIKE MAGIC. YOU CAN'T LEARN IT.
THEY'RE LIKE KIRIË'S ABILITY.
UNIQUE MYSTICAL POWERS—GREATER THAN MAGIC—THAT CANNOT BE TAUGHT OR TRANSFERRED TO ANYONE.
AWW, I CAN'T LEARN IT?
UGH. YOU KNOW HE TECHNICALLY KILLED YOU, RIGHT?
IN OUR WORLD, WE DON'T CALL THEM PSYCHIC POWERS; WE CALL THEM UNIQUE SKILLS.
THEY ARE EXTREMELY RARE, AND THERE IS VERY LITTLE INFORMATION ON UNIQUE SKILL HOLDERS. THEY SAY THERE ARE ONLY A FEW ON EARTH, AND NO MORE THAN 20 IN THE ENTIRE SOLAR SYSTEM.

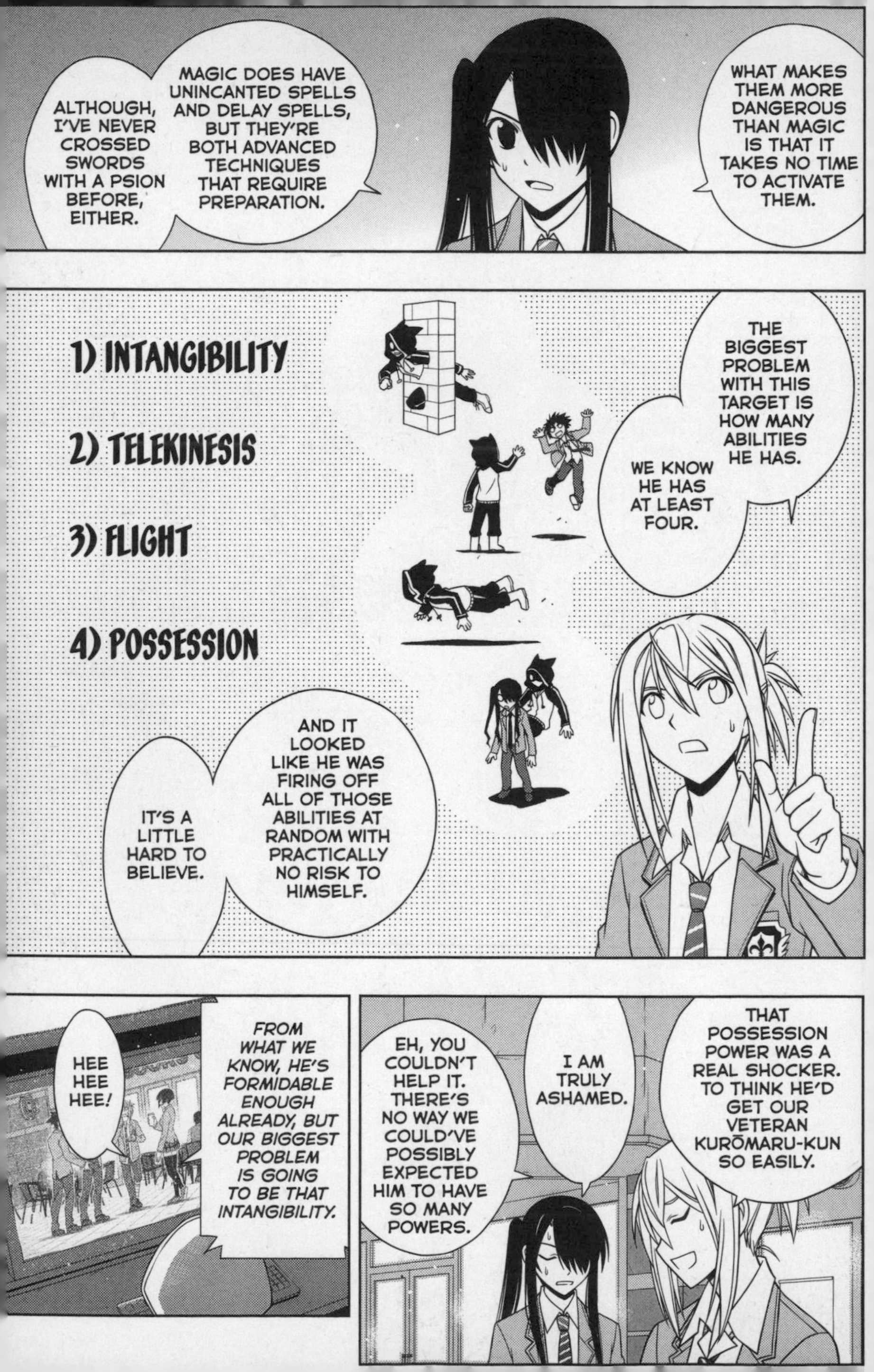
WHAT MAKES THEM MORE DANGEROUS THAN MAGIC IS THAT IT TAKES NO TIME TO ACTIVATE THEM.
MAGIC DOES HAVE UNINCANTED SPELLS AND DELAY SPELLS, BUT THEY'RE BOTH ADVANCED TECHNIQUES THAT REQUIRE PREPARATION.
ALTHOUGH, I'VE NEVER CROSSED SWORDS WITH A PSION BEFORE, EITHER.
THE BIGGEST PROBLEM WITH THIS TARGET IS HOW MANY ABILITIES HE HAS.
WE KNOW HE HAS AT LEAST FOUR.
1) INTANGIBILITY
2) TELEKINESIS
3) FLIGHT
4) POSSESSION
AND IT LOOKED LIKE HE WAS FIRING OFF ALL OF THOSE ABILITIES AT RANDOM WITH PRACTICALLY NO RISK TO HIMSELF.
IT'S A LITTLE HARD TO BELIEVE.
THAT POSSESSION POWER WAS A REAL SHOCKER. TO THINK HE'D GET OUR VETERAN KURŌMARU-KUN SO EASILY.
I AM TRULY ASHAMED.
EH, YOU COULDN'T HELP IT. THERE'S NO WAY WE COULD'VE POSSIBLY EXPECTED HIM TO HAVE SO MANY POWERS.
FROM WHAT WE KNOW, HE'S FORMIDABLE ENOUGH ALREADY, BUT OUR BIGGEST PROBLEM IS GOING TO BE THAT INTANGIBILITY.
HEE HEE HEE!

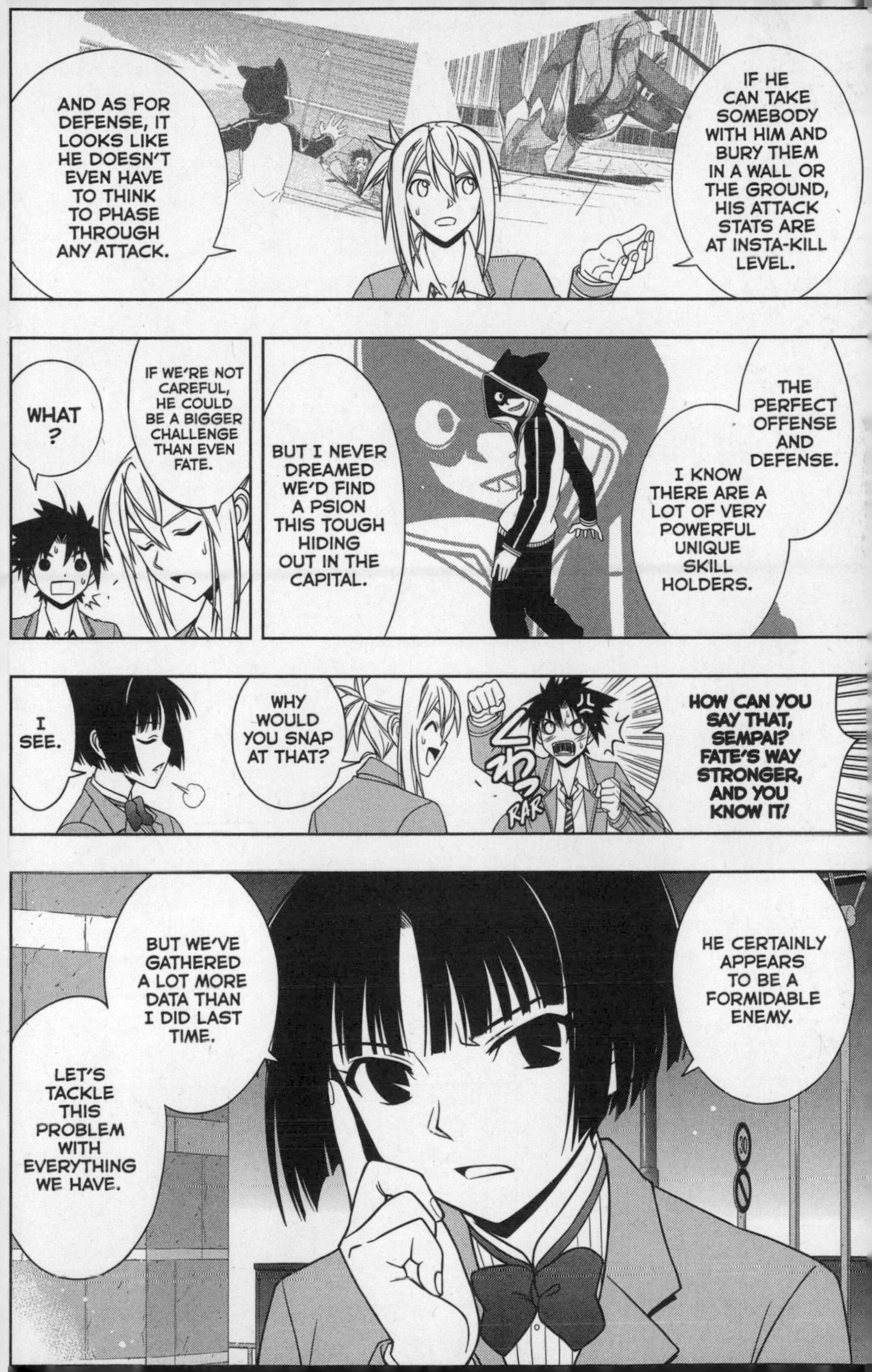
IF HE CAN TAKE SOMEBODY WITH HIM AND BURY THEM IN A WALL OR THE GROUND, HIS ATTACK STATS ARE AT INSTA-KILL LEVEL.
AND AS FOR DEFENSE, IT LOOKS LIKE HE DOESN'T EVEN HAVE TO THINK TO PHASE THROUGH ANY ATTACK.
THE PERFECT OFFENSE AND DEFENSE.
I KNOW THERE ARE A LOT OF VERY POWERFUL UNIQUE SKILL HOLDERS.
BUT I NEVER DREAMED WE'D FIND A PSION THIS TOUGH HIDING OUT IN THE CAPITAL.
IF WE'RE NOT CAREFUL, HE COULD BE A BIGGER CHALLENGE THAN EVEN FATE.
WHAT?
HOW CAN YOU SAY THAT, SEMPAI? FATE'S WAY STRONGER, AND YOU KNOW IT!
RAR
WHY WOULD YOU SNAP AT THAT?
I SEE.
HE CERTAINLY APPEARS TO BE A FORMIDABLE ENEMY.
BUT WE'VE GATHERED A LOT MORE DATA THAN I DID LAST TIME.
LET'S TACKLE THIS PROBLEM WITH EVERYTHING WE HAVE.
30

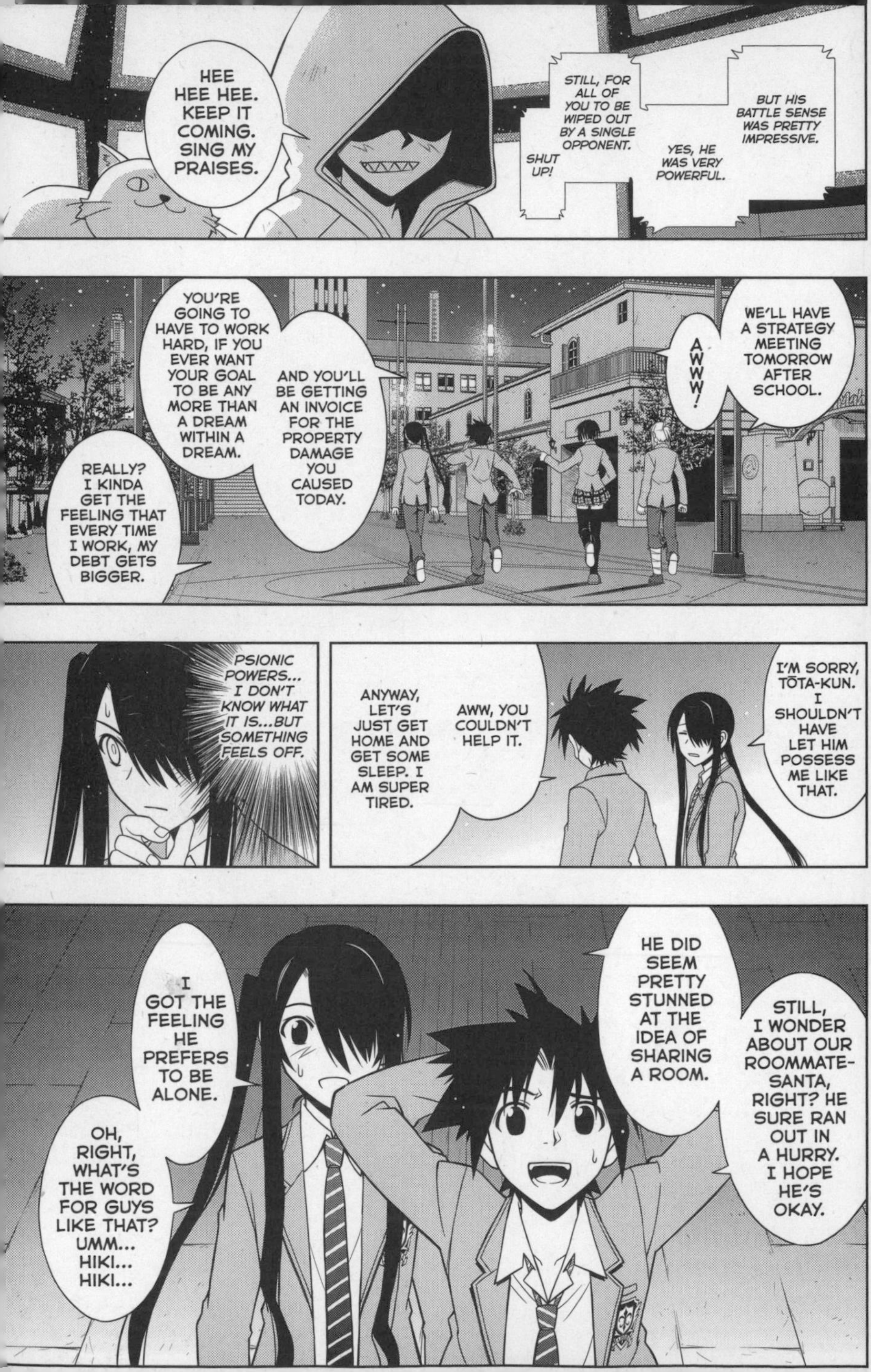
BUT HIS BATTLE SENSE WAS PRETTY IMPRESSIVE.
YES, HE WAS VERY POWERFUL.
STILL, FOR ALL OF YOU TO BE WIPED OUT BY A SINGLE OPPONENT.
SHUT UP!
HEE HEE HEE. KEEP IT COMING. SING MY PRAISES.
WE'LL HAVE A STRATEGY MEETING TOMORROW AFTER SCHOOL.
AWWW!
AND YOU'LL BE GETTING AN INVOICE FOR THE PROPERTY DAMAGE YOU CAUSED TODAY.
YOU'RE GOING TO HAVE TO WORK HARD, IF YOU EVER WANT YOUR GOAL TO BE ANY MORE THAN A DREAM WITHIN A DREAM.
REALLY? I KINDA GET THE FEELING THAT EVERY TIME I WORK, MY DEBT GETS BIGGER.
I'M SORRY, TŌTA-KUN. I SHOULDN'T HAVE LET HIM POSSESS ME LIKE THAT.
AWW, YOU COULDN'T HELP IT.
ANYWAY, LET'S JUST GET HOME AND GET SOME SLEEP. I AM SUPER TIRED.
PSIONIC POWERS... I DON'T KNOW WHAT IT IS...BUT SOMETHING FEELS OFF.
STILL, I WONDER ABOUT OUR ROOMMATE-SANTA, RIGHT? HE SURE RAN OUT IN A HURRY. I HOPE HE'S OKAY.
HE DID SEEM PRETTY STUNNED AT THE IDEA OF SHARING A ROOM.
I GOT THE FEELING HE PREFERS TO BE ALONE.
OH, RIGHT, WHAT'S THE WORD FOR GUYS LIKE THAT? UMM... HIKI... HIKI...

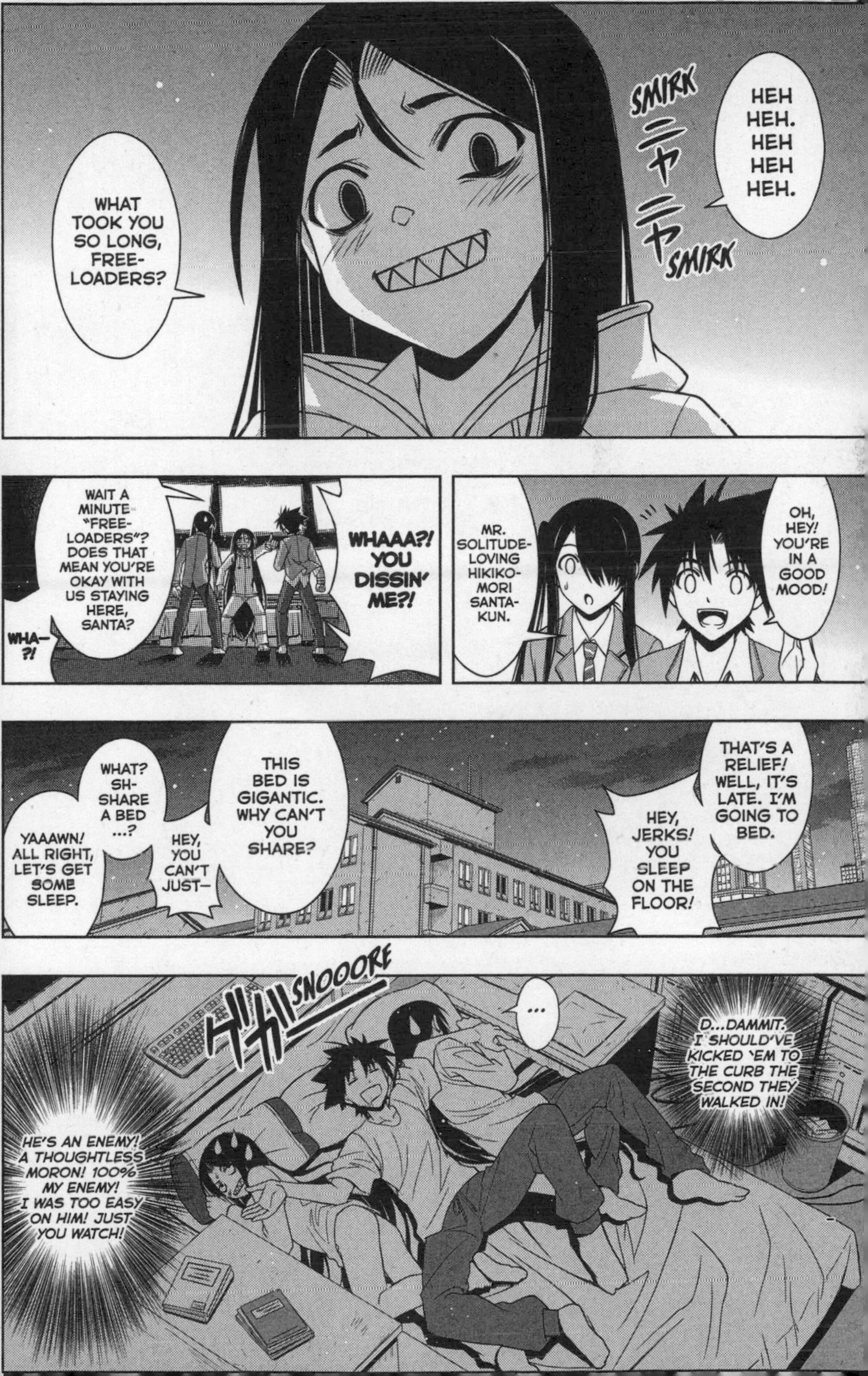
HEH HEH. HEH HEH HEH.
SMIRK
ニヤニヤ
SMIRK
WHAT TOOK YOU SO LONG, FREE-LOADERS?
OH, HEY! YOU'RE IN A GOOD MOOD!
MR. SOLITUDE-LOVING HIKIKOMORI SANTA-KUN.
WHAAA?! YOU DISSIN' ME?!
WAIT A MINUTE— "FREE-LOADERS"? DOES THAT MEAN YOU'RE OKAY WITH US STAYING HERE, SANTA?
WHA—?!
THAT'S A RELIEF! WELL, IT'S LATE. I'M GOING TO BED.
HEY, JERKS! YOU SLEEP ON THE FLOOR!
THIS BED IS GIGANTIC. WHY CAN'T YOU SHARE?
HEY, YOU CAN'T JUST—
WHAT? SH-SHARE A BED ...?
YAAAWN! ALL RIGHT, LET'S GET SOME SLEEP.
D...DAMMIT. I SHOULD'VE KICKED 'EM TO THE CURB THE SECOND THEY WALKED IN!
...
SNOOORE
HE'S AN ENEMY! A THOUGHTLESS MORON! 100% MY ENEMY! I WAS TOO EASY ON HIM! JUST YOU WATCH!

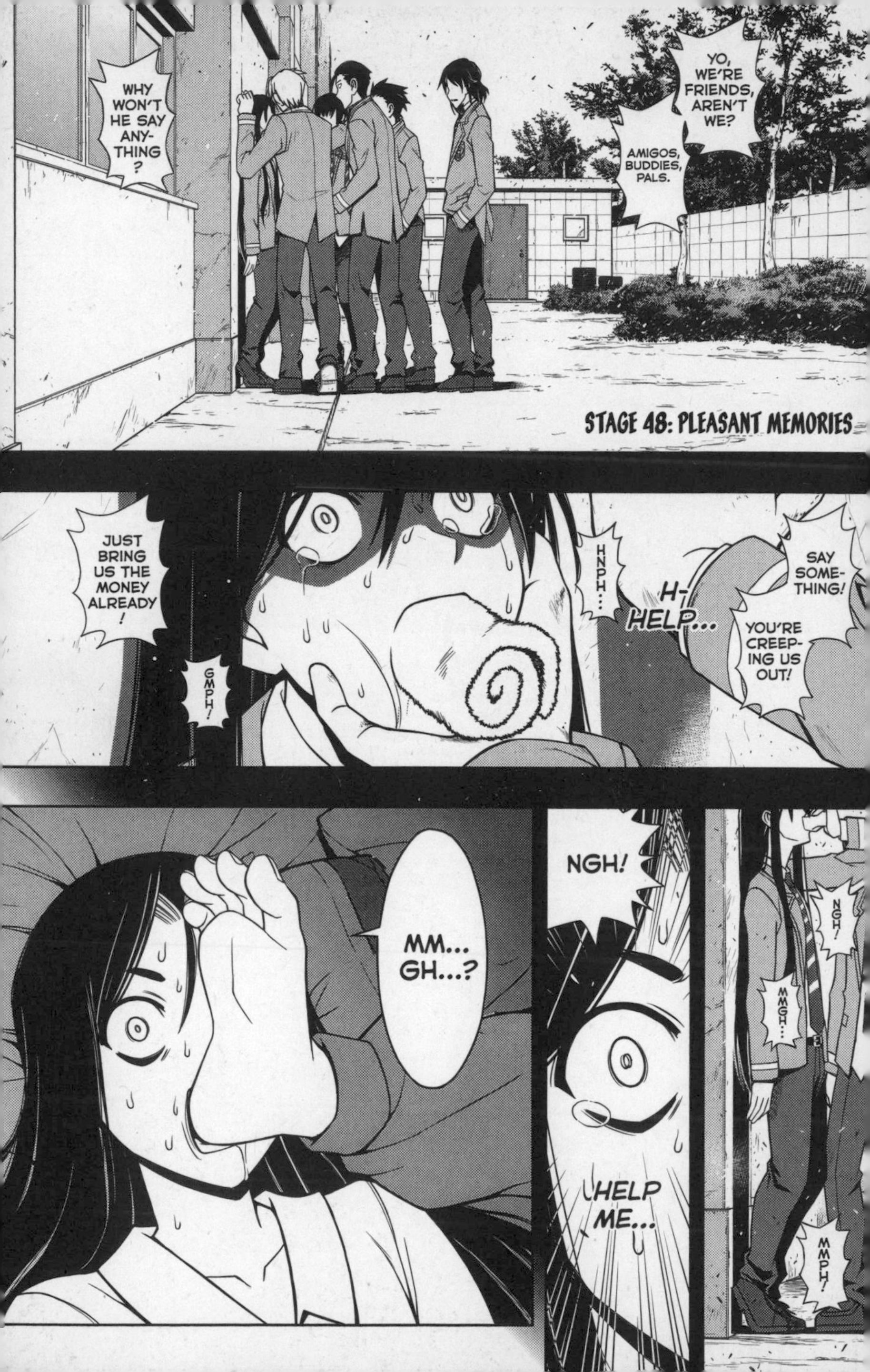
YO, WE'RE FRIENDS, AREN'T WE?
AMIGOS, BUDDIES, PALS.
WHY WON'T HE SAY ANY-THING?
STAGE 48: PLEASANT MEMORIES
SAY SOME-THING!
YOU'RE CREEP-ING US OUT!
H-HELP...
HNPH...
JUST BRING US THE MONEY ALREADY!
GMPH!
NGH!
MMGH...
MMPH!
NGH!
HELP ME...
MM... GH...?

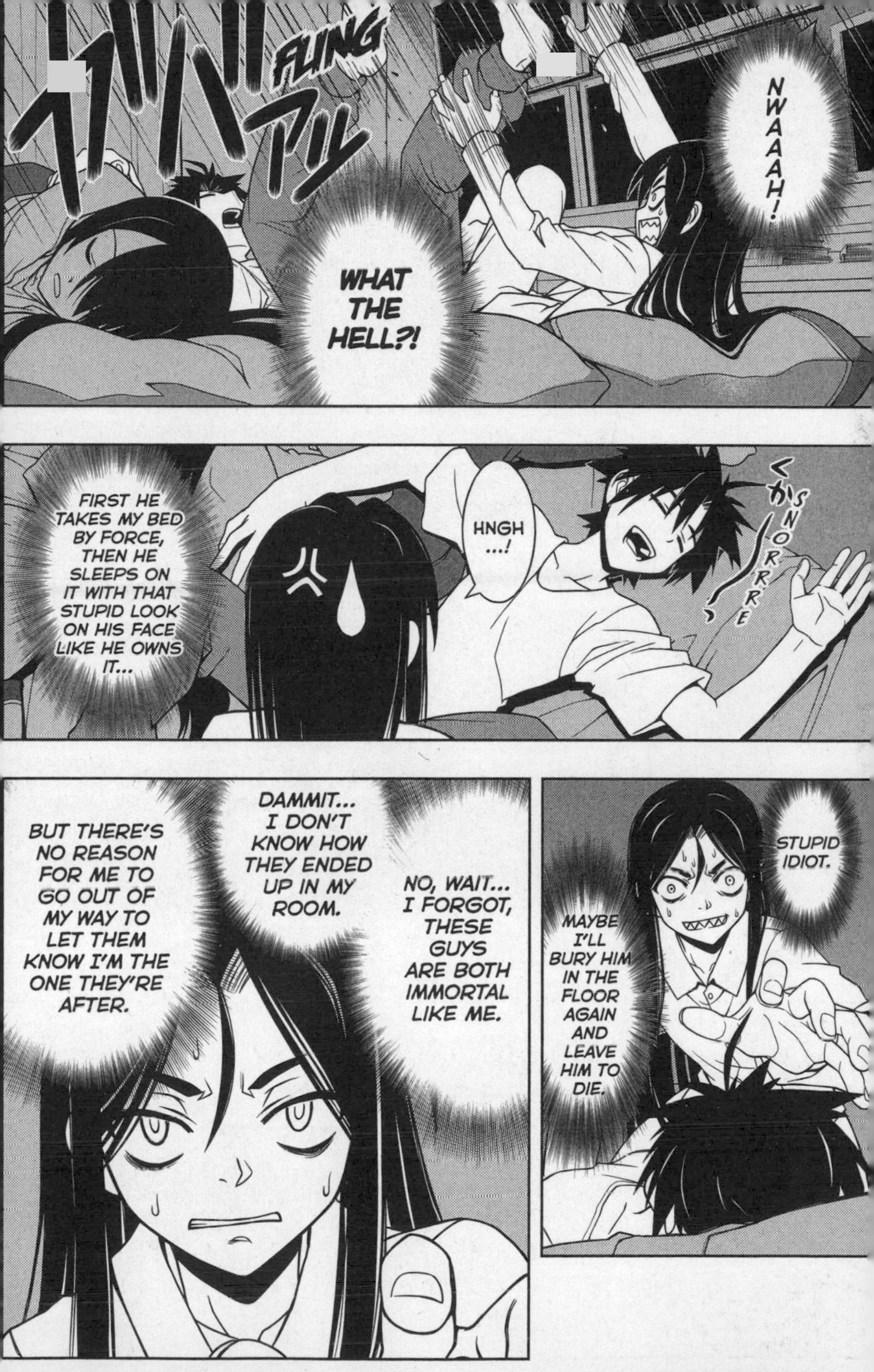
NWAAAH!
FLING
WHAT THE HELL?!
SNORRRE
HNGH ...!
FIRST HE TAKES MY BED BY FORCE, THEN HE SLEEPS ON IT WITH THAT STUPID LOOK ON HIS FACE LIKE HE OWNS IT...
STUPID IDIOT.
MAYBE I'LL BURY HIM IN THE FLOOR AGAIN AND LEAVE HIM TO DIE.
DAMMIT... I DON'T KNOW HOW THEY ENDED UP IN MY ROOM.
NO, WAIT... I FORGOT, THESE GUYS ARE BOTH IMMORTAL LIKE ME.
BUT THERE'S NO REASON FOR ME TO GO OUT OF MY WAY TO LET THEM KNOW I'M THE ONE THEY'RE AFTER.

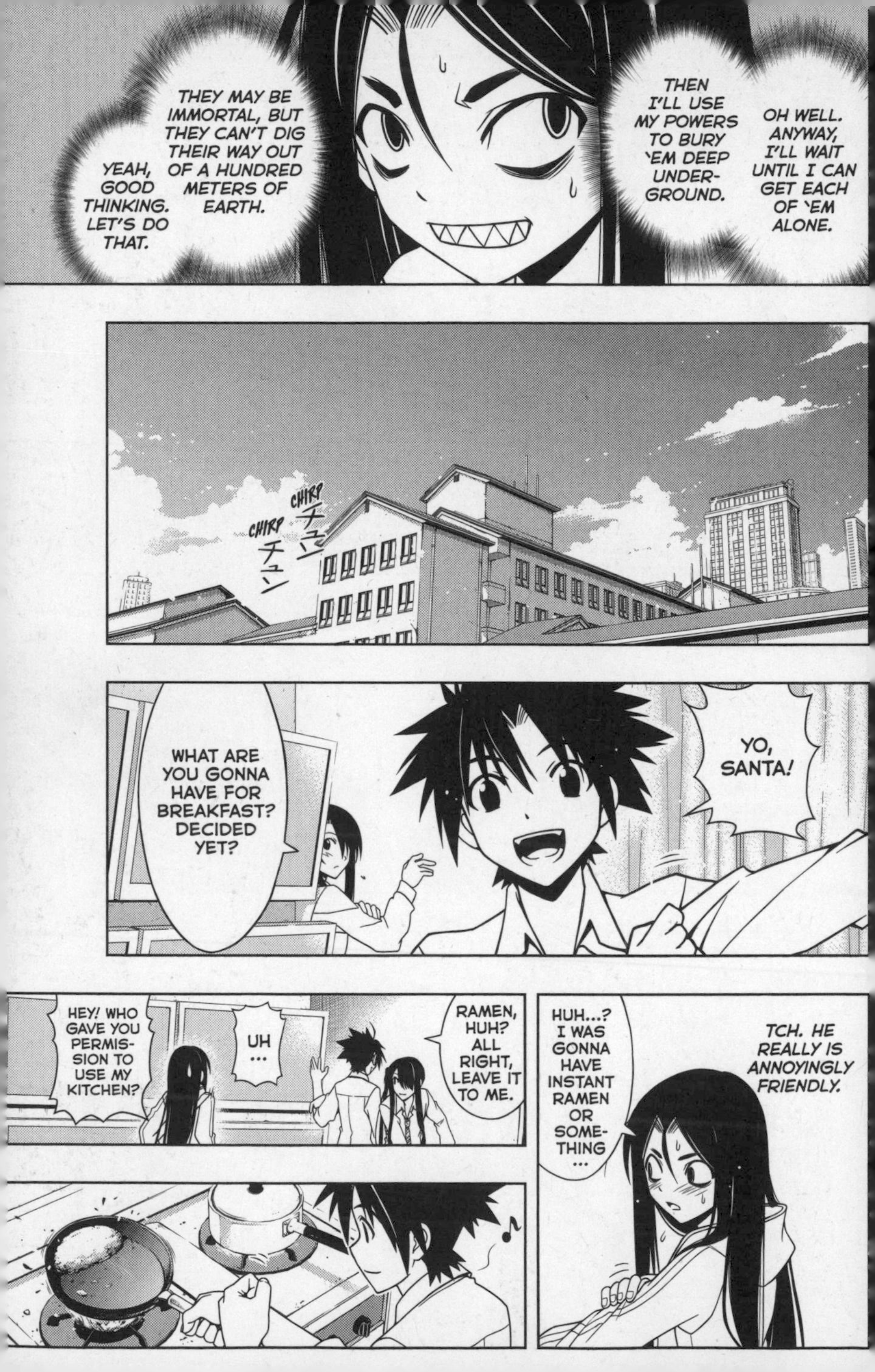
OH WELL. ANYWAY, I'LL WAIT UNTIL I CAN GET EACH OF 'EM ALONE.
THEN I'LL USE MY POWERS TO BURY 'EM DEEP UNDER-GROUND.
THEY MAY BE IMMORTAL, BUT THEY CAN'T DIG THEIR WAY OUT OF A HUNDRED METERS OF EARTH.
YEAH, GOOD THINKING. LET'S DO THAT.
CHIRP チュン
CHIRP チュン
YO, SANTA!
WHAT ARE YOU GONNA HAVE FOR BREAKFAST? DECIDED YET?
TCH. HE REALLY IS ANNOYINGLY FRIENDLY.
HUH...? I WAS GONNA HAVE INSTANT RAMEN OR SOME-THING...
RAMEN, HUH? ALL RIGHT, LEAVE IT TO ME.
UH...
HEY! WHO GAVE YOU PERMIS-SION TO USE MY KITCHEN?

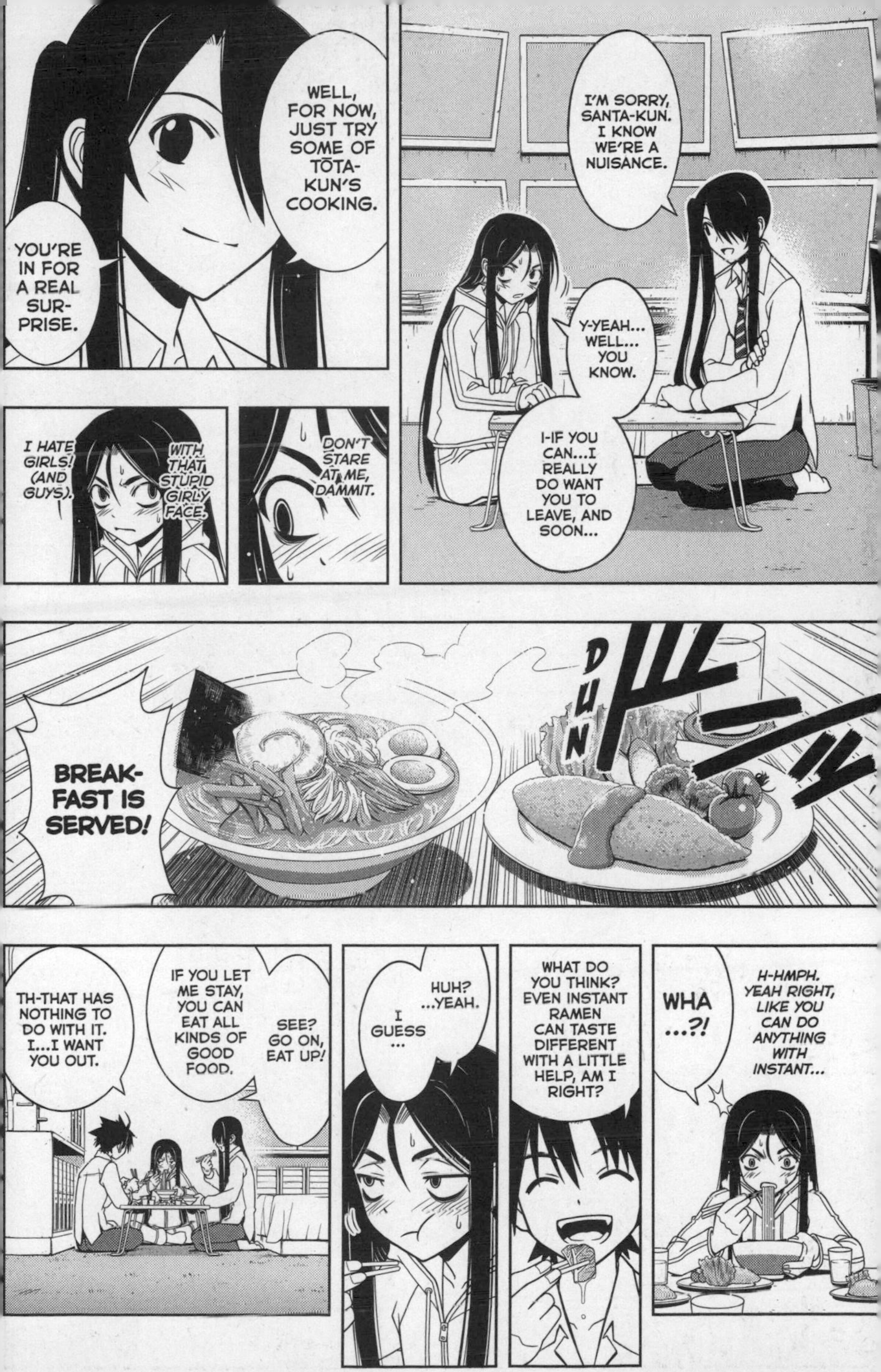
I'M SORRY, SANTA-KUN. I KNOW WE'RE A NUISANCE.
Y-YEAH... WELL... YOU KNOW.
I-IF YOU CAN...I REALLY DO WANT YOU TO LEAVE, AND SOON...
WELL, FOR NOW, JUST TRY SOME OF TŌTA-KUN'S COOKING.
YOU'RE IN FOR A REAL SURPRISE.
DON'T STARE AT ME, DAMMIT.
WITH THAT STUPID GIRLY FACE.
I HATE GIRLS! (AND GUYS).
DUN
BREAKFAST IS SERVED!
H-HMPH. YEAH RIGHT, LIKE YOU CAN DO ANYTHING WITH INSTANT...
WHA ...?!
WHAT DO YOU THINK? EVEN INSTANT RAMEN CAN TASTE DIFFERENT WITH A LITTLE HELP, AM I RIGHT?
HUH? ...YEAH.
I GUESS ...
SEE? GO ON, EAT UP!
IF YOU LET ME STAY, YOU CAN EAT ALL KINDS OF GOOD FOOD.
TH-THAT HAS NOTHING TO DO WITH IT. I...I WANT YOU OUT.

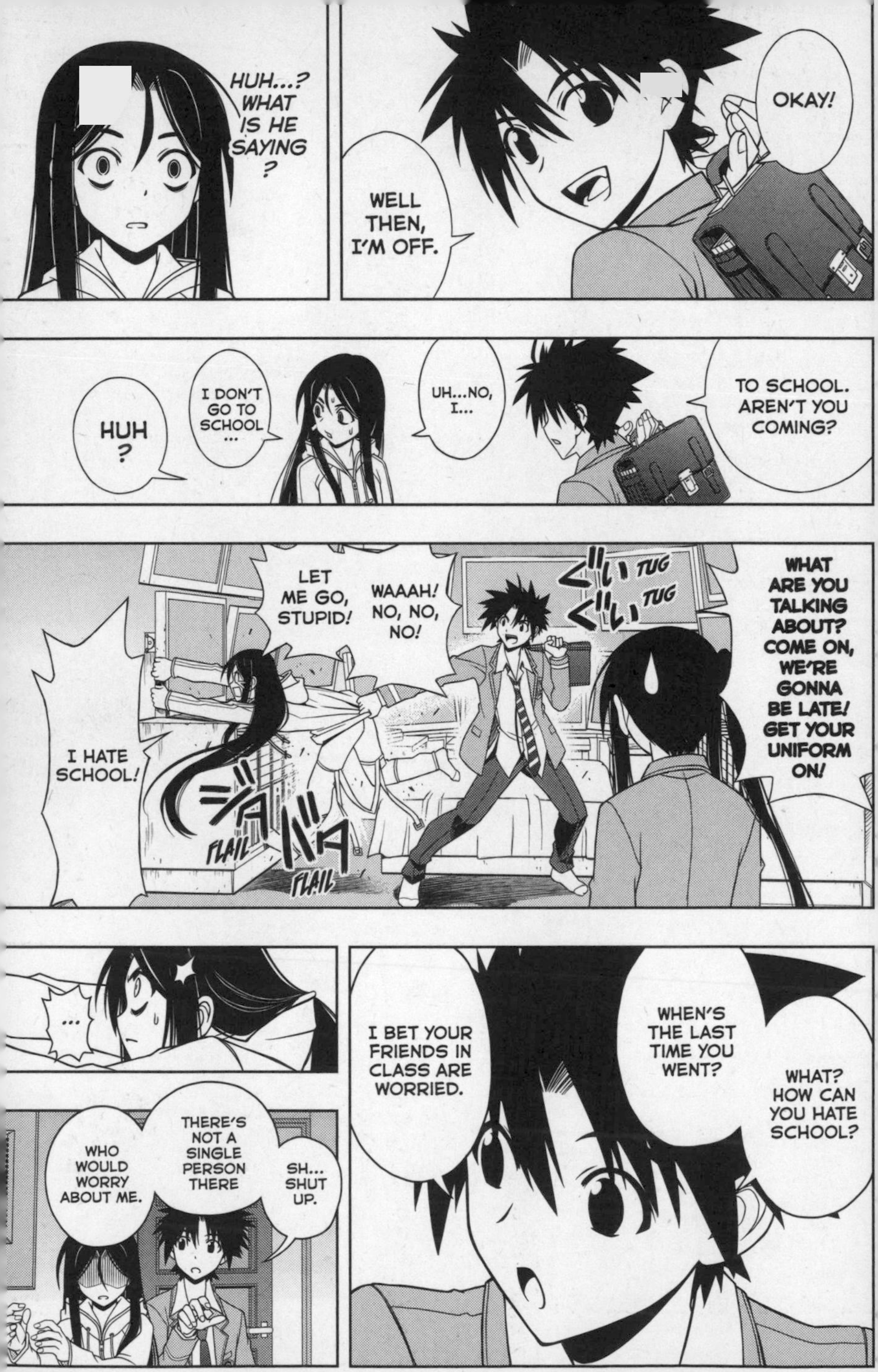
OKAY!
WELL THEN, I'M OFF.
HUH...? WHAT IS HE SAYING?
TO SCHOOL. AREN'T YOU COMING?
UH...NO, I...
I DON'T GO TO SCHOOL...
HUH?
WHAT ARE YOU TALKING ABOUT? COME ON, WE'RE GONNA BE LATE! GET YOUR UNIFORM ON!
TUG
TUG
WAAAH! NO, NO, NO!
LET ME GO, STUPID!
I HATE SCHOOL!
FLAIL
FLAIL
WHAT? HOW CAN YOU HATE SCHOOL?
WHEN'S THE LAST TIME YOU WENT?
I BET YOUR FRIENDS IN CLASS ARE WORRIED.
...
SH... SHUT UP.
THERE'S NOT A SINGLE PERSON THERE
WHO WOULD WORRY ABOUT ME.

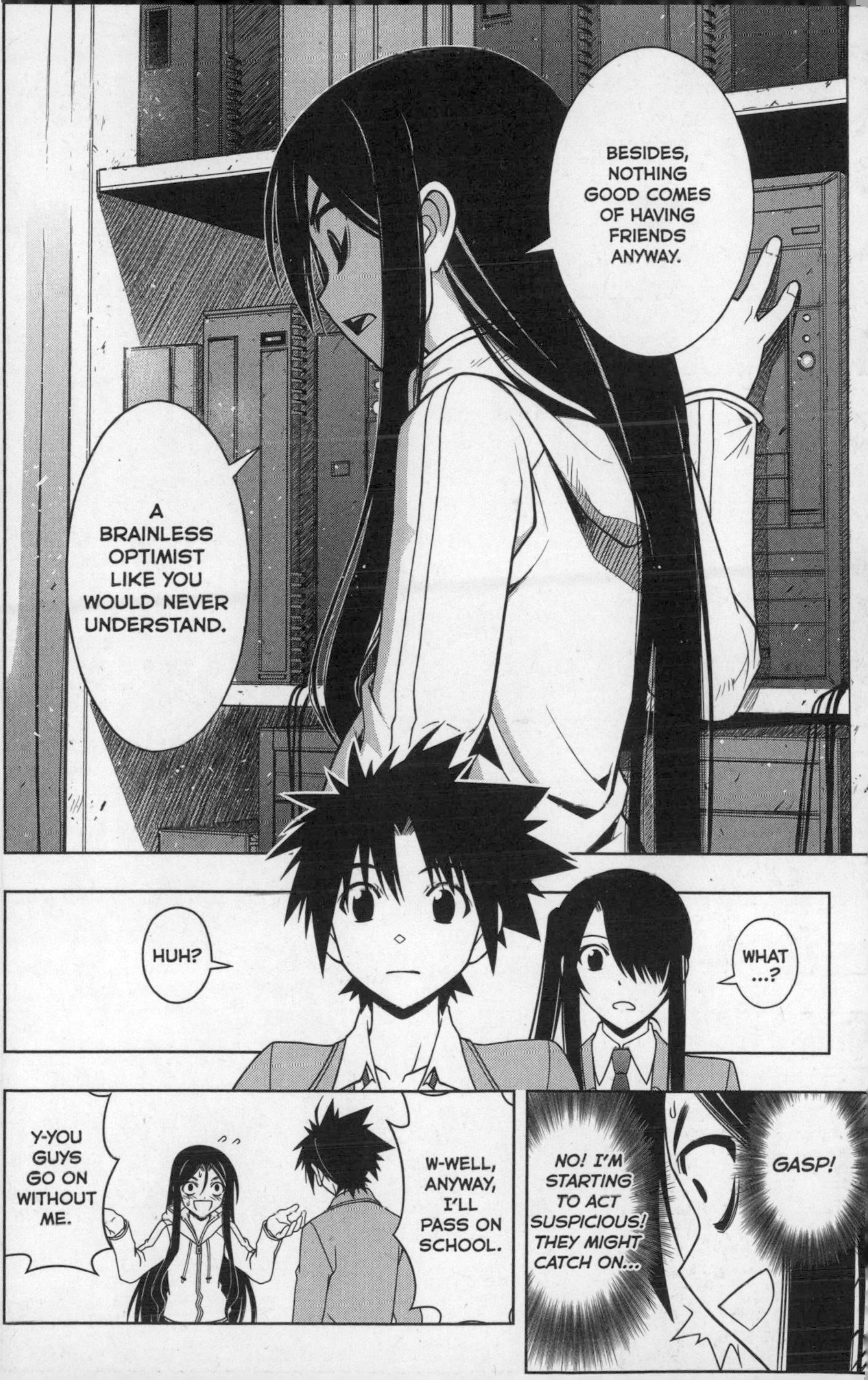
BESIDES, NOTHING GOOD COMES OF HAVING FRIENDS ANYWAY.
A BRAINLESS OPTIMIST LIKE YOU WOULD NEVER UNDERSTAND.
WHAT ...?
HUH?
GASP!
NO! I'M STARTING TO ACT SUSPICIOUS! THEY MIGHT CATCH ON...
W-WELL, ANYWAY, I'LL PASS ON SCHOOL.
Y-YOU GUYS GO ON WITHOUT ME.

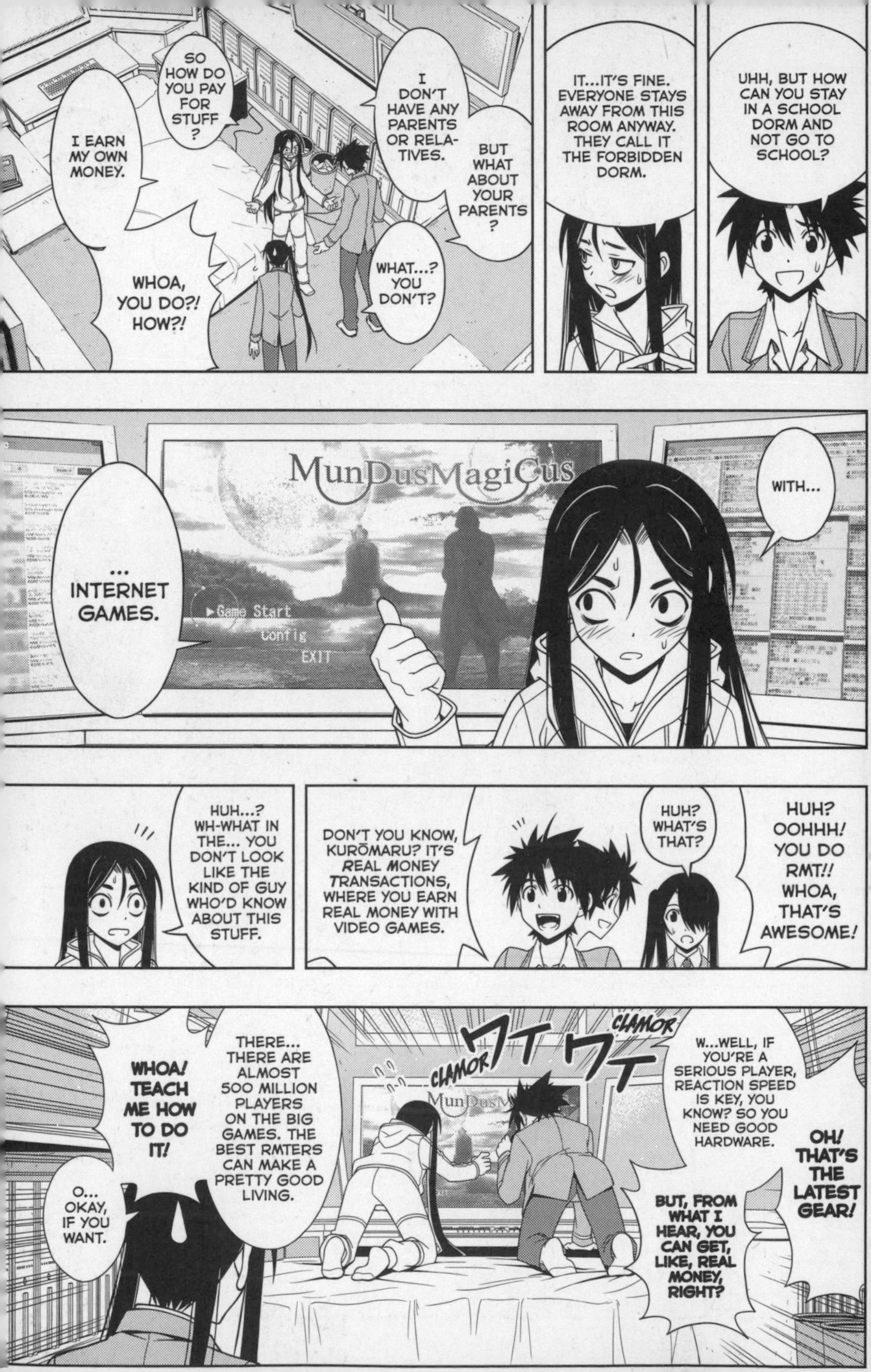
UHH, BUT HOW CAN YOU STAY IN A SCHOOL DORM AND NOT GO TO SCHOOL?
IT...IT'S FINE. EVERYONE STAYS AWAY FROM THIS ROOM ANYWAY. THEY CALL IT THE FORBIDDEN DORM.
BUT WHAT ABOUT YOUR PARENTS?
I DON'T HAVE ANY PARENTS OR RELATIVES.
WHAT...? YOU DON'T?
SO HOW DO YOU PAY FOR STUFF?
I EARN MY OWN MONEY.
WHOA, YOU DO?! HOW?!
WITH...
MunDusMagiCus
▶Game Start
Config
EXIT
... INTERNET GAMES.
HUH? OOHHH! YOU DO RMT!! WHOA, THAT'S AWESOME!
HUH? WHAT'S THAT?
DON'T YOU KNOW, KURŌMARU? IT'S REAL MONEY TRANSACTIONS, WHERE YOU EARN REAL MONEY WITH VIDEO GAMES.
HUH...? WH-WHAT IN THE... YOU DON'T LOOK LIKE THE KIND OF GUY WHO'D KNOW ABOUT THIS STUFF.
OH! THAT'S THE LATEST GEAR!
W...WELL, IF YOU'RE A SERIOUS PLAYER, REACTION SPEED IS KEY, YOU KNOW? SO YOU NEED GOOD HARDWARE.
BUT, FROM WHAT I HEAR, YOU CAN GET, LIKE, REAL MONEY, RIGHT?
CLAMOR
CLAMOR
THERE... THERE ARE ALMOST 500 MILLION PLAYERS ON THE BIG GAMES. THE BEST RMTERS CAN MAKE A PRETTY GOOD LIVING.
WHOA! TEACH ME HOW TO DO IT!
O... OKAY, IF YOU WANT.

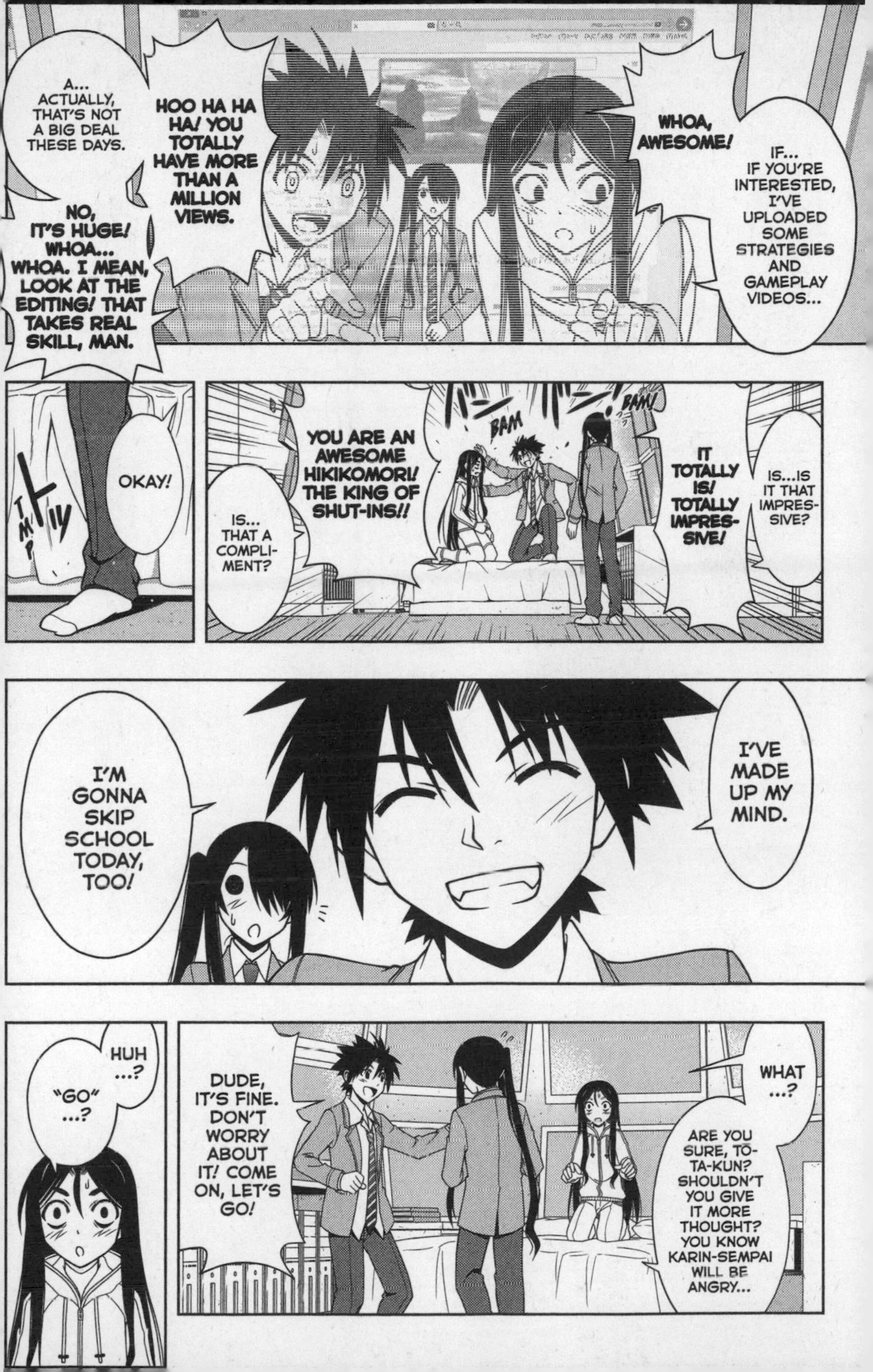
WHOA, AWESOME!
IF... IF YOU'RE INTERESTED, I'VE UPLOADED SOME STRATEGIES AND GAMEPLAY VIDEOS...
HOO HA HA HA! YOU TOTALLY HAVE MORE THAN A MILLION VIEWS.
A... ACTUALLY, THAT'S NOT A BIG DEAL THESE DAYS.
NO, IT'S HUGE! WHOA... WHOA. I MEAN, LOOK AT THE EDITING! THAT TAKES REAL SKILL, MAN.
IS...IS IT THAT IMPRESSIVE?
BAM!
IT TOTALLY IS! TOTALLY IMPRESSIVE!
BAM
YOU ARE AN AWESOME HIKIKOMORI! THE KING OF SHUT-INS!!
IS... THAT A COMPLIMENT?
OKAY!
TMP
I'VE MADE UP MY MIND.
I'M GONNA SKIP SCHOOL TODAY, TOO!
WHAT ...?
ARE YOU SURE, TO-TA-KUN? SHOULDN'T YOU GIVE IT MORE THOUGHT? YOU KNOW KARIN-SEMPAI WILL BE ANGRY...
DUDE, IT'S FINE. DON'T WORRY ABOUT IT! COME ON, LET'S GO!
HUH ...?
"GO" ...?

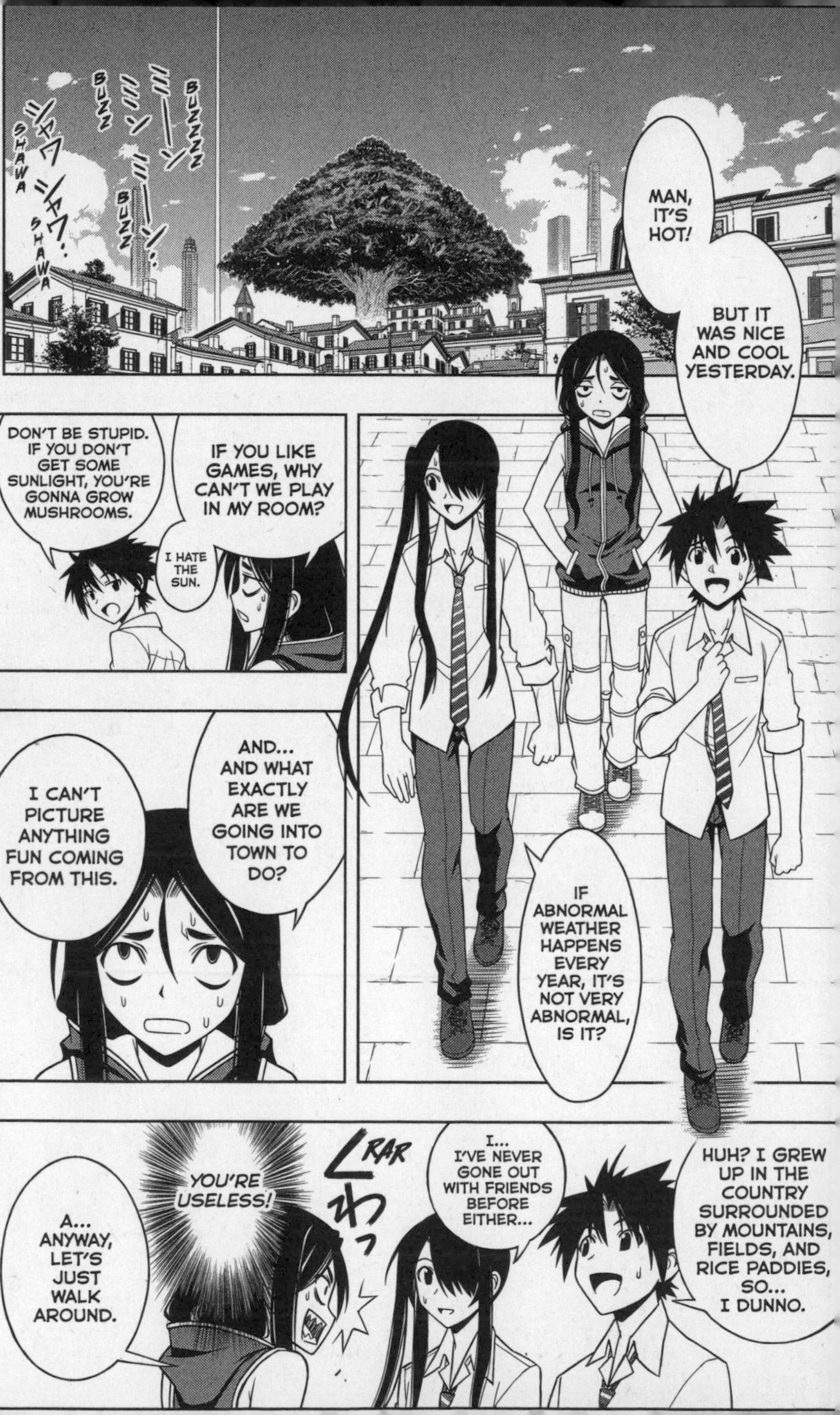
MAN, IT'S HOT!
BUT IT WAS NICE AND COOL YESTERDAY.
BUZZZZ
BUZZ
BUZZ
SHAWA
SHAWA
IF ABNORMAL WEATHER HAPPENS EVERY YEAR, IT'S NOT VERY ABNORMAL, IS IT?
IF YOU LIKE GAMES, WHY CAN'T WE PLAY IN MY ROOM?
I HATE THE SUN.
DON'T BE STUPID. IF YOU DON'T GET SOME SUNLIGHT, YOU'RE GONNA GROW MUSHROOMS.
AND... AND WHAT EXACTLY ARE WE GOING INTO TOWN TO DO?
I CAN'T PICTURE ANYTHING FUN COMING FROM THIS.
HUH? I GREW UP IN THE COUNTRY SURROUNDED BY MOUNTAINS, FIELDS, AND RICE PADDIES, SO... I DUNNO.
I... I'VE NEVER GONE OUT WITH FRIENDS BEFORE EITHER...
RAR
YOU'RE USELESS!
A... ANYWAY, LET'S JUST WALK AROUND.

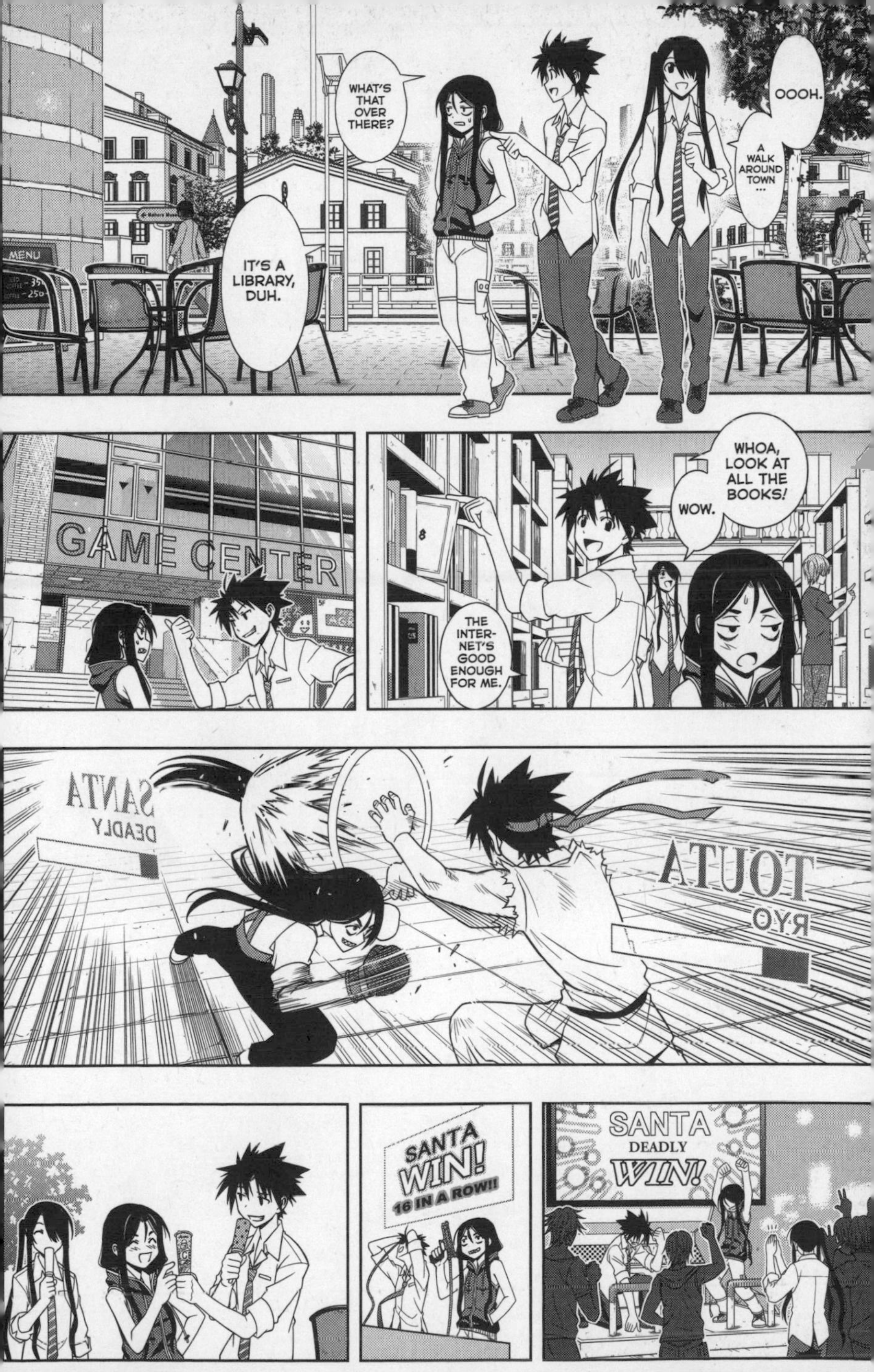
OOOH.
A WALK AROUND TOWN...
WHAT'S THAT OVER THERE?
IT'S A LIBRARY, DUH.
MENU
WHOA, LOOK AT ALL THE BOOKS!
WOW.
THE INTER-NET'S GOOD ENOUGH FOR ME.
GAME CENTER
5F
TOUTA
RYO
SANTA
DEADLY
SANTA
DEADLY
WIN!
SANTA
WIN!
16 IN A ROW!!

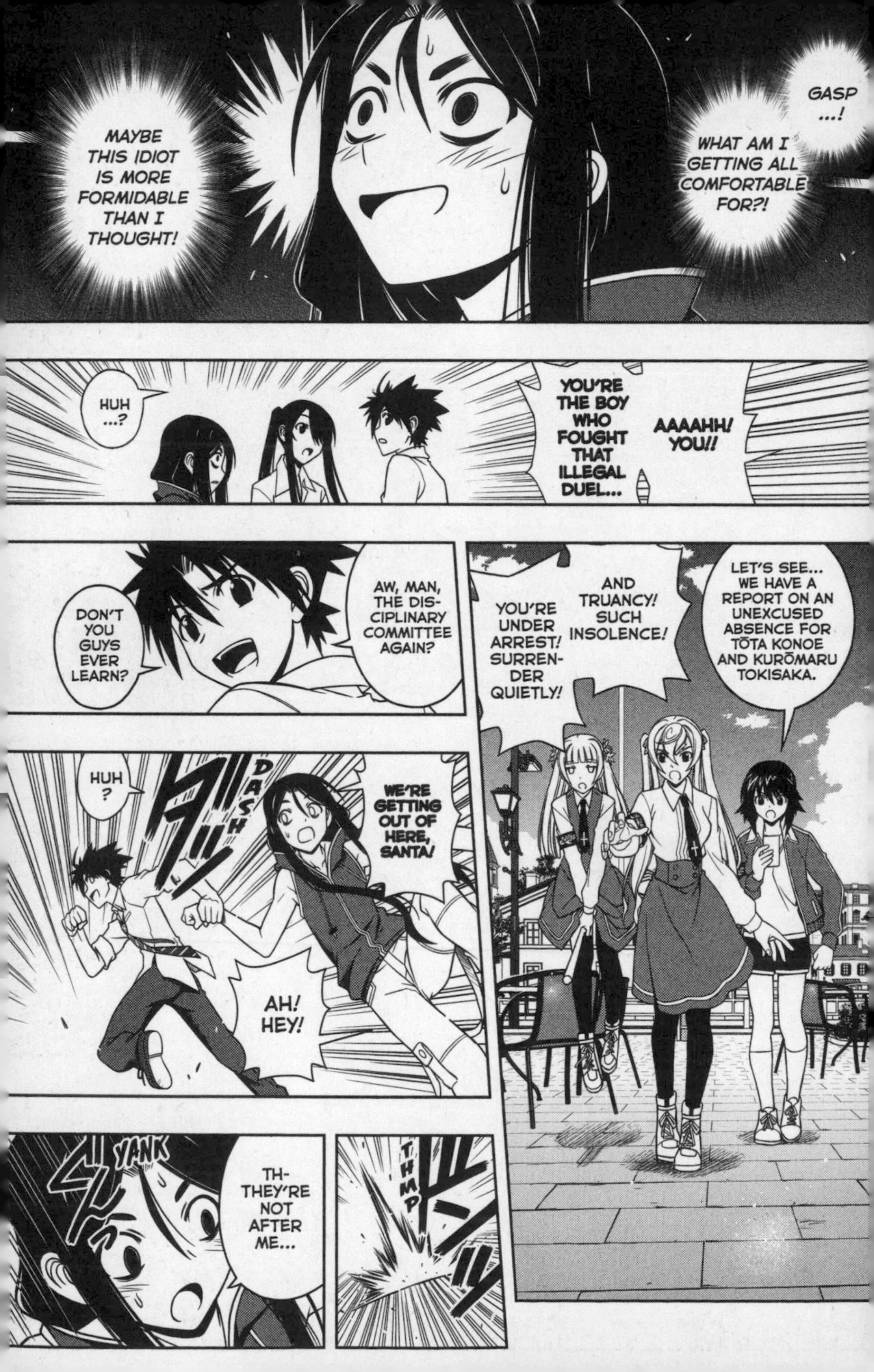
GASP ...!
WHAT AM I GETTING ALL COMFORTABLE FOR?!
MAYBE THIS IDIOT IS MORE FORMIDABLE THAN I THOUGHT!
AAAAHH! YOU!!
YOU'RE THE BOY WHO FOUGHT THAT ILLEGAL DUEL...
HUH ...?
LET'S SEE... WE HAVE A REPORT ON AN UNEXCUSED ABSENCE FOR TŌTA KONOE AND KURŌMARU TOKISAKA.
AND TRUANCY! SUCH INSOLENCE!
YOU'RE UNDER ARREST! SURREN-DER QUIETLY!
AW, MAN, THE DIS-CIPLINARY COMMITTEE AGAIN?
DON'T YOU GUYS EVER LEARN?
WE'RE GETTING OUT OF HERE, SANTA!
DASH
HUH ?
AH! HEY!
THMP
YANK
TH- THEY'RE NOT AFTER ME...

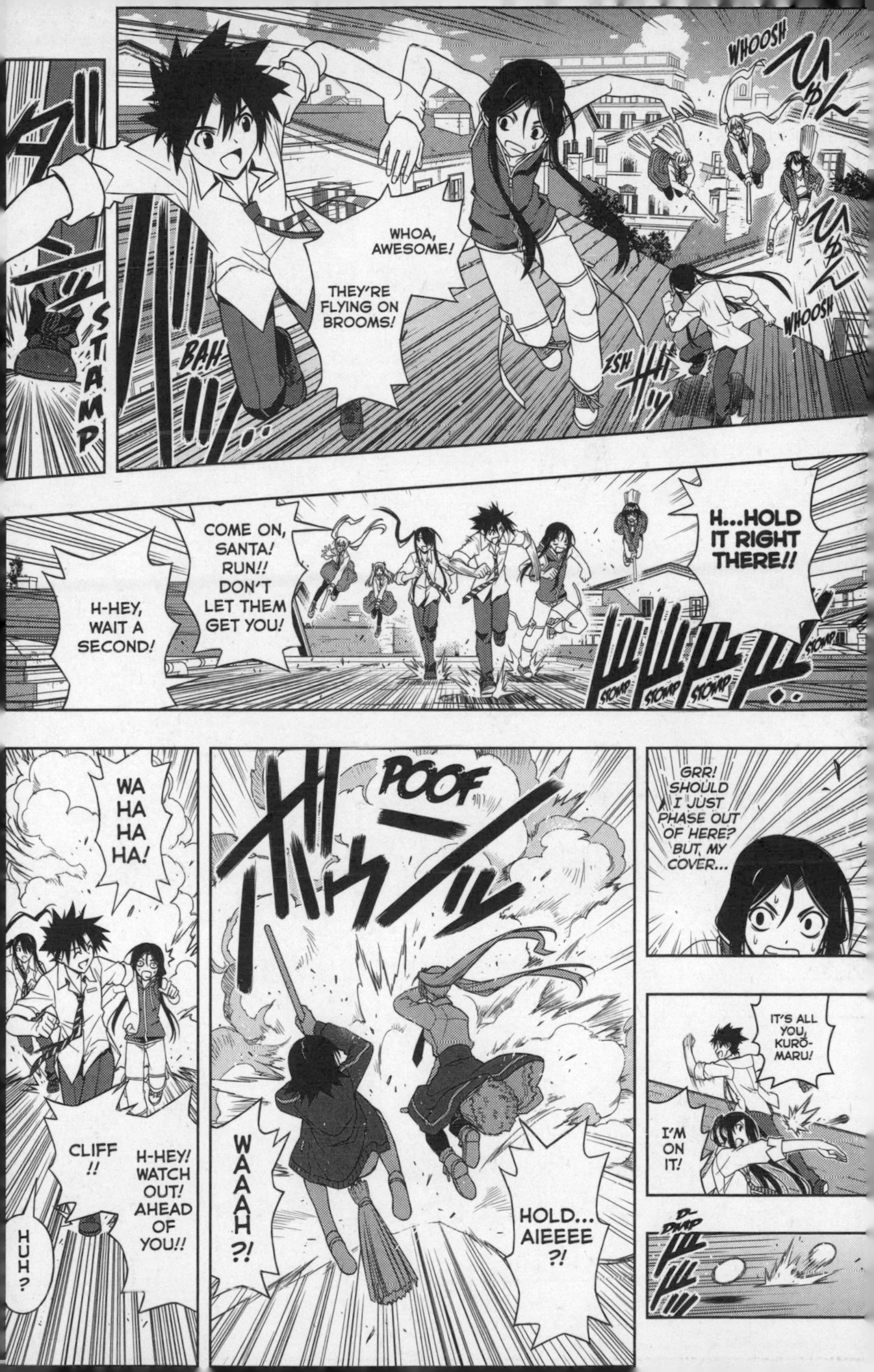
WHOOSH
WHOOSH
WHOA, AWESOME!
THEY'RE FLYING ON BROOMS!
ZSH
BAH
STAMP
H...HOLD IT RIGHT THERE!!
STOMP STOMP STOMP STOMP
COME ON, SANTA! RUN!! DON'T LET THEM GET YOU!
H-HEY, WAIT A SECOND!
GRR! SHOULD I JUST PHASE OUT OF HERE? BUT, MY COVER...
IT'S ALL YOU, KURŌ-MARU!
I'M ON IT!
D-DWAP
POOF
HOLD... AIEEEE?!
WAAAH?!
WA HA HA HA!
H-HEY! WATCH OUT! AHEAD OF YOU!!
CLIFF!!
HUH?

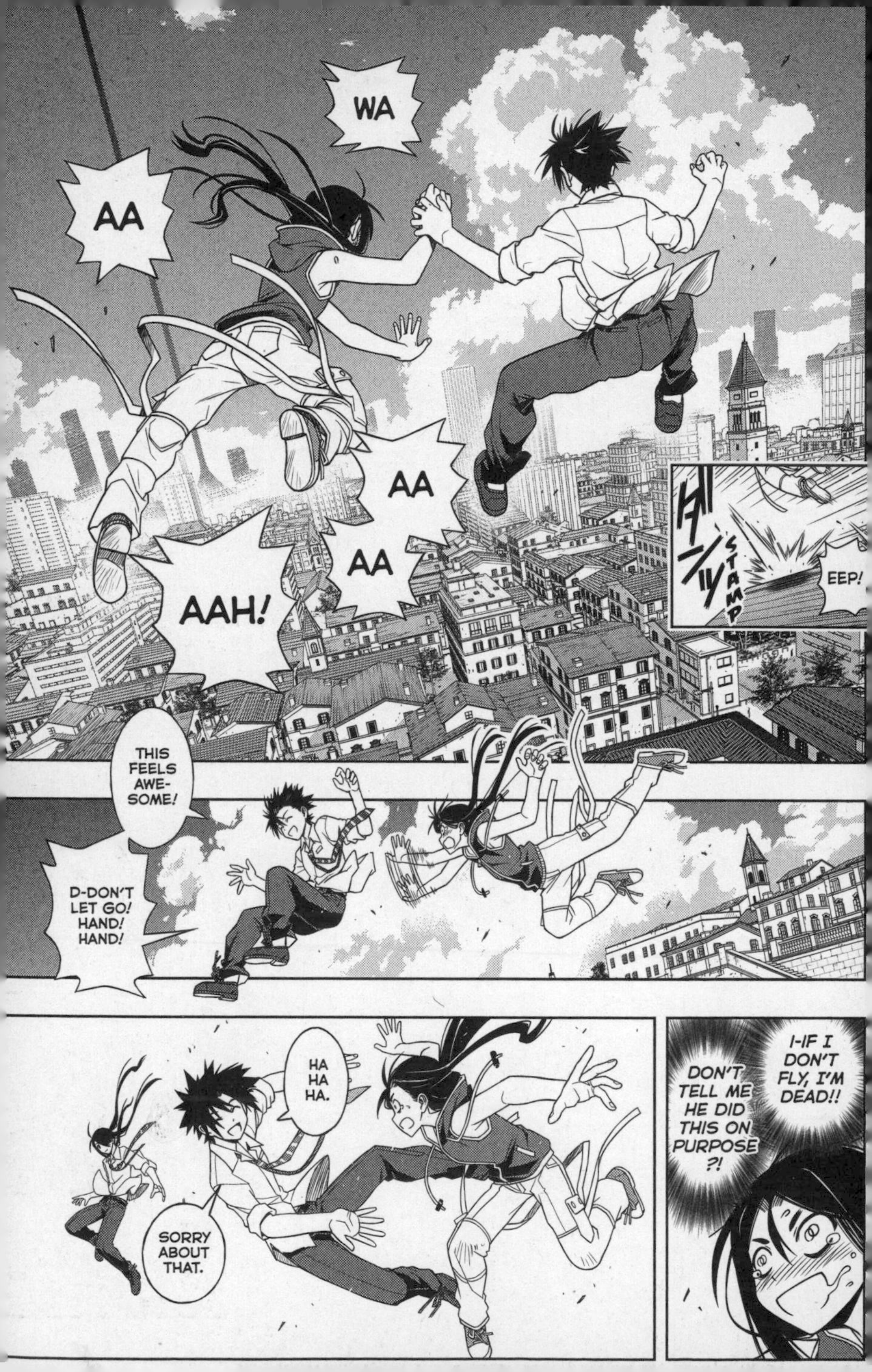
WA
AA
AA
AA
AAH!
STAMP
EEP!
THIS FEELS AWE-SOME!
D-DON'T LET GO! HAND! HAND!
I-IF I DON'T FLY, I'M DEAD!!
DON'T TELL ME HE DID THIS ON PURPOSE?!
HA HA HA.
SORRY ABOUT THAT.

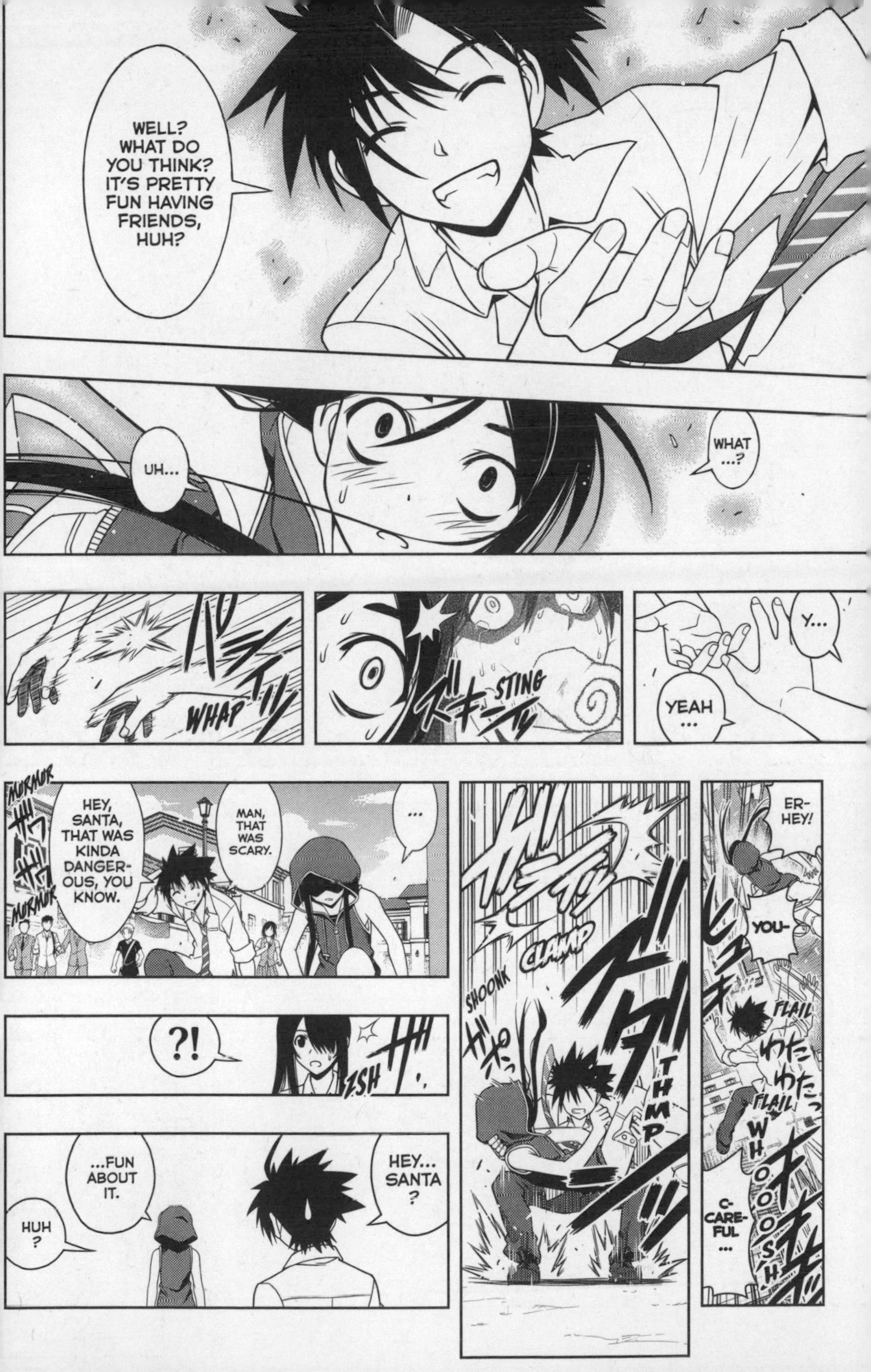
WELL? WHAT DO YOU THINK? IT'S PRETTY FUN HAVING FRIENDS, HUH?
WHAT ...?
UH...
Y...
YEAH ...
STING
WHAP
ER-HEY!
YOU-
FLAIL
FLAIL
WHOOOSH
C-CAREFUL ...
CLAMP
SHOONK
THUMP
...
MAN, THAT WAS SCARY.
HEY, SANTA, THAT WAS KINDA DANGER-OUS, YOU KNOW.
MURMUR
MURMUR
?!
ZSH
HEY... SANTA ?
...FUN ABOUT IT.
HUH ?

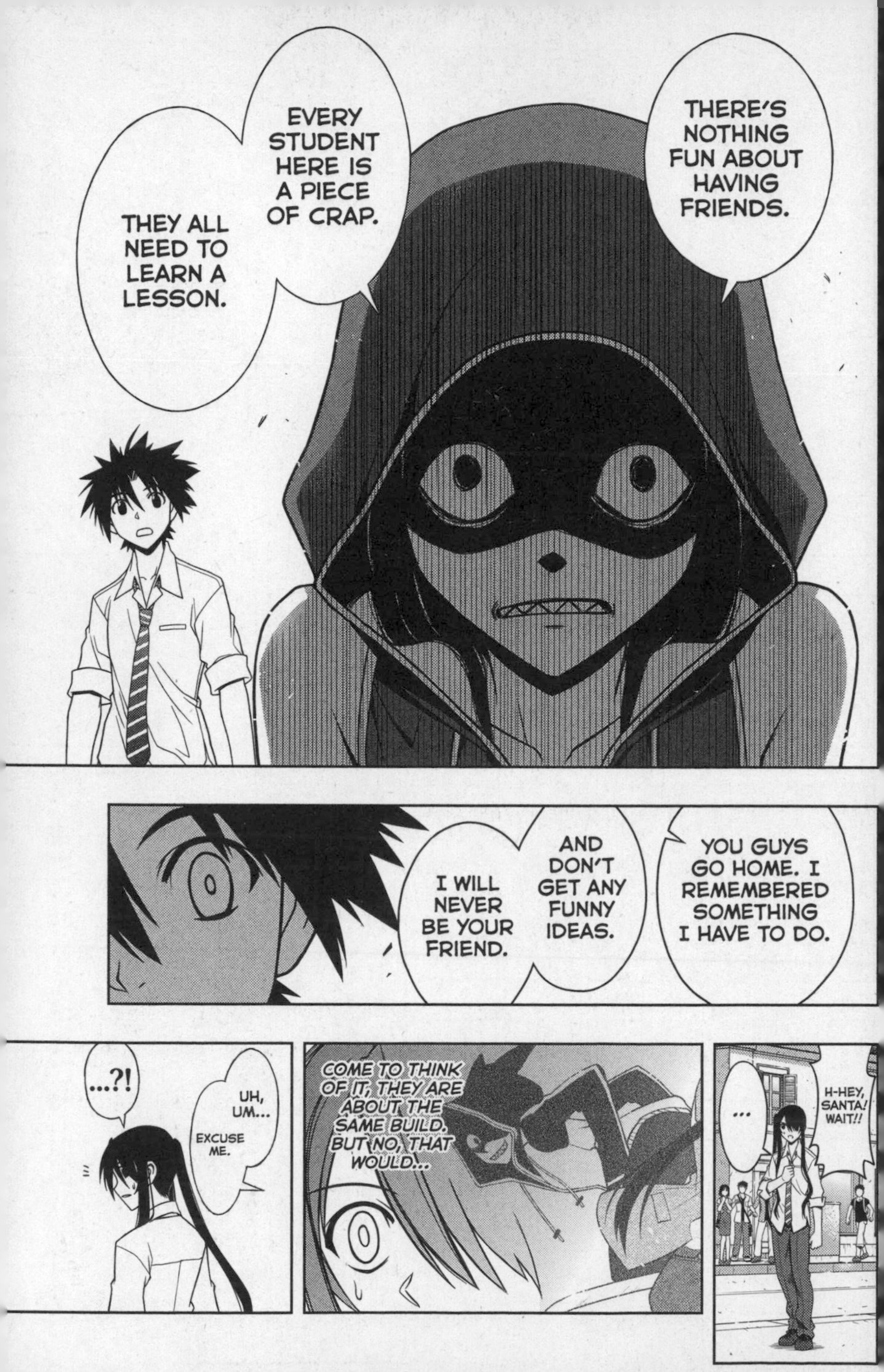
THERE'S NOTHING FUN ABOUT HAVING FRIENDS.
EVERY STUDENT HERE IS A PIECE OF CRAP.
THEY ALL NEED TO LEARN A LESSON.
YOU GUYS GO HOME. I REMEMBERED SOMETHING I HAVE TO DO.
AND DON'T GET ANY FUNNY IDEAS.
I WILL NEVER BE YOUR FRIEND.
H-HEY, SANTA! WAIT!!
...
COME TO THINK OF IT, THEY ARE ABOUT THE SAME BUILD. BUT NO, THAT WOULD...
...?!
UH, UM... EXCUSE ME.

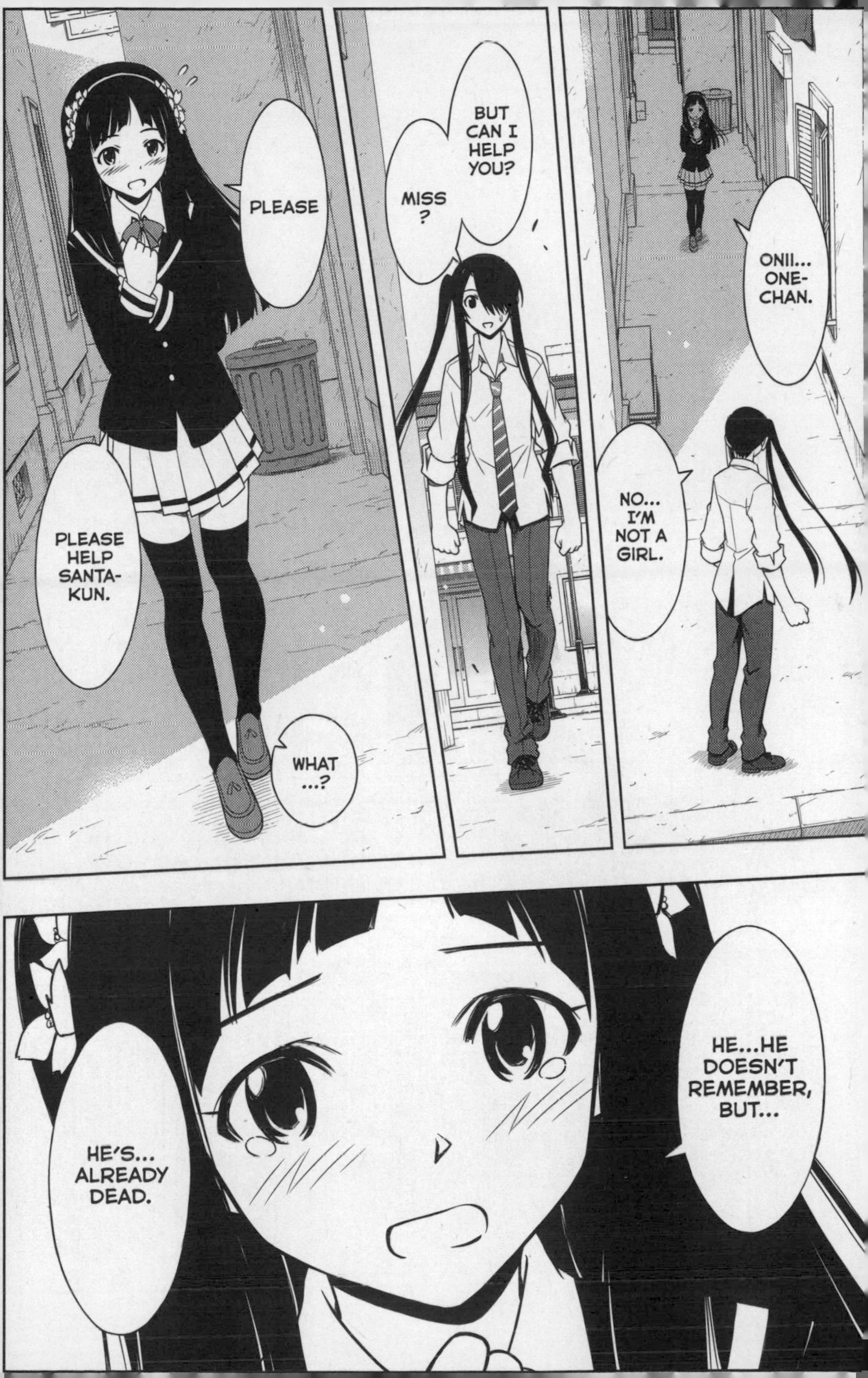
ONII... ONE-CHAN.
NO... I'M NOT A GIRL.
BUT CAN I HELP YOU?
MISS?
PLEASE
PLEASE HELP SANTA-KUN.
WHAT ...?
HE...HE DOESN'T REMEMBER, BUT...
HE'S... ALREADY DEAD.

悠 UQ HOLDER!

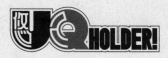

STAGE 49: THE TRUTH OF THE MATTER

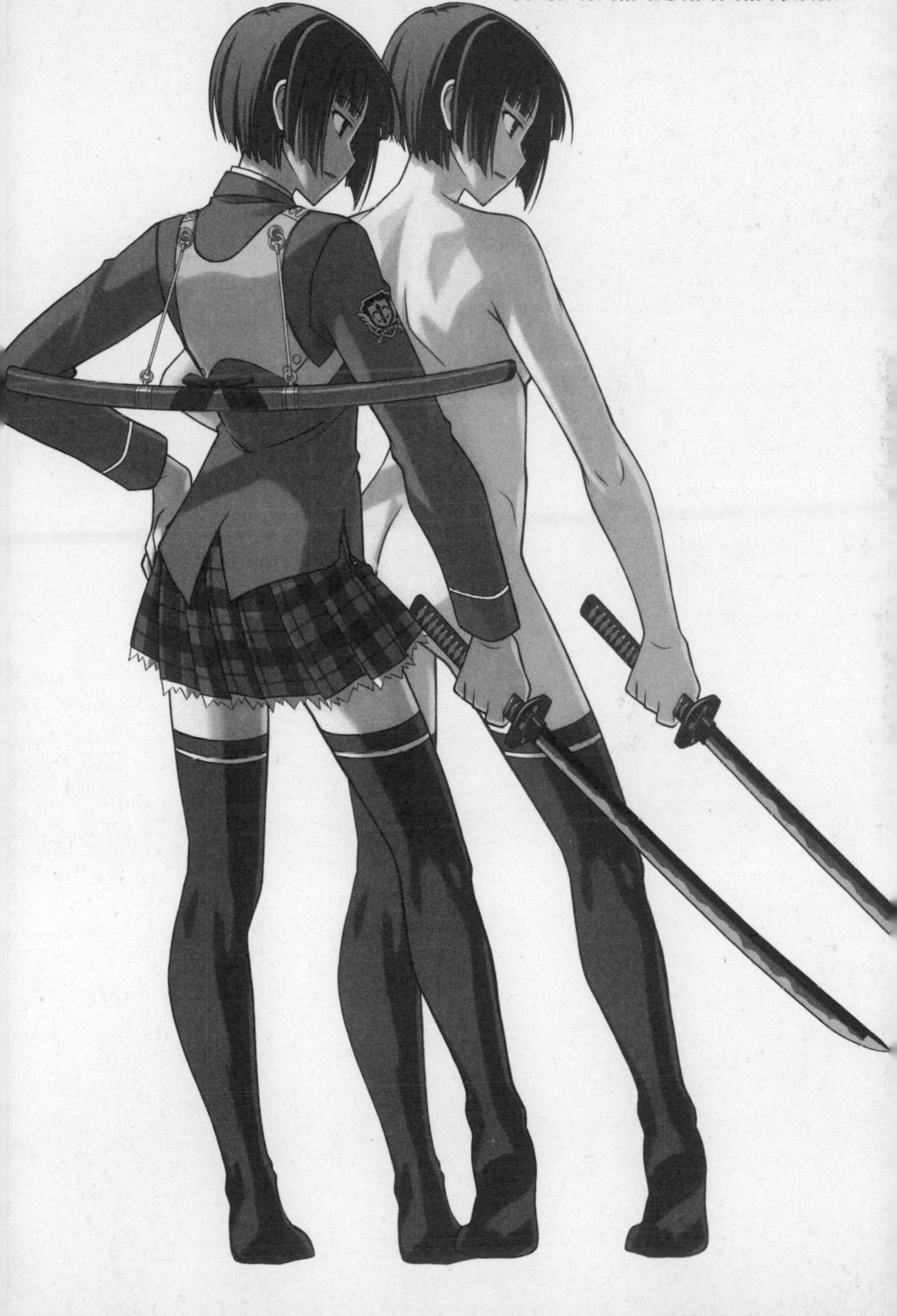

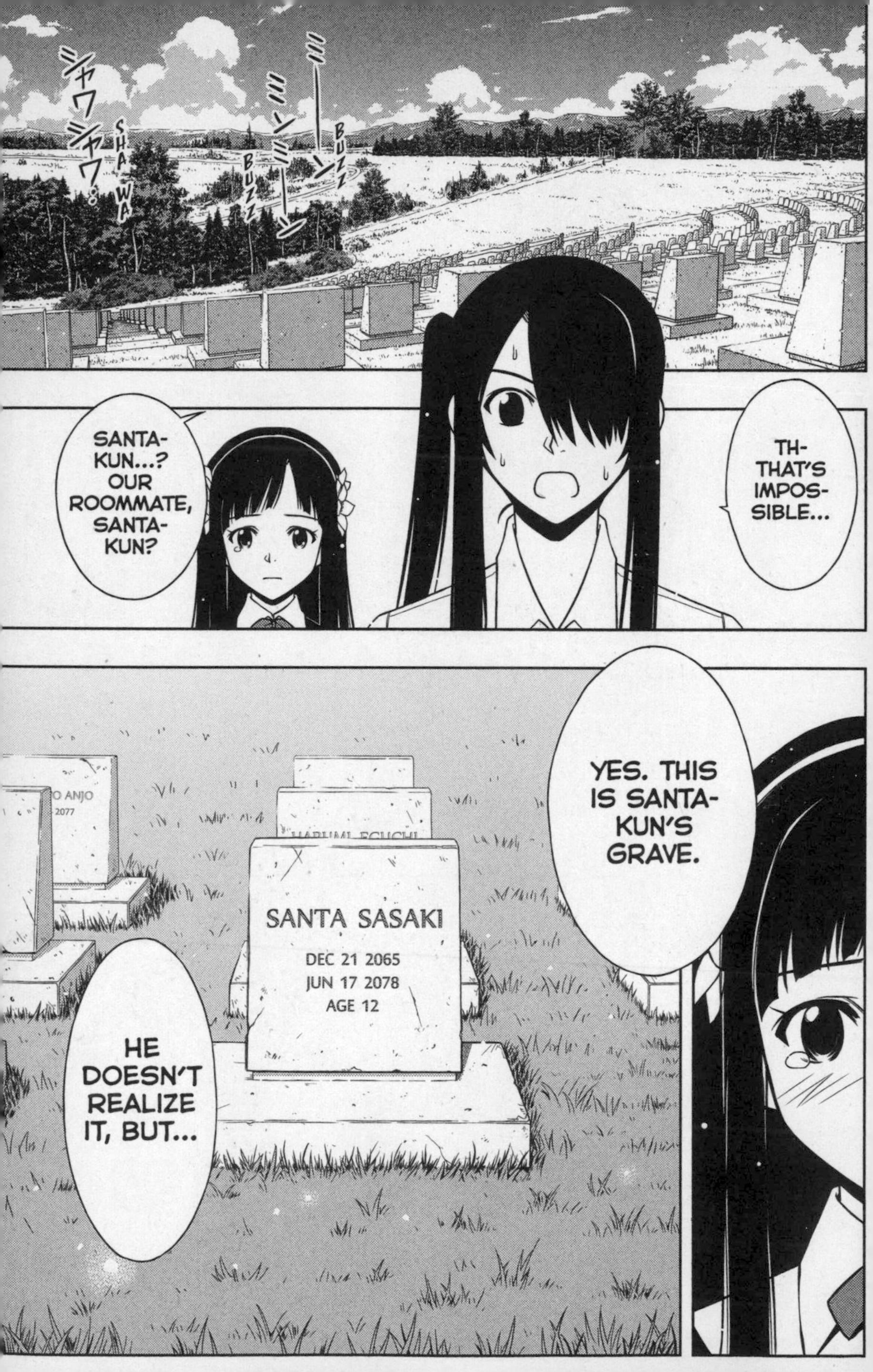
ミーン
BUZZ
ミンミーン
BUZZ
シャワシャワ
SHA WA
TH-THAT'S IMPOSSIBLE...
SANTA-KUN...? OUR ROOMMATE, SANTA-KUN?
YES. THIS IS SANTA-KUN'S GRAVE.
SANTA SASAKI
DEC 21 2065
JUN 17 2078
AGE 12
HE DOESN'T REALIZE IT, BUT...

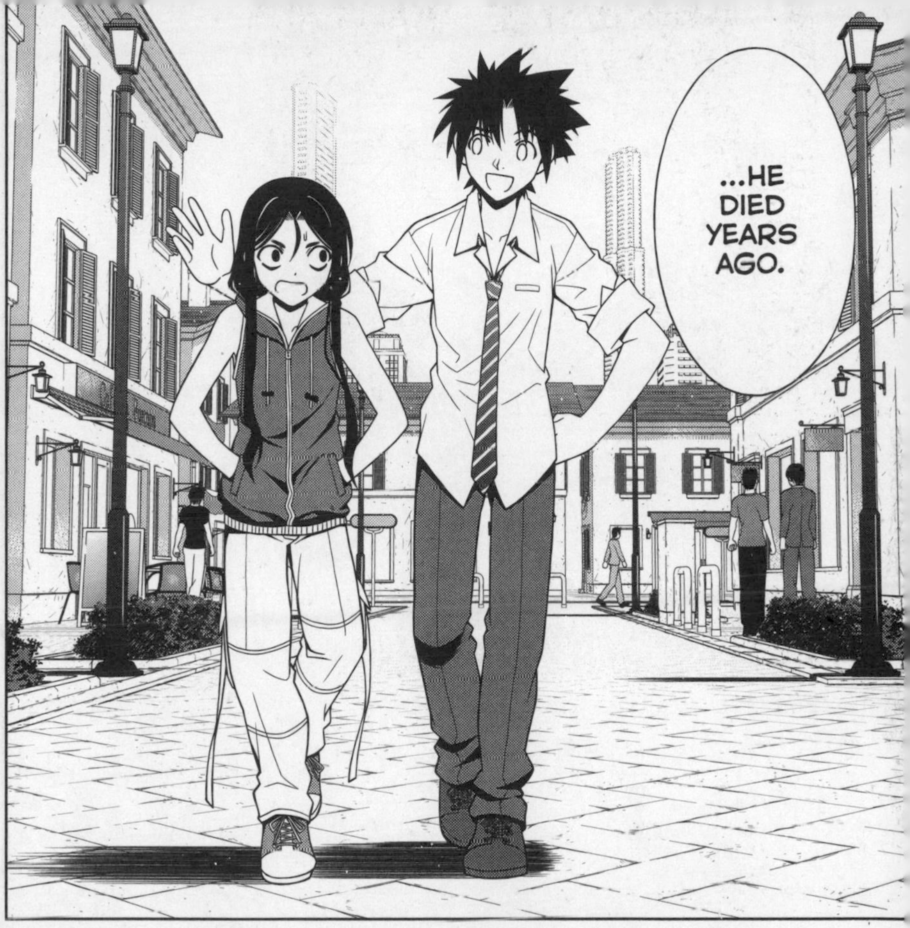
...HE DIED YEARS AGO.

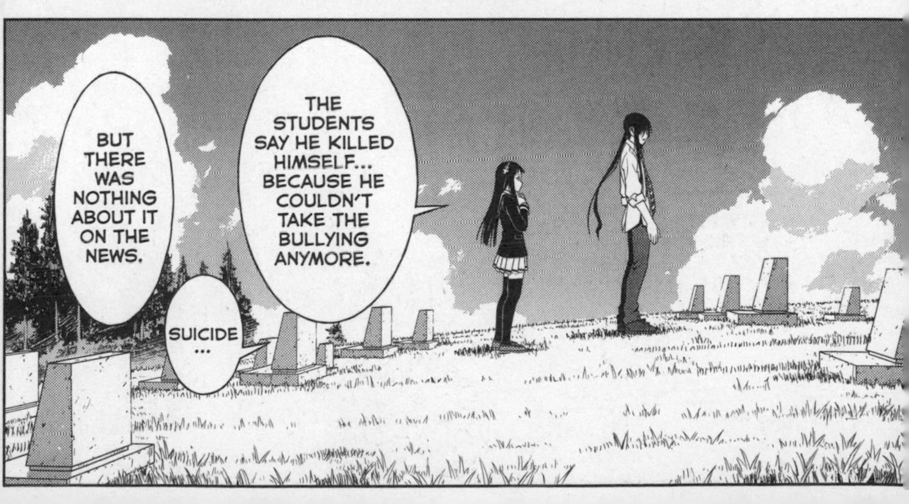
THE STUDENTS SAY HE KILLED HIMSELF... BECAUSE HE COULDN'T TAKE THE BULLYING ANYMORE.
BUT THERE WAS NOTHING ABOUT IT ON THE NEWS.
SUICIDE...

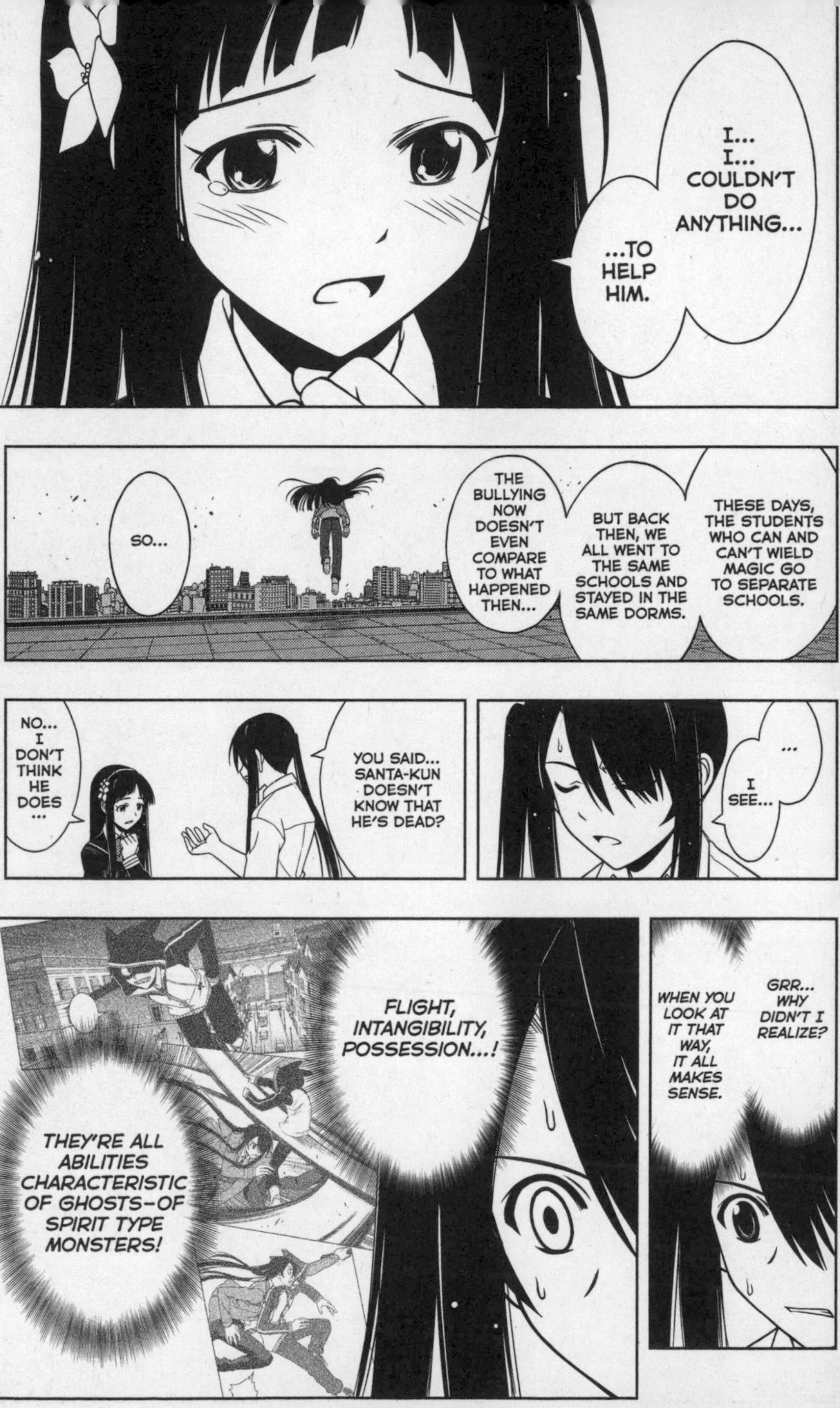
I... I... COULDN'T DO ANYTHING...
...TO HELP HIM.
THESE DAYS, THE STUDENTS WHO CAN AND CAN'T WIELD MAGIC GO TO SEPARATE SCHOOLS.
BUT BACK THEN, WE ALL WENT TO THE SAME SCHOOLS AND STAYED IN THE SAME DORMS.
THE BULLYING NOW DOESN'T EVEN COMPARE TO WHAT HAPPENED THEN...
SO...
...
I SEE...
YOU SAID... SANTA-KUN DOESN'T KNOW THAT HE'S DEAD?
NO... I DON'T THINK HE DOES...
GRR... WHY DIDN'T I REALIZE?
WHEN YOU LOOK AT IT THAT WAY, IT ALL MAKES SENSE.
FLIGHT, INTANGIBILITY, POSSESSION...!
THEY'RE ALL ABILITIES CHARACTERISTIC OF GHOSTS—OF SPIRIT TYPE MONSTERS!

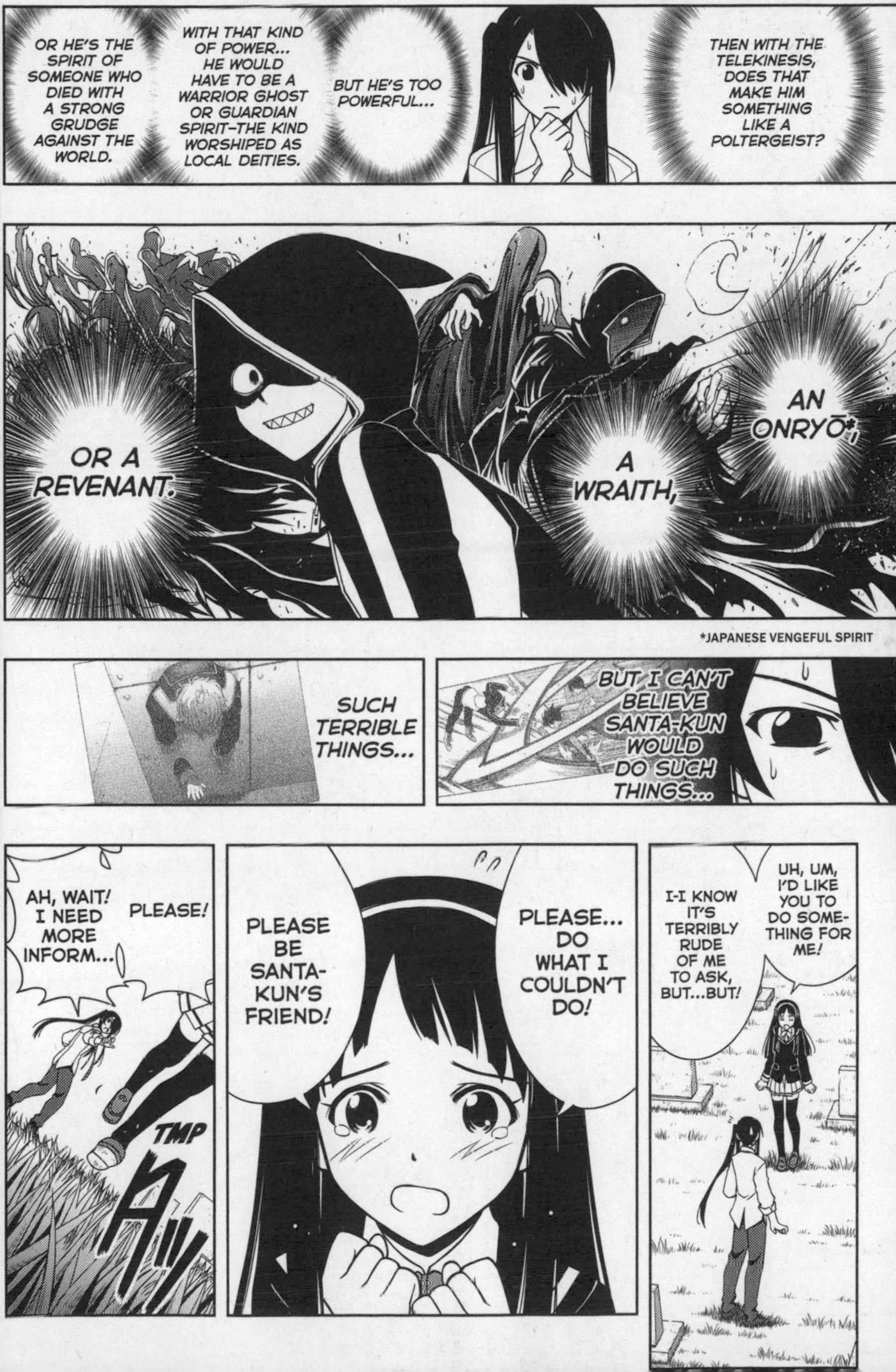
THEN WITH THE TELEKINESIS, DOES THAT MAKE HIM SOMETHING LIKE A POLTERGEIST?
BUT HE'S TOO POWERFUL...
WITH THAT KIND OF POWER... HE WOULD HAVE TO BE A WARRIOR GHOST OR GUARDIAN SPIRIT–THE KIND WORSHIPED AS LOCAL DEITIES.
OR HE'S THE SPIRIT OF SOMEONE WHO DIED WITH A STRONG GRUDGE AGAINST THE WORLD.
AN ONRYŌ*,
A WRAITH,
OR A REVENANT.
*JAPANESE VENGEFUL SPIRIT
BUT I CAN'T BELIEVE SANTA-KUN WOULD DO SUCH THINGS...
SUCH TERRIBLE THINGS...
UH, UM, I'D LIKE YOU TO DO SOME-THING FOR ME!
I-I KNOW IT'S TERRIBLY RUDE OF ME TO ASK, BUT...BUT!
PLEASE... DO WHAT I COULDN'T DO!
PLEASE BE SANTA-KUN'S FRIEND!
PLEASE!
AH, WAIT! I NEED MORE INFORM...
TMP

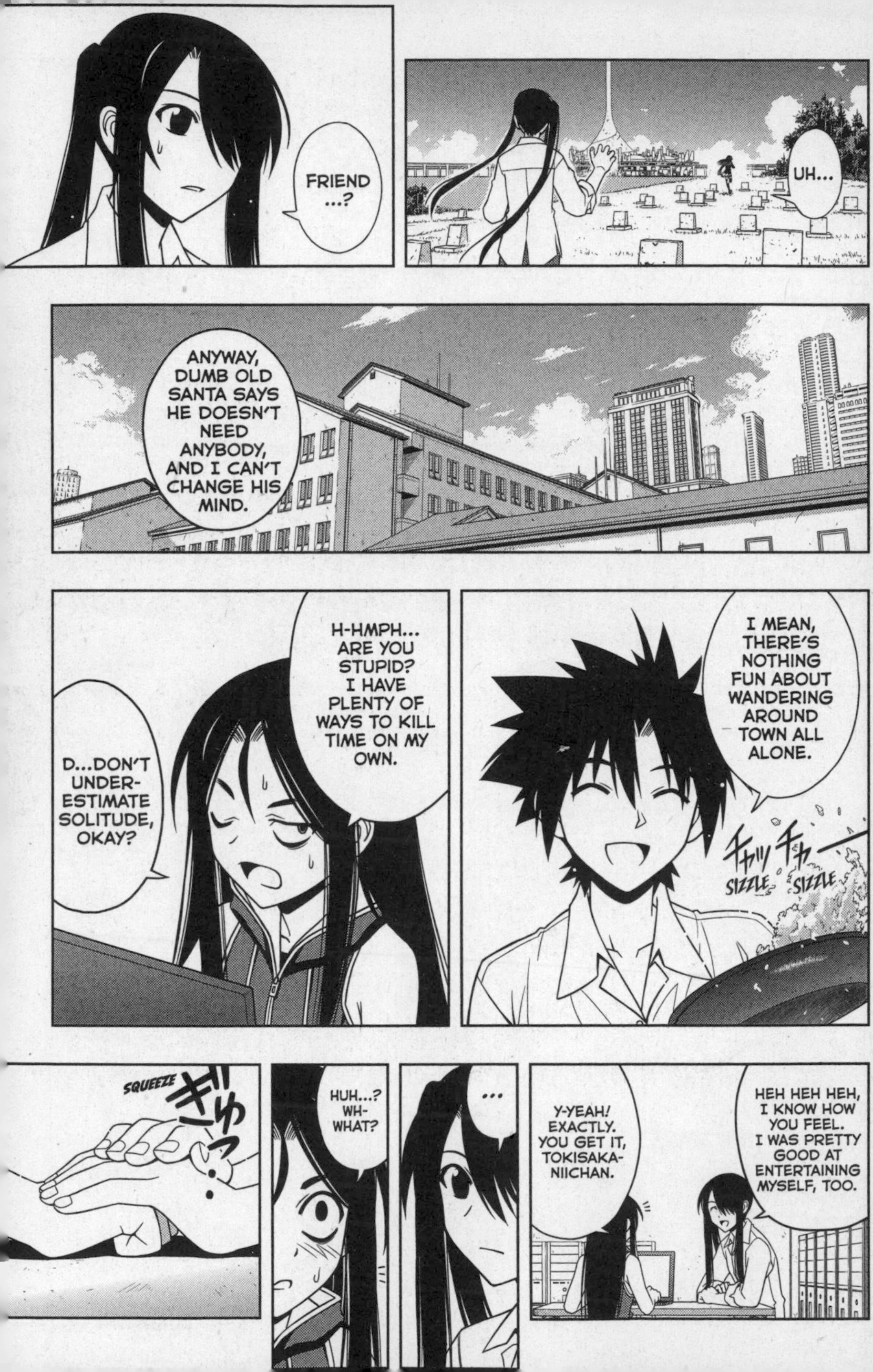

UH...
FRIEND ...?
ANYWAY, DUMB OLD SANTA SAYS HE DOESN'T NEED ANYBODY, AND I CAN'T CHANGE HIS MIND.
I MEAN, THERE'S NOTHING FUN ABOUT WANDERING AROUND TOWN ALL ALONE.
SIZZLE SIZZLE
H-HMPH... ARE YOU STUPID? I HAVE PLENTY OF WAYS TO KILL TIME ON MY OWN.
D...DON'T UNDER-ESTIMATE SOLITUDE, OKAY?
HEH HEH HEH, I KNOW HOW YOU FEEL. I WAS PRETTY GOOD AT ENTERTAINING MYSELF, TOO.
Y-YEAH! EXACTLY. YOU GET IT, TOKISAKA-NIICHAN.
...
HUH...? WH-WHAT?
SQUEEZE

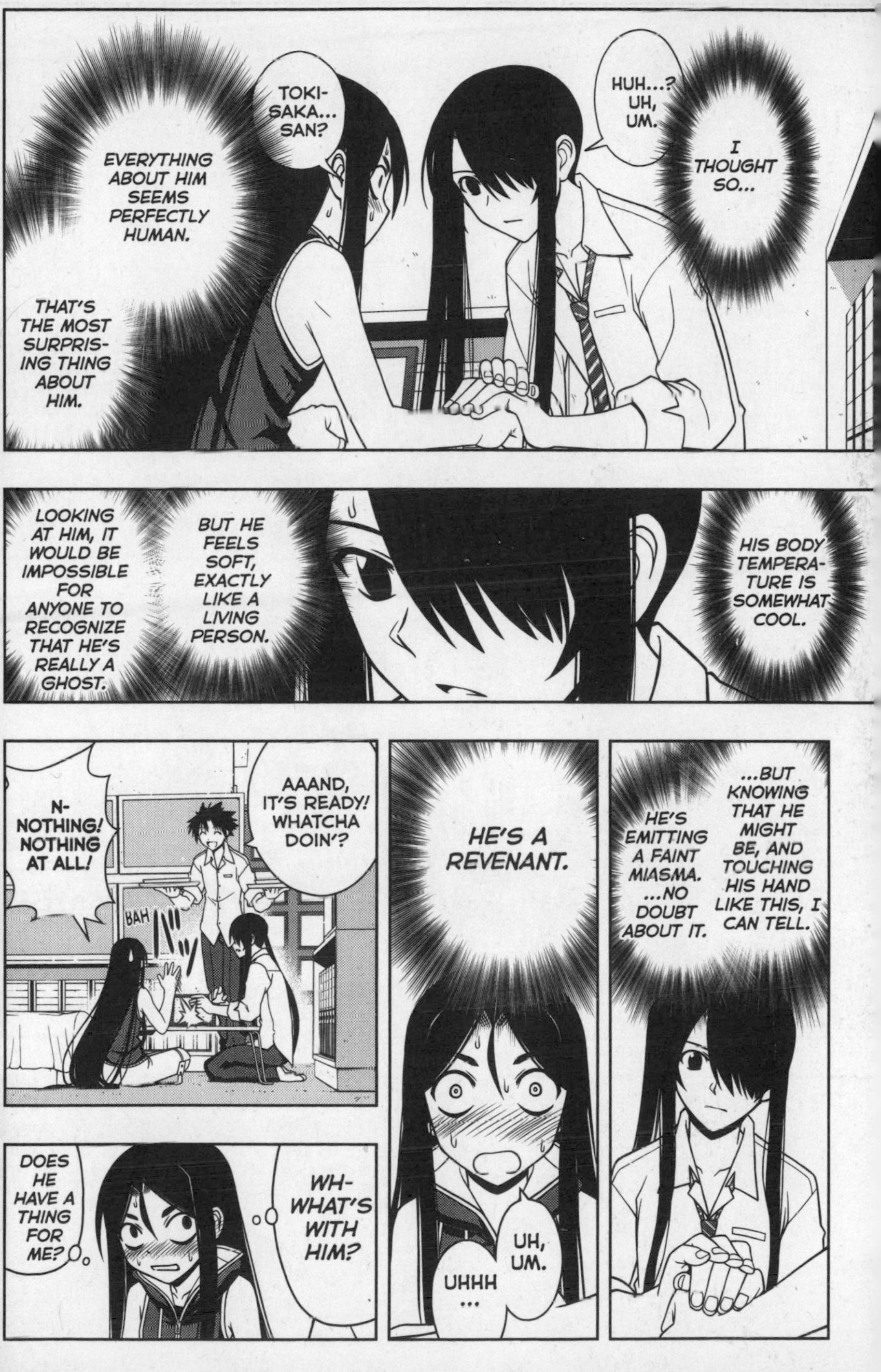
I THOUGHT SO...
HUH...? UH, UM.
TOKI-SAKA... SAN?
EVERYTHING ABOUT HIM SEEMS PERFECTLY HUMAN.
THAT'S THE MOST SURPRIS-ING THING ABOUT HIM.
HIS BODY TEMPERA-TURE IS SOMEWHAT COOL.
BUT HE FEELS SOFT, EXACTLY LIKE A LIVING PERSON.
LOOKING AT HIM, IT WOULD BE IMPOSSIBLE FOR ANYONE TO RECOGNIZE THAT HE'S REALLY A GHOST.
...BUT KNOWING THAT HE MIGHT BE, AND TOUCHING HIS HAND LIKE THIS, I CAN TELL.
HE'S EMITTING A FAINT MIASMA. ...NO DOUBT ABOUT IT.
HE'S A REVENANT.
UH, UM.
UHHH...
AAAND, IT'S READY! WHATCHA DOIN'?
N-NOTHING! NOTHING AT ALL!
BAH
WH-WHAT'S WITH HIM?
DOES HE HAVE A THING FOR ME?

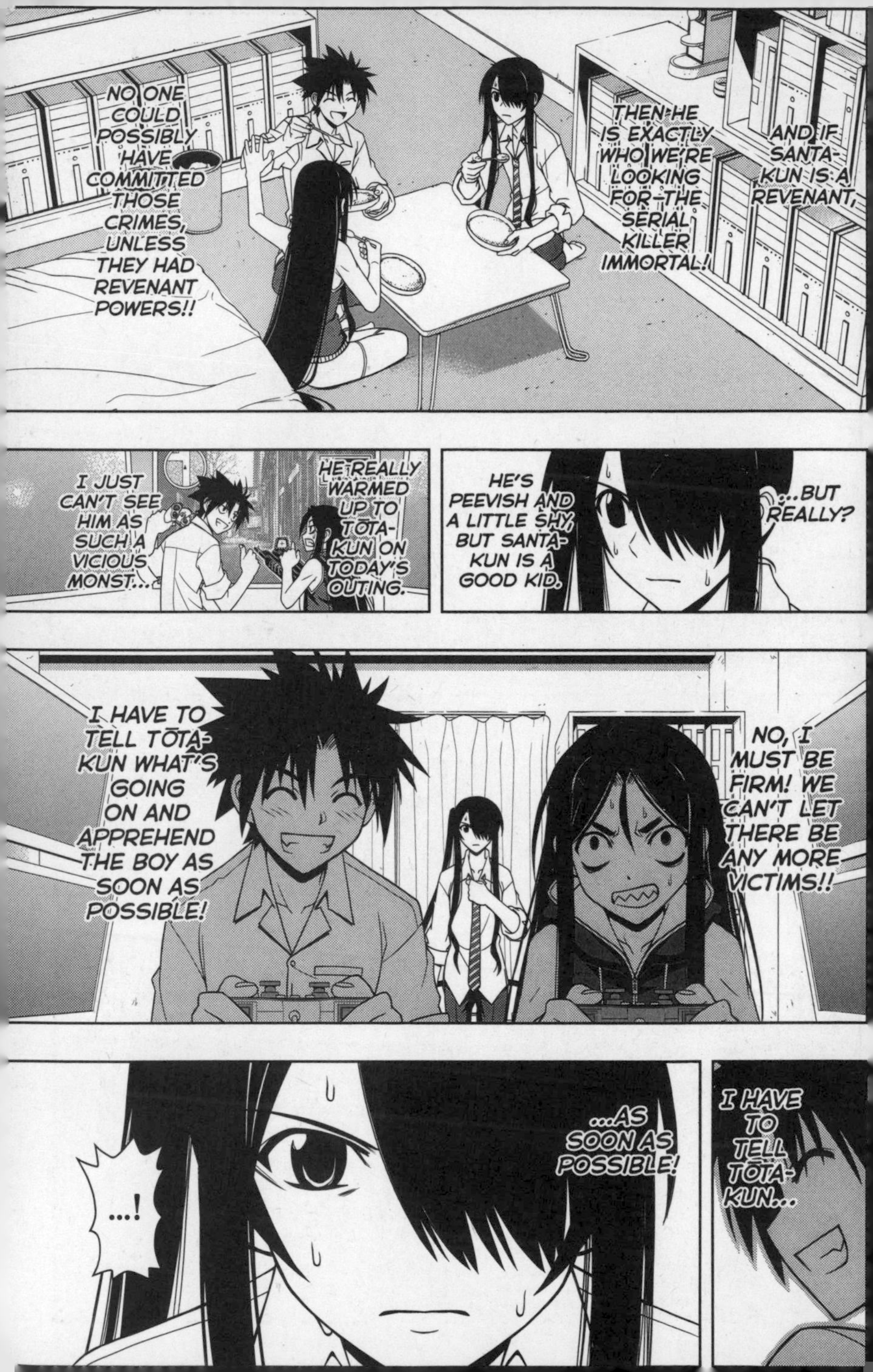
AND IF SANTA-KUN IS A REVENANT,
THEN HE IS EXACTLY WHO WE'RE LOOKING FOR—THE SERIAL KILLER IMMORTAL!
NO ONE COULD POSSIBLY HAVE COMMITTED THOSE CRIMES, UNLESS THEY HAD REVENANT POWERS!!
...BUT REALLY?
HE'S PEEVISH AND A LITTLE SHY, BUT SANTA-KUN IS A GOOD KID.
HE REALLY WARMED UP TO TŌTA-KUN ON TODAY'S OUTING.
I JUST CAN'T SEE HIM AS SUCH A VICIOUS MONST...
NO, I MUST BE FIRM! WE CAN'T LET THERE BE ANY MORE VICTIMS!!
I HAVE TO TELL TŌTA-KUN WHAT'S GOING ON AND APPREHEND THE BOY AS SOON AS POSSIBLE!
I HAVE TO TELL TŌTA-KUN...
...AS SOON AS POSSIBLE!
...!

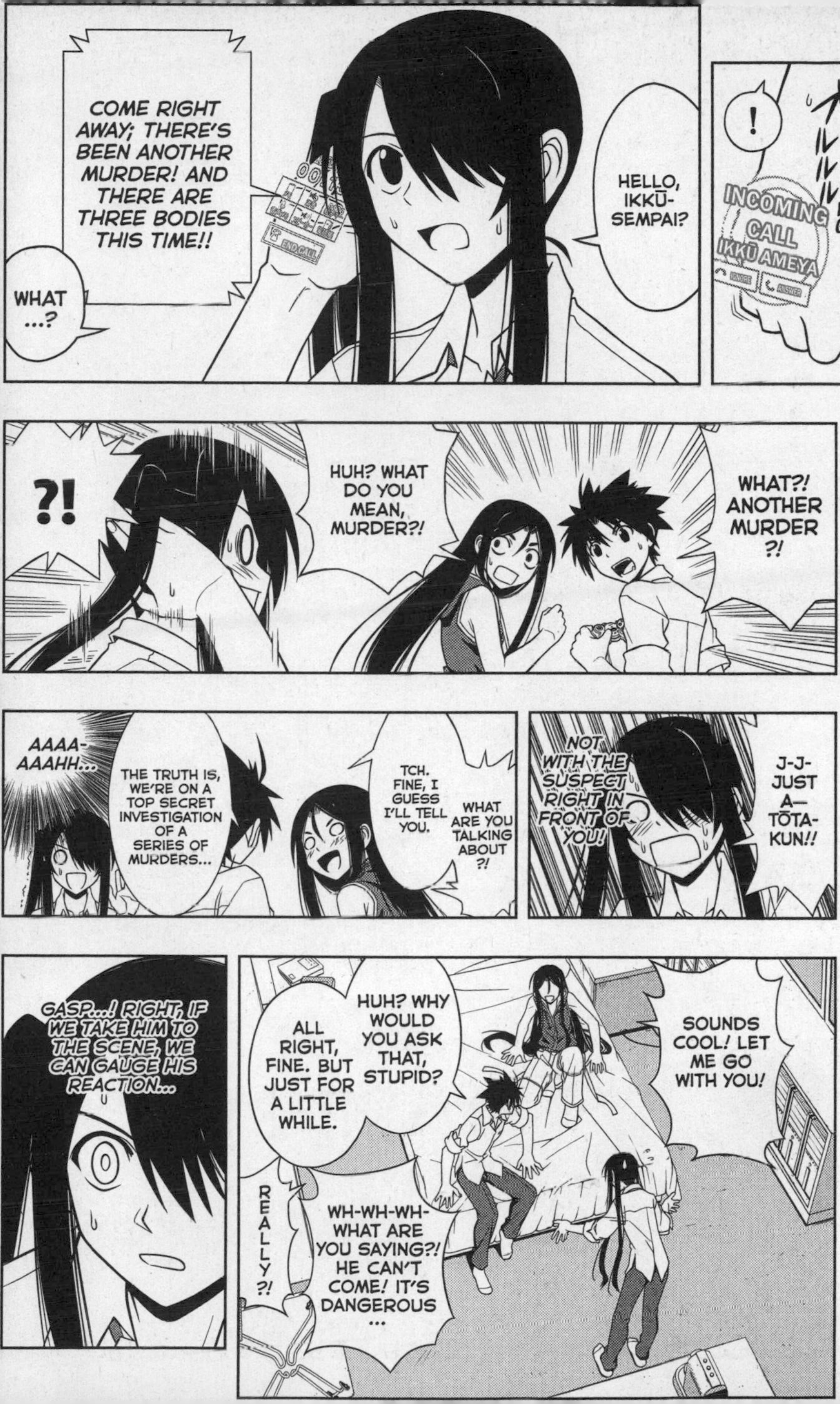
!
BRRRING
INCOMING CALL
IKKŪ AMEYA
IGNORE
ANSWER
HELLO, IKKŪ-SEMPAI?
COME RIGHT AWAY; THERE'S BEEN ANOTHER MURDER! AND THERE ARE THREE BODIES THIS TIME!!
END CALL
WHAT ...?
WHAT?! ANOTHER MURDER ?!
HUH? WHAT DO YOU MEAN, MURDER?!
?!
J-J-JUST A— TŌTA-KUN!!
NOT WITH THE SUSPECT RIGHT IN FRONT OF YOU!
WHAT ARE YOU TALKING ABOUT ?!
TCH. FINE, I GUESS I'LL TELL YOU.
THE TRUTH IS, WE'RE ON A TOP SECRET INVESTIGATION OF A SERIES OF MURDERS...
AAAA-AAAHH...
SOUNDS COOL! LET ME GO WITH YOU!
HUH? WHY WOULD YOU ASK THAT, STUPID?
ALL RIGHT, FINE. BUT JUST FOR A LITTLE WHILE.
WH-WH-WH-WHAT ARE YOU SAYING?! HE CAN'T COME! IT'S DANGEROUS ...
REALLY ?!
GASP...! RIGHT, IF WE TAKE HIM TO THE SCENE, WE CAN GAUGE HIS REACTION...

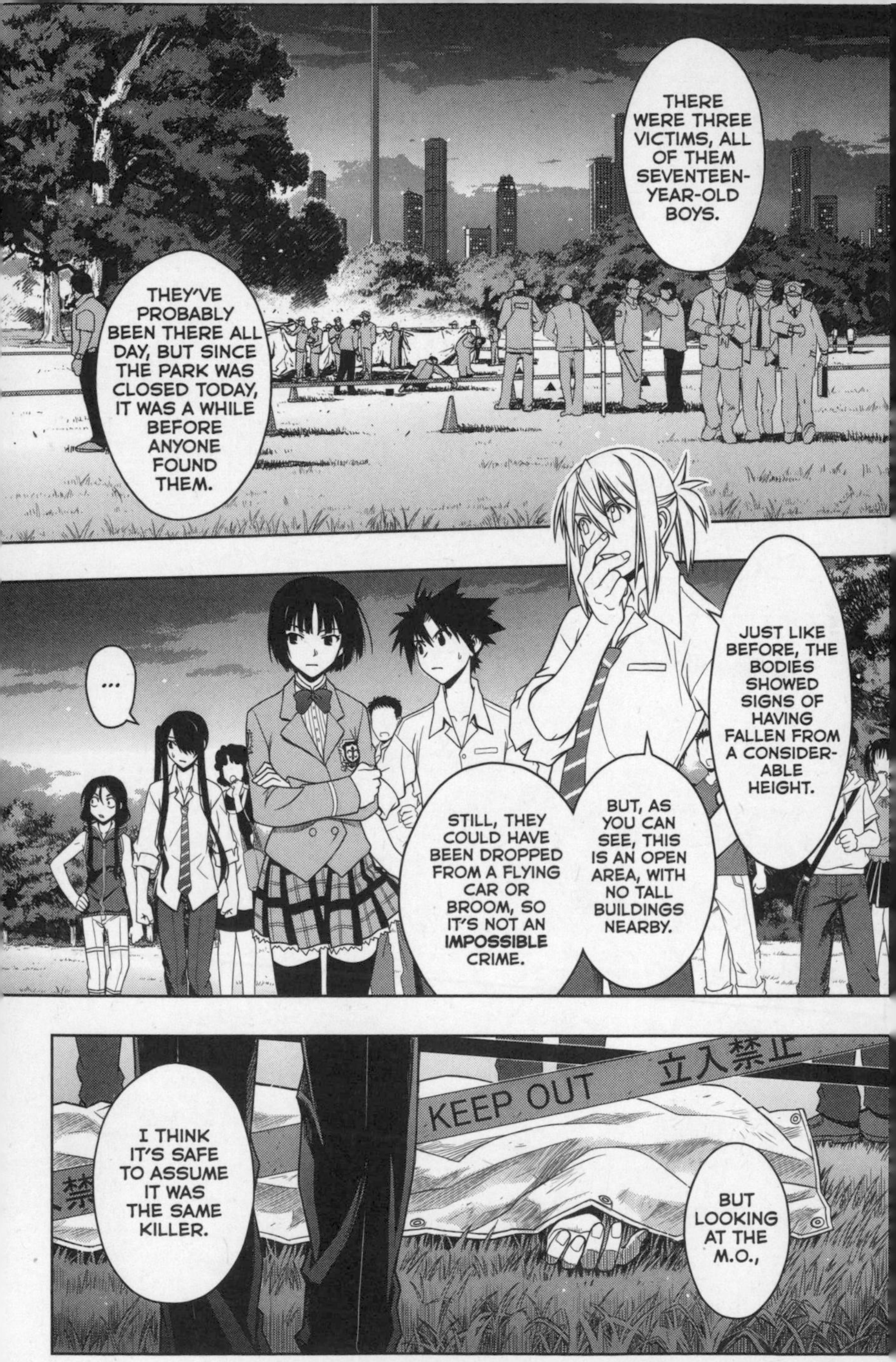
THERE WERE THREE VICTIMS, ALL OF THEM SEVENTEEN-YEAR-OLD BOYS.
THEY'VE PROBABLY BEEN THERE ALL DAY, BUT SINCE THE PARK WAS CLOSED TODAY, IT WAS A WHILE BEFORE ANYONE FOUND THEM.
JUST LIKE BEFORE, THE BODIES SHOWED SIGNS OF HAVING FALLEN FROM A CONSIDER-ABLE HEIGHT.
BUT, AS YOU CAN SEE, THIS IS AN OPEN AREA, WITH NO TALL BUILDINGS NEARBY.
STILL, THEY COULD HAVE BEEN DROPPED FROM A FLYING CAR OR BROOM, SO IT'S NOT AN IMPOSSIBLE CRIME.
...
KEEP OUT 立入禁止
BUT LOOKING AT THE M.O.,
I THINK IT'S SAFE TO ASSUME IT WAS THE SAME KILLER.

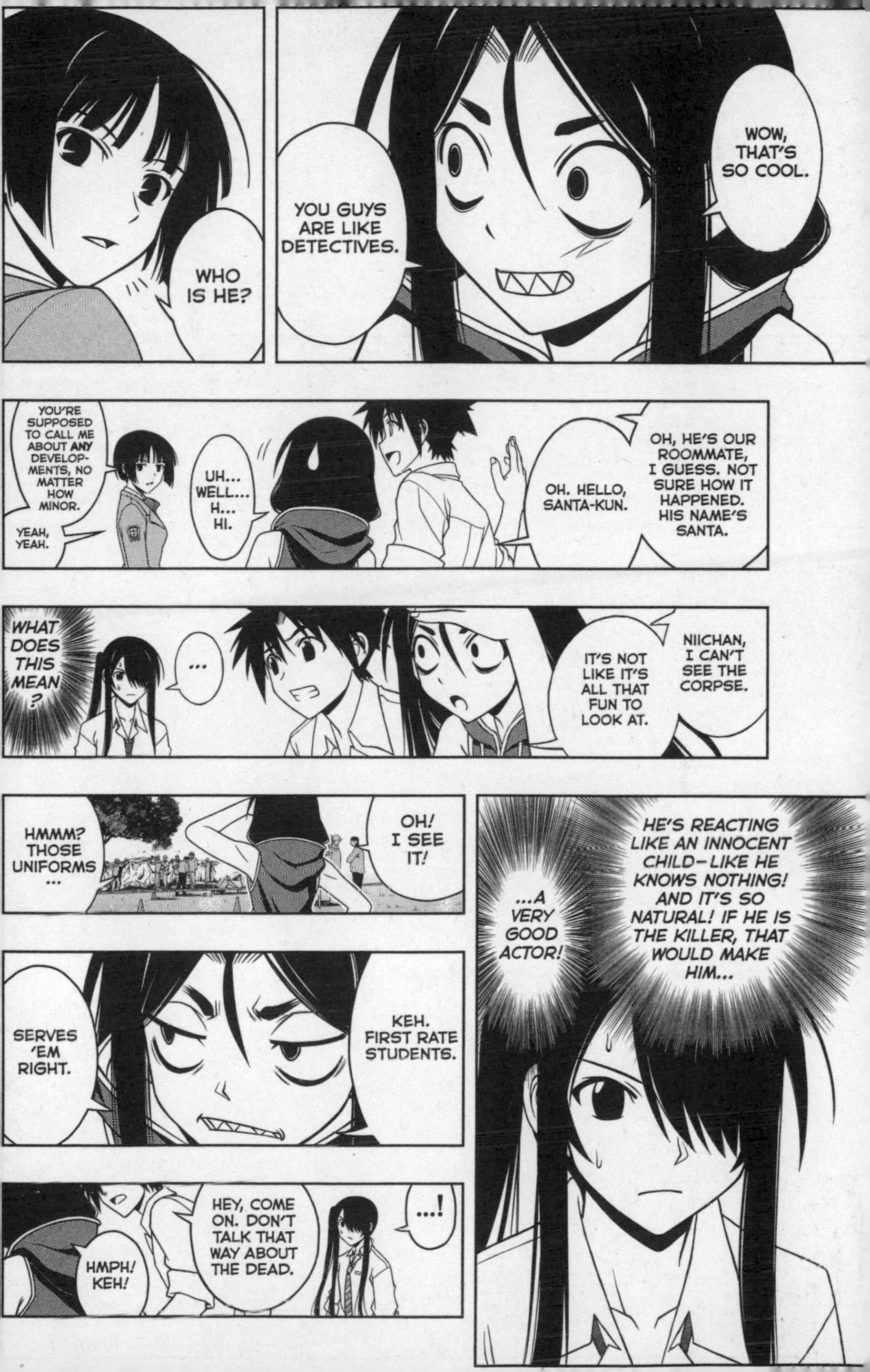
WOW, THAT'S SO COOL.
YOU GUYS ARE LIKE DETECTIVES.
WHO IS HE?
OH, HE'S OUR ROOMMATE, I GUESS. NOT SURE HOW IT HAPPENED. HIS NAME'S SANTA.
OH. HELLO, SANTA-KUN.
UH... WELL... H... HI.
YOU'RE SUPPOSED TO CALL ME ABOUT ANY DEVELOPMENTS, NO MATTER HOW MINOR.
YEAH, YEAH.
NIICHAN, I CAN'T SEE THE CORPSE.
IT'S NOT LIKE IT'S ALL THAT FUN TO LOOK AT.
...
WHAT DOES THIS MEAN?
HE'S REACTING LIKE AN INNOCENT CHILD–LIKE HE KNOWS NOTHING! AND IT'S SO NATURAL! IF HE IS THE KILLER, THAT WOULD MAKE HIM...
...A VERY GOOD ACTOR!
OH! I SEE IT!
HMMM? THOSE UNIFORMS...
KEH. FIRST RATE STUDENTS.
SERVES 'EM RIGHT.
...!
HEY, COME ON. DON'T TALK THAT WAY ABOUT THE DEAD.
HMPH! KEH!

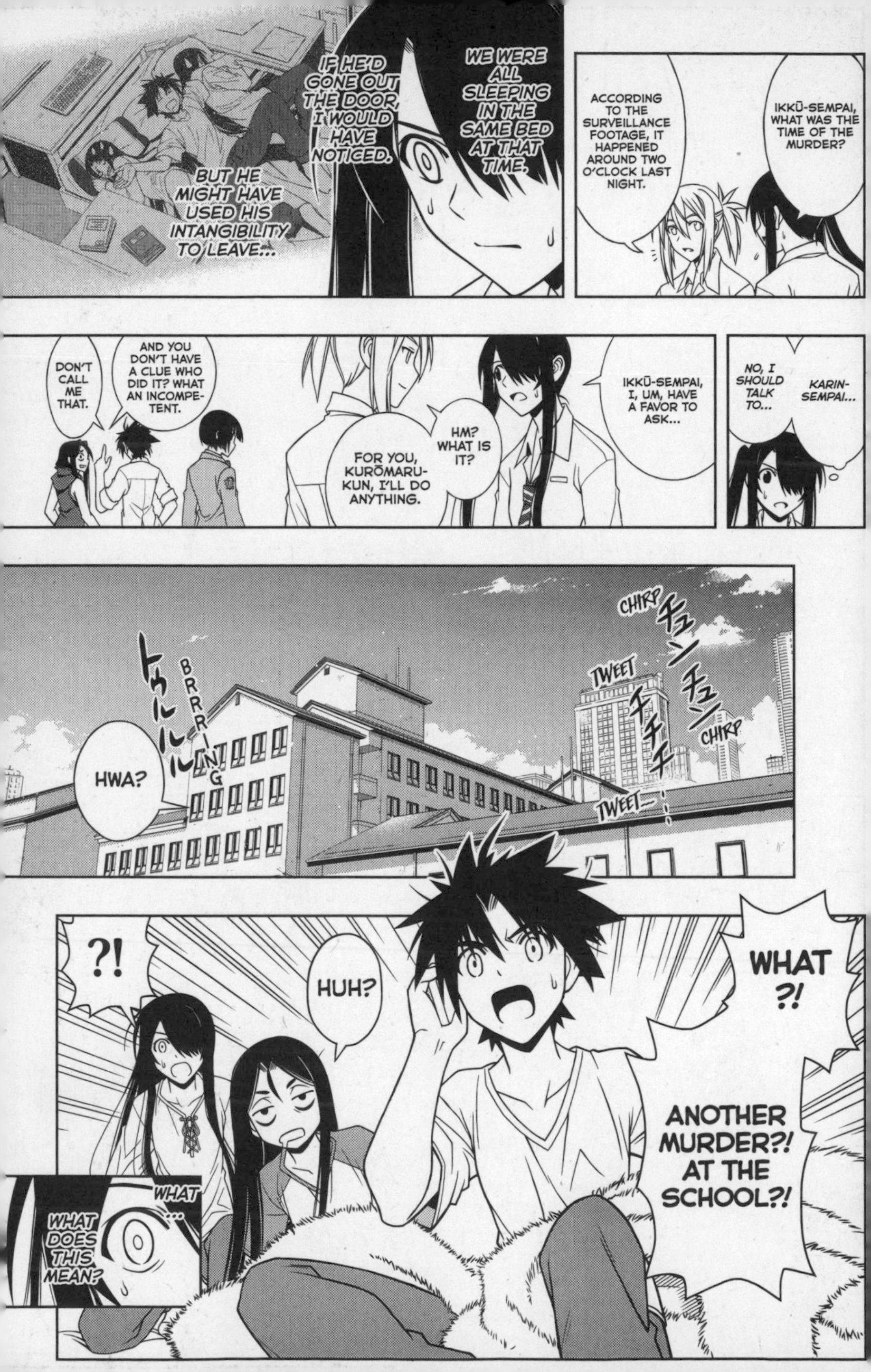
IKKŪ-SEMPAI, WHAT WAS THE TIME OF THE MURDER?
ACCORDING TO THE SURVEILLANCE FOOTAGE, IT HAPPENED AROUND TWO O'CLOCK LAST NIGHT.
WE WERE ALL SLEEPING IN THE SAME BED AT THAT TIME.
IF HE'D GONE OUT THE DOOR, I WOULD HAVE NOTICED.
BUT HE MIGHT HAVE USED HIS INTANGIBILITY TO LEAVE...
KARIN-SEMPAI...
NO, I SHOULD TALK TO...
IKKŪ-SEMPAI, I, UM, HAVE A FAVOR TO ASK...
HM? WHAT IS IT?
FOR YOU, KURŌMARU-KUN, I'LL DO ANYTHING.
AND YOU DON'T HAVE A CLUE WHO DID IT? WHAT AN INCOMPETENT.
DON'T CALL ME THAT.
チュン CHIRP
チュン CHIRP
チチチ TWEET TWEET...
トゥルルル BRRRING
HWA?
WHAT ?!
ANOTHER MURDER?! AT THE SCHOOL?!
HUH?
?!
WHAT...
WHAT DOES THIS MEAN?

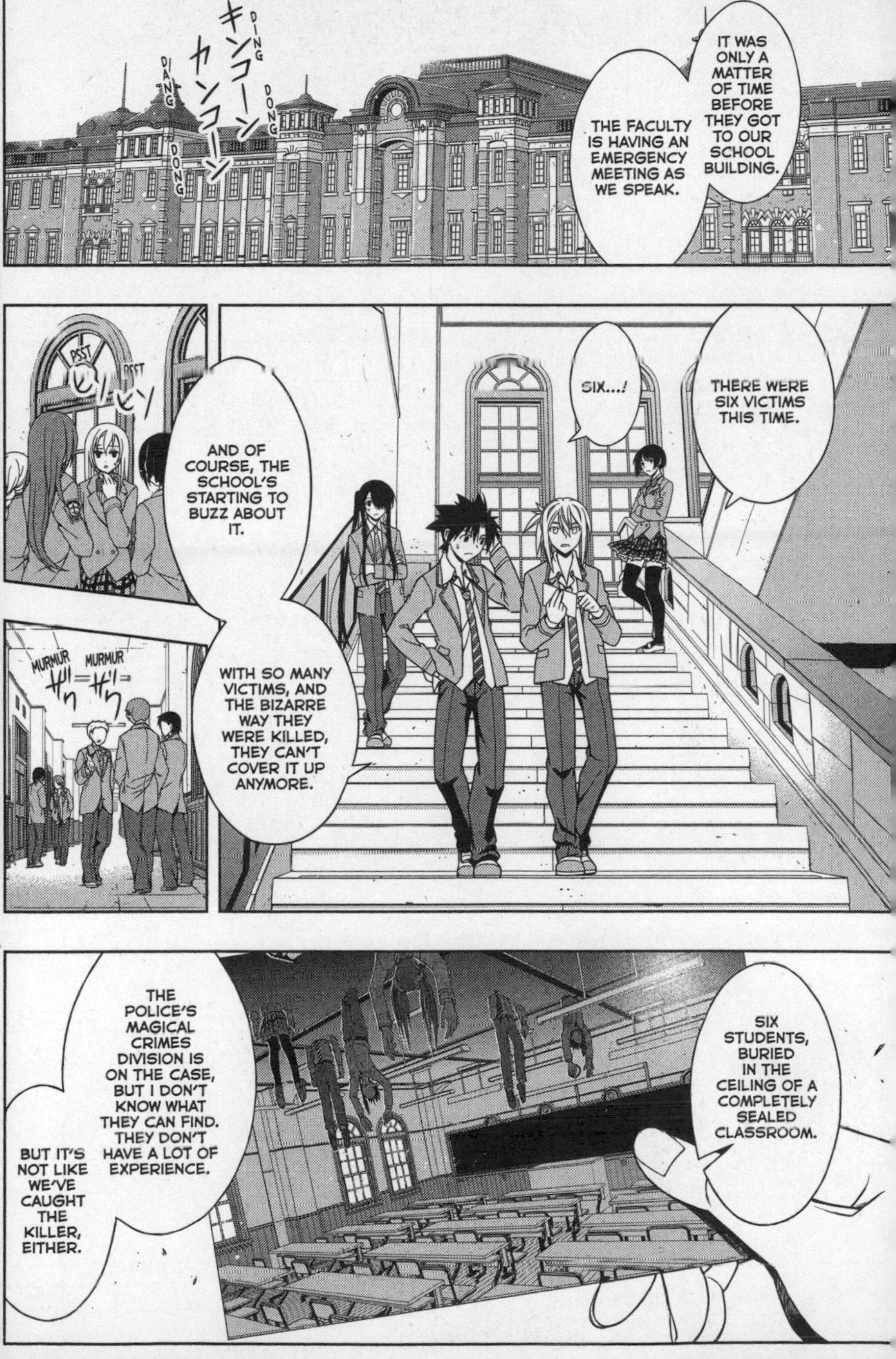
IT WAS ONLY A MATTER OF TIME BEFORE THEY GOT TO OUR SCHOOL BUILDING.
THE FACULTY IS HAVING AN EMERGENCY MEETING AS WE SPEAK.
DING DONG
キンコーン
DIANG DONG
カンコーン
THERE WERE SIX VICTIMS THIS TIME.
SIX...!
AND OF COURSE, THE SCHOOL'S STARTING TO BUZZ ABOUT IT.
WITH SO MANY VICTIMS, AND THE BIZARRE WAY THEY WERE KILLED, THEY CAN'T COVER IT UP ANYMORE.
PSST
ヒソ
PSST
ヒソ
MURMUR
ザワ
MURMUR
ザワ
SIX STUDENTS, BURIED IN THE CEILING OF A COMPLETELY SEALED CLASSROOM.
THE POLICE'S MAGICAL CRIMES DIVISION IS ON THE CASE, BUT I DON'T KNOW WHAT THEY CAN FIND. THEY DON'T HAVE A LOT OF EXPERIENCE.
BUT IT'S NOT LIKE WE'VE CAUGHT THE KILLER, EITHER.

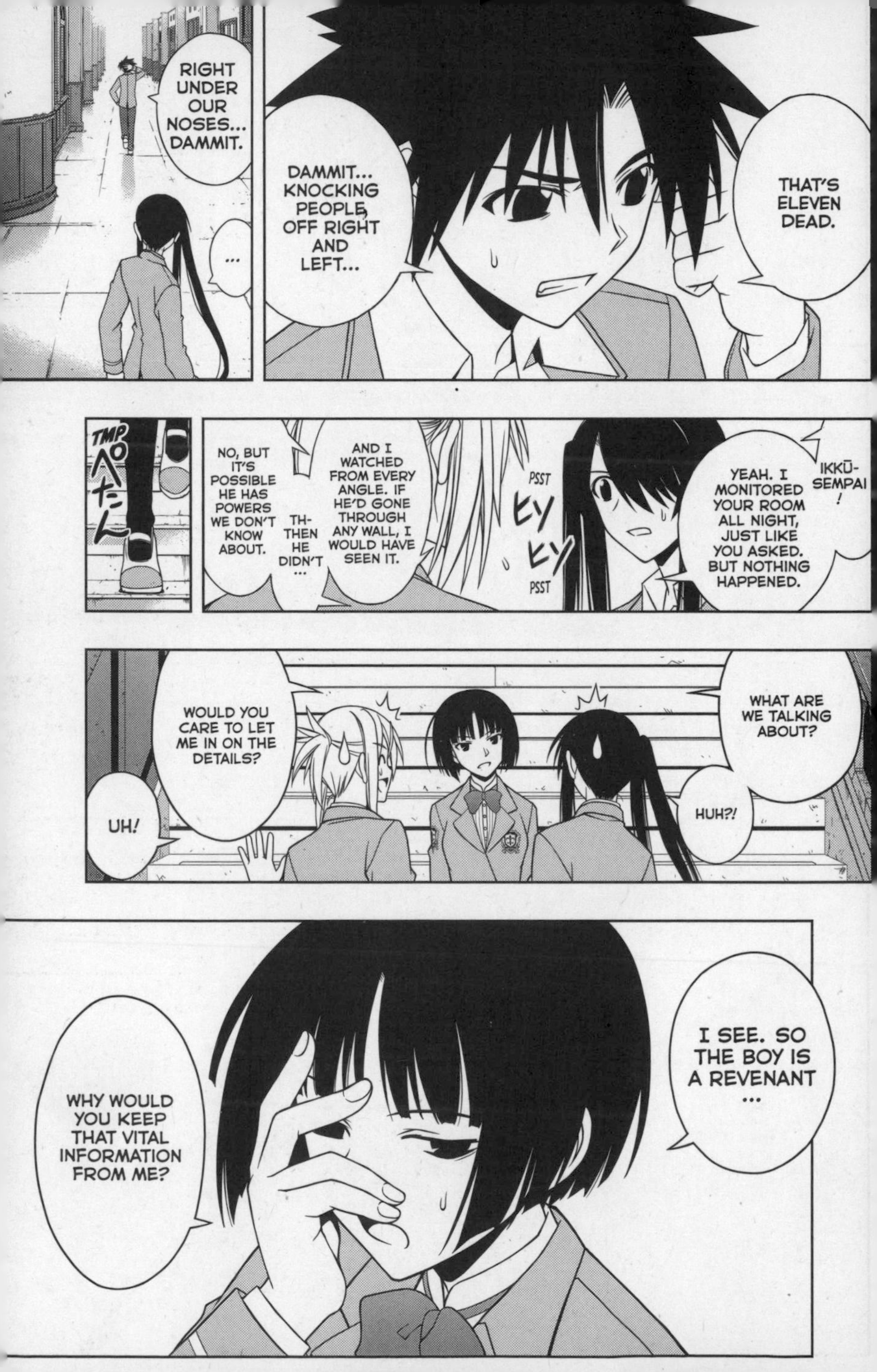
THAT'S ELEVEN DEAD.
DAMMIT... KNOCKING PEOPLE OFF RIGHT AND LEFT...
RIGHT UNDER OUR NOSES... DAMMIT.
...
IKKŪ-SEMPAI!
YEAH. I MONITORED YOUR ROOM ALL NIGHT, JUST LIKE YOU ASKED. BUT NOTHING HAPPENED.
PSST ヒソ
ヒソ PSST
AND I WATCHED FROM EVERY ANGLE. IF HE'D GONE THROUGH ANY WALL, I WOULD HAVE SEEN IT.
TH-THEN HE DIDN'T ...
NO, BUT IT'S POSSIBLE HE HAS POWERS WE DON'T KNOW ABOUT.
TMP へたん
WHAT ARE WE TALKING ABOUT?
HUH?!
WOULD YOU CARE TO LET ME IN ON THE DETAILS?
UH!
I SEE. SO THE BOY IS A REVENANT ...
WHY WOULD YOU KEEP THAT VITAL INFORMATION FROM ME?

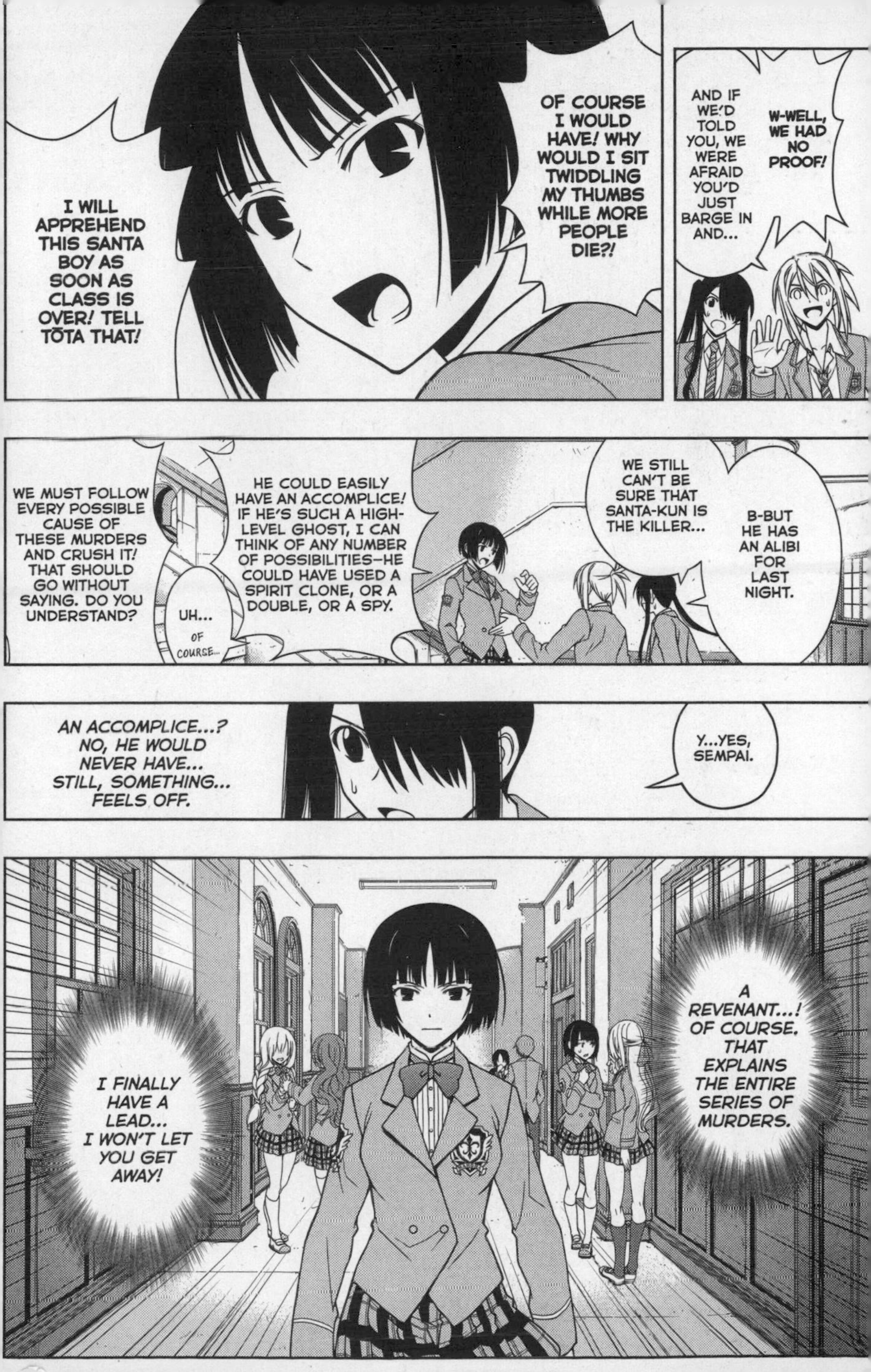
W-WELL, WE HAD NO PROOF!
AND IF WE'D TOLD YOU, WE WERE AFRAID YOU'D JUST BARGE IN AND...
OF COURSE I WOULD HAVE! WHY WOULD I SIT TWIDDLING MY THUMBS WHILE MORE PEOPLE DIE?!
I WILL APPREHEND THIS SANTA BOY AS SOON AS CLASS IS OVER! TELL TŌTA THAT!
B-BUT HE HAS AN ALIBI FOR LAST NIGHT.
WE STILL CAN'T BE SURE THAT SANTA-KUN IS THE KILLER...
HE COULD EASILY HAVE AN ACCOMPLICE! IF HE'S SUCH A HIGH-LEVEL GHOST, I CAN THINK OF ANY NUMBER OF POSSIBILITIES—HE COULD HAVE USED A SPIRIT CLONE, OR A DOUBLE, OR A SPY.
WE MUST FOLLOW EVERY POSSIBLE CAUSE OF THESE MURDERS AND CRUSH IT! THAT SHOULD GO WITHOUT SAYING. DO YOU UNDERSTAND?
UH... OF COURSE...
Y...YES, SEMPAI.
AN ACCOMPLICE...? NO, HE WOULD NEVER HAVE... STILL, SOMETHING... FEELS OFF.
A REVENANT...! OF COURSE. THAT EXPLAINS THE ENTIRE SERIES OF MURDERS.
I FINALLY HAVE A LEAD... I WON'T LET YOU GET AWAY!

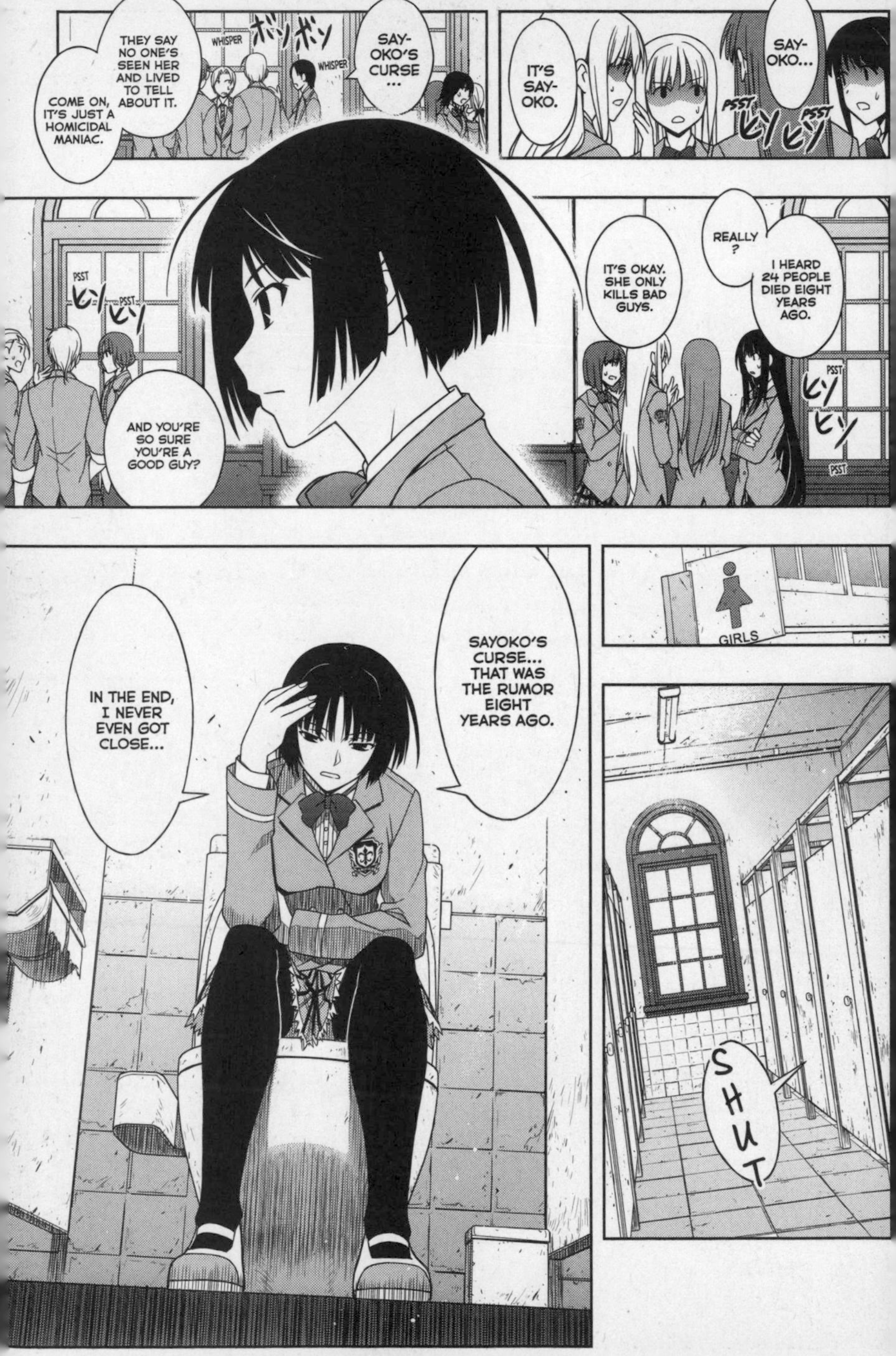
SAY-OKO...
PSST
PSST
IT'S SAY-OKO.
SAY-OKO'S CURSE ...
WHISPER
WHISPER
THEY SAY NO ONE'S SEEN HER AND LIVED TO TELL ABOUT IT.
COME ON, IT'S JUST A HOMICIDAL MANIAC.
REALLY ?
I HEARD 24 PEOPLE DIED EIGHT YEARS AGO.
IT'S OKAY. SHE ONLY KILLS BAD GUYS.
PSST
PSST
PSST
PSST
AND YOU'RE SO SURE YOU'RE A GOOD GUY?
GIRLS
SHUT
SAYOKO'S CURSE... THAT WAS THE RUMOR EIGHT YEARS AGO.
IN THE END, I NEVER EVEN GOT CLOSE...

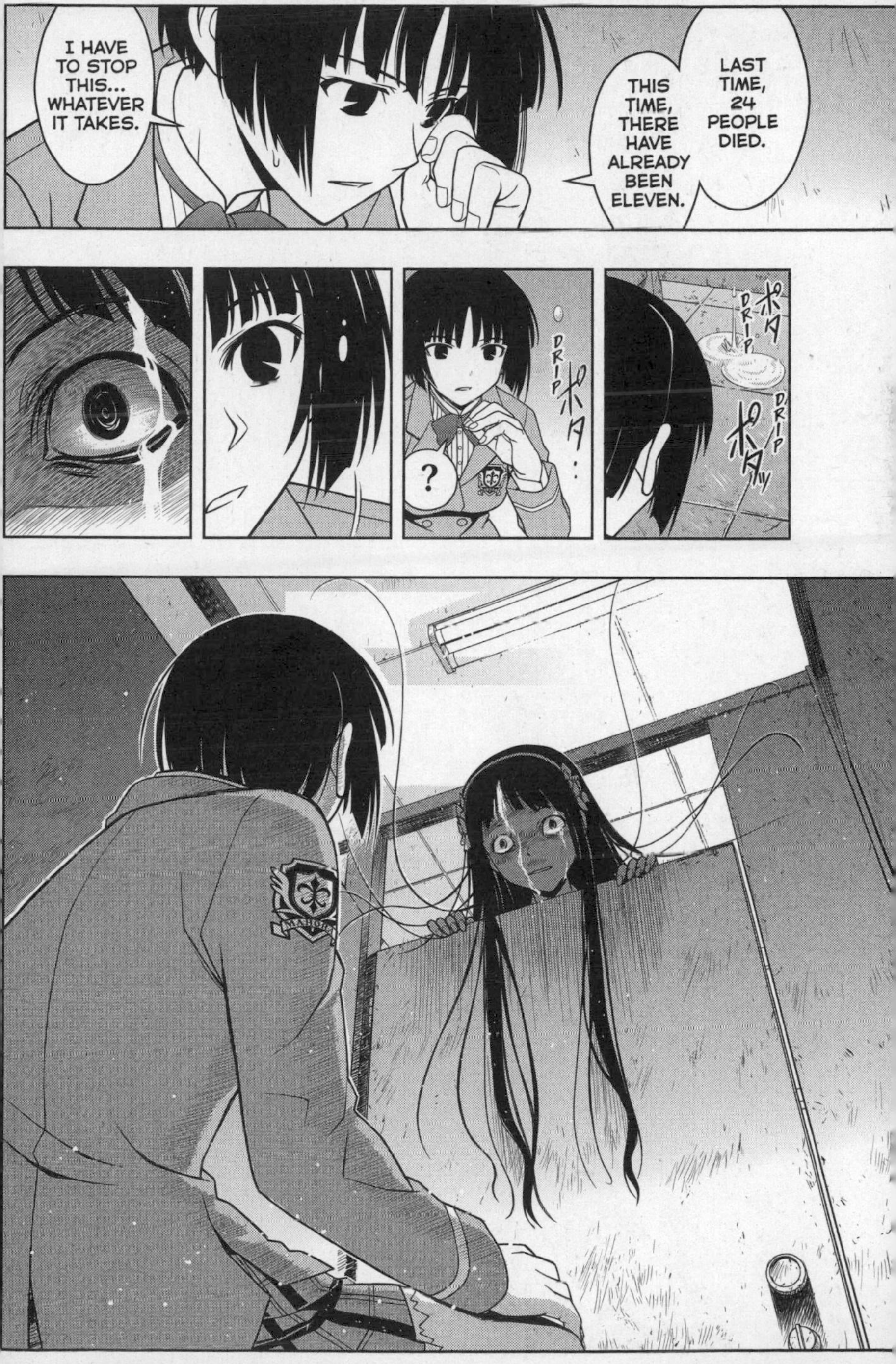
LAST TIME, 24 PEOPLE DIED.
THIS TIME, THERE HAVE ALREADY BEEN ELEVEN.
I HAVE TO STOP THIS... WHATEVER IT TAKES.
ポタ
DRIP
ポタッ
DRIP
DRIP
ポタ・・
?

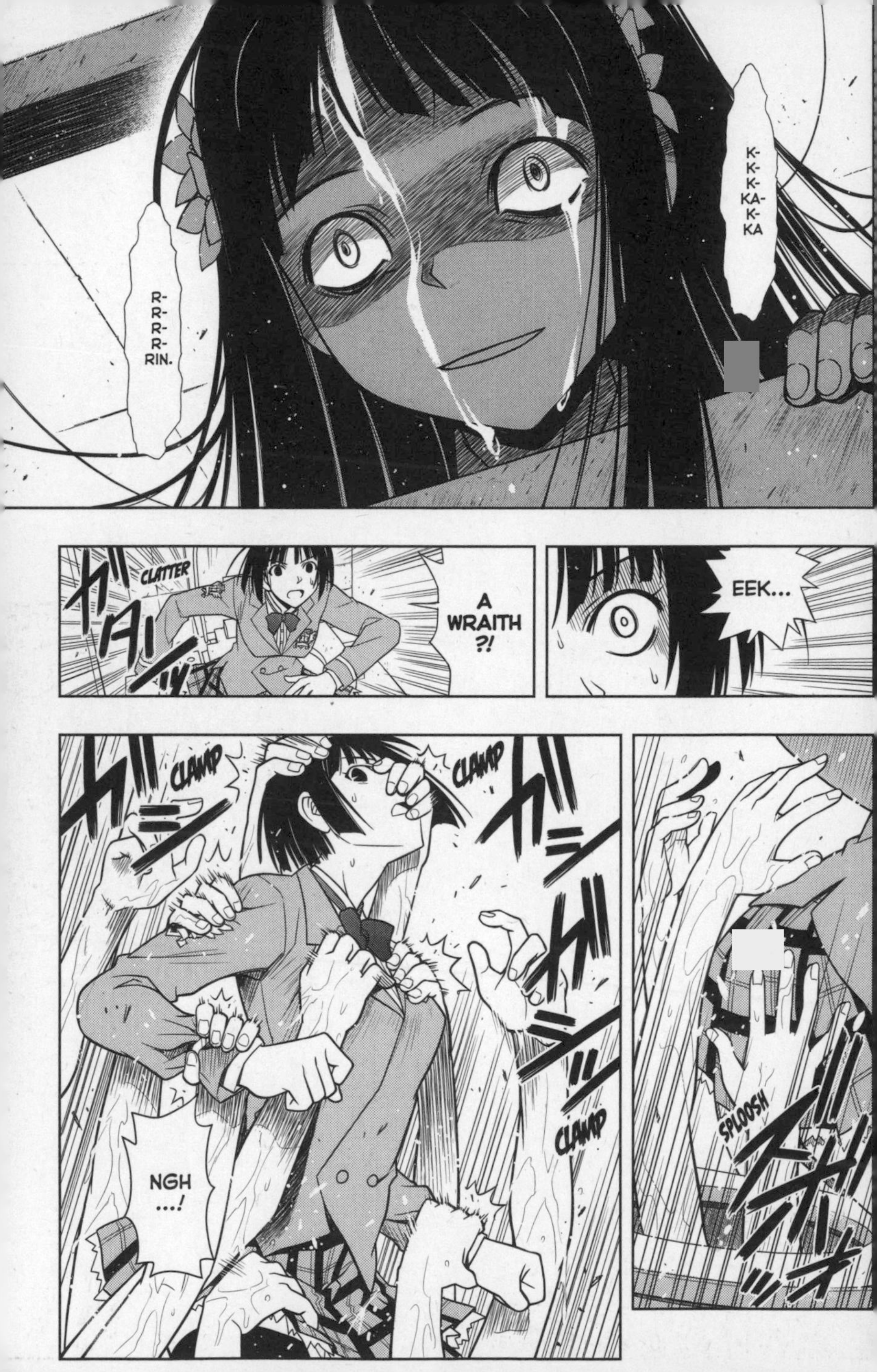
K-K-K-KA-K-KA
R-R-R-R-RIN.
EEK...
CLATTER
A WRAITH ?!
SPLOOSH
CLAMP
CLAMP
CLAMP
NGH ...!

UQ HOLDER!

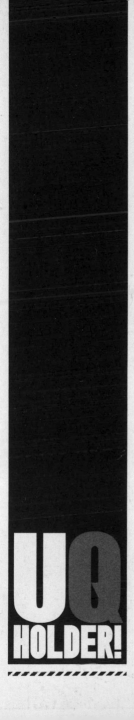

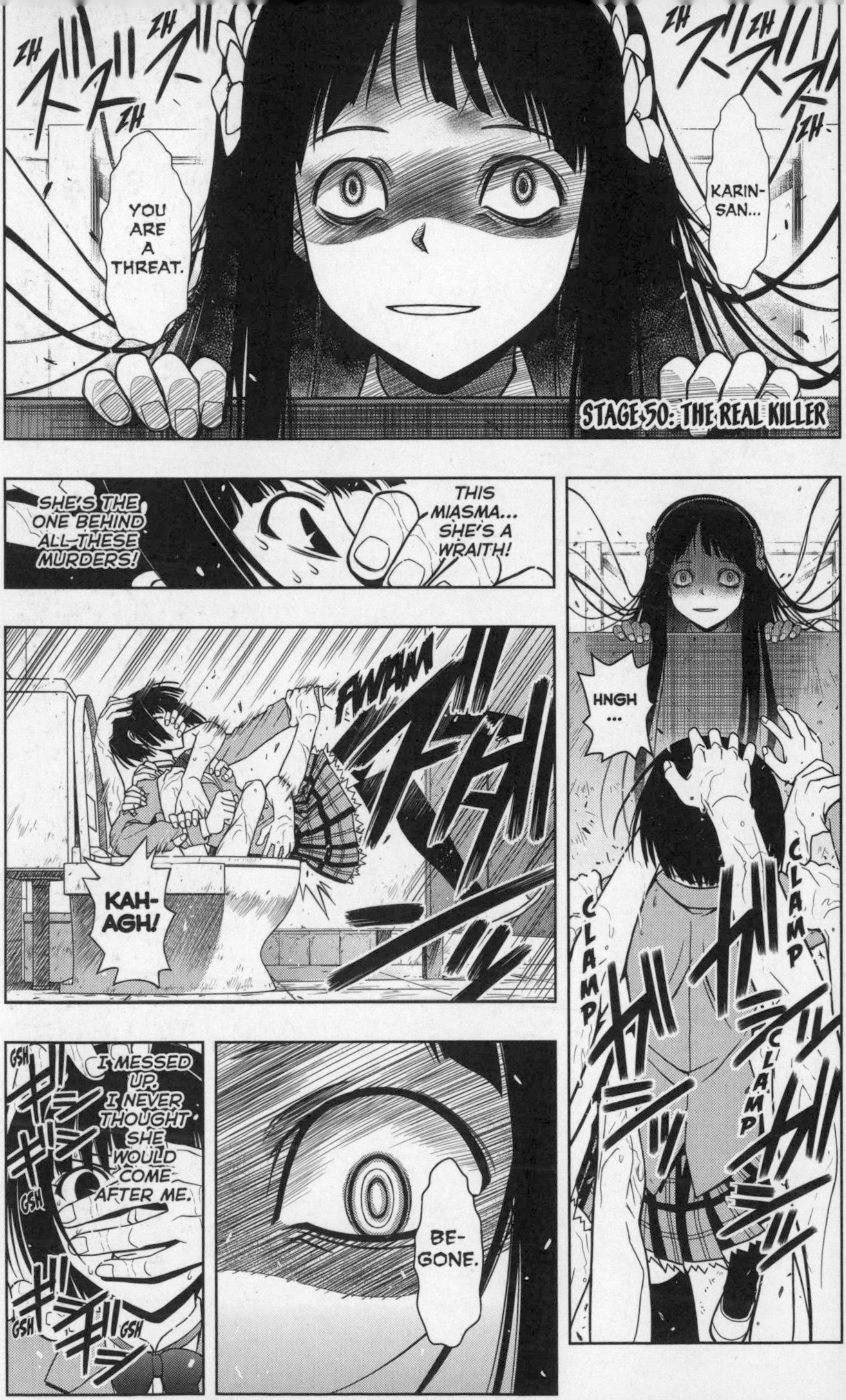
ZH
KARIN-SAN...
ZH
YOU ARE A THREAT.
STAGE 50: THE REAL KILLER
HNGH...
CLAMP
CLAMP
CLAMP
CLAMP
THIS MIASMA... SHE'S A WRAITH!
SHE'S THE ONE BEHIND ALL THESE MURDERS!
FWAM
KAH-AGH!
BE-GONE.
I MESSED UP. I NEVER THOUGHT SHE WOULD COME AFTER ME.
GSH
GSH
GSH
GSH

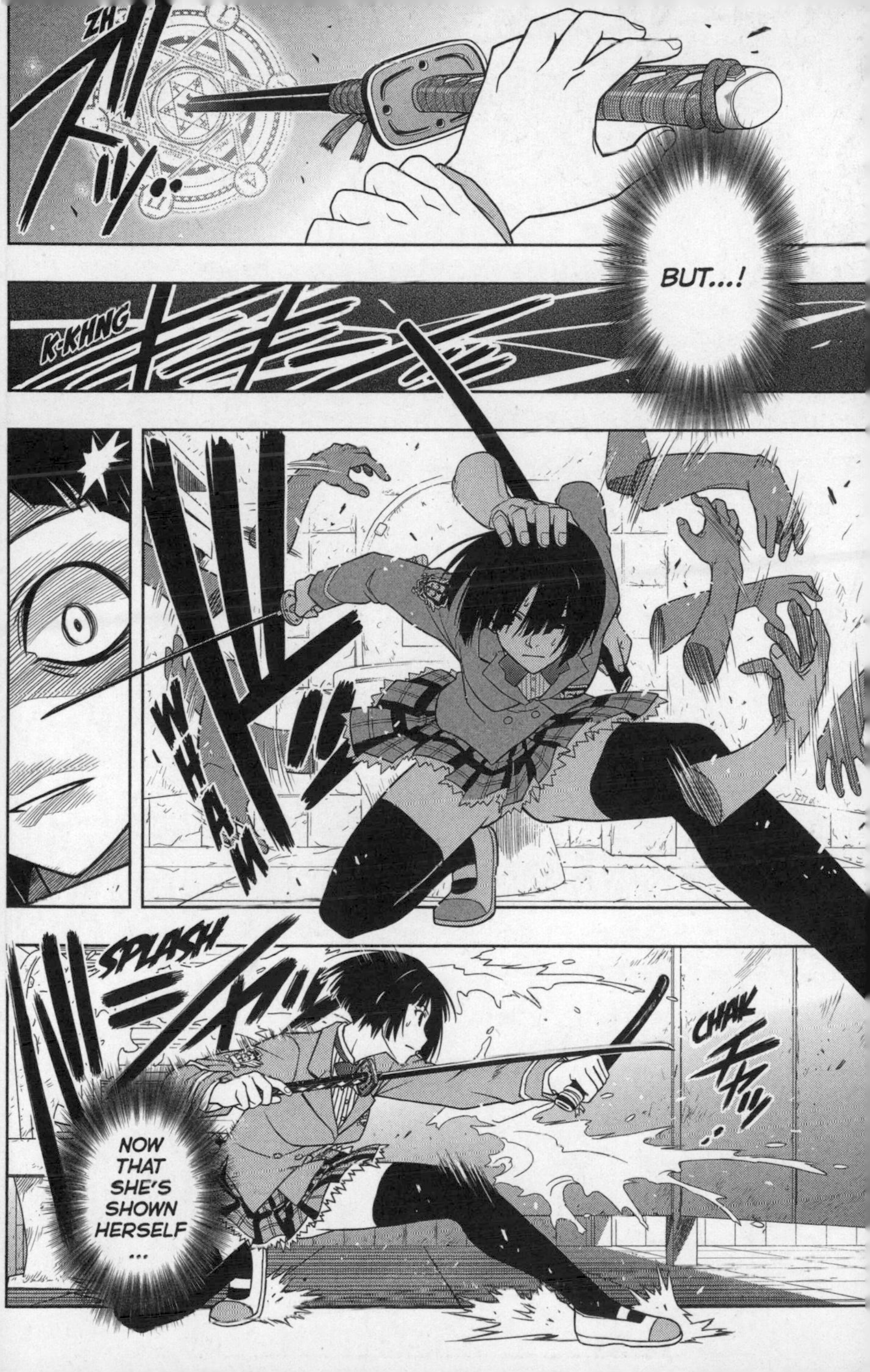
ZH
BUT...!
K-KHNG
WHAM
CHAK
SPLASH
NOW THAT SHE'S SHOWN HERSELF ...

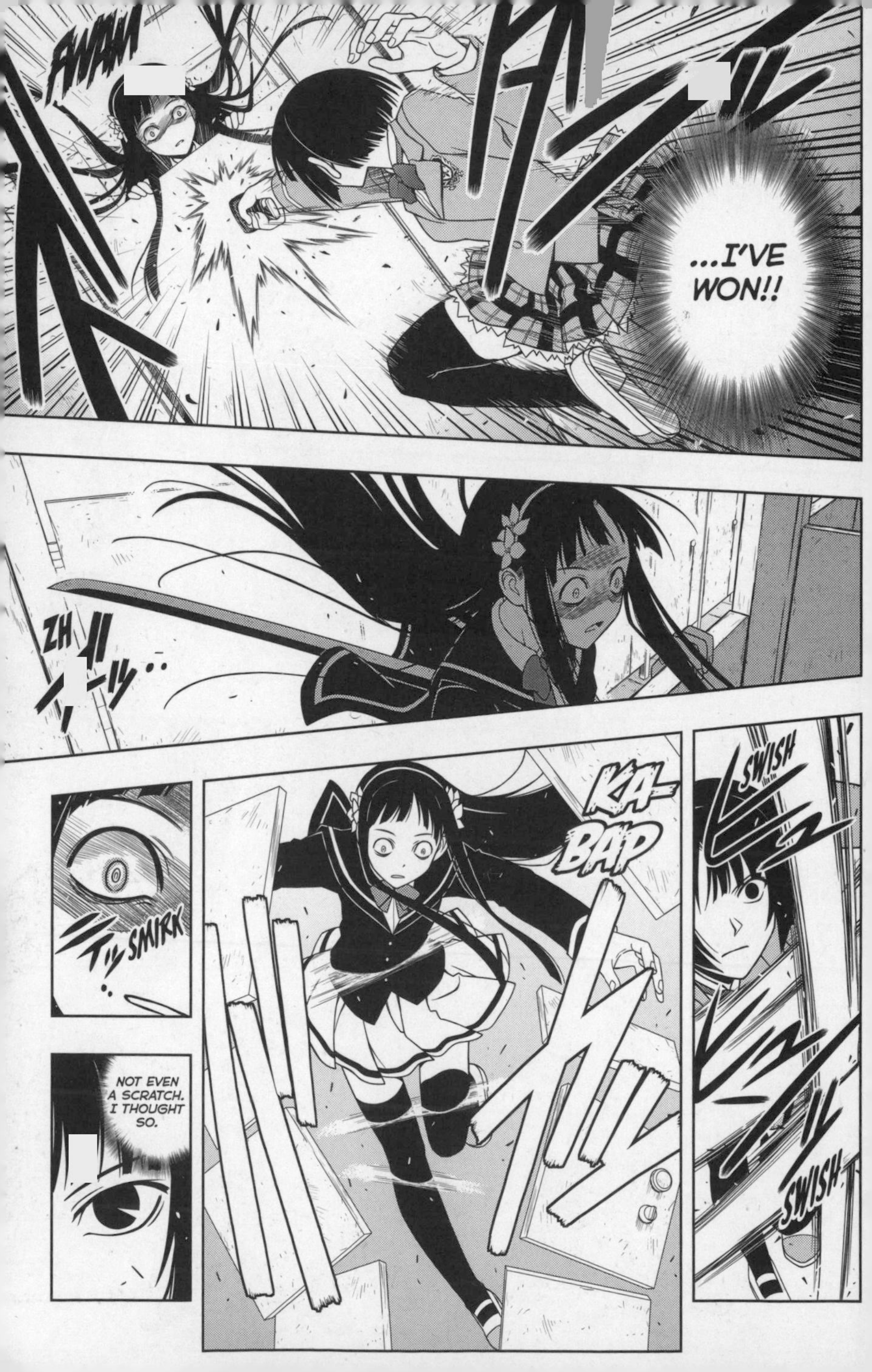
...I'VE WON!!
FWAAA
ZH
SWISH
SWISH
KA-BAP
SMIRK
NOT EVEN A SCRATCH. I THOUGHT SO.

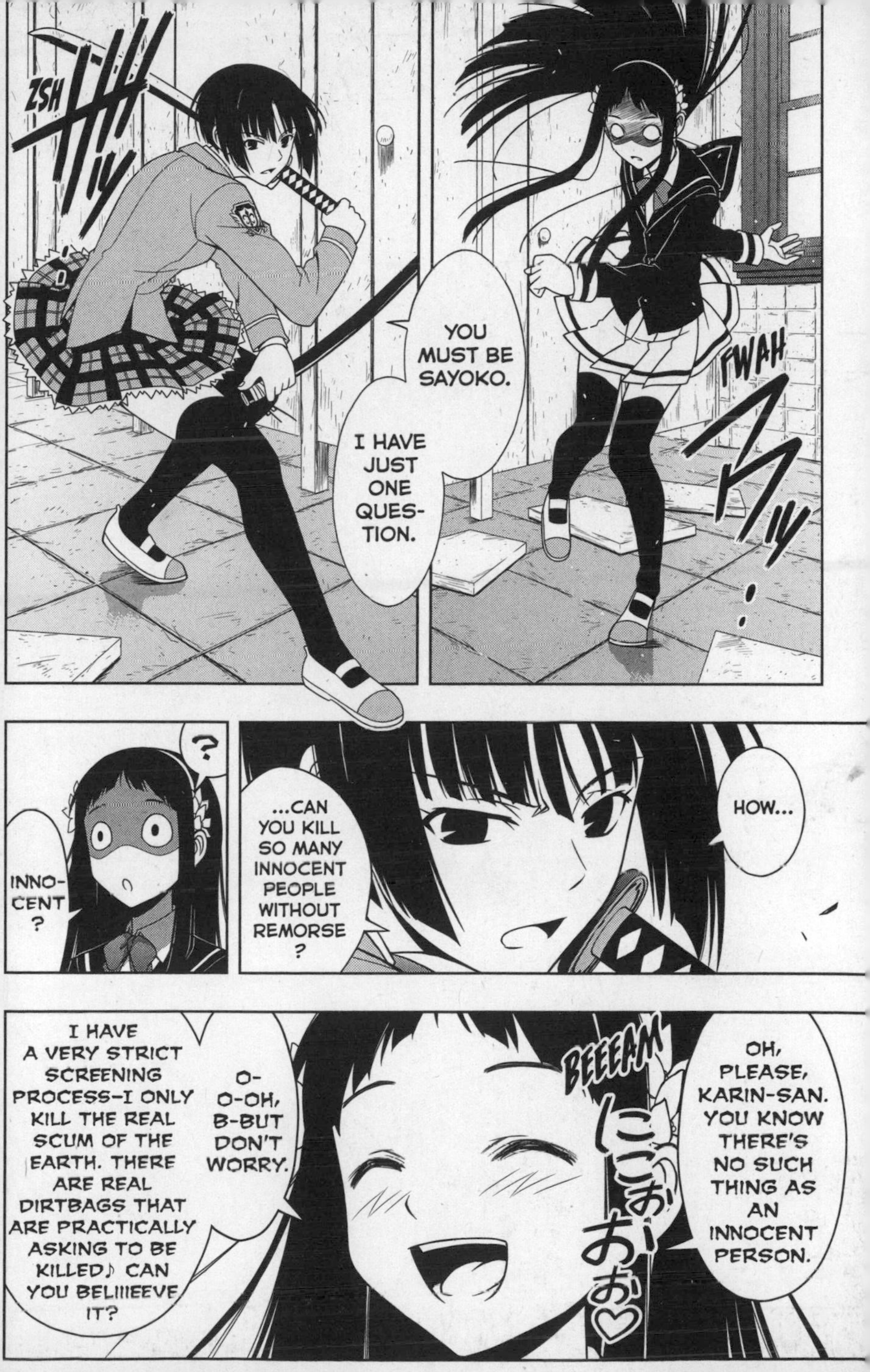
YOU MUST BE SAYOKO.
I HAVE JUST ONE QUES-TION.
FWAH
ZSH
HOW...
...CAN YOU KILL SO MANY INNOCENT PEOPLE WITHOUT REMORSE?
?
INNO-CENT?
OH, PLEASE, KARIN-SAN. YOU KNOW THERE'S NO SUCH THING AS AN INNOCENT PERSON.
BEEEAM
にこぉぉ♡
O-O-OH, B-BUT DON'T WORRY.
I HAVE A VERY STRICT SCREENING PROCESS—I ONLY KILL THE REAL SCUM OF THE EARTH. THERE ARE REAL DIRTBAGS THAT ARE PRACTICALLY ASKING TO BE KILLED♪ CAN YOU BELIIIEEVE IT?

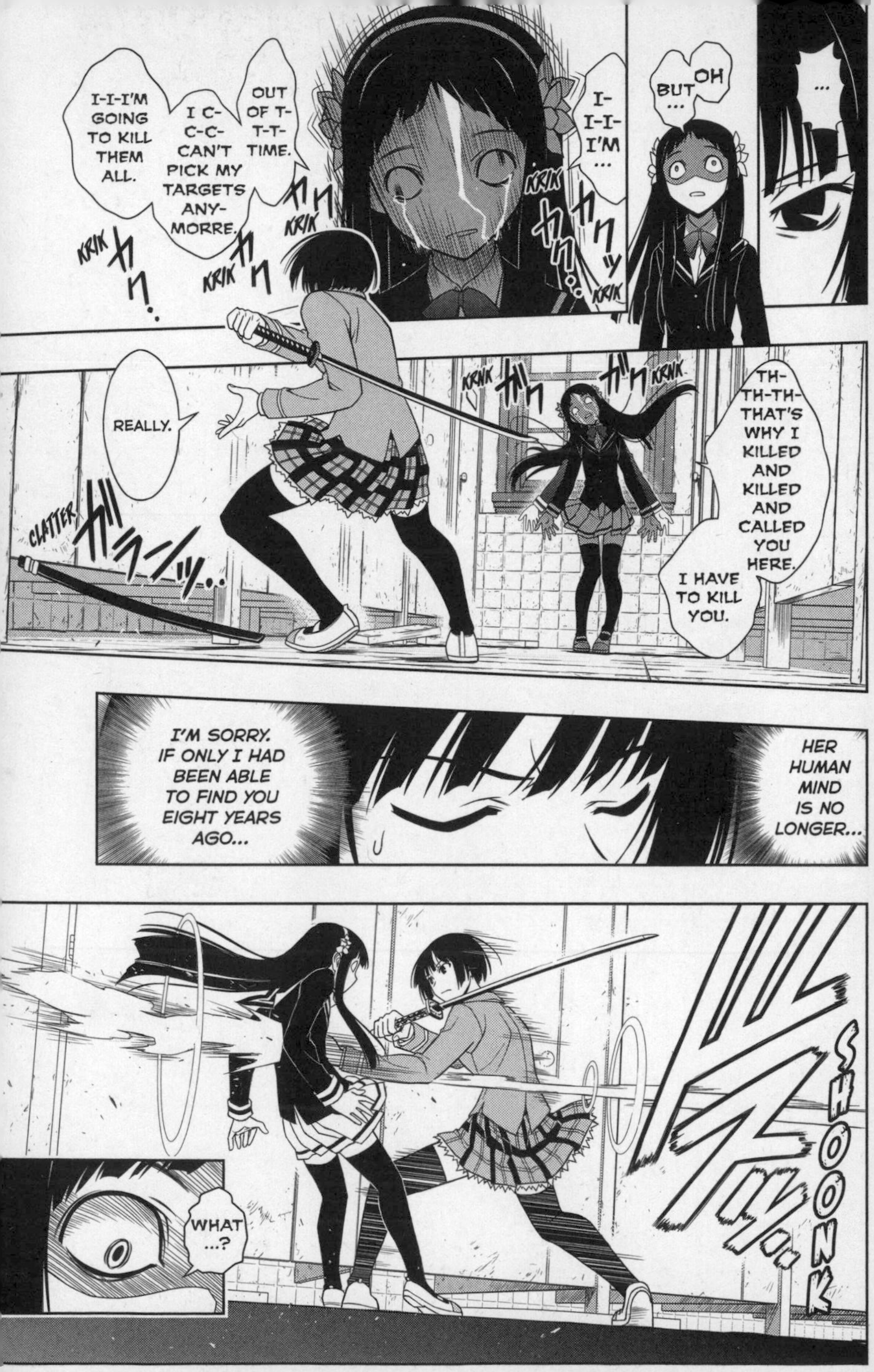
...
OH BUT ...
I-I-I-I'M ...
KRIK
KRIK
OUT OF T-T-T-TIME.
I C-C-C-CAN'T PICK MY TARGETS ANY-MORRE.
I-I-I'M GOING TO KILL THEM ALL.
KRIK
KRIK
TH-TH-TH-THAT'S WHY I KILLED AND KILLED AND CALLED YOU HERE.
I HAVE TO KILL YOU.
KRNK
KRNK
REALLY.
CLATTER
HER HUMAN MIND IS NO LONGER...
I'M SORRY. IF ONLY I HAD BEEN ABLE TO FIND YOU EIGHT YEARS AGO...
SHOONK
WHAT ...?

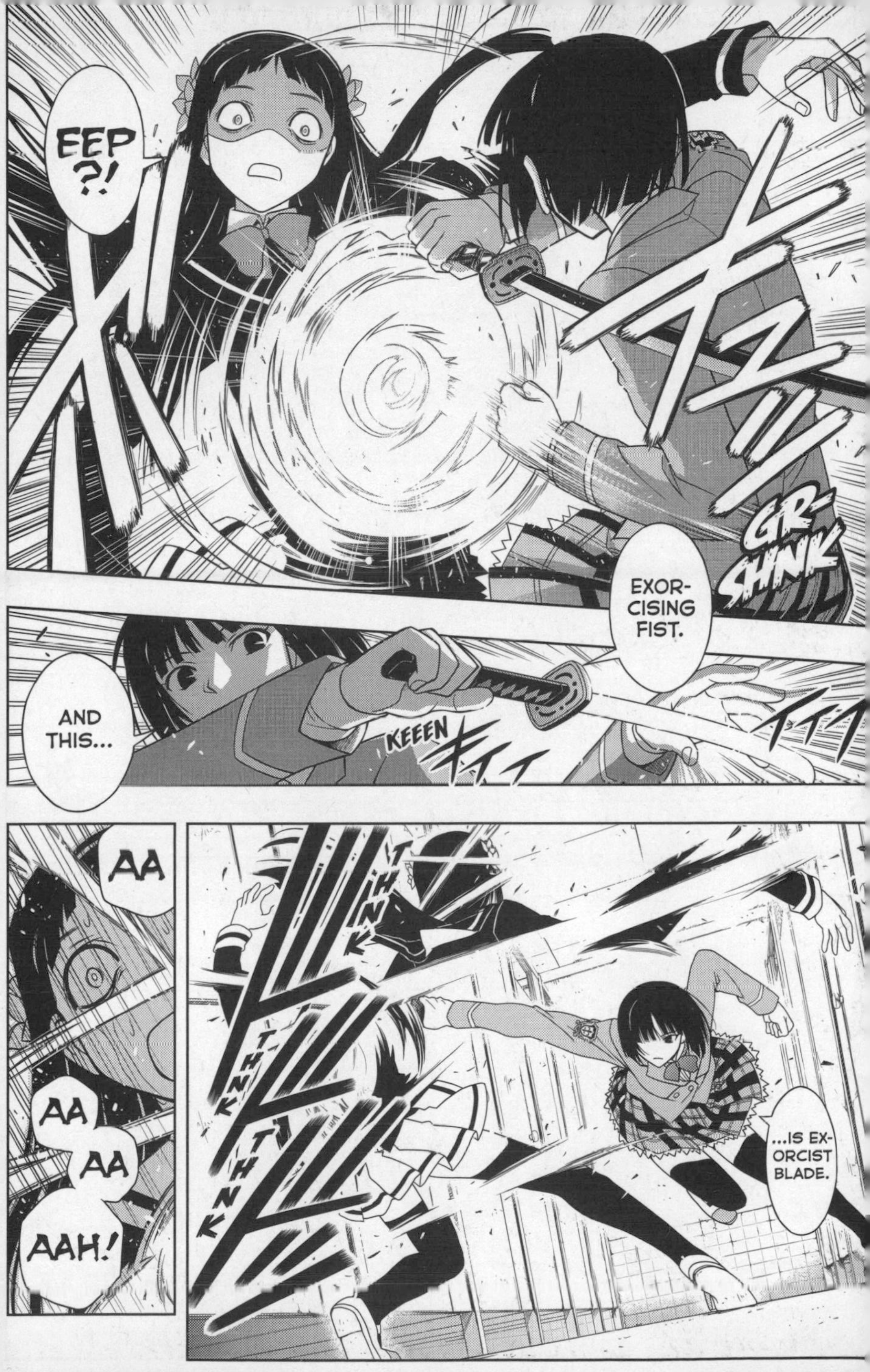
EEP ?!
GR-SHNK
EXOR-CISING FIST.
KEEEN
AND THIS...
THNK
THNK
THNK
...IS EX-ORCIST BLADE.
AA
AA
AA
AAH!

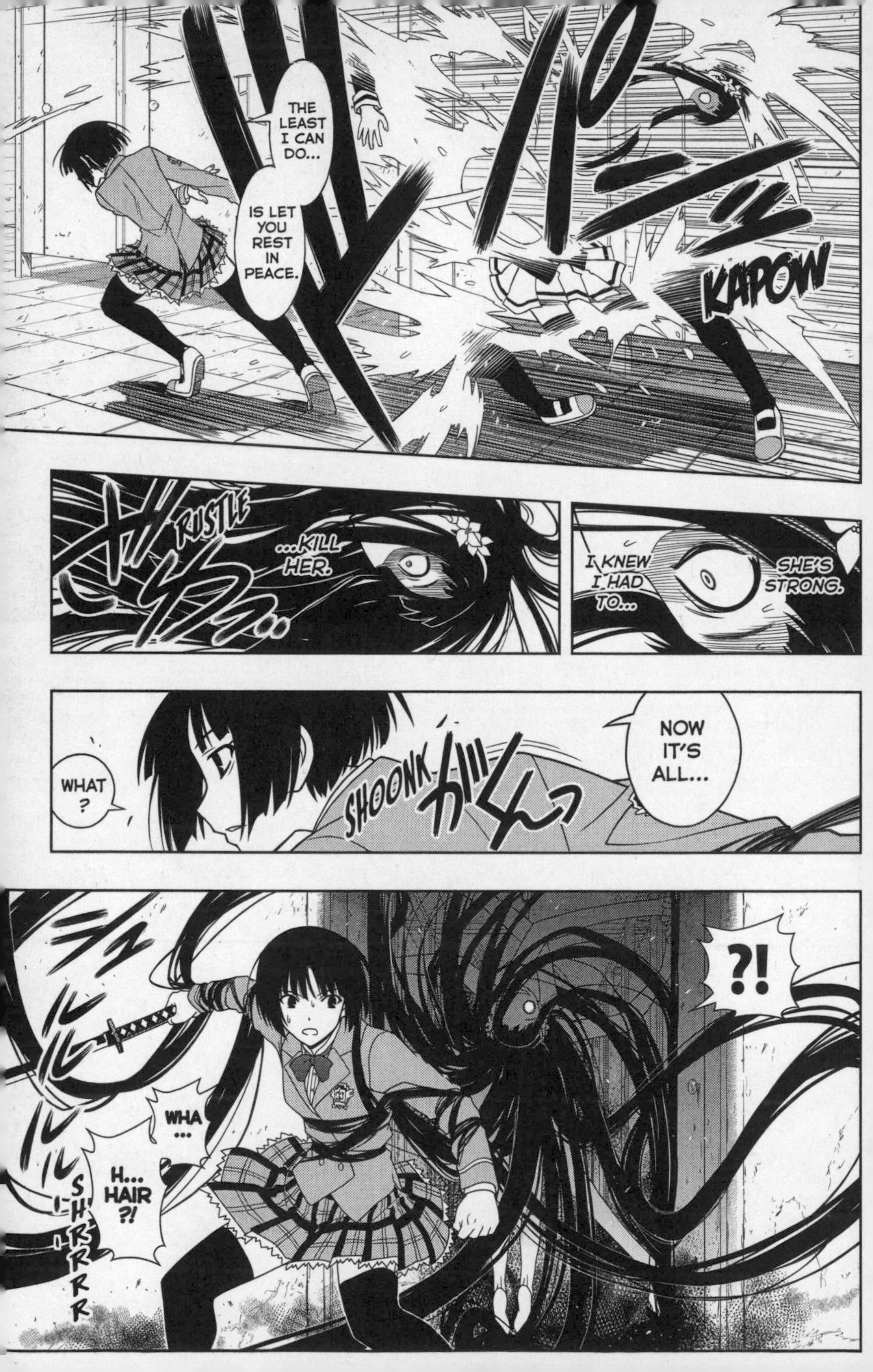
THE LEAST I CAN DO...
IS LET YOU REST IN PEACE.
KAPOW
SHE'S STRONG.
I KNEW I HAD TO...
...KILL HER.
RUSTLE
NOW IT'S ALL...
SHOONK
WHAT?
?!
WHA...
H... HAIR?!
SHRRRR

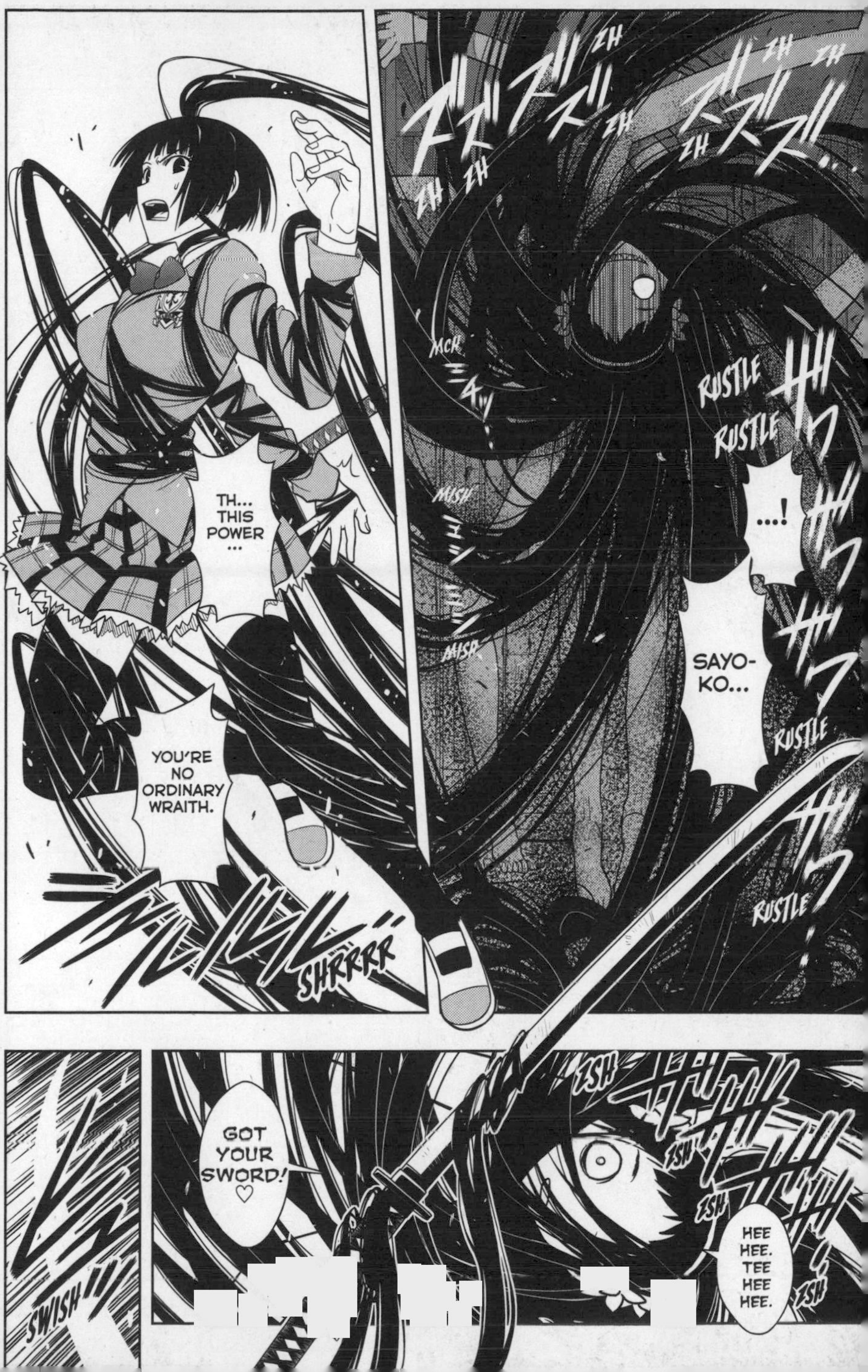
ZH ZH ZH ZH ZH ZH ZH
MCH
MISH
MISH
RUSTLE
RUSTLE
...!
SAYO-KO...
RUSTLE
RUSTLE
TH... THIS POWER...
YOU'RE NO ORDINARY WRAITH.
SHRRRR
TSH
GOT YOUR SWORD! ♡
TSH
TSH
HEE HEE. TEE HEE HEE.
TSH
SWISH

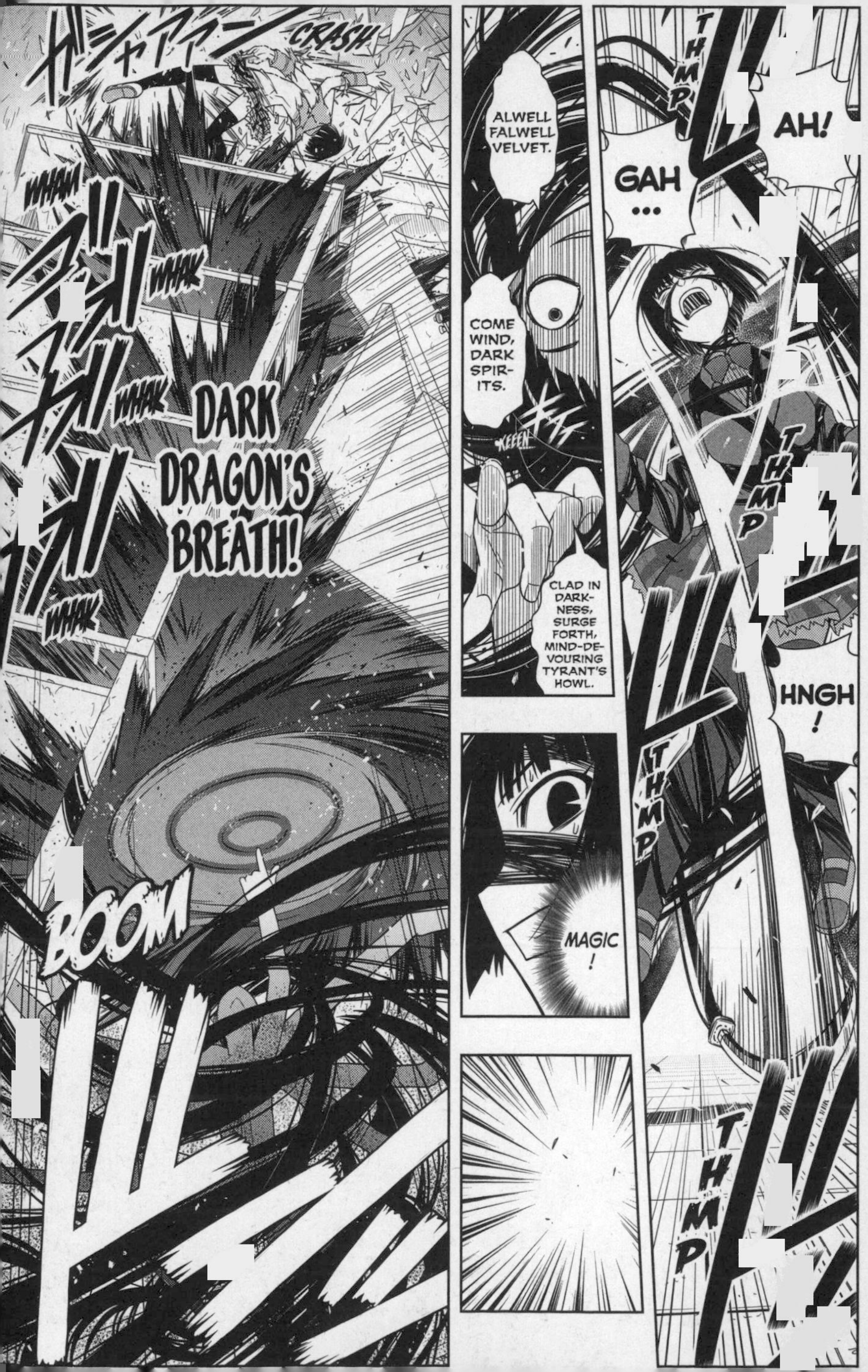
THMP
AH!
GAH...
THMP
HNGH!
THMP
THMP
ALWELL FALWELL VELVET.
COME WIND, DARK SPIRITS.
KEEEN
CLAD IN DARKNESS, SURGE FORTH, MIND-DEVOURING TYRANT'S HOWL.
MAGIC!
ガシャアーン
CRASH
WHAM
WHAK
WHAK
DARK DRAGON'S BREATH!
WHAK
BOOM

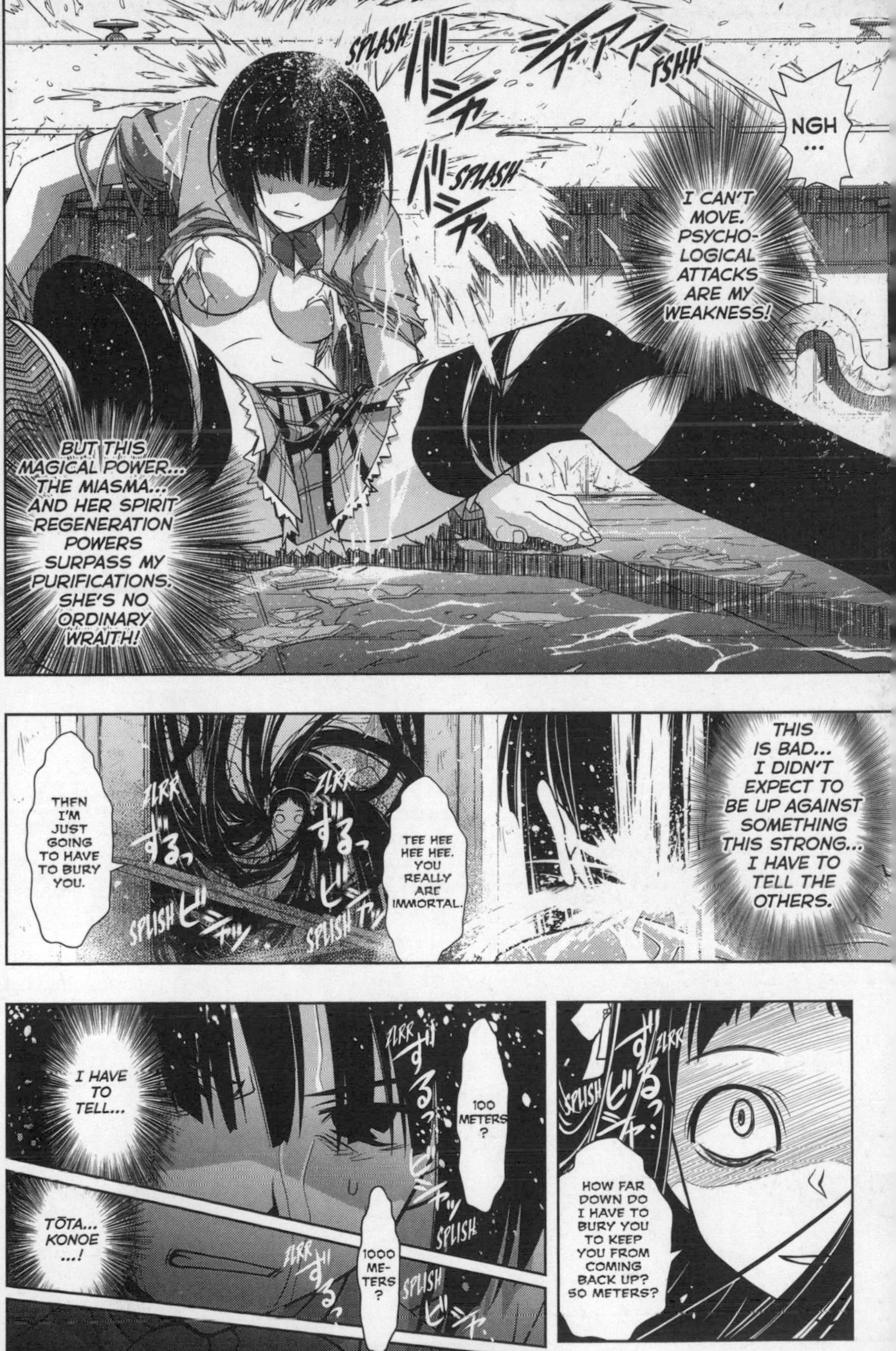
FSHH
SPLASH
SPLASH
NGH ...
I CAN'T MOVE. PSYCHO-LOGICAL ATTACKS ARE MY WEAKNESS!
BUT THIS MAGICAL POWER... THE MIASMA... AND HER SPIRIT REGENERATION POWERS SURPASS MY PURIFICATIONS. SHE'S NO ORDINARY WRAITH!
THIS IS BAD... I DIDN'T EXPECT TO BE UP AGAINST SOMETHING THIS STRONG... I HAVE TO TELL THE OTHERS.
ZLRR
TEE HEE HEE HEE. YOU REALLY ARE IMMORTAL.
SPLISH
THEN I'M JUST GOING TO HAVE TO BURY YOU.
SPLISH
ZLRR
SPLISH
HOW FAR DOWN DO I HAVE TO BURY YOU TO KEEP YOU FROM COMING BACK UP? 50 METERS?
ZLRR
100 METERS?
SPLISH
I HAVE TO TELL...
ZLRR
1000 METERS?
SPLISH
TŌTA... KONOE ...!

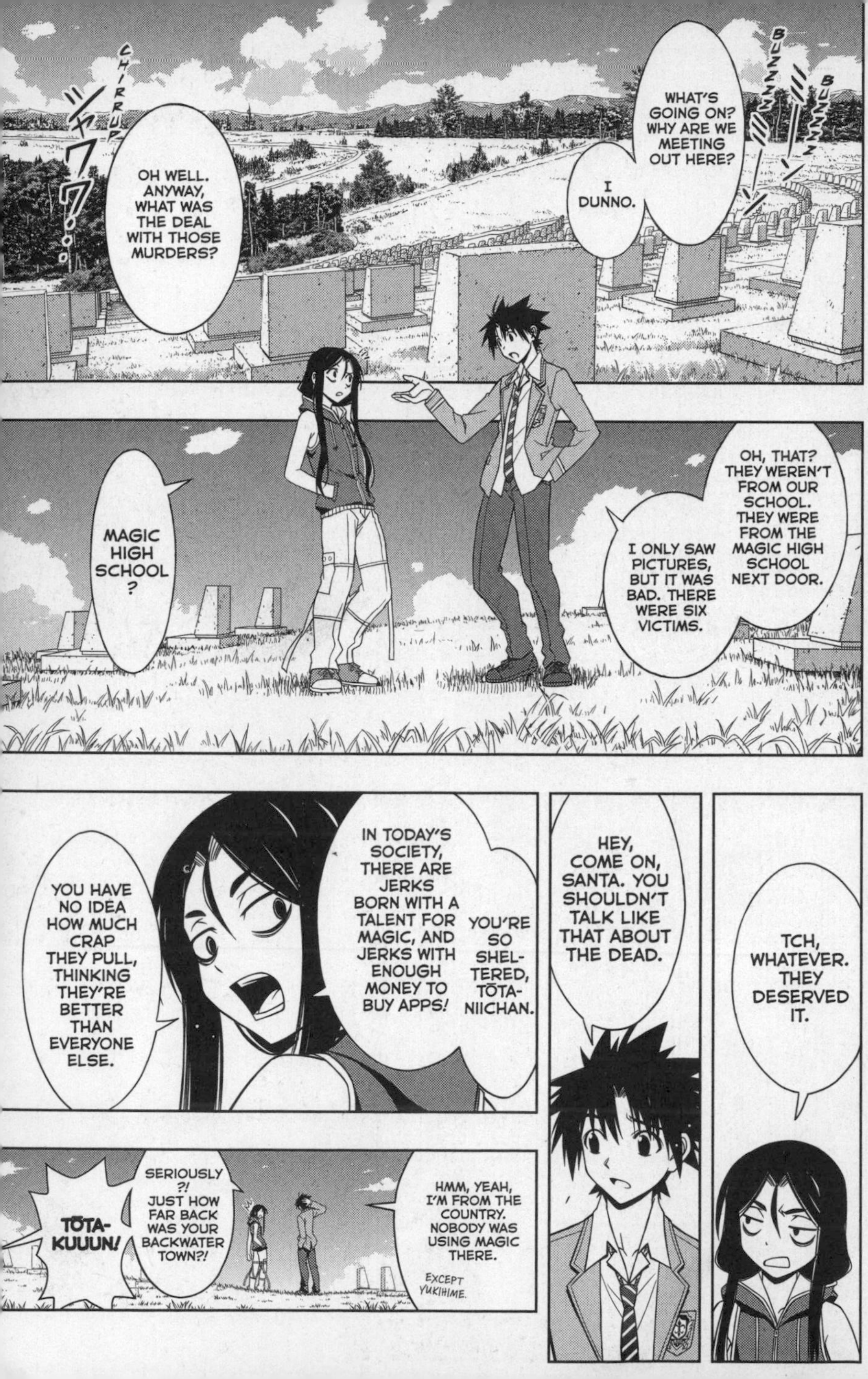
BUZZZZ
BUZZZZ
WHAT'S GOING ON? WHY ARE WE MEETING OUT HERE?
I DUNNO.
OH WELL. ANYWAY, WHAT WAS THE DEAL WITH THOSE MURDERS?
CHIRRUP
OH, THAT? THEY WEREN'T FROM OUR SCHOOL. THEY WERE FROM THE MAGIC HIGH SCHOOL NEXT DOOR.
I ONLY SAW PICTURES, BUT IT WAS BAD. THERE WERE SIX VICTIMS.
MAGIC HIGH SCHOOL?
TCH, WHATEVER. THEY DESERVED IT.
HEY, COME ON, SANTA. YOU SHOULDN'T TALK LIKE THAT ABOUT THE DEAD.
YOU'RE SO SHEL-TERED, TŌTA-NIICHAN.
IN TODAY'S SOCIETY, THERE ARE JERKS BORN WITH A TALENT FOR MAGIC, AND JERKS WITH ENOUGH MONEY TO BUY APPS!
YOU HAVE NO IDEA HOW MUCH CRAP THEY PULL, THINKING THEY'RE BETTER THAN EVERYONE ELSE.
HMM, YEAH, I'M FROM THE COUNTRY. NOBODY WAS USING MAGIC THERE.
EXCEPT YUKIHIME.
SERIOUSLY?! JUST HOW FAR BACK WAS YOUR BACKWATER TOWN?!
TŌTA-KUUUN!

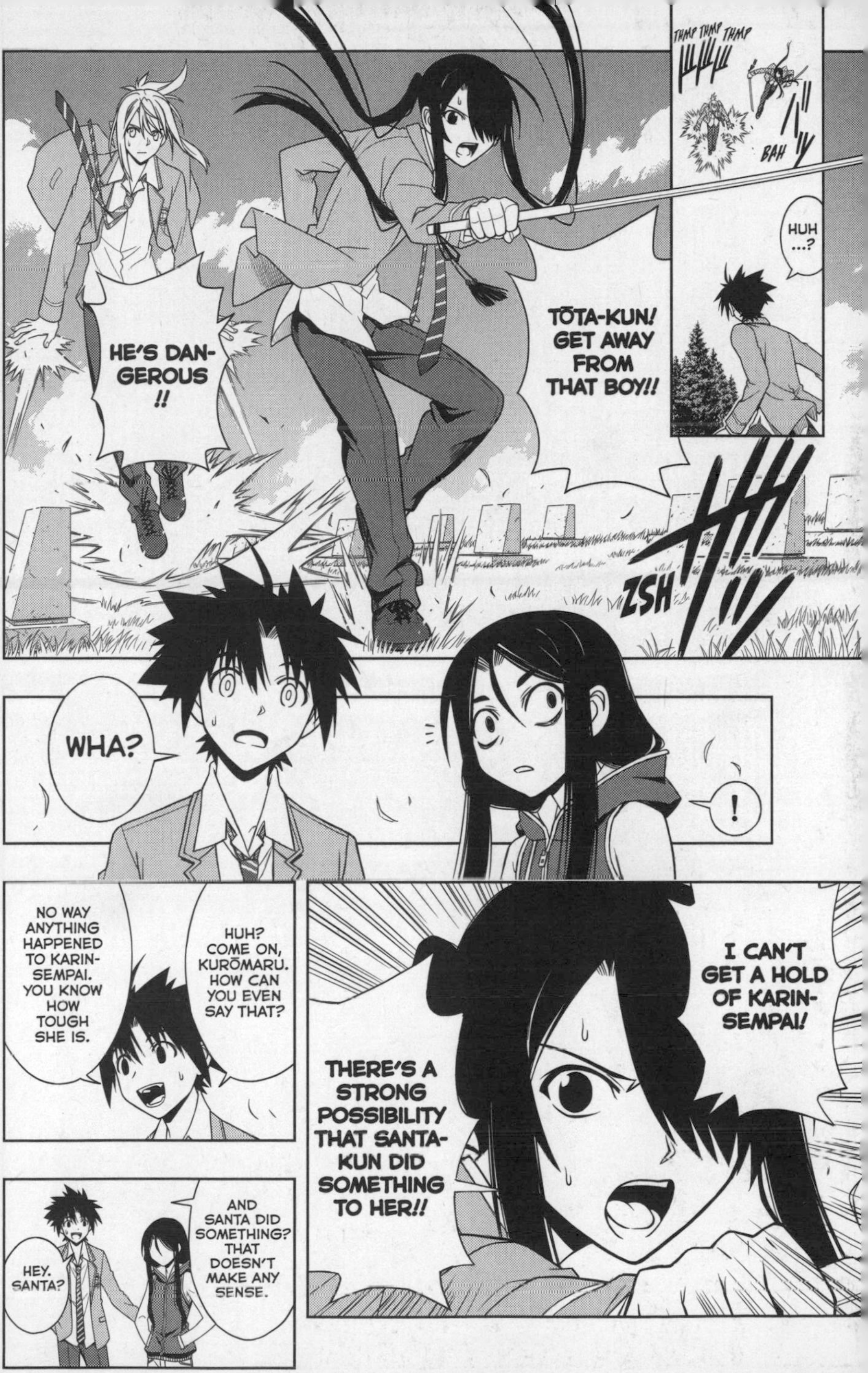
THMP THMP THMP
BAH
HUH ...?
TŌTA-KUN! GET AWAY FROM THAT BOY!!
HE'S DAN-GEROUS !!
ZSH
WHA?
!
I CAN'T GET A HOLD OF KARIN-SEMPAI!
THERE'S A STRONG POSSIBILITY THAT SANTA-KUN DID SOMETHING TO HER!!
HUH? COME ON, KURŌMARU. HOW CAN YOU EVEN SAY THAT?
NO WAY ANYTHING HAPPENED TO KARIN-SEMPAI. YOU KNOW HOW TOUGH SHE IS.
AND SANTA DID SOMETHING? THAT DOESN'T MAKE ANY SENSE.
HEY. SANTA?

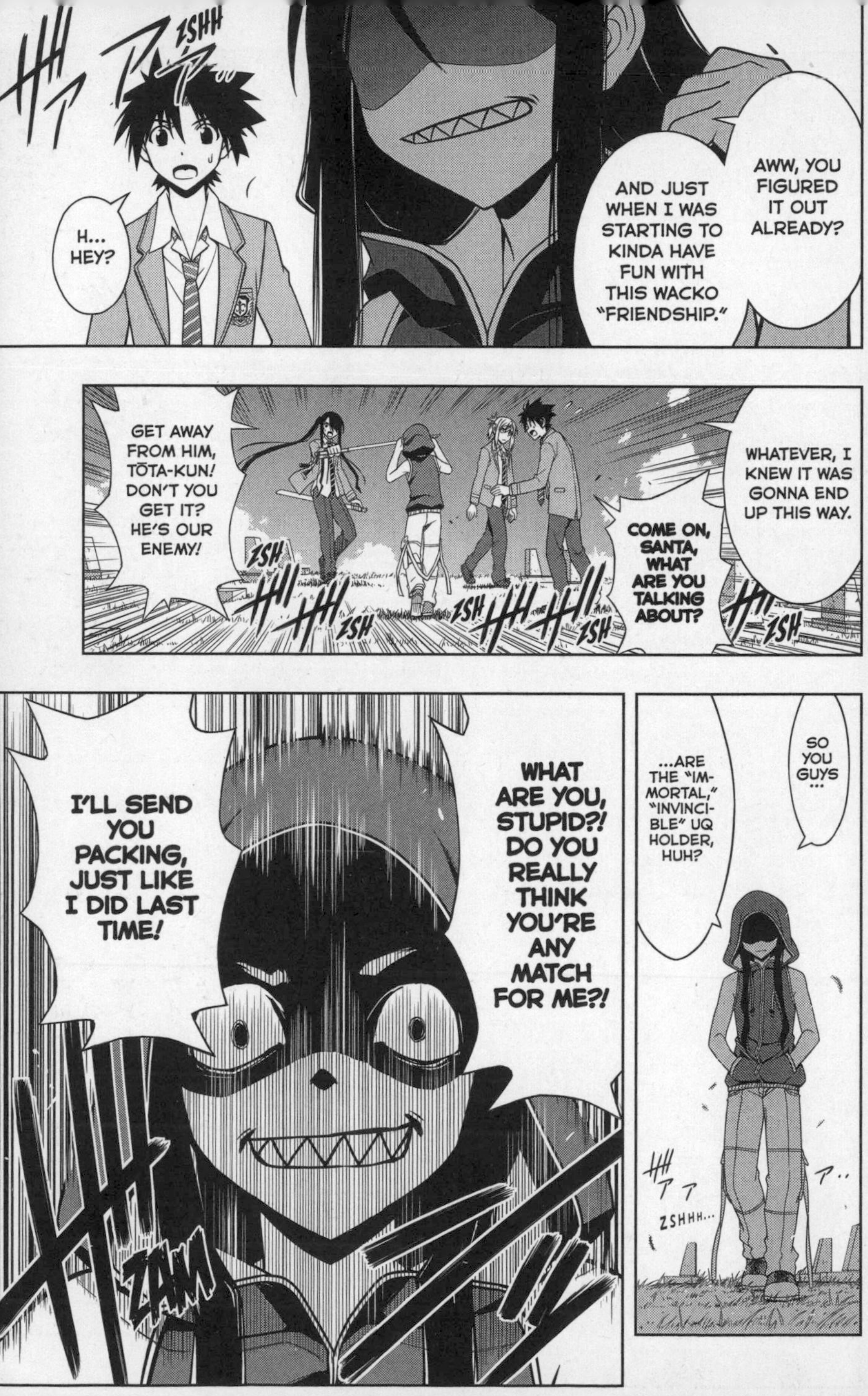
ZSHH
AWW, YOU FIGURED IT OUT ALREADY?
AND JUST WHEN I WAS STARTING TO KINDA HAVE FUN WITH THIS WACKO "FRIENDSHIP."
H... HEY?
WHATEVER, I KNEW IT WAS GONNA END UP THIS WAY.
ZSH
COME ON, SANTA, WHAT ARE YOU TALKING ABOUT?
ZSH
ZSH
GET AWAY FROM HIM, TŌTA-KUN! DON'T YOU GET IT? HE'S OUR ENEMY!
ZSH
SO YOU GUYS...
...ARE THE "IM-MORTAL," "INVINCI-BLE" UQ HOLDER, HUH?
ZSHHH...
WHAT ARE YOU, STUPID?! DO YOU REALLY THINK YOU'RE ANY MATCH FOR ME?!
I'LL SEND YOU PACKING, JUST LIKE I DID LAST TIME!
ZAM

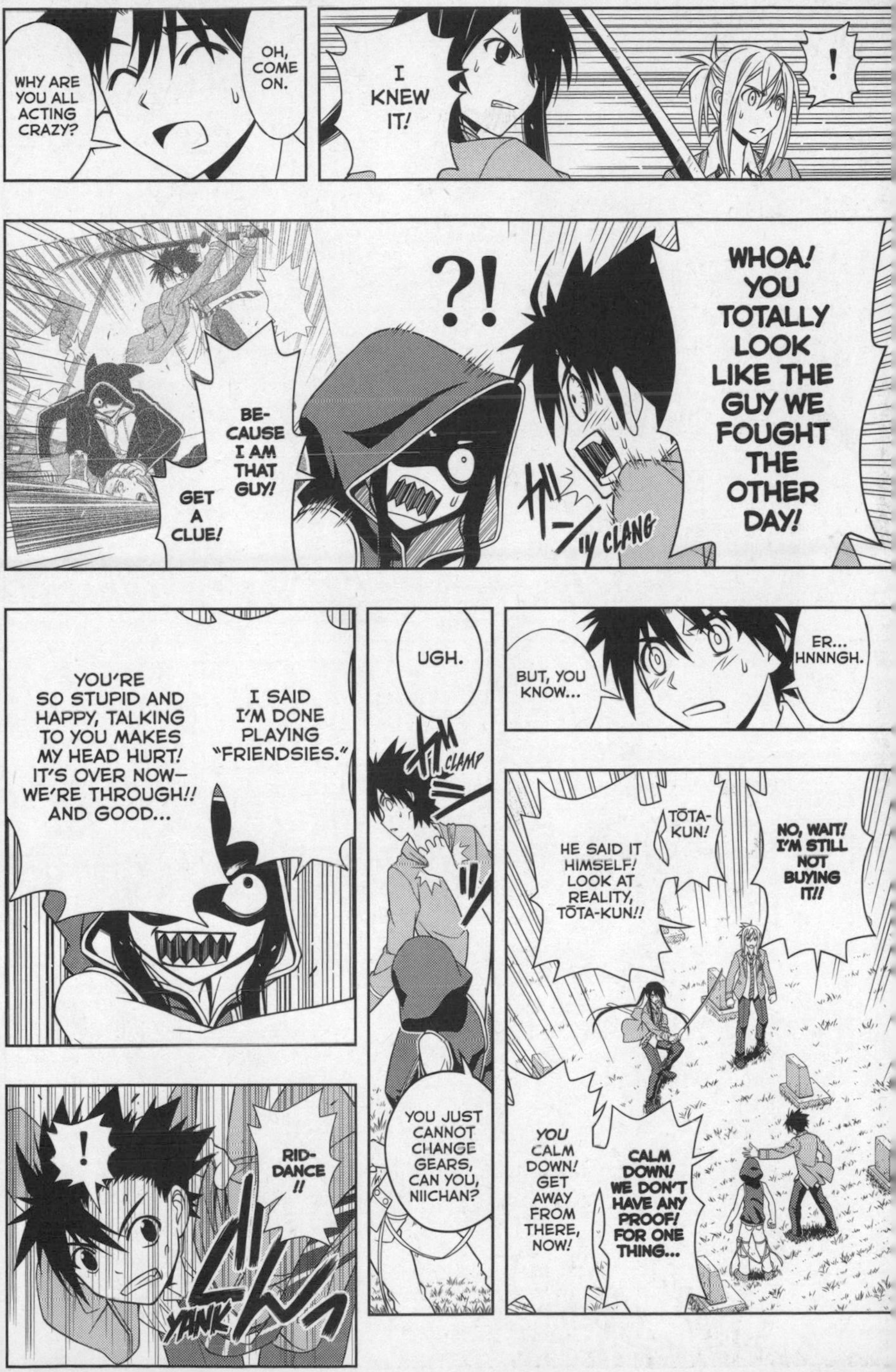
!
I KNEW IT!
OH, COME ON.
WHY ARE YOU ALL ACTING CRAZY?
WHOA! YOU TOTALLY LOOK LIKE THE GUY WE FOUGHT THE OTHER DAY!
?!
CLANG
BE-CAUSE I AM THAT GUY!
GET A CLUE!
ER... HNNNGH.
BUT, YOU KNOW...
NO, WAIT! I'M STILL NOT BUYING IT!!
TŌTA-KUN!
HE SAID IT HIMSELF! LOOK AT REALITY, TŌTA-KUN!!
CALM DOWN! WE DON'T HAVE ANY PROOF! FOR ONE THING...
YOU CALM DOWN! GET AWAY FROM THERE, NOW!
UGH.
CLAMP
YOU JUST CANNOT CHANGE GEARS, CAN YOU, NIICHAN?
I SAID I'M DONE PLAYING "FRIENDSIES."
YOU'RE SO STUPID AND HAPPY, TALKING TO YOU MAKES MY HEAD HURT! IT'S OVER NOW—WE'RE THROUGH!! AND GOOD...
RID-DANCE!!
!
YANK

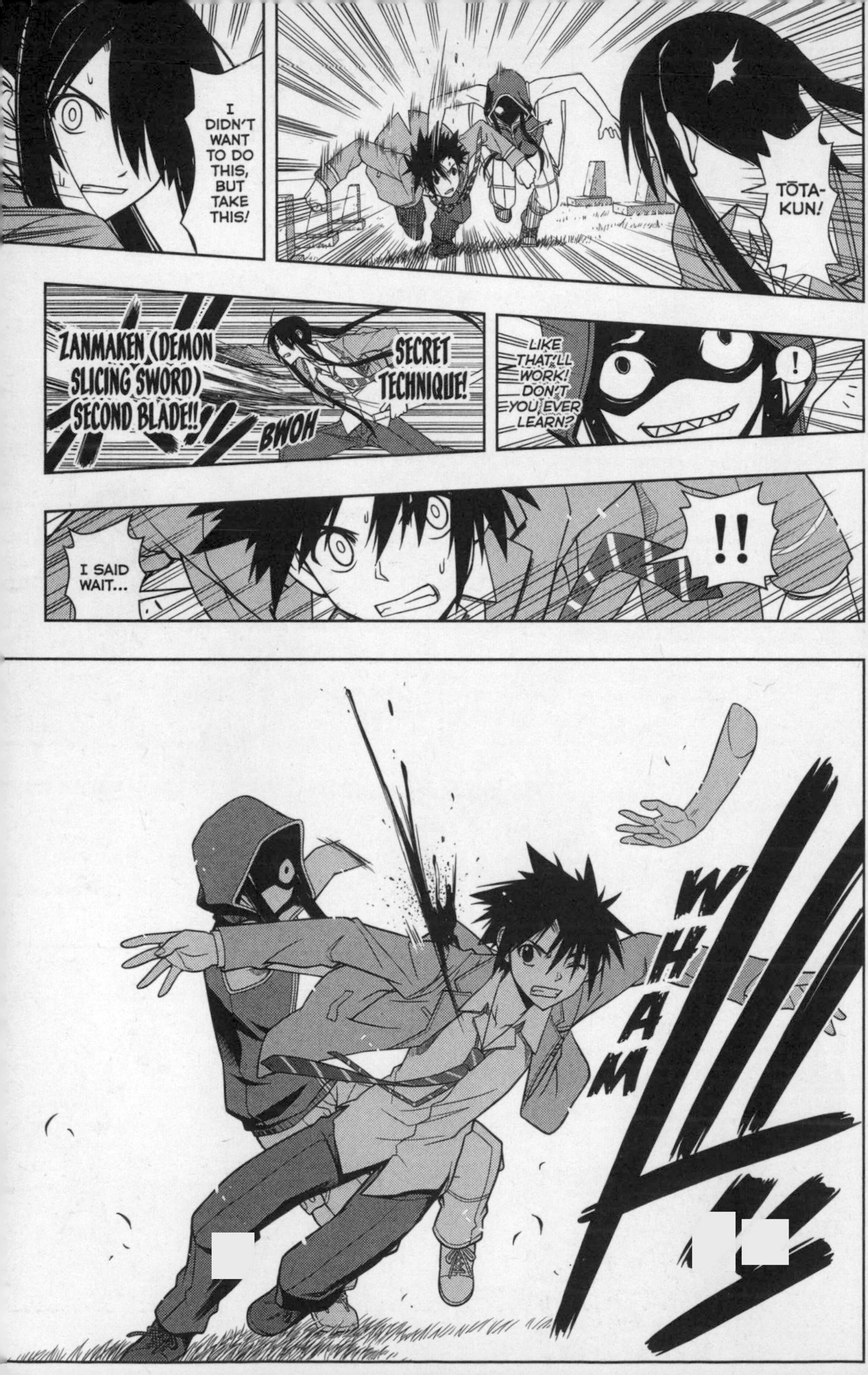
TŌTA-KUN!
I DIDN'T WANT TO DO THIS, BUT TAKE THIS!
!
LIKE THAT'LL WORK! DON'T YOU EVER LEARN?
SECRET TECHNIQUE!
ZANMAKEN (DEMON SLICING SWORD) SECOND BLADE!!
BWOH
!!
I SAID WAIT...
WHAM

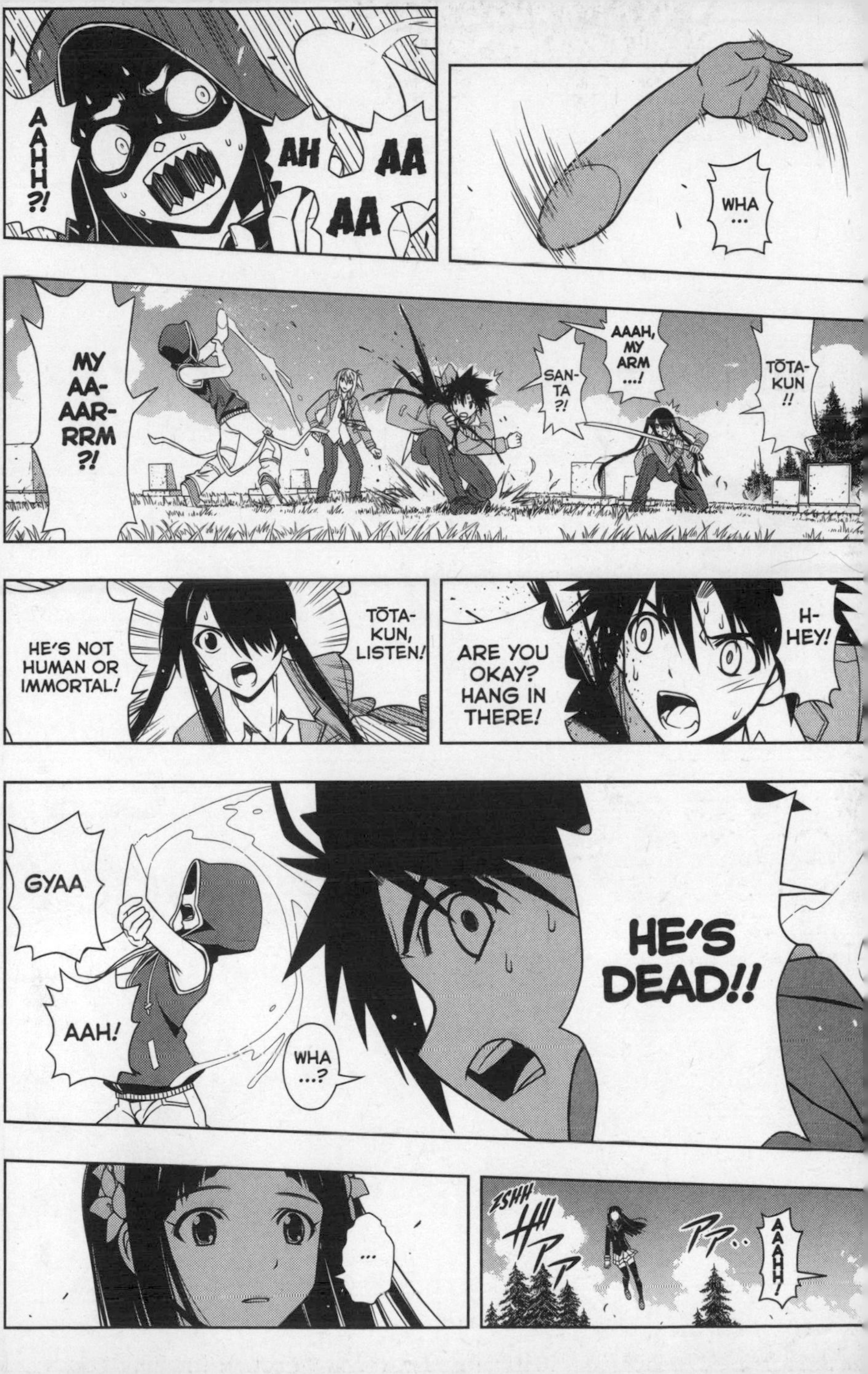
WHA ...
AAHH?!
AH AA AA
TŌTA-KUN!!
AAAH, MY ARM ...!
SAN-TA?!
MY AA-AAR-RRM?!
H-HEY!
ARE YOU OKAY? HANG IN THERE!
TŌTA-KUN, LISTEN!
HE'S NOT HUMAN OR IMMORTAL!
HE'S DEAD!!
WHA ...?
GYAA
AAH!
AAAHH!
ZSHH
...

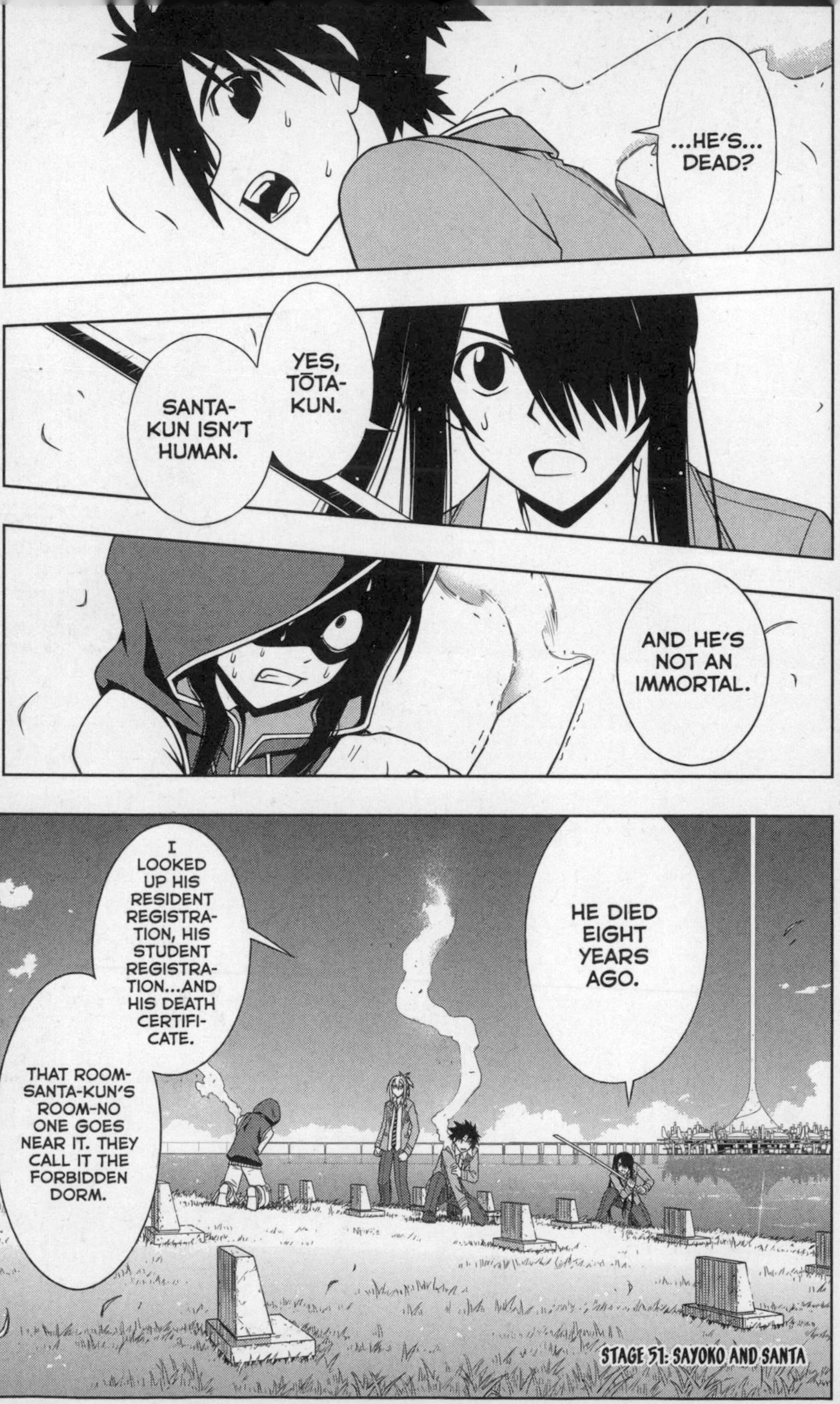
...HE'S... DEAD?
YES, TŌTA-KUN.
SANTA-KUN ISN'T HUMAN.
AND HE'S NOT AN IMMORTAL.
HE DIED EIGHT YEARS AGO.
I LOOKED UP HIS RESIDENT REGISTRATION, HIS STUDENT REGISTRATION...AND HIS DEATH CERTIFICATE.
THAT ROOM-SANTA-KUN'S ROOM-NO ONE GOES NEAR IT. THEY CALL IT THE FORBIDDEN DORM.
STAGE 51: SAYOKO AND SANTA

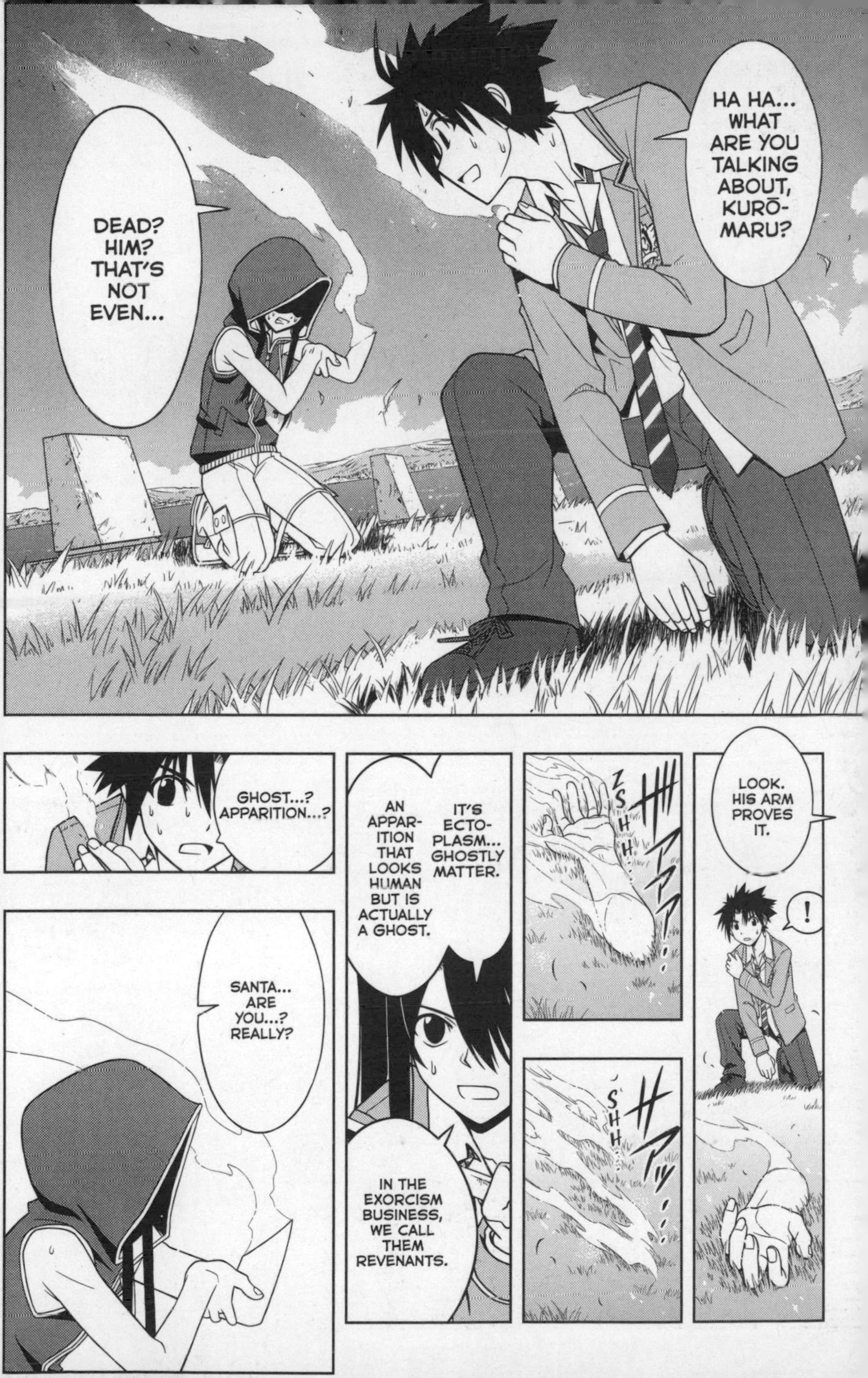
HA HA... WHAT ARE YOU TALKING ABOUT, KURŌ-MARU?
DEAD? HIM? THAT'S NOT EVEN...
LOOK. HIS ARM PROVES IT.
!
ZSHH...
SHH...
IT'S ECTO-PLASM... GHOSTLY MATTER.
AN APPAR-ITION THAT LOOKS HUMAN BUT IS ACTUALLY A GHOST.
IN THE EXORCISM BUSINESS, WE CALL THEM REVENANTS.
GHOST...? APPARITION...?
SANTA... ARE YOU...? REALLY?

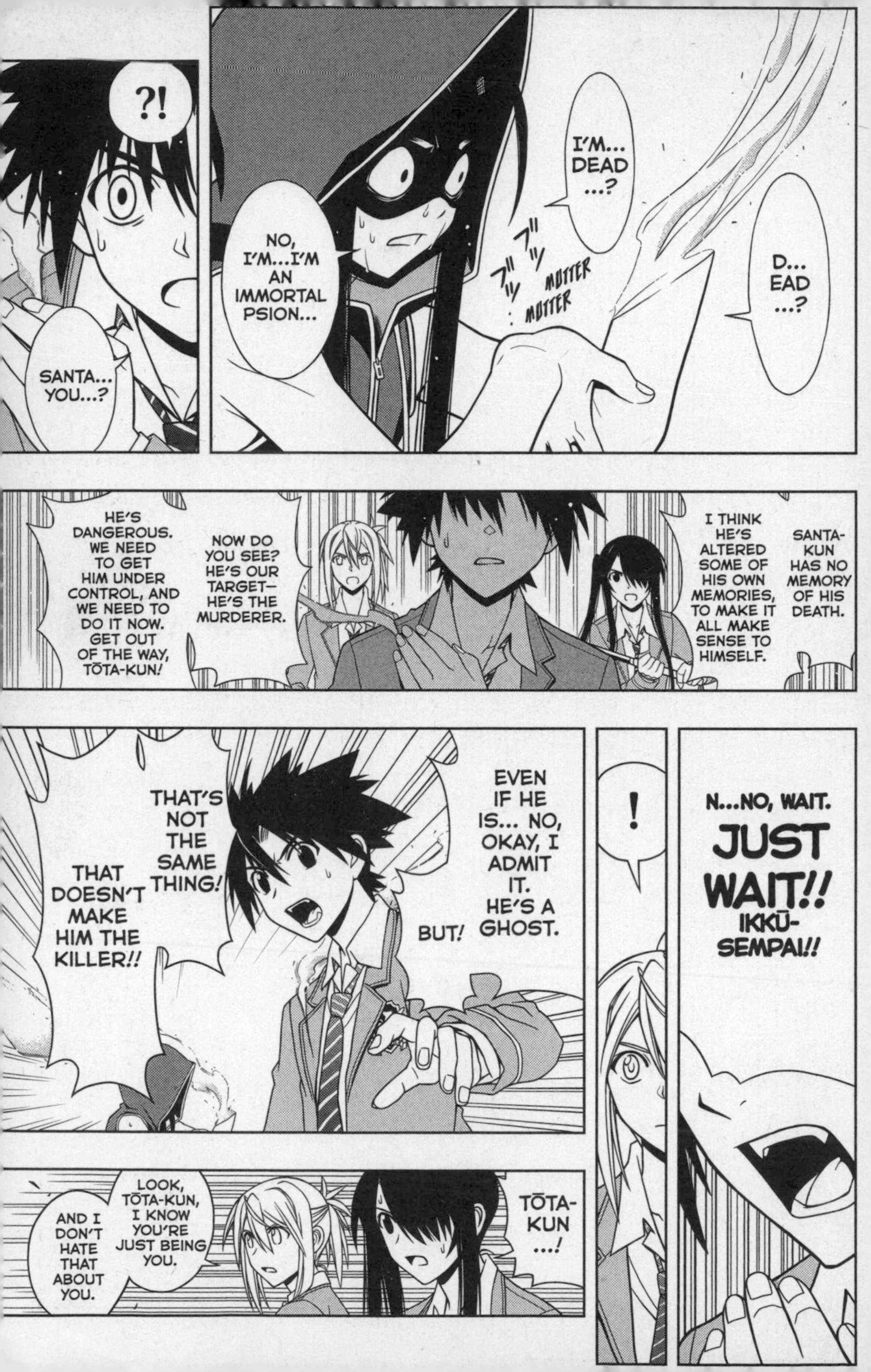
D... EAD ...?
I'M... DEAD ...?
ブツブツ
MUTTER MUTTER
NO, I'M...I'M AN IMMORTAL PSION...
?!
SANTA... YOU...?
SANTA-KUN HAS NO MEMORY OF HIS DEATH.
I THINK HE'S ALTERED SOME OF HIS OWN MEMORIES, TO MAKE IT ALL MAKE SENSE TO HIMSELF.
NOW DO YOU SEE? HE'S OUR TARGET—HE'S THE MURDERER.
HE'S DANGEROUS. WE NEED TO GET HIM UNDER CONTROL, AND WE NEED TO DO IT NOW. GET OUT OF THE WAY, TŌTA-KUN!
N...NO, WAIT. JUST WAIT!! IKKŪ-SEMPAI!!
!
EVEN IF HE IS... NO, OKAY, I ADMIT IT. HE'S A GHOST.
BUT!
THAT'S NOT THE SAME THING!
THAT DOESN'T MAKE HIM THE KILLER!!
TŌTA-KUN ...!
LOOK, TŌTA-KUN, I KNOW YOU'RE JUST BEING YOU.
AND I DON'T HATE THAT ABOUT YOU.

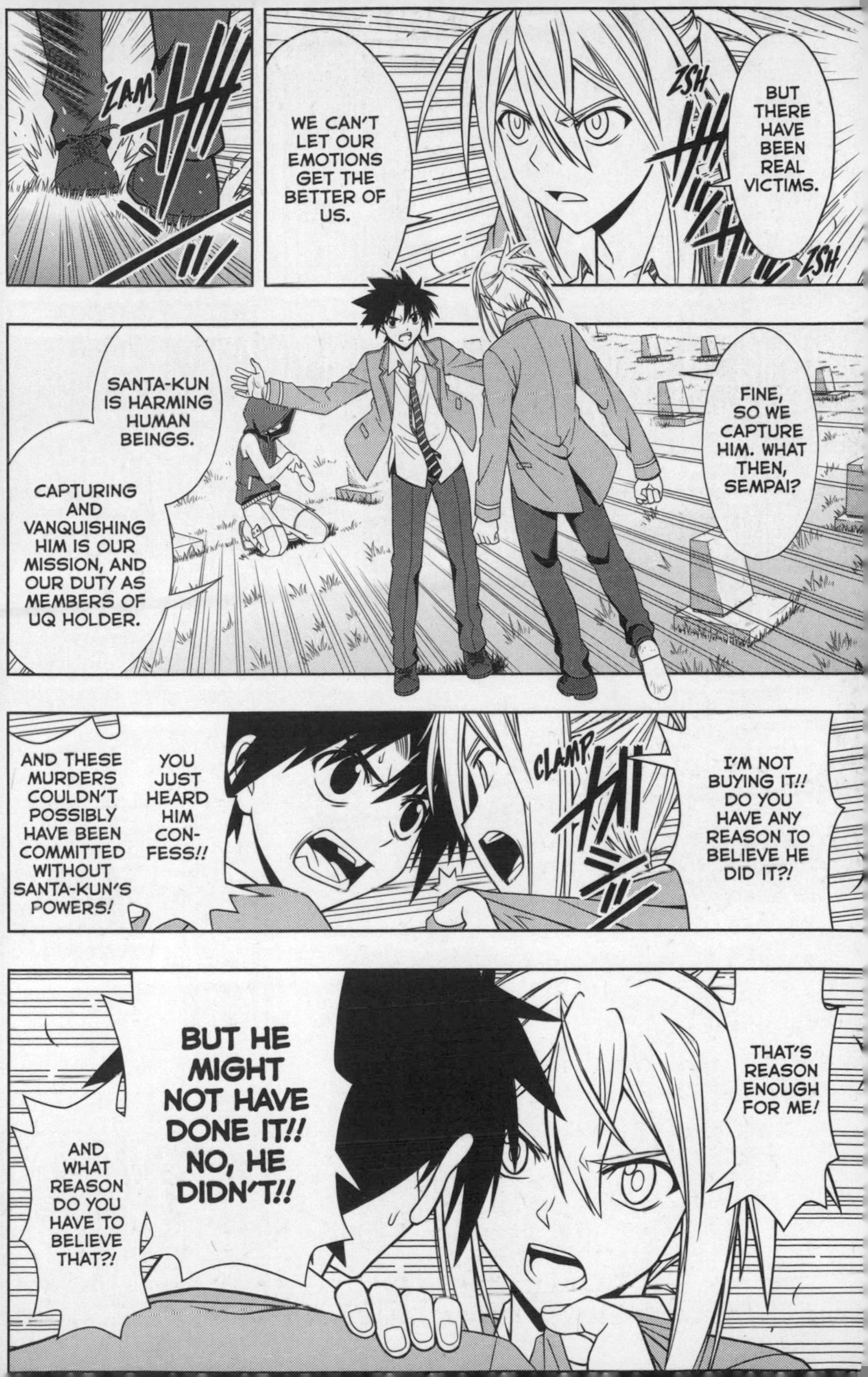
ZSH
BUT THERE HAVE BEEN REAL VICTIMS.
WE CAN'T LET OUR EMOTIONS GET THE BETTER OF US.
ZSH
ZAM
FINE, SO WE CAPTURE HIM. WHAT THEN, SEMPAI?
SANTA-KUN IS HARMING HUMAN BEINGS.
CAPTURING AND VANQUISHING HIM IS OUR MISSION, AND OUR DUTY AS MEMBERS OF UQ HOLDER.
CLAMP
I'M NOT BUYING IT!! DO YOU HAVE ANY REASON TO BELIEVE HE DID IT?!
YOU JUST HEARD HIM CON-FESS!!
AND THESE MURDERS COULDN'T POSSIBLY HAVE BEEN COMMITTED WITHOUT SANTA-KUN'S POWERS!
THAT'S REASON ENOUGH FOR ME!
BUT HE MIGHT NOT HAVE DONE IT!! NO, HE DIDN'T!!
AND WHAT REASON DO YOU HAVE TO BELIEVE THAT?!

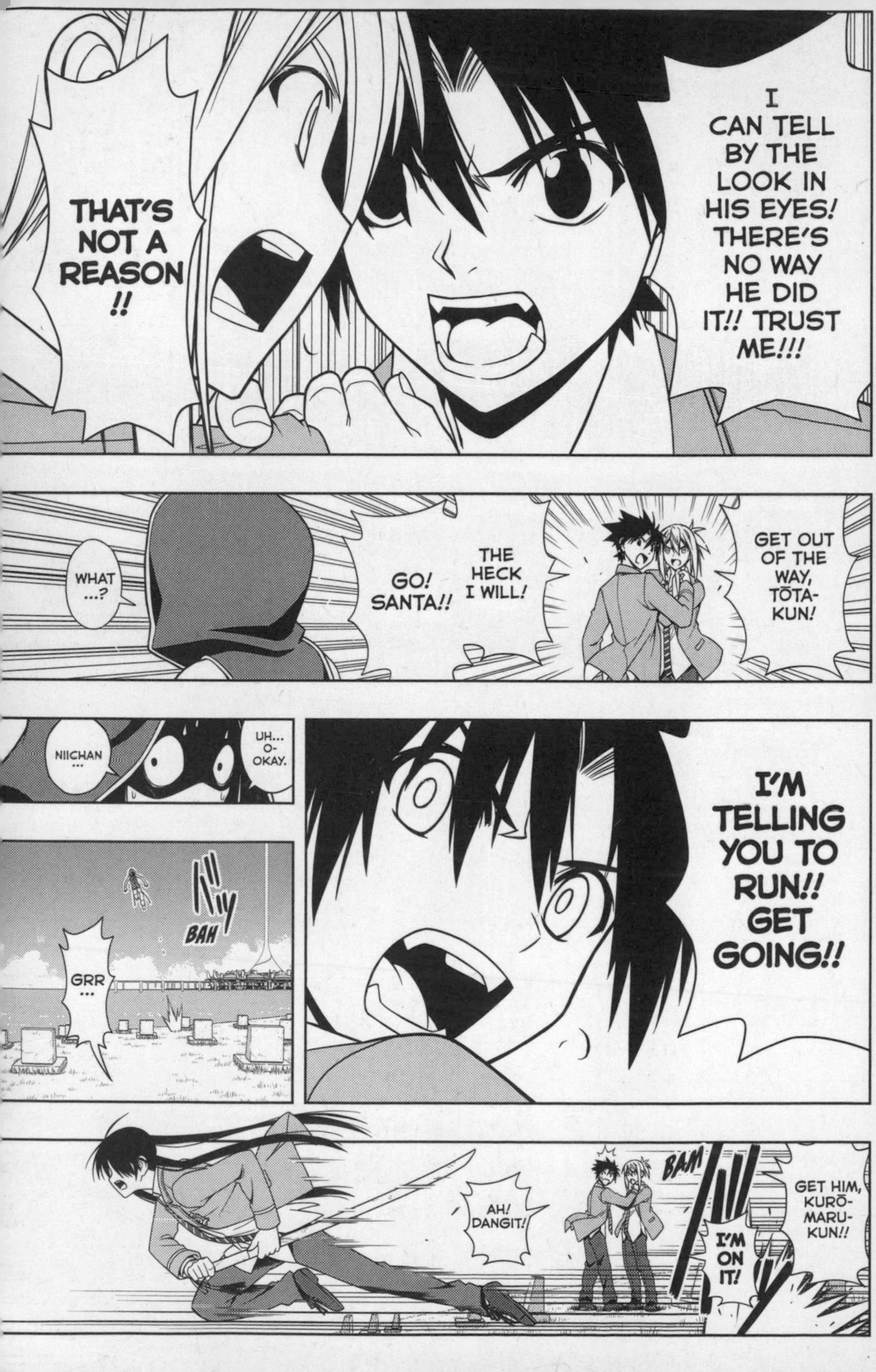
I CAN TELL BY THE LOOK IN HIS EYES! THERE'S NO WAY HE DID IT!! TRUST ME!!!
THAT'S NOT A REASON!!
GET OUT OF THE WAY, TŌTA-KUN!
THE HECK I WILL!
GO! SANTA!!
WHAT...?
I'M TELLING YOU TO RUN!! GET GOING!!
UH... O-OKAY.
NIICHAN...
BAH
GRR...
GET HIM, KURŌ-MARU-KUN!!
I'M ON IT!
BAM
AH! DANGIT!

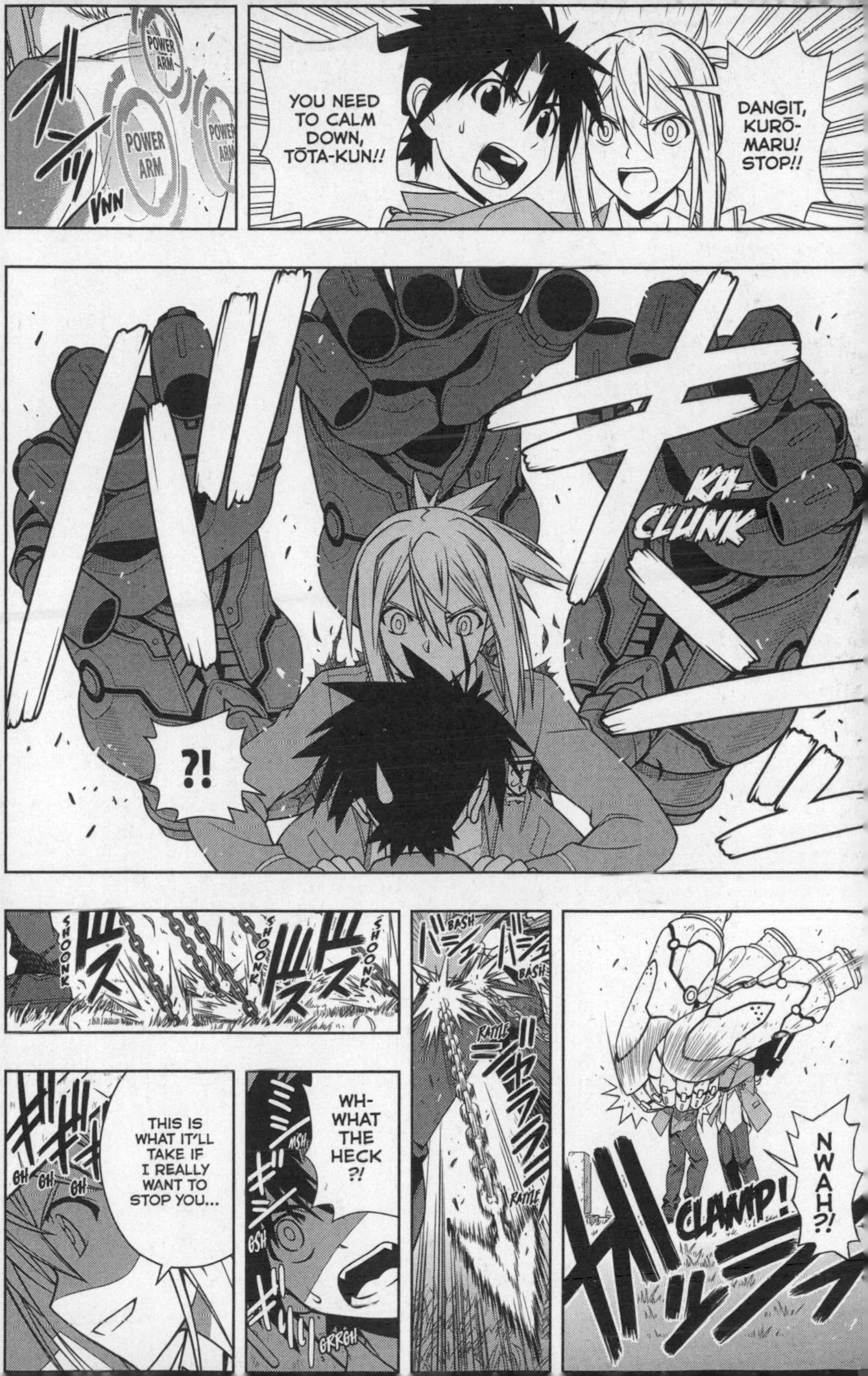
DANGIT, KURŌ-MARU! STOP!!
YOU NEED TO CALM DOWN, TŌTA-KUN!!
POWER ARM
POWER ARM
POWER ARM
VNN
KA-CLUNK
?!
NWAH?!
CLAMP!
BASH
BASH
RATTLE
RATTLE
SHOONK
SHOONK
SHOONK
WH-WHAT THE HECK?!
MSH
GSH
GRRGH
THIS IS WHAT IT'LL TAKE IF I REALLY WANT TO STOP YOU...
GH
GH
GH

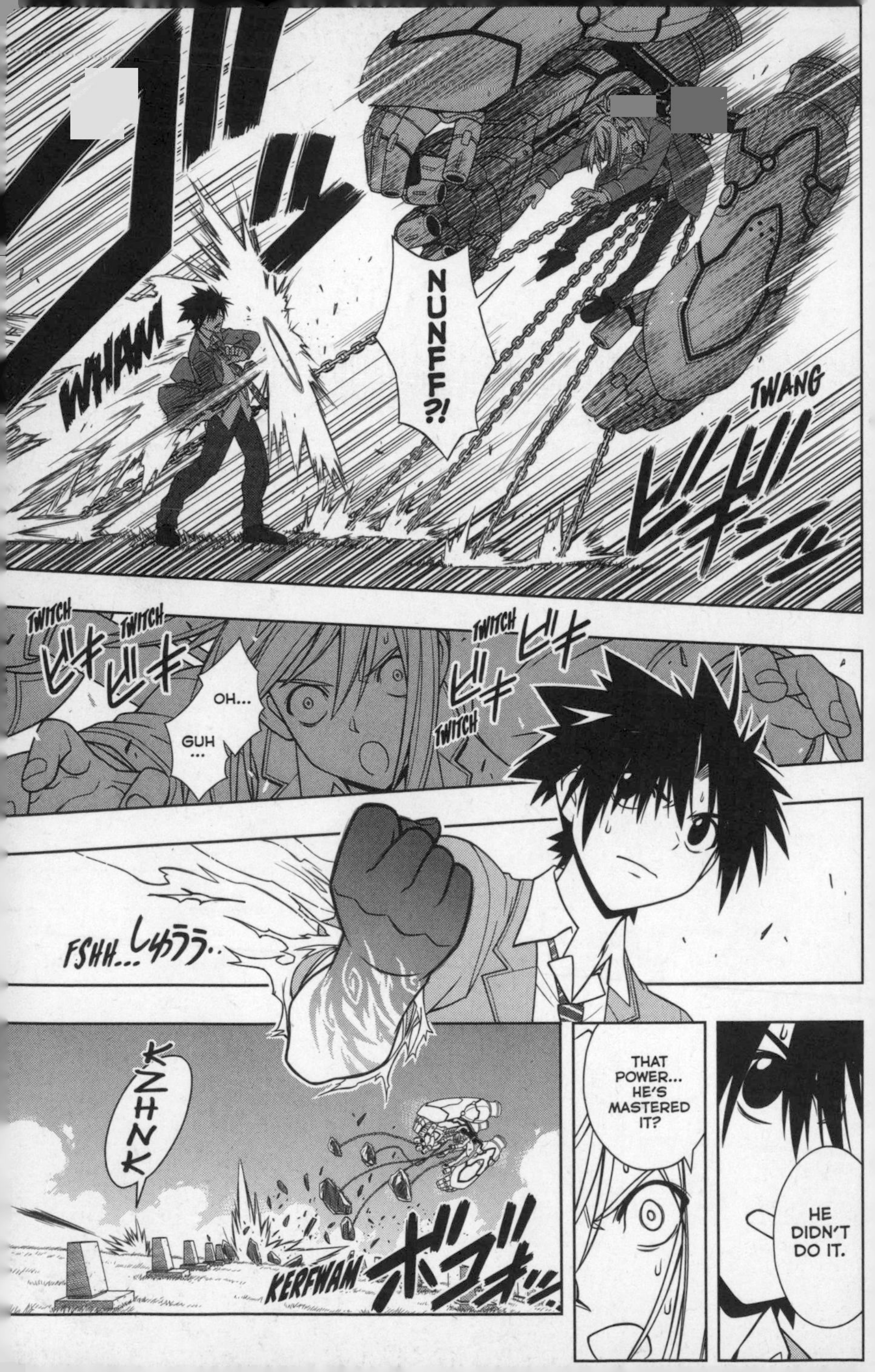

TWANG
ビギーッ
NUNFF?!
WHAM
ゴッ
TWITCH
ビキ
ビキ
TWITCH
OH... GUH ...
TWITCH
ビキ
TWITCH
ビキ
FSHH... しゅうう..
HE DIDN'T DO IT.
THAT POWER... HE'S MASTERED IT?
KZHNK
KERFWAM
オゴォッ

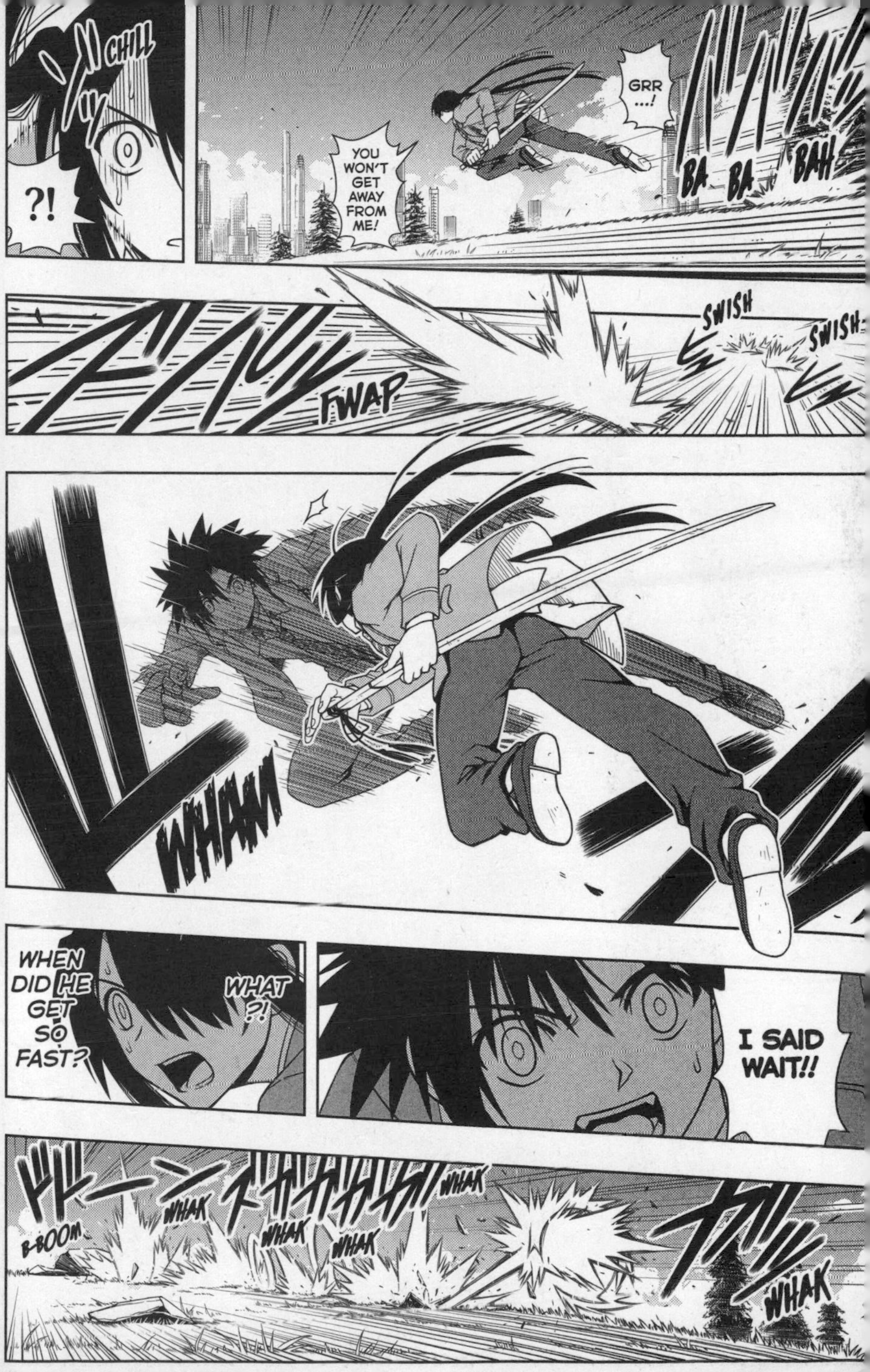
BA BA BAH
GRR ...!
YOU WON'T GET AWAY FROM ME!
CHILL
?!
SWISH
SWISH
FWAP
WHAM
I SAID WAIT!!
WHAT ?!
WHEN DID HE GET SO FAST?
WHAK
WHAK
WHAK
WHAK
WHAK
B-BOOM

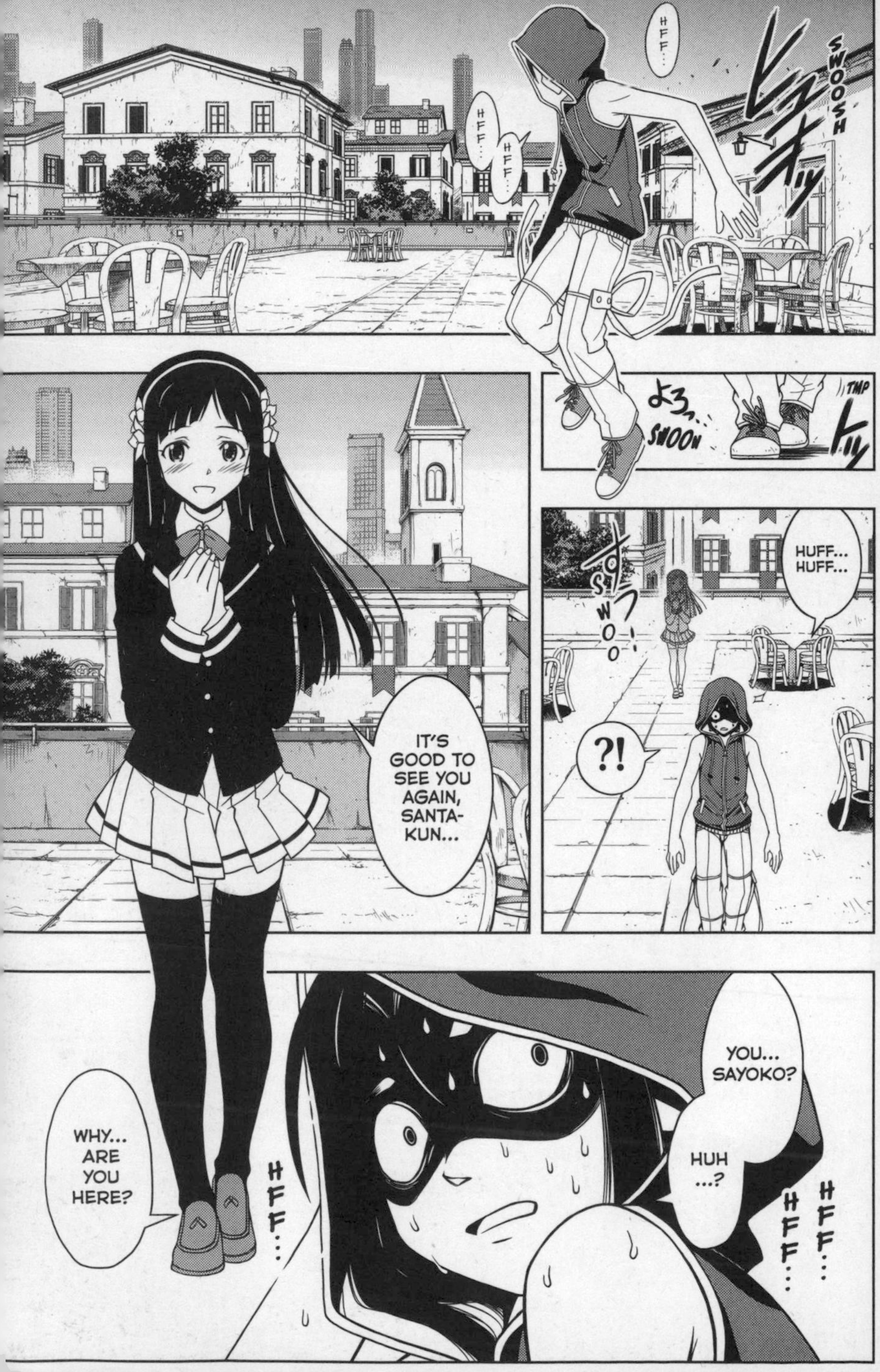

SWOOSH
HFF...
HFF...
HFF...
TMP
SWOON
HUFF... HUFF...
SWOO
?!
IT'S GOOD TO SEE YOU AGAIN, SANTA-KUN...
HFF... HFF...
YOU... SAYOKO?
HUH ...?
WHY... ARE YOU HERE?
HFF...

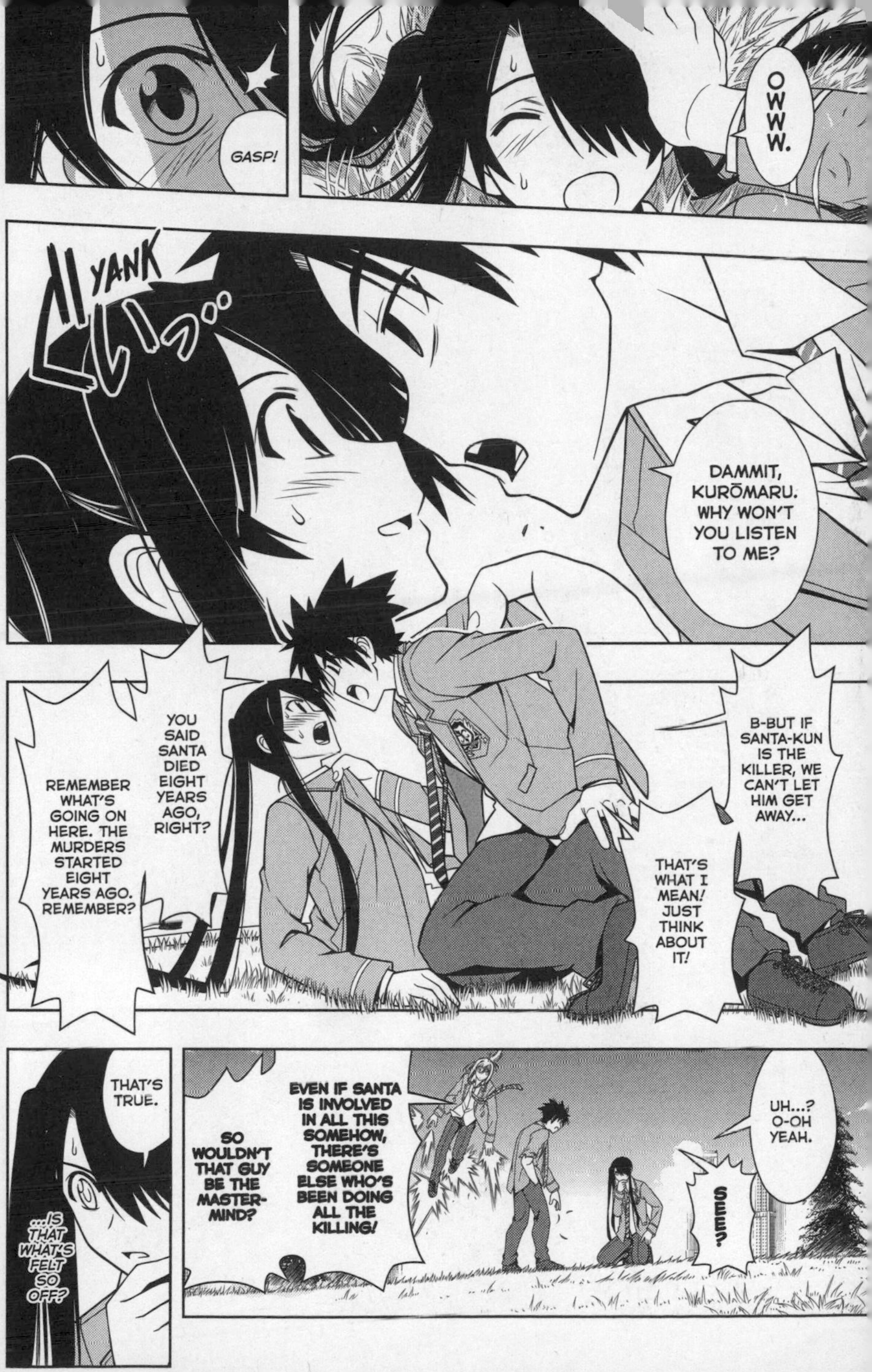
OWWW.
GASP!
YANK
DAMMIT, KURŌMARU. WHY WON'T YOU LISTEN TO ME?
B-BUT IF SANTA-KUN IS THE KILLER, WE CAN'T LET HIM GET AWAY...
THAT'S WHAT I MEAN! JUST THINK ABOUT IT!
YOU SAID SANTA DIED EIGHT YEARS AGO, RIGHT?
REMEMBER WHAT'S GOING ON HERE. THE MURDERS STARTED EIGHT YEARS AGO. REMEMBER?
UH...? O-OH YEAH.
SEE?
EVEN IF SANTA IS INVOLVED IN ALL THIS SOMEHOW, THERE'S SOMEONE ELSE WHO'S BEEN DOING ALL THE KILLING!
SO WOULDN'T THAT GUY BE THE MASTER-MIND?
THAT'S TRUE.
...IS THAT WHAT'S FELT SO OFF?

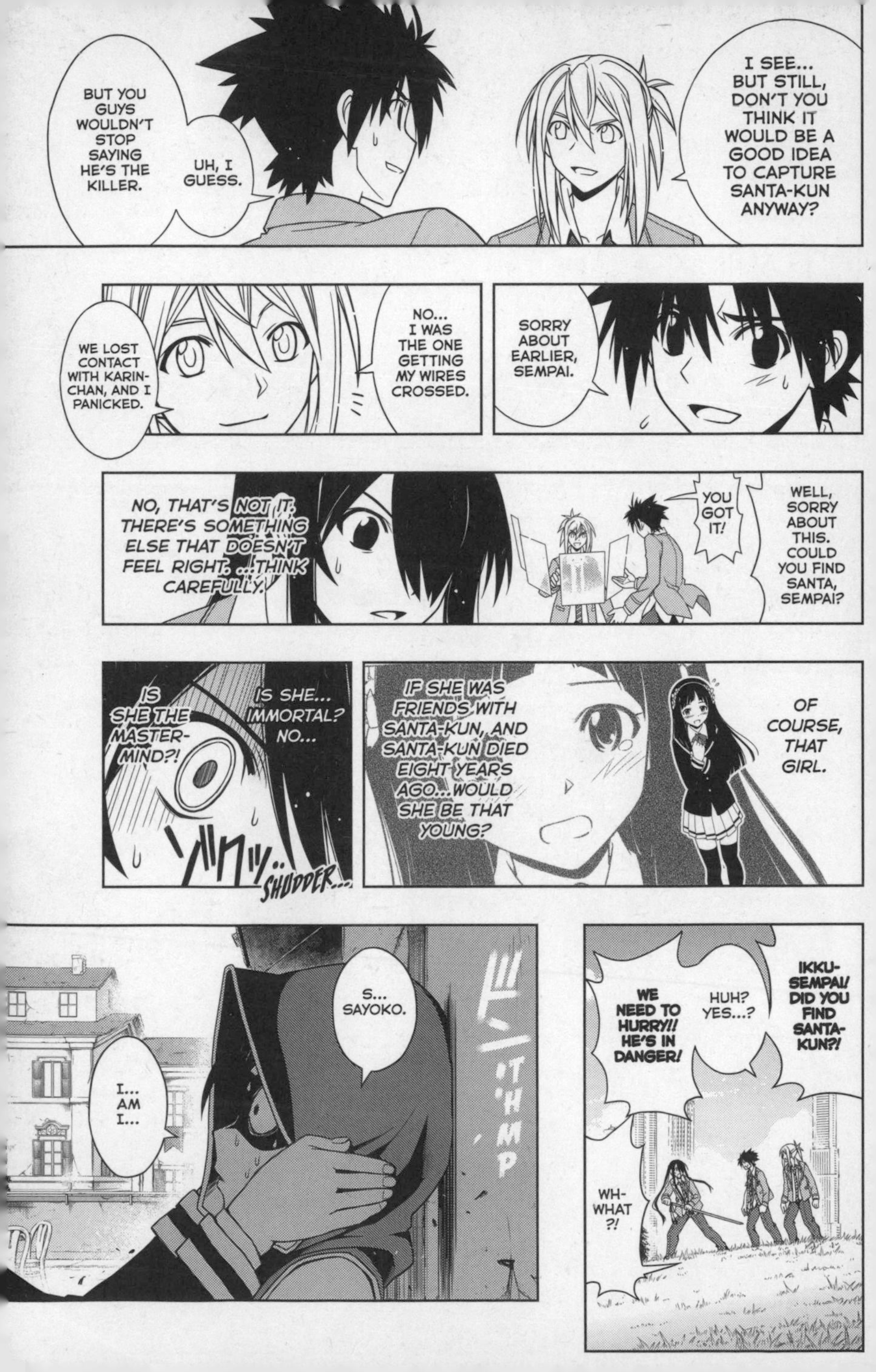
I SEE... BUT STILL, DON'T YOU THINK IT WOULD BE A GOOD IDEA TO CAPTURE SANTA-KUN ANYWAY?
UH, I GUESS.
BUT YOU GUYS WOULDN'T STOP SAYING HE'S THE KILLER.
SORRY ABOUT EARLIER, SEMPAI.
NO... I WAS THE ONE GETTING MY WIRES CROSSED.
WE LOST CONTACT WITH KARIN-CHAN, AND I PANICKED.
WELL, SORRY ABOUT THIS. COULD YOU FIND SANTA, SEMPAI?
YOU GOT IT!
NO, THAT'S NOT IT. THERE'S SOMETHING ELSE THAT DOESN'T FEEL RIGHT. ...THINK CAREFULLY.
OF COURSE, THAT GIRL.
IF SHE WAS FRIENDS WITH SANTA-KUN, AND SANTA-KUN DIED EIGHT YEARS AGO...WOULD SHE BE THAT YOUNG?
IS SHE... IMMORTAL? NO...
IS SHE THE MASTER-MIND?!
SHUDDER...
IKKU-SEMPAI! DID YOU FIND SANTA-KUN?!
HUH? YES...?
WE NEED TO HURRY!! HE'S IN DANGER!
WH-WHAT?!
THMP
S... SAYOKO.
I... AM I...

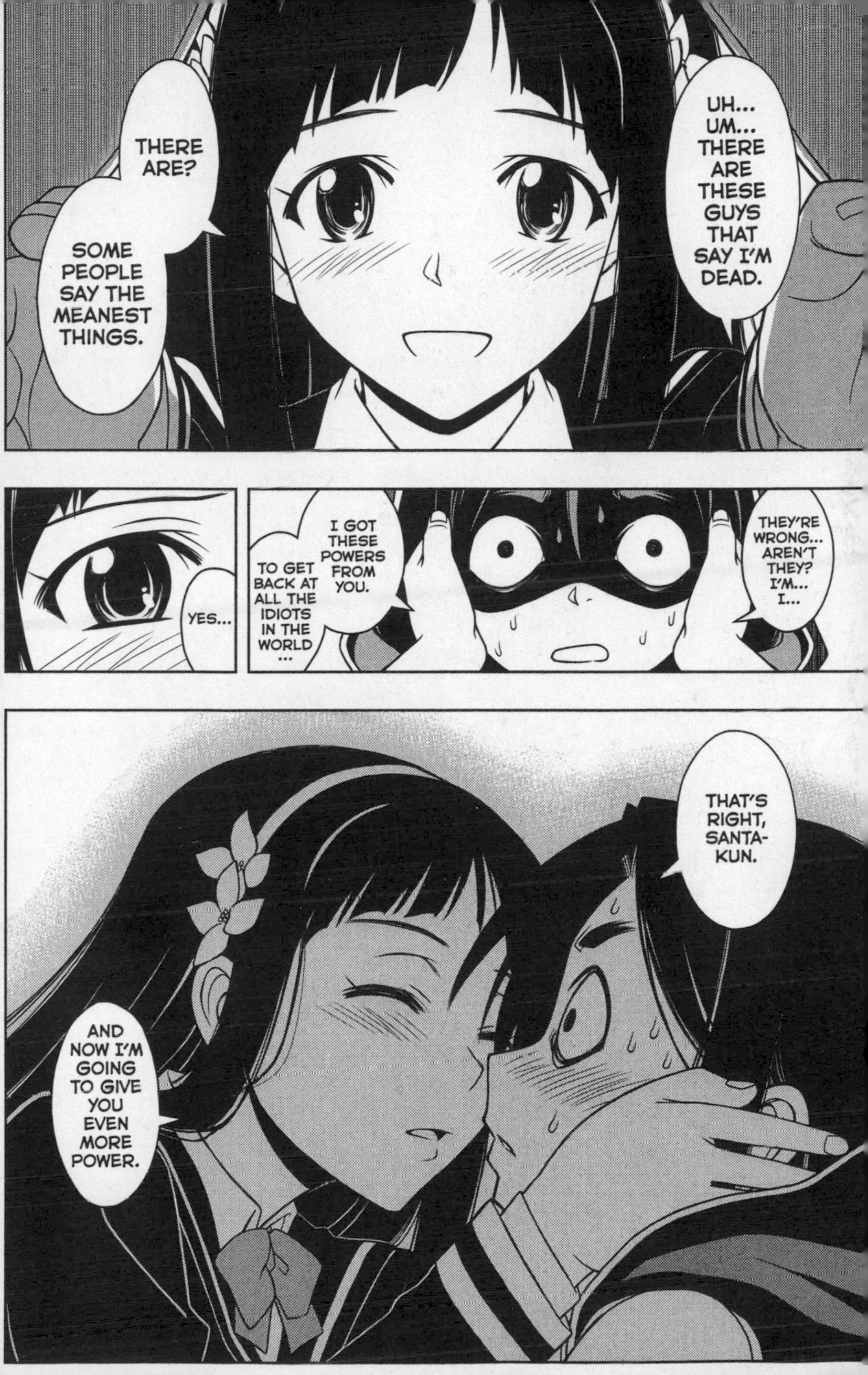
UH... UM... THERE ARE THESE GUYS THAT SAY I'M DEAD.
THERE ARE?
SOME PEOPLE SAY THE MEANEST THINGS.
THEY'RE WRONG... AREN'T THEY? I'M... I...
I GOT THESE POWERS FROM YOU.
TO GET BACK AT ALL THE IDIOTS IN THE WORLD...
YES...
THAT'S RIGHT, SANTA-KUN.
AND NOW I'M GOING TO GIVE YOU EVEN MORE POWER.

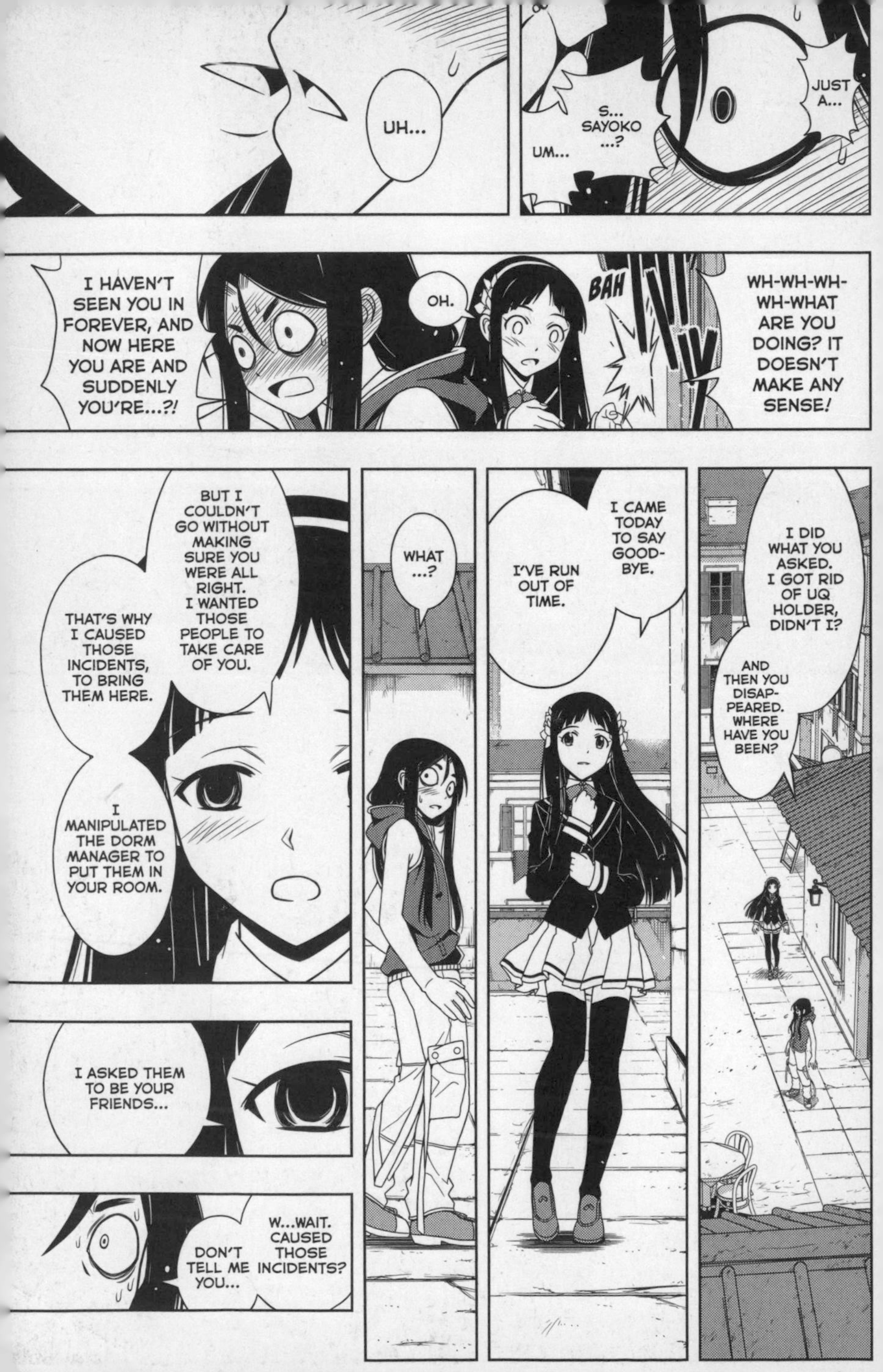
JUST A...
S... SAYOKO ...?
UM...
UH...
WH-WH-WH-WH-WHAT ARE YOU DOING? IT DOESN'T MAKE ANY SENSE!
BAH
OH.
I HAVEN'T SEEN YOU IN FOREVER, AND NOW HERE YOU ARE AND SUDDENLY YOU'RE...?!
I DID WHAT YOU ASKED. I GOT RID OF UQ HOLDER, DIDN'T I?
AND THEN YOU DISAPPEARED. WHERE HAVE YOU BEEN?
I CAME TODAY TO SAY GOOD-BYE.
I'VE RUN OUT OF TIME.
WHAT ...?
BUT I COULDN'T GO WITHOUT MAKING SURE YOU WERE ALL RIGHT. I WANTED THOSE PEOPLE TO TAKE CARE OF YOU.
THAT'S WHY I CAUSED THOSE INCIDENTS, TO BRING THEM HERE.
I MANIPULATED THE DORM MANAGER TO PUT THEM IN YOUR ROOM.
I ASKED THEM TO BE YOUR FRIENDS...
W...WAIT. CAUSED THOSE INCIDENTS?
DON'T TELL ME YOU...

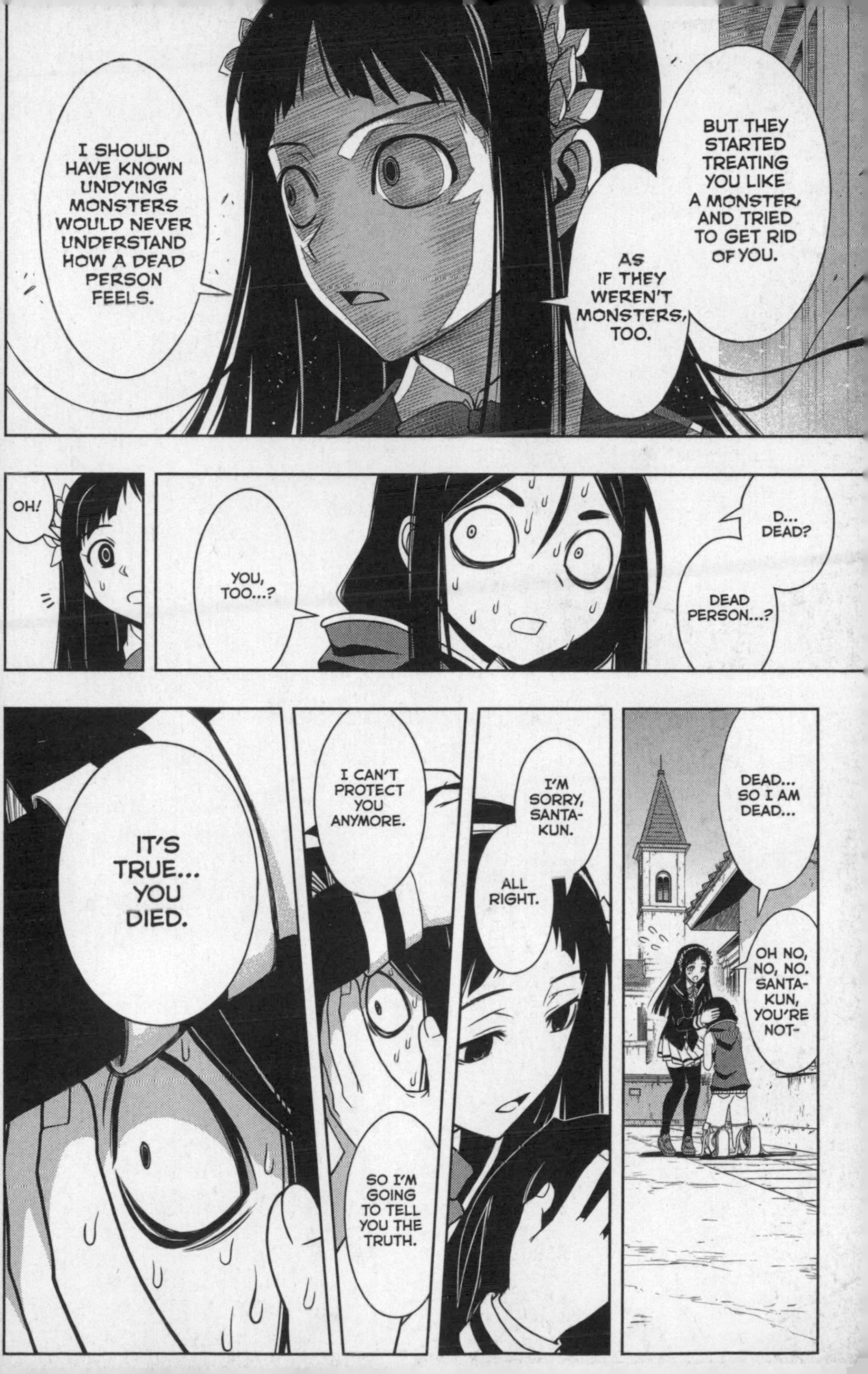
BUT THEY STARTED TREATING YOU LIKE A MONSTER AND TRIED TO GET RID OF YOU.
AS IF THEY WEREN'T MONSTERS, TOO.
I SHOULD HAVE KNOWN UNDYING MONSTERS WOULD NEVER UNDERSTAND HOW A DEAD PERSON FEELS.
D... DEAD?
DEAD PERSON...?
YOU, TOO...?
OH!
DEAD... SO I AM DEAD...
OH NO, NO, NO. SANTA-KUN, YOU'RE NOT-
I'M SORRY, SANTA-KUN.
ALL RIGHT.
I CAN'T PROTECT YOU ANYMORE.
SO I'M GOING TO TELL YOU THE TRUTH.
IT'S TRUE... YOU DIED.

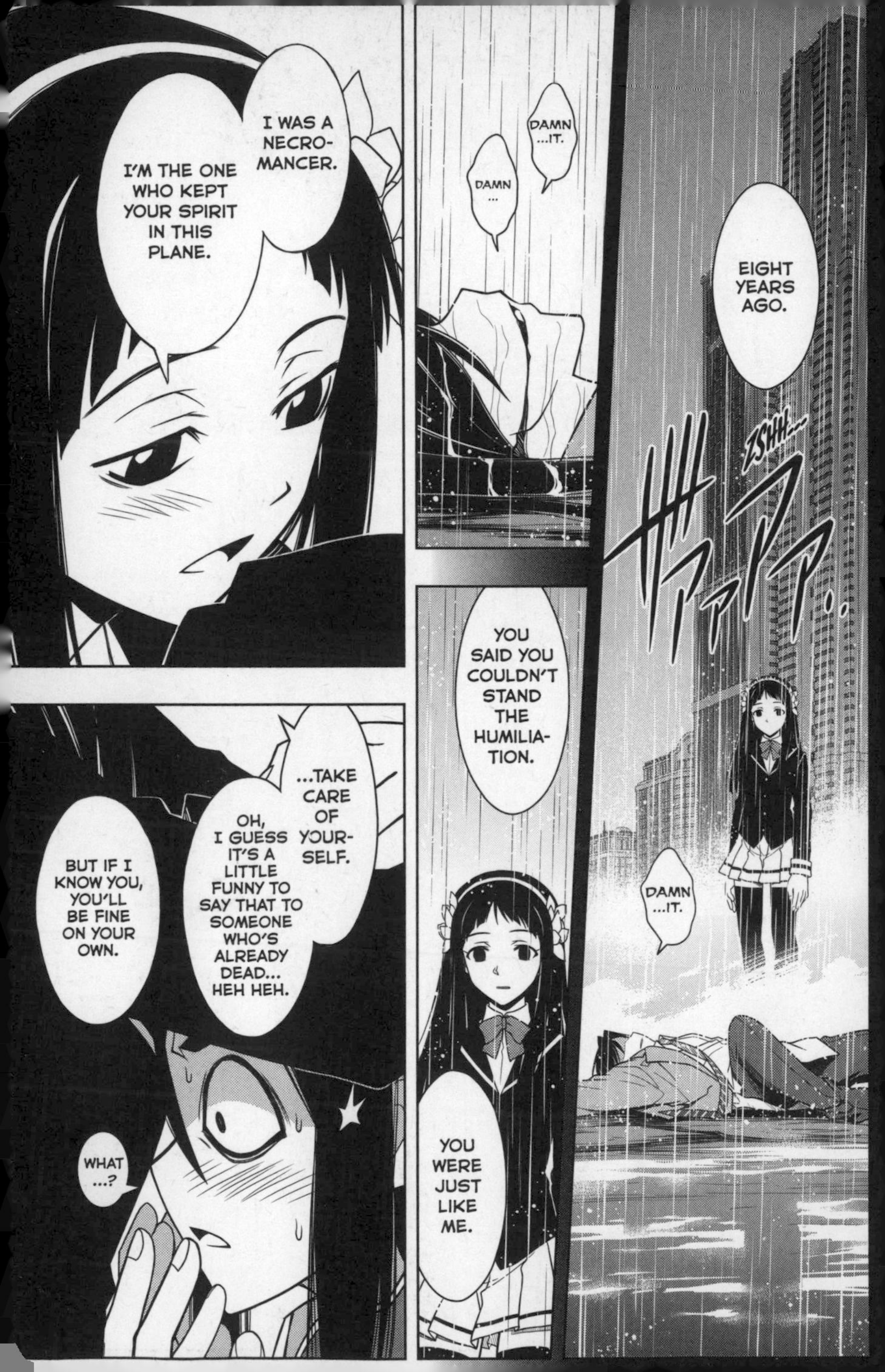
EIGHT YEARS AGO.
ZSHH...
DAMN ...IT.
DAMN ...IT.
DAMN ...
YOU SAID YOU COULDN'T STAND THE HUMILIA-TION.
YOU WERE JUST LIKE ME.
I WAS A NECRO-MANCER.
I'M THE ONE WHO KEPT YOUR SPIRIT IN THIS PLANE.
...TAKE CARE OF YOUR-SELF.
OH, I GUESS IT'S A LITTLE FUNNY TO SAY THAT TO SOMEONE WHO'S ALREADY DEAD... HEH HEH.
BUT IF I KNOW YOU, YOU'LL BE FINE ON YOUR OWN.
WHAT ...?

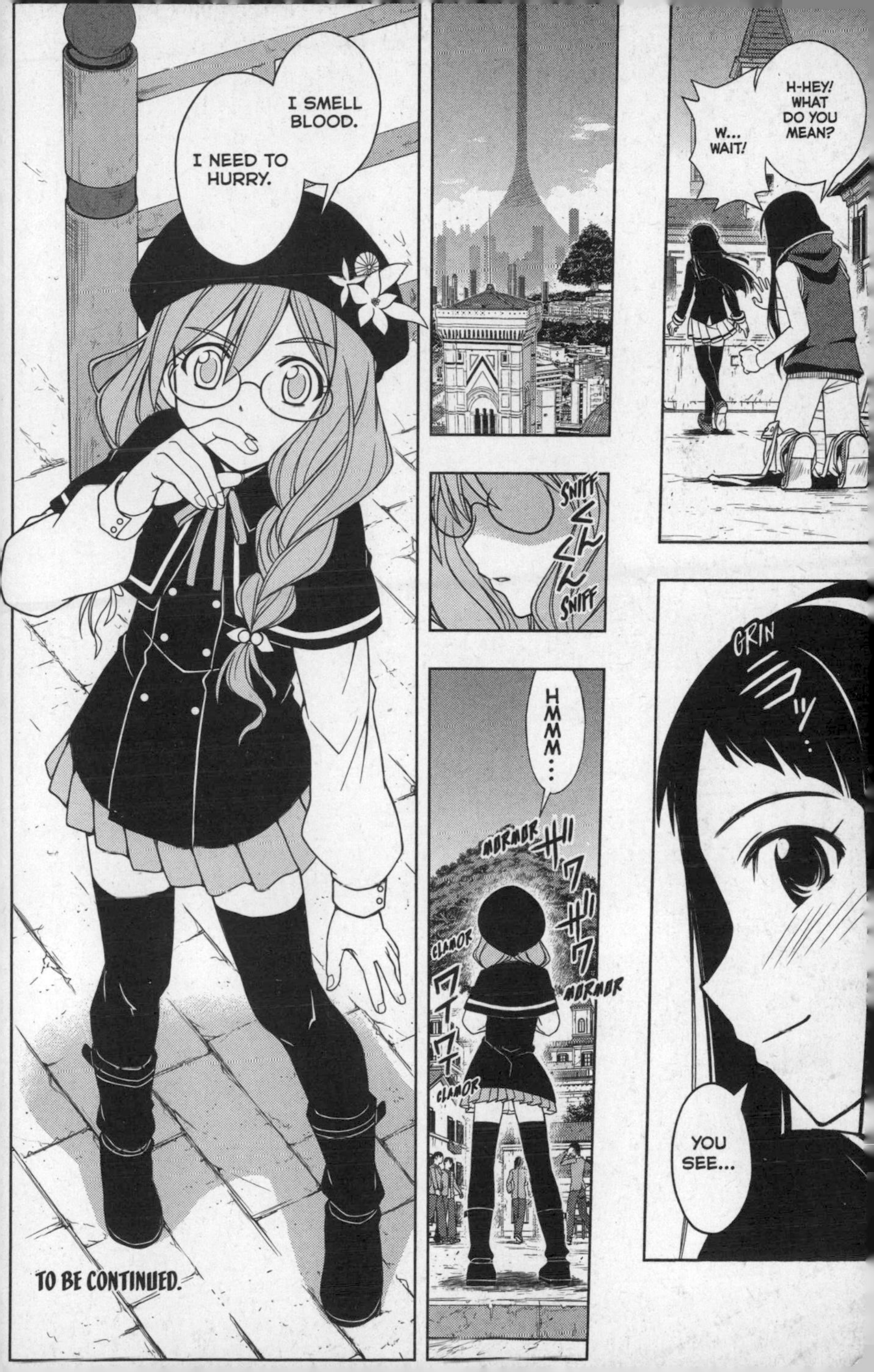
H-HEY! WHAT DO YOU MEAN?
W... WAIT!
GRIN
YOU SEE...
SNIFF
SNIFF
HMMM...
MURMUR
MURMUR
CLAMOR
CLAMOR
I SMELL BLOOD.
I NEED TO HURRY.
TO BE CONTINUED.

UQ HOLDER!

STAFF

Ken Akamatsu
Takashi Takemoto
Kenichi Nakamura
Keiichi Yamashita
Tohru Mitsuhashi
Susumu Kuwabara
Yuri Sasaki

Thanks to Ran Ayanaga

NO.6

A PERFECT LIFE IN A PERFECT CITY

For Shion, an elite student in the technologically sophisticated city No. 6, life is carefully choreographed. One fateful day, he takes a misstep, sheltering a fugitive his age from a typhoon. Helping this boy throws Shion's life down a path to discovering the appalling secrets behind the "perfection" of No. 6.

KC
KODANSHA
COMICS

UQ HOLDER! VOLUME 5 IS A WORK OF FICTION. NAMES, CHARACTERS, PLACES, AND INCIDENTS ARE THE PRODUCTS OF THE AUTHOR'S IMAGINATION OR ARE USED FICTITIOUSLY. ANY RESEMBLANCE TO ACTUAL EVENTS, LOCALES, OR PERSONS, LIVING OR DEAD, IS ENTIRELY COINCIDENTAL.

A KODANSHA COMICS TRADE PAPERBACK ORIGINAL

PUBLISHED IN THE UNITED STATES BY KODANSHA COMICS, AN IMPRINT OF KODANSHA USA PUBLISHING, LLC, NEW YORK.

PUBLICATION RIGHTS FOR THIS ENGLISH EDITION ARRANGED THROUGH KODANSHA LTD., TOKYO.

FIRST PUBLISHED IN JAPAN IN 2014 BY KODANSHA LTD., TOKYO.

ISBN 978-1-61262-833-2

PRINTED IN THE UNITED STATES OF AMERICA.

WWW.KODANSHACOMICS.COM

9 8 7 6 5 4 3 2 1

TRANSLATOR: ALETHEA NIBLEY AND ATHENA NIBLEY
LETTERING: JAMES DASHIELL